Frenzy and Betrayal

To Carol, Dylan, Kelly & Jane.

Truth is on the march and nothing can stop it – Emile Zola, *J'Accuse*, extract from a letter on the Dreyfus Affair to the President of the French Republic, *L'Aurore*, 13 January 1898.

Frenzy and Betrayal

THE ANATOMY
OF A
POLITICAL ASSASSINATION

ALAN SHATTER

MERRION
PRESS

First published in 2019 by
Merrion Press
An imprint of Irish Academic Press
10 George's Street
Newbridge
Co. Kildare
Ireland
www.merrionpress.ie

9781785372377 (Paper)
9781785372384 (Kindle)
9781785372391 (Epub)
9781785372407 (PDF)

British Library Cataloguing in Publication Data
An entry can be found on request

Library of Congress Cataloging in Publication Data
An entry can be found on request

Typeset in Minion Pro 11.5/15 pt

Cover front: Minister for Justice Alan Shatter TD, 2011.
Photograph: Bryan O'Brien/*The Irish Times*.

Cover back: Minister for Justice Alan Shatter TD at a press
conference on the subject of allegations of improper cancellation
of Fixed Charge Notices by members of an Garda Síochána, 2013.
Photograph: Bryan O'Brien/*The Irish Times*.

Contents

Introduction

The arc of the moral universe is long but it bends towards justice
–From a sermon delivered by Martin Luther King Jr, in Wesleyan
University, Middleton, Connecticut, USA, in 1964.

This famous, much-quoted optimistic insight of Martin Luther King Jr
is inscribed on the King Memorial in Washington DC. While I am an
admirer of King's courageous legacy, I am not a great believer in divine
providence, the force of a universal morality, or in historical inevitability
ultimately ensuring that justice is achieved and that truth prevails. I
believe, in today's complex multimedia age, that truth is a daily casualty, a
pliable commodity readily rejected or distorted by those who, for a variety
of reasons, favour or have a vested interest in promoting alternative
realities. This is not an entirely new phenomenon. It did not first emerge,
as some would have us believe, with Donald Trump's presidency of the
United States of America. It is a feature of human discourse since time
immemorial. It has merely achieved greater public prominence since
Trump's inauguration and as a result of contemporary intellectual and
political battles over fake news. I use the phrase 'fake news' with some
reluctance as it has evolved into a Trumpian catchphrase all too regularly
deployed by one of the world's greatest exponents of falsity to denigrate
truth. It is the importance of truth that is central to my story.

Truth and justice matter but they do not inevitably win out. Facts can
too easily be manipulated and distorted. Lies can too readily be skilfully
camouflaged, disseminated and within moments travel around the world
to be accessed by many millions of people. There have always been those
who use deceit to gain personal benefit or advantage. The difference in
today's world is the way in which global communications and the internet
enable lives and reputations to be destroyed in an instant by lies and
falsehoods.

The perceptions of good people are formed by the truths or lies they
read in newspapers, glean from television and radio broadcasts or access
online. As Peter Charleton SC, now a Supreme Court judge, observed
in 2006 in his scholarly book *Lies in a Mirror*, lies or false news whip
up emotions, generate hatred and infect cognitive capacity. He correctly
asserted 'deceit causes injustices, big and small, to those with whom
we interact'. However, lies that do so are not confined to deceit. False
allegations for which there is no evidence made by individuals who are

delusional, mistaken, or misled by others also cause injustice. Opinions expressed by journalists, commentators and experts all add to the mix and their opinions substantially derive from the truths, half-truths or lies available to them and their capacity to digest and assess what they believe they know. Unfortunately, too often, controversial opinion is valued more than the tedium of careful analysis and fact checking. Constant, online competition between journalists, broadcasters and social media narratives complicate matters in a 24/7 news media cycle. Greater importance is too frequently attached to breaking news, speed of publication and sensationalising, rather than accuracy and research.

In the world of Irish politics that I inhabited as Ireland's Minister for Justice, Equality and Defence, during the period February to May 2014, fake news was in the ascendancy. Truth, if inconvenient, was sidelined and denigrated. This was not a sudden development. Some time had elapsed before we arrived at that point and both politicians on the Opposition benches in Leinster House and a select group of journalists, broadcasters and commentators played a central role. Attention-seeking politicians in search of public praise became addicted to desired, exaggerated and fictitious narratives and allegations they opportunistically contrived or promoted. Too many journalists and broadcasters abandoned their rational and objective faculties to uncritically embrace the same narratives and allegations and radiate in their glow. Fiction replaced fact in an unprecedented political and media frenzy that dominated political discourse and viciously targeted and demonised those who would not opt into the prevailing popularised orthodoxy. Plaudits were readily available for those who opted into the approved mythology while nothing but opprobrium greeted those who resisted doing so. Eventually, the political and media onslaught together with the public's perspective, gleaned from opinion polls, contaminated and affected the judgement and actions of those I most admired and with whom I worked closest as a Cabinet minister in the Irish Government – the Taoiseach, Enda Kenny, and the Attorney General, Máire Whelan. It also negatively influenced the insights and conduct of some of my other cabinet colleagues.

February 2014 brought together a perfect storm of issues focusing on my ministerial competence and conduct and that of An Garda Síochána, the Irish police force. After a brief lull, the storm regained its momentum in mid-March of that year and then evolved in the first week in May 2014 into a category five hurricane which destroyed my reputation and laid the foundations for ending my over thirty years of active involvement in Irish politics.

An outsider who knows nothing of the events that occurred would suspect that I was guilty of serious criminal misconduct or that I was responsible for major political wrongdoing or dishonesty or gross incompetence or had engaged in some terrible political row with the Taoiseach or my Fine Gael colleagues. The outsider would also expect that by now I would be serving time in prison for my wrongdoing or that any uncertainty about my guilt or failures would have long ago been dispelled. Of course, he or she would be mistaken. What the outsider would not expect is that in the aftermath of my resignation from government all of the allegations that led to my political downfall would be discredited and established to be entirely untrue by two different independent statutory Judicial Commissions of Investigation (see the *O'Higgins and Fennelly Reports*) and one independent non-statutory judicial inquiry (see the *Cooke Report*). None of their reports voiced a word of criticism of my ministerial behaviour and the expertise I applied to my ministerial duties, although to this day there remain some still wedded to and heavily invested in a critical false narrative. Ironically, as a result of the inquiry and investigations conducted, I believe that when it comes to allegations of bad conduct, I am the most exonerated and vindicated politician in the Irish State's history, an accolade in which I take no pleasure.

Our unidentified outsider would also be surprised to learn that in the Ireland of 2014 it was possible for me, as a Government minister, to be wrongly criticised and arbitrarily condemned in a report written by a Government-appointed lawyer who exceeded the boundaries of his Terms of Reference when conducting a preliminary, informal, non-statutory inquiry at the government's request and at the State's expense. The lawyer, Sean Guerin SC, completed his report without affording me an opportunity to express my views or to defend myself and the Guerin Report, as it became known, resulted in my forced resignation from government. It might also be unexpected that as a minister I could be wrongly condemned for breaking the law by the State's Data Protection Commissioner, Billy Hawkes, who publicly and arbitrarily prejudged an important issue of contention, fundamentally misapplied the law he was appointed to administer and denied me a fair hearing. Some might also find surprising the coincidence that the reports of both Guerin and Hawkes were delivered on the same day, 6 May 2014, one to the Department of Justice, the other to the Taoiseach's Department, each containing deeply flawed and mistaken conclusions. The outsider might expect that such extraordinary events could not occur in a long-established constitutional democracy which traditionally respects the rule of law and is a member of the European Union. It is likely our stranger would expect that in a democratic state, when an independent inquiry is conducted, no one could be condemned without due process and a fair hearing and not anticipate it could take almost five years of costly litigation through the Irish courts for the rule of law to prevail.

If I am guilty of anything, I am guilty of naive truth telling when political theatrics or a political parable compatible with or which pandered to the desired false narratives of others might have avoided much of the trouble that led to my political downfall in 2014. Political pragmatism rather than fastidious truth telling could have avoided or possibly diminished the impact of the political and media frenzy that occurred or at least enabled me to survive its spotlight. Aficionados of Niccolo Machiavelli's *The Prince* would advise that all that mattered was my personal political survival in Cabinet and that that imperative required that I abandon any concern for the truth, which can be a variable commodity, and that I should have resorted to any deception required to retain my position. But I believe in the importance of truth, justice, the rule of law and constitutional and democratic values. I dedicated over forty years of my life to those principles, which I believe are central to the political health of a democratic state and to the well-being of its citizens. I had fought countless legal and political battles on behalf of others to uphold those principles and was not prepared as either a lawyer or a politician to jettison my principles and surrender to those who either attached no value to them or simply forgot their value and importance. I would also not bend the knee to those who inhabit Irish politics and are so consumed by political position and obsessed with political power or blinded by ideology, partisanship, bias or ambition that they are impervious to the damage done by their non-observance.

This book is focused on the unprecedented garda-related controversies that exploded into public view in the early months of 2014, events of relevance that preceded them, the role of whistle-blowers, Opposition politicians and the media and what happened inside government. It examines the complexity of what occurred and how simplistic narratives of good and evil, together with ignoring inconvenient truths, created a toxic mix of harmful fantasies. It describes how the gardaí were wrongly accused of bugging the offices of the Garda Síochána Ombudsman Commission, a police oversight body, and how I came to be wrongly accused of covering up espionage that never took place. It details how legitimate complaints made by garda whistle-blower, Sergeant Maurice McCabe about garda incompetence, negligence, failures, maladministration and oversight dysfunction were accompanied by exaggerated and unfounded allegations many of which received widespread currency. The latter included unfounded allegations that Garda Commissioner, Martin Callinan, and other garda officers behaved corruptly; that he had been assaulted and imprisoned by an Assistant Garda Commissioner; that, had gardai not wrongly cancelled motorists ticket charges and penalty points, identified road fatalities may not have occurred and that I had ignored McCabe's allegations and concerns. It also discusses the revelation of previously unknown recordings of telephone conversations in garda stations across the country for over thirty years, how as Minister for Justice I was sidelined by the Taoiseach when he first learned of the recordings from an alarmist Attorney General and the circumstances which resulted in the early retirement of Garda Commissioner, Martin Callinan. It examines how I came to be wrongly accused of covering up alleged garda wrongdoing and failures, of how senior Department of Justice officials failed to furnish me with important communications and information, the relevance to it all of the conduct of whistle-blowers and the dangers of injustice resulting by rushing to judgement and assuming that every allegation made by a whistle-blower is correct and should never be questioned. It looks beyond the allegations and accusations of that period to the outcome of inquiries and investigations into controversies in which I and others were involved, including the recent Disclosures Tribunal presided over by Judge Peter Charleton, and my first learning during its hearings of conversations in which Martin Callinan engaged denigrating Maurice McCabe when I was Justice Minister. The book also discusses the circumstances which resulted in my losing my Dáil seat having been a Fine Gael TD for over thirty years and the role played in my doing so by then Taoiseach and Fine Gael leader, Enda Kenny. It gives an insider's insight into the dysfunctional relationship between truth and politics and the judiciary's crucial role in ensuring adherence to and respect for the rule of law. This is my unvarnished account of the truth of dramatic and unprecedented events that occurred from my own personal experiences and involvement in them.

In January 2015 I commenced writing this book, as I believed in the importance of a factual, fully informed chronological account unburdened by any agenda other than to tell the truth. Early chapters were written in anticipation of the outcome of unfinished judicial investigations then underway, and of likely future political events and dramas. I had little doubt that inevitably Leo Varadkar, who was Minister for Transport, Tourism and Sport during my time in cabinet, would ultimately replace Enda Kenny as leader of Fine Gael and, possibly, as Taoiseach and I anticipated that former colleagues in government would become embroiled in future Garda and McCabe-related controversy. I optimistically hoped that the truth of my account of events in which I became embroiled would ultimately be established. However, it would be untruthful not to admit that as time passed I became increasingly despondent and doubted my judgement and it was an enormous relief when this occurred. I initially believed that within a couple of years court proceedings commenced by me would irrefutably establish that the inquiries conducted by Sean Guerin and Billy Hawkes, which resulted in my being wrongly criticised and condemned, were both fatally flawed, that the rule of law and my right to due process and a fair hearing would prevail and that my conduct and initiation of court actions would be vindicated. What I did not anticipate was that when first heard, both of my court applications would be unceremoniously rejected and that it would take almost five years for that litigation to successfully conclude.

In writing this book I start from the premise that no one gets everything right all of the time and that as we go through life we all make mistakes. This premise not only applies to me but, in so far as it is relevant to my story, also applies to Taoisigh, cabinet ministers, politicians on all sides of the political spectrum, members of An Garda Síochána, whistle-blowers, lawyers, judges, journalists and all involved in the news media. All of those referenced have varied and important roles, which include preserving the integrity of our democracy, respecting and valuing the rule of law, protecting constitutional norms, ensuring justice is not arbitrary, questioning perceived wisdom and challenging and exposing wrongdoing. Obligations and responsibilities accompany such roles, which include not making or endorsing allegations for which there is not a scintilla of evidence, not engaging in deception, not promoting pernicious falsehood and not giving credibility to fabricated, unfounded or mistaken narratives nor to those solely based on leaks of selective incomplete documentation and unsubstantiated assumption. Researching allegations made, recognising the important value of due process and not rushing to judgement to condemn others without a fair hearing is a crucial public interest. Respecting the role of a free press and media and its duty 'to speak truth to power' is a vital democratic and constitutional bulwark that must never be undervalued. However, the importance of factual 'truth' should never be forgotten and that respect should never be abused nor taken for granted by members of the fourth estate. The significance of fact checking, research, investigative reporting and the questioning of a dominant media consensus should never be ignored or devalued. Truth should never be sacrificed to reward those granted anonymity, who leak false self-serving information or serve up unsubstantiated accusation or rumour. On occasions, the overwhelming temptation to simply buy into the favoured narrative of friends and colleagues within the media bubble or the editorially encouraged narrative should be resisted.

If there are lessons to be learned from the events in which I was involved they are that both those in power and their accusers should, when complaints or allegations are made and controversies arise, be subject to the same level of scrutiny. No one, regardless of title, status or profession should be regarded as infallible or elevated to a level of virtue that demands that those who disagree with or challenge them should be automatically demonised. Critical faculties should never be suspended by elevating any whistle-blower, politician or journalist to a mythological level of sainthood. It is right that the courage of those who blow the whistle on wrongdoing or maladministration should be recognised but no one should ever become so invested in their story as to ignore the egregious impact of false or mistaken allegations. The news media, in a democracy, also should not be so precious as to regard itself immune to criticism and should not greet any questioning of its accuracy or professionalism with howls of outrage and condemnation. To retain the public's trust and maintain credibility there is a need to truly recognise the value of an apology and a correction when something clearly false or mistaken is published or broadcast and to not contemptuously or automatically reject complaints made, while adopting a defensive posture.

There is a vital public interest in the preservation of standards both in public life and in journalism and they should never be betrayed or undermined by the entertainment, commercial or political value of dramatising allegations of uncertain validity or by the loss of all sense of proportion. The importance of this I believe is starkly illustrated in the chapters that follow.

Alan Shatter
April 2019

CHAPTER 1

Plane Sailing

Truth can be stranger than fiction but fiction dressed up as truth often attracts more online attention and sells more newspapers!
–Alan Shatter

News devoid of or loosely associated with fact which is intended for the general public –Definition of 'fake news', Urban Dictionary

Humour is like exercise for the brain, and just as physical exercise strengthens the body, keeping a funny outlook is the healthiest way to stay cognitively sharp
–Scott Weems, HA! The Science of When We Laugh and Why

'INEARLY SHATTERED MYSELF'. I suspect the Irish Sun newspaper had been waiting a long time to publish that headline and they deserved a mazeltov for finally getting there ahead of the rest of the media pack. The story was not just billed 'an EXCLUSIVE', but a 'RUNWAY EXCLUSIVE' – even more impressive!

It was 6 August 2014 and, unexpectedly, that morning I was given front-page top billing by the *Irish Sun*. A photograph of me accompanied the story. In it, my mouth was open and I looked as if I was awaiting a tooth inspection by my favourite dental hygeneist. There was also a photograph of a plane. For those not in the know and who suffer from planerecophobia or an inability to recognise planes, there was the helpful caption 'SCARE ... SHATTER' and, in case there was any doubt 'below, a plane'. Unfortunately, we will never know whether many of the paper's loyal readers truly appreciated the explanation that the winged configuration on the bottom right-hand corner of the page with an Aer Lingus logo was indeed a plane. No doubt some subeditor was concerned it could be mistaken for a turkey, even though Christmas was still almost five months away.

A sub-headline helpfully explained 'Former Justice Minister in Take-Off Terror'. Adding two and two, readers might have been led to believe that, having ceased to be Minister for Justice, Equality and Defence in May 2014, I had totally lost my marbles and attempted to hijack a plane or, perhaps, had been a passenger on a plane hijacked by terrorists. It turned out to be neither.

Sun journalist Eavan Murray informed readers that the previous day I had a lucky escape when an Aer Lingus carrier jet narrowly avoided a catastrophic collision. The jet, it was reported, had to 'slam on the brakes as it hurtled down a Dublin runway to dodge an incoming aircraft'. The front page was merely the teaser for the far more detailed 'full story' inside.

Page five was really impressive. 'SHATTER SECONDS FROM DISASTER', blared the headline, missing the irony that the entirety of 2014, so far, could be accurately depicted as a personal disaster. I was again pictured with my mouth open (why the prurient interest in my teeth?) but this time sitting in a plane with my head transplanted onto a body I did not recognise, wearing a tie I did not own or like and there was no sign of my feet! I was manically staring at a woman I had never met. The quote in a bubble beside the photo of my transferred noggin explained 'This was a terrifying experience for the passengers and crew'. The caption on the photo read 'Terror at Zero Feet'.

I would have thought common sense dictated that anyone unexpectedly seated next to an open-mouthed borrowed head lodged on a footless body would be petrified. But, of course, this was the *Irish Sun* and, in the interests of accuracy, there was a further caption explaining the picture. It read 'How Shatter might look on an Airplane'. And I thought I looked so much better than that when in full flight! But at least the Photoshopped picture got my hair right and, for once, I was not having a bad hair day.

Eavan Murray's graphic detailed account left no room for doubt that those aboard the plane had suffered a bad experience, 'The former Justice Minister was on board a Heathrow bound jet forced to abort take-off to avoid a collision with a delayed plane'. Further on, we were told 'the plane was almost at full throttle when it was ordered to abort. It was extremely shocking for everyone on board'. An Aer Lingus spokesperson was quoted confirming the incident saying 'Flight EI 152 Dublin to London, Heathrow pushed back for departure at 6.38 this morning. Shortly thereafter air traffic control instructed the crew to abort take-off. This was due to the delayed landing of another aircraft. EI 152 returned to stand and subsequently took off at 7.56.' An Irish Aviation Authority spokesperson was also reported: 'This morning Dublin Air Traffic Control instructed an Aer Lingus aircraft to abort its take-off when an incoming aircraft advised that it would perform a go-around for technical reasons. This was done to ensure the highest levels of safety were maintained.'

An unidentified 'informed source' was quoted as labelling 'the incident' 'the stuff of nightmares', saying that there could have been 'scores if not hundreds of casualties'. It is not clear whether the informed source was the scripted equivalent of Photoshopping. It may be there was an incident and, if so, I sympathise with those who were on board but in the interests of truth and accuracy I should make one thing clear: I was not there.

I first learned of Eavan Murray's story when I discovered texts on my mobile phone inquiring after my health and welfare from friends and a number of texts and phone messages from various Irish journalists and radio shows seeking interviews or comments from me about the *Irish Sun*'s reported plane incident. Unsurprisingly, none of those connected with the media who left phone messages sympathised or expressed any concern for my well-being. They were simply chasing the *Sun*'s story for newsworthy follow-up on a slow news day.

When I discovered what all the fuss was about, I thought the *Irish Sun*'s front page that day eloquently encapsulated the year so far. Like so much media reportage and commentary since the start of 2014, all references to me in the story were as fictitious as the Photoshopped picture. I had flown to Florida seven days earlier and was over 4,000 miles away from Dublin Airport when the alleged incident occurred. This explained the only accurate reference to me in the entire story, which was 'Shatter could not be reached for comment last night.'

My office having emailed me the *Irish Sun*'s fake news story, I discovered at the bottom of page five another story focussed on identifiable flying objects. The headline read 'Nut Allergy forces Jet to Return'. Fortuitously, the paper had neither alleged that I had fuelled a plane with nuts nor that I was responsible for its aborted flight. That at least was a promising sign that the insanity in which I had been embroiled since the start of the year might eventually end. It held out the promise that the remaining months of 2014 could be plain sailing. Of course, in the world of politics, promises are a debased currency of little value and should not be relied upon.

CHAPTER 2

Joined at the Hip

GSOC under High-Tech Surveillance
–Headline of report by John Mooney, *Sunday Times*, 9 February 2014

A lie will go round the world while truth is pulling its boots on
–Charles Haddon Spurgeon, *Spurgeon's Gems*

Padraig MacLochlainn TD, Sinn Féin's Spokesperson on Justice, Equality and Defence was obsessed with a body part and he mentioned it as often as possible. The tactic worked and it became a staple reference for reporters and political commentators. Omitting it would have been tantamount to confessing you were not truly on the inside track and in the know.

The body part, until February 2014, had not been mentioned in political circles nor come to national prominence in the context of policing. Reference to it in previous times was usually confined to arthritic pain, personal and sporting injuries and surgical intervention. The focus on it was essentially physiological and surgical and not ideological and political.

It is not clear when the Deputy first developed his intense interest in this body part but, as far as he was concerned, the then Garda Commissioner, Martin Callinan and I were 'joined at the hip' or, to use an acronym, JATH. This was surprising, as we had not known each other until I became Minister for Justice in March 2011 and we are unrelated. If we were or had been conjoined, it is likely that at least one of us would have noticed. Nevertheless, Padraig was clearly in love with the idea of JATH and it fitted the narrative that he and other Opposition Deputies were anxious to promote. It was enthusiastically embraced and adopted by many in the news media and some other Opposition TDs who viewed it as manna from a Shinner heaven. Incredibly, it seems that ultimately MacLochlainn's hip construct impacted, as we shall discover, on the perception of the Taoiseach, Enda Kenny, his praetorian guard of special advisers and the Attorney General, Máire Whelan.

In Padraig's world, the Garda Commissioner and I were joined at the hip because, as Minister for Justice, I was not prepared to pass instant judgement and publicly criticise the gardaí and the commissioner every time an allegation of garda misconduct was made and I required that allegations be fully and properly investigated. Where criticism was warranted, I also was of the view that it was usually more productive and less damaging to the public's confidence in the gardaí and to garda morale to voice it privately rather than denigrate the gardaí in public, despite the media plaudits enthusiastically awarded for doing so. I did not then, as now, believe in rushing to judgement for the sake of either a media headline or media applause.

In the Sinn Féin world of kangaroo courts and cynical political posturing, as in a different but related world inhabited by some other TDs and commentators, all allegations made against the gardaí were to be treated as absolute truth and required instant validation. Any questioning of their veracity was synonymous with a cover-up.

We had essentially pivoted from a world of decades earlier where allegations of misconduct made against members of An Garda Síochána were given a hostile media reception and nearly always automatically dismissed, to one in which the news media demanded that all such allegations be instantly validated and believed. This paradigm requires that politicians generally, and government ministers in particular, respond with immediacy, publicly expressing 'concern' and 'shock' about allegations of which they know nothing. The reality is that the more a story can be sensationalised, the better it is for generating interest in online news sites and traditional print newspapers and for attracting commercial advertising.

In politics a failure to express instant concern and alarm about an issue unknown to you diminishes your popularity ratings with some members of the media pack and editors desperately in search of copy. From the political perspective, the more willing you are to offer up instant comment and to buy into a journalist's desired narrative, the more often your comments will be sought, the more journalistic acclaim you are likely to receive and the more recognisable and popular you hope to become. It may also increase your prospect of one day, perhaps, becoming leader of your political party, if you are a member of one. There are few rewards in politics for only speaking when you truly know the facts and for only speaking the truth. Far too frequently alternative facts are preferred and readily reported and inconvenient truths avoided. The events in which I was involved as an Irish government minister in the pre-Trumpian year of 2014 when fake news was king, starkly illustrate this.

So how come the commissioner and I were depicted as a pair of hippies or JATH? To put it succinctly it could be said we were GSOCed! We each committed the ultimate sin of failing to opt into the media's wished-for narrative when an unexpected revelation was published in *The Sunday Times* on 9 February 2014. In particular, I failed to initially voice the demanded 'concern and alarm' sought by journalists to elevate the importance of the story and to provide front-page headlines. In the days that followed I further sinned by failing to endorse and validate the favoured promoted narrative.

For those who know nothing of GSOC, let me explain. It is the Garda Síochána Ombudsman Commission, a garda oversight body composed of three commissioners, including its chairperson. Its job is to independently investigate allegations of garda misconduct. It could do so, during my time as Minister for Justice, upon receipt of a complaint from a member of the general public or could commence an investigation on its own initiative where it decided to do so in the public interest. Where a serving member of An Garda Síochána complained of garda misconduct, the complaint could not be made directly to GSOC, but came to GSOC, as I will explain, in a roundabout way, via the Garda Confidential Recipient. In the last week of January 2014, I announced that legislation under which GSOC operated was to be amended, to allow it to receive complaints directly from a garda. The required legislation was later enacted.

Since its establishment in 2007, there had been understandable tensions between An Garda Síochána and GSOC. One of my concerns as Minister for Justice was to ensure the fullest co-operation between the two organisations. This was important so that when GSOC, as an independent body, investigated a complaint, all information requested from An Garda Síochána was provided speedily and gardaí fully co-operated. There had been ongoing difficulties between the two bodies many but not all of which had been the fault of the gardaí. In July 2013, I had convened a meeting in the Department of Justice with the Garda Commissioner and then Chairperson of GSOC, Simon O'Brien. Its purpose was to encourage them to conclude unduly drawn out discussions on new to-be-agreed protocols to resolve their difficulties. Each had their own independent statutory roles and functions but it was crucial to end disputes occurring between them. I insisted their discussions should be completed before the end of September 2013. This was achieved and the new working protocols were announced and published on 23 September 2013. This coincided with the date of my wedding anniversary but, as I was unfortunately to discover, the coming together of the two bodies was not a match made in heaven!

GSOC's then Chairperson, Simon O'Brien, was formerly Deputy Chief Inspector of the Garda Síochána Inspectorate and, prior to that, Territorial Policing Commander in the UK's London Metropolitan Police. The two other GSOC Commissioners were Carmel Foley and Kieran Fitzgerald. Foley had been on GSOC since its inception. She had previously served as Chief Executive of both the Employment Equality Agency and the Council for the Status of Women. She had also been the Director of Consumer Affairs. Fitzgerald, prior to his appointment as a commissioner, had been Head of Communications and Research at GSOC and previously was a journalist and a senior reporter on RTÉ's *Prime Time*. He had been named News and Current Affairs Journalist of the Year 2000. Subsequent to my becoming Minister for Justice, the positions on GSOC had for the first time been advertised on the Public Appointments Service website. All three had been nominated by the government on my recommendation, having been designated to me as appropriate for appointment as GSOC Commissioners. Their appointments had been approved by resolutions in both Houses of the Oireachtas in December 2011.

By the end of September 2013, I believed we were entering a new era and that the new protocols would ensure both GSOC and the Garda Síochána would properly fulfil their statutory duties. Then came Sunday, 9 February 2014.

'GSOC under High-Tech Surveilliance' was the incendiary front-page headline on a *Sunday Times* story written by crime journalist John Mooney. Mooney reported that 'The Garda Síochána Ombudsman Commission (GSOC) was targeted as part of a sophisticated surveillance operation which used "Government-level technology" to look into its emails, Wi-Fi and phone systems.' There were no 'ifs', 'buts' or 'maybes' about this report. Its content was presented as absolute, sensational fact.

It continued:

The espionage was uncovered last year after GSOC hired a British security consultancy to investigate whether its headquarters in Abbey Street, Dublin, and its internal communications systems were bugged.

The consultants, among them former counter-surveillance specialists with Britain's GCHQ Spying Agency, found a speaker phone on the upper floor of the GSOC building was bugged. The room was regularly used to hold case conferences on sensitive investigations. A test of the line confirmed the phone was being used to eavesdrop on meetings, according to sources.

The investigation also found that those responsible for the surveillance had compromised GSOC's Wi-Fi network in order to steal emails, data, confidential reports and possibly eavesdrop on mobile phone calls. The US National Security Agency (NSA) has used this technique to spy on targets in the past.

Investigators discovered that a second Wi-Fi system had been created to harvest GSOC data. It was operated using an IP address in Britain which electronically concealed the identities and whereabouts of those spying on the Garda watchdog, say sources.

Another device, which worked off GSOC's broadband network, was also found to have been compromised. However, it was wiped of all data by those involved in the spying operation, known in security circles as a 'black operation', when it became clear their activities had been detected.

Further on the report asserted: 'A report prepared for the three-person commission found there were specific indicators to prove it was being targeted using controlled technology, which was not commercially available or sold to non-Government agencies.'

According to Mooney, it was 'not clear if mobile phones and computers used by the three Commissioners were specifically targeted but this is suspected to be the case'. He also said that the duration 'of the espionage could not be established by the investigators'.

The unnamed British security company who investigated the 'sophisticated surveillance' of GSOC was stated to have 'secretly shipped' to Dublin specialist counter-surveillance and telecommunication equipment 'to integrity test the Garda watchdog's communication system as part of the inquiry'. GSOC, we were told, had spent €50,000 on the investigation and had 'stepped up internal security measures'.

As Mooney presented it, the 'surveillance' of GSOC's offices and 'espionage' conducted was all very cloak and dagger in the John Le Carré mould. Mooney reported that 'details of what happened were withheld from the Department of Justice and Garda Headquarters as the spying techniques used to mount the surveillance had left no clues which could categorically identify those involved'.

While those responsible for the surveillance and espionage could not, according to the story, be categorically identified, Mooney's story was definitive in its assertion that it had occurred. To further enhance the narrative he was not slow to hint at who was likely to be responsible. Towards the end of his report he reminded readers that GSOC had investigated 'allegations of collusion between Gardai and Kieran Boylan, an international drug dealer' and 'was currently investigating the cancellation of penalty points by senior gardai'. The latter was a task I had requested of GSOC thirteen days earlier on 27 January 2014 and which had no relevance of any nature. Mooney was clearly implying both investigations were connected to the covert activity that he reported had occurred.

Mooney concluded the report:

The Gardai, Customs and Military are permitted to use intrusive surveillance techniques to spy on people involved in organised crime and terrorism, but only for legitimate reasons and if permitted to do so by a judge.

Telephone intercepts require Ministerial approval which must set out the reasons for the surveillance.

Senior security and military sources last night said that no Government agency would mount surveillance on another. Other security sources said it would be impossible for a private individual to organise such surveillance.

The clear implication of the story was that either An Garda Síochána itself or a group of rogue garda members were responsible for the surveillance, which Mooney was absolutely certain had occurred.

The Sunday Times speculated that 'the surveillance appeared to have been organised after O'Brien, Fitzgerald and Foley had been appointed to head up the Garda Watchdog'. Mooney predicted that 'the disclosure that GSOC *was targeted* [author's italics] is likely to cause concern at the highest level of Government and civil rights groups'. [*sic*]

Although the newspaper acknowledged that information about the surveillance and investigation into it was withheld from the Department of Justice and, by implication, from me as Minister for Justice, both broadcast and print media sought instant expressions of concern from me as Mooney predicted. I decided to say nothing of substance until I knew the full facts. I recognised that even an expression of concern by me, as Minister for Justice, would add credibility and legs to a story which, if untrue, could substantially undermine public confidence in both the Garda Síochána and in GSOC. I did not anticipate that if the surveillance story turned out to be untrue, some members of the Oireachtas and sections of the media would remain intractably wedded to a false narrative.

Having read the *Sunday Times* report, I asked Department of Justice officials to urgently arrange a meeting with Simon O'Brien so that I could be fully briefed by him on what had occurred. It was clearly very serious if the story were true and if GSOC had been under any form of surveillance. Moreover, if the gardaí were involved at any level, it would be an enormous scandal. It was imperative to bring clarity to what had occurred as rapidly as possible and to not fuel inaccurate speculation.

I contacted the Taoiseach, Enda Kenny TD, who understandably requested a report on the alleged espionage and surveillance for the following Tuesday morning's Cabinet meeting. I informed him that I would be meeting Simon O'Brien the next day, Monday, for a full briefing. The media, in response to queries, were also informed of the meeting by the Department of Justice press office. Meanwhile, predictably, some Cabinet colleagues added hype to the story by being reported on *RTÉ News* at 6pm and 9pm, as expressing concern about the alleged surveillance of GSOC. That was at a time when all they and I knew was dependent on the *Sunday Times* report. The Labour Party Leader, Tánaiste and Minister for Foreign Affairs, Eamon Gilmore TD, while acknowledging 'I don't know anything about it' stated 'as a general principle, I don't think any public official should be bugged or have their phones bugged'. In the next day's *Irish Times* he was reported as describing suggestions of surveillance on GSOC as 'quite sinister'.

By Monday morning, all of the print and broadcast media presumed that GSOC had been a victim of espionage, had been bugged and that the *Sunday Times* story was accurate. According to *The Sunday Times*, GSOC had recruited a British security consultancy firm, which included counter-surveillance specialists, who formerly worked for 'Britain's GCHQ spying agency' and it was they who had confirmed the surveillance of GSOC. I was surprised to read that former members of a British Government intelligence agency had been requested to undertake a counter-surveillance assignment in the Republic of Ireland at the request of an independent Irish police watchdog. It was even more surprising, if it was discovered that GSOC was under surveillance, that I had not been informed by the GSOC Commissioners. If there was either credible evidence or proof that An Garda Síochána were the culprits, it was beyond comprehension that such information had been withheld from me and the Department of Justice.

The legislation under which GSOC operated contained express provision to facilitate the commission bringing important issues to the Justice Minister's attention. Section 80 (5) of the Garda Síochána Act 2005 enabled the commission to make any report 'it considered appropriate' to draw an issue to the minister's attention because of its 'gravity or other exceptional circumstances'. The Act also required the minister 'as soon as practicable' after receipt of any such report to place it before both Houses of the Oireachtas. I believed that a discovery that GSOC either is or was under covert surveillance could be described as nothing other than a grave matter or one of exceptional importance. I so informed the Taoiseach, who publicly stated that GSOC should explain why it had failed to report the matter to me.

Bizarrely, in the days that followed, the issue of whether GSOC had a responsibility to report its concerns about covert surveillance of its offices to me as minister, under section 80(5) of the 2005 Act, became the subject of controversy generated by Opposition politicians and media commentators. The issue should have become irrelevant following GSOC issuing a statement after my meeting Simon O'Brien, GSOC's Chairperson, on the Monday afternoon. He informed me that not only had GSOC recruited the service of a British intelligence consulting firm, Verimus, but it had also, on 8 October 2013, formally commenced a public interest investigation under Section 102 of the Garda Síochána Act 2005. This was on the assumption that, not only had their offices been bugged, but the bugging had been undertaken by members of An Garda. Section 103 of the Act specifically prescribed that both the Minister for Justice and the Garda Commissioner be informed of the commencement of any such investigation and of its outcome and neither of us had been. During the controversy that ensued over whether GSOC was or was not obliged to keep me informed as Minister for Justice, both Opposition politicians and the media carefully averted their eyes from this express statutory obligation.

I could not have met Simon O'Brien on the Sunday as he was in England. My meeting with him took place in the Department of Justice, together with Justice officials, at 3pm on the afternoon of Monday, 10 February 2014. He informed me that GSOC for some considerable time had not arranged for a security check of their offices. Following their appointment in December 2011, this was a concern to him and the other commissioners. They had done little about the matter until 2013 when, to ensure the independence of any security check undertaken, a UK security firm had been contracted. He informed me that, following a security check undertaken by Verrimus operatives in September 2013, the commissioners had received a report identifying what he described as two security 'vulnerabilities' and that later a third had been identified. It was not clear to me from his briefing how the discovery of the 'vulnerabilities' had evolved into a conclusion that GSOC had been subject to some form of covert surveillance. Nevertheless, as a consequence of Verrimus's initial report of the two alleged vulnerabilities, GSOC had initiated a formal investigation assuming that, if under surveillance, such surveillance originated from An Garda Síochána. He explained that some weeks later, GSOC concluded that there was no evidence of any such surveillance and the matter was dropped, but they had implemented measures to beef up their security.

I asked detailed questions about the nature of the alleged 'vulnerabilities' and the technology involved. I was concerned by his lack of clarity. I was not convinced O'Brien fully understood the technology we were discussing. I decided it was crucial that I receive a written report from GSOC that could be relied upon to brief the Taoiseach, the Cabinet and for any Dáil statement I would have to make and requested that one be provided to me that evening. O'Brien apologised for not informing me earlier of what had occurred and, towards the end of the meeting, said he thought I might be seeking his resignation.

My focus at that stage was to obtain as comprehensive a report as possible and not on the future of the chairperson or the other two commissioners. I was anxious to ascertain whether there was any solid factual basis for concern that GSOC had been under surveillance and whether any evidence existed of any garda involvement. I would reserve judgement until I received the chairperson's report.

I anticipated that if O'Brien's report confirmed that there was no evidence of surveillance, or of Garda involvement, the whole thing might be a storm in a teacup. However, I was unclear why exactly the gardaí had come under suspicion or why, as Minister for Justice, I had not been informed of the public interest investigation GSOC had initiated.

It was not my style to berate or lose my temper with any individual with whom I worked or engaged but I quietly made it clear to O'Brien that I should not have first learnt of GSOC's surveillance concerns from what now appeared to be a grossly inaccurate report in *The Sunday Times*. Following his apology, I assumed that both he and the other commissioners would provide a comprehensive and straightforward briefing to me and, as an independent body, detail clearly in public exactly what had occurred and GSOC's conclusions. This prophetic assumption would prove wildly inaccurate.

At 6.45 that evening, GSOC released a statement to the press with the unfortunate title 'Security at and Surveillance of Garda Síochána Ombudsman Commission' which I believe helped fuel the narrative that the organisation had been under surveillance. In it GSOC said it 'has always been conscious of the need for appropriate confidentiality and proper levels of security'. It detailed that 'on two occasions since commencing operations, security experts have been consulted', and that sweeps of their building and 'tests on the integrity' of their telecommunication security had been undertaken. According to the commission, a security sweep of their offices had been conducted on the evenings of 23–27 September 2013 by 'a specialist UK security firm' (Verrimus was not named). The firm's 'expert advice' had also been sought 'on the sorts of capabilities that exist in relation to the interception of communications, including telephones'. The press release continued 'the investigation was completed on 17 December 2013.' (This would later prove inaccurate as the investigation effectively ended four weeks earlier.) It confirmed the existence of three technical and electronic anomalies. These could not be conclusively explained and raised concerns among the investigation team in terms of GSOC's communications security. 'However, GSOC is satisfied its databases were not compromised. Since the investigation we have been working to review and enhance our security systems in the light of what the investigation revealed.'

This part of the statement referencing 'three technical and electronic anomalies', and contradicting the *Sunday Times*'s story, unambiguously asserted that GSOCs 'Databases' had not been compromised and made no mention of GSOC being under surveillance at any time. Inexplicably, the 'surveillance' word appeared only in the title of GSOC's press release which totally failed to explain what was meant by 'three technical and electronic anomalies'. Moreover, without explanation, GSOC then baldly and explosively stated 'There was no evidence of garda misconduct.' The commission, it was explained, 'decided to discontinue the investigation' on the basis that 'no further action was necessary or reasonably practicable'. It was unclear from this whether 'no further action was necessary' because there had been no wrongdoing by any member of the gardaí or anyone else or whether the investigation was discontinued because there was no 'practicable' possibility of identifying those engaged in wrongdoing.

The overall cost of the security checks undertaken was said to be €18,000 not the €50,000 claimed in the *Sunday Times* report. While the press release did not substantiate *The Sunday Times*' definitive assertion that GSOC had been under surveillance, that its meetings had been bugged or its data compromised, the reference to 'three technical and electronic anomalies' that could not be conclusively explained, the appearance of the word 'surveillance' in its title and the bald reference to there being 'no evidence of Garda misconduct' was used by Opposition politicians, reporters and media commentators to give the story legs. For some it simply lent credibility to the claim that GSOC's offices had been bugged.

The initial understandable demands that I, as Minister for Justice, explain what if anything had occurred, something I could not do without first meeting Simon O'Brien, within twenty-four hours of our meeting morphed into an allegation that my meeting with him violated the independence of GSOC and undermined his position as chairperson of an independent body. Not only did some commentators ignore the true statutory background, they also ignored what GSOC first officially said about this in the final paragraph of their press release that Monday evening:

> We took the difficult decision not to report this matter to other parties. We did not wish to point fingers unnecessarily and we did not believe wide-spread reporting would be conducive to public confidence. We took the decision not to report in good faith. We regret that now

and this was communicated to the Minister for Justice, Equality and Defence by Simon O'Brien, chairman of the Commission, this afternoon.

This explanation, later repeated by Simon O'Brien when addressing a Joint Oireachtas Committee, should have conclusively established that GSOC retrospectively recognised that it had a duty to report to me as Minister for Justice on its security concerns and the action taken by it. However, as we shall see, GSOC's own explanation and expression of regret did not suit the narrative that some journalists and commentators were anxious to peddle and develop. Nor did it inhibit Opposition TDs from criticising my temerity in speedily arranging to meet Simon O'Brien the day after publication of the *Sunday Times* story. This was Catch 22 stuff. How I could have otherwise explained the events that had occurred to the Dáil, the Cabinet or the general public was entirely ignored in this criticism. Had I not met with O'Brien, no doubt I would have been accused of dereliction of my ministerial duties!

CHAPTER 3

Vulnerabilities, Anomalies and Threats

At any given moment there is an orthodoxy, a body of ideas which it is assumed all right thinking people will accept without question ... Anyone who challenges the prevailing orthodoxy finds himself silenced with surprising effectiveness. A genuinely unfashionable opinion is never given a fair hearing, either in the popular press or in the highbrow periodicals –George Orwell's preface to *Animal Farm*, omitted when originally published in 1945 and first published in *The Times Literary Supplement*, 15 September 1972

Something difficult, abnormal, peculiar or not easily classified –Definition of 'anomaly', *Merriam-Webster Dictionary*

Two and a half hours after GSOC's press release issued, I received from Simon O'Brien the typed brief I had requested. In it GSOC detailed two 'potential threats' identified during the security sweep of 23–27 September 2013. O'Brien at our meeting had made no reference to any 'threats' nor had GSOC's earlier press release. What were originally described to me by O'Brien as 'vulnerabilities' and then in GSOC's press statement as 'technical and electronic anomalies' had inexplicably evolved into 'potential threats'.

These were described as follows:

Threat 1: A Wi-Fi device located in the Boardroom [the Commission's conference room], was found to have connected to an external Wi-Fi network. Access to this Wi-Fi device was protected by a password; absent this password, the device should not have been able to connect to that external Wi-Fi network. As GSOC does not have a Wi-Fi network, this device had never been activated by GSOC and its password was unknown. Its connection to an external network was, therefore, a concern. This device, although Wi-Fi enabled was unable to communicate with any of GSOC's databases or electronic systems.

Threat 2: As part of the security checks, the conference call telephone unit located in the Chairman's office was subjected to a number of tests. One of the tests involved sending an audio signal down the telephone line; this is known as an 'alerting' test as it presents the possibility that a listener will hear this audio signal. Immediately after the transmission of the audio signal, the conference phone line rang. The Verrimus operator judged that the likelihood of a 'wrong number' being called at that time, to that exact unknown number at the time of an alerting test, was so small as to be at virtually zero. GSOC conducted a number of telecoms checks to seek to establish the source of this telephone call but was unable to do so. Further checks revealed no additional anomalies or matters of concern.

The briefing detailed that, on 7 October 2013 after 'confirmation paperwork' was received from Verrimus, 'the [GSOC] investigation team assessed these two threats' and the next day, 8 October 'a public interest investigation was launched pursuant to section 102(4) of the Garda Síochána Act 2005'. The briefing continued:

> the investigation was launched on the basis that the Acting Director of Investigations was of the opinion that, to the extent that these threats could be proven, section 102(4) engaged [*sic*] – that is to say that such surveillance may have originated with An Garda Síochána [AGS] and if so, a member of AGS may have committed an offence or behaved in a manner that justified disciplinary proceedings.

At this point the briefing had jumped from referencing two 'potential threats' to a preliminary conclusion that GSOC had been or was under surveillance and that either the gardaí as a force, a group of rogue guards or an individual garda 'may' be the culprit. Not only was it unclear how a preliminary conclusion of a potential threat evolved into a view that surveillance had been attempted or had occurred, it was also unclear why it was presumed, without any evidence of any nature whatsoever, that gardaí could be the culprits and no one else. If GSOC was under surveillance, it could equally have been by an individual with a grievance against the gardaí or GSOC, by members of a subversive or criminal organisation or by individuals associated with a media group. In light of the then recent revelations in England in the Leveson Report about the conduct of the tabloid press, the latter could not be ruled out. It was also possible that GSOC could have fallen victim to any number of potential hackers. It was subsequently to become clear that whatever about the difficulties in identifying why the conference phone line in the chairman's office rang as referenced in 'Threat 2', the background to 'Threat 1' was known and readily explainable but omitted from GSOC's briefing note. It not only posed no threat of any nature to GSOC, it bordered on the farcical.

Subsequent to the 8 October decision, I was told Verrimus were re-engaged and, during a visit by their operatives on 19–20 October, a third 'potential threat' was identified, in that 'A UK 3G network' was detected. The report continued:

> UK networks do not operate within Ireland except in border areas. They advised that such a network can only be simulated through a service called an 'IMSI catcher'. An IMSI catcher, in simulating a UK mobile phone network, will pick up UK phones registered to that network. Once a phone has been connected to an IMSI catcher, it can be forced to disable call encryption making the call data vulnerable to interception and recording. The specialist firm indicated that this level of technology is only available to government agencies.

According to the briefing, analysis of all three 'potential threats' was 'inconclusive'. Acknowledging that GSOC was operating at the limits of its technical knowledge and on information from security professionals, the report continued 'the Commission did not rule out that there could be reasonable explanations for any/all of these issues, for example':

> *Connection by the Wi-Fi device in the conference room with an external Wi-Fi network was occurring randomly and no discernible pattern or agent apparent

> *The anomaly in the telephone unit in the Chairman's office could not be repeated – the Commission could not rule out the possibility that an innocent call was made to the office at 1am. Telecoms data could not identify a number from which the call originated or even that a call had been made

> *Considering IMSI catcher, the Commission could not rule out that such a device was being lawfully used in the vicinity of Capel Street to, for example, counter subversion or organised crime.

I was informed that a specific operational test concluded on 19 November yielded no results and added no clarity. GSOC concluded stating that 'no definitive evidence of unauthorised or electronic surveillance was found', important information omitted from GSOC's 'surveillance' press release issued 2.5 hours earlier. Omitted from GSOC's written brief to me was its conclusion that 'There was no evidence of Garda misconduct' contained in its press release.

To ensure the story I told fully reflected all the information received by me from GSOC, I incorporated both conclusions into my cabinet briefing and subsequent statement to the Dáil.

Within a short time, the term 'GSOC Bugging Scandal' entered the political lexicon. It was used by some to denote as a fact that the gardaí had GSOC under surveillance and to pillory me as Minister for Justice for allegedly both covering up such surveillance and treating GSOC and its chairperson disgracefully by seeking a briefing following publication of the *Sunday Times* story. The fact that GSOC itself, in its very first public comment to the media, stated that it was 'satisfied its data bases were not compromised' and that 'there is no evidence of Garda misconduct' was conveniently ignored. The reference to the gardaí in GSOC's press release understandably angered Martin Callinan, who issued a swift response criticising GSOC for implying that 'An Garda Síochána was in some way suspected of complicity' in the suspected bugging of GSOC's offices. The commissioner's statement was issued without my receiving any forewarning. It was just in time to be reported by RTÉ television on that Monday evening's *Nine O'Clock News* and shortly before receipt by me at approximately 9.15 pm of the report I had requested from Simon O'Brien. The commissioner and the Garda Press Office had been under pressure to respond since publication of the *Sunday Times* story and GSOC's statement earlier that evening had added to that pressure. There was nothing out of the ordinary in Callinan's statement and, had he remained silent, his silence in the days that followed would undoubtedly have been interpreted as the gardaí having something to hide. He could not have anticipated that the fact that he had responded so speedily would be interpreted the same way by some. Unfortunately, as a result of an unconnected but long-running controversy over motorists fixed charge notices and penalty points, Martin Callinan was by then perceived as fair game for criticism no matter what he said, while GSOC was regarded as beyond reproach.

In the days that followed, the Garda Commissioner and I were to be repeatedly wrongly accused of being involved in some sort of conspiratorial cover up of serious garda misconduct. References to the GSOC bugging scandal became a code, which included this portrayal. Of course, the real GSOC scandal was the totally incompetent manner in which GSOC dealt with the 'vulnerabilities' or 'anomalies' revealed by Verrimus, how they were elevated into being 'potential' then later, as we shall see, 'credible threats', the failure of GSOC's commissioners to comply with their statutory reporting obligations, their cavalier approach to the commencement of a public interest investigation, the extraordinary divergence between the content of GSOC's original public statement on the evening of 10 February 2014 and its briefing to me two and a half hours later, the incapacity of GSOC's commissioners to carefully publicly explain what occurred and their abject failure, as an independent body, during the days of controversy that followed, to directly and accurately publicly address and correct misinformation repetitively reported and broadcast.

CHAPTER 4

The Media Frenzy Begins

In the past 48 hours, the guns have been trained on the GSOC because it did not report to the Minister even though it had no obligation to –Micheál Martin, leader of Fianna Fáil, Dáil Éireann, 12 February 2014

There is no provision in the law which insists that GSOC must report to the Minister –Gerry Adams TD, leader of Sinn Féin, Dáil Éireann, 12 February 2014

Truth does not become more true by virtue of the fact that the entire world agrees with it, nor less so even if the whole world disagrees with it –Moses Maimonides, *The Guide for the Perplexed*

A temporary madness: violent mental or emotional agitation: intense usually wild and often disorderly compulsive or agitated activity –Definition of 'frenzy', *Merriam-Webster Dictionary*

The morning after *The Sunday Times'* GSOC surveillance revelations, Sinn Féin's Padraig MacLochlainn, in his capacity as Chairperson of the Joint Oireachtas Committee on Public Service Oversight and Petitions (the Petitions Committee), announced that he would be contacting GSOC to ask the commissioners to appear before his committee to explain what it had found. It was, he said, 'quite extraordinary' that bugging had been detected last year (2013) and the Government knew nothing about it until a report in *The Sunday Times*. Fianna Fáil's Justice Spokesperson Niall Collins TD described the matter as so serious I should immediately 'explain what on earth is going on'.

It was assumed by most of the media on Monday that the *Sunday Times* story, which was widely reported, was true and that GSOC had been bugged. The Department of Justice was peppered with questions throughout the day and, by the Tuesday morning the frenzied media juggernaut was on the road and gathering speed.

All that was in the public domain at that stage was the GSOC press release of 6.45pm Monday, and the Garda Commissioner's furious reaction.

He expressed 'grave concern' that GSOC's statement 'contains a clear indication that an Garda Síochána was in some way suspected of complicity in this matter, despite GSOC's overall finding that the existence of technical and electronic anomalies could not be conclusively explained'.

He stated he was seeking clarification from GSOC of the nature and extent of the anomalies, whether they amounted to a security breach, whether a criminal offence was suspected and the basis for suspicion of garda misconduct.

I regarded his reaction understandable, particularly considering the protocols detailing working arrangements between GSOC and An Garda Síochána agreed only two weeks prior to GSOC's commencement of its secret public interest investigation on 8 October 2013. Of course, when the commissioner issued his statement he did not know that GSOC, on a preliminary basis, suspected that the gardaí had its offices under surveillance without having a shred of evidence on which they could rely. I believed, in the interests of both GSOC and An Garda Síochána and in the public interest, the main focus should be on obtaining the full facts and bringing the growing controversy to an end. I also knew that its continuation could only fuel the narrative that GSOC and An Garda Síochána were still at war with each other and that nothing had been done by me as minister to ensure, when required, that each organisation respected the other and fully co-operated to enable GSOC to properly undertake its garda oversight functions.

The Tuesday morning papers included further comment from Opposition politicians. I was accused of wrongly shifting the debate (what debate?) to GSOC's obligation to inform me of their surveillance concerns accompanied by demands that I recognise 'the seriousness of the situation'. Fianna Fáil's Niall Collins TD, assuming the *Sunday Times* story to be accurate, insisted that I 'move quickly to establish who was responsible for this surveillance and on whose authority the individual or organisation was acting'. It suited the Opposition's political narrative to be critical of my lack of knowledge of what had occurred, while ignoring GSOC's public expression of regret for its failure to report to me what had happened. It also suited them to subsequently criticise my seeking a briefing from GSOC's chairperson to obtain the full picture. This was political *Alice in Wonderland* stuff but media commentators bought into it all – hook, line and sinker.

Ruairi Quinn TD, the Labour Party's Minister for Education, was reported that Tuesday morning as expressing surprise that I had not been informed of the alleged bugging stating: 'I would get briefings on a regular basis about confidential matters'. Fine Gael's Frances Fitzgerald, the Minister for Children was reported as being 'shocked' and 'astounded' by the allegations, terminology I had deliberately refrained from using, and was quoted stating 'we have to get the details of what are the allegations at this stage and to discuss them at Cabinet'.

The Irish Times, which regards itself as 'the paper of record', editorialised on the 'covert surveillance of the Commission's office [which] is believed to have started two years ago'. It authoritatively informed readers that upon a British security firm confirming GSOC's 'communication's system had been compromised, those engaged in the surveillance became aware that they had been detected ... and had removed traceable evidence'. Asserting 'the Commission did not bug itself' the paper demanded 'an independent investigation', ignoring the fact that GSOC as an independent investigating body had conducted and concluded its own independent investigation.

At the Tuesday morning Cabinet meeting I fully briefed colleagues on the bugging controversy and we agreed there would be statements in the Dáil Chamber around 6pm that evening. Prior to that there was a preliminary skirmish on the issue in the Dáil during Leaders' Questions between the Taoiseach, Enda Kenny, and Opposition leaders. Nothing new of substance emerged other than Kenny referencing GSOC's attendance the next day before the Petitions Committee and rather optimistically stating that, at that meeting, he expected 'that the matters that need to be addressed in respect of giving absolute clarity about this fundamentally important office will be addressed'. By the end of the exchanges, it was absolutely clear that the Opposition intended to use the issue as a political football aimed both at me and the Government.

In my Dáil statement, I detailed the facts I then knew, based entirely on the information supplied by GSOC. I believed it important to use the occasion to recognise and endorse the important role of both An Garda Síochána and GSOC, while lowering the temperature.

I expressly acknowledged that 'each is a crucial pillar in our constitutional democracy and each plays a vital role in the public interest' and stated the need to ensure 'conclusions reached when investigations are undertaken based on well-founded and solid evidence'.

I emphasised the importance of both the gardaí and GSOC complying with their statutory reporting obligations and the need for each to be 'mindful of the service they perform in the public interest' and 'conscious of how their actions and words may affect public confidence in each organisation'. I was, however, emphatic that they should 'show no fear nor favour when seeking to ascertain the truth on issues, no matter how difficult or potentially controversial'.

Acknowledging that if GSOC 'were, in fact, subject to surveillance from any quarter, it would be a matter of the greatest concern' I stated that it was 'unfortunate that An Garda Síochána has found itself, during the last 48 hours, the subject of what appears to be completely baseless innuendo'. I concluded, asserting that 'concerns which GSOC had in regard to the security of its communications have been investigated by it, no definitive evidence of unauthorised technical or electronic surveillance was uncovered, it deemed no further action was necessary and took steps to review its systems with a view to further enhancing its security'.

In response, Niall Collins alleged that Simon O'Brien had 'been forced to apologise to me the previous day' and that the independence of GSOC had been undermined by his 'being dragged into meet the Minister'. While he demanded answers to a variety of questions surrounding the *Sunday Times* story, Collins exonerated GSOC for not informing me of what had occurred, while being critical of my seeking answers to the very questions he had asked during the preceding forty-eight hours. There was no logic to his contribution but this is the Dáil chamber and his hyperbole provided the desired sound bites.

Padraig MacLochlainn continued in the same vein. 'People,' he stated 'will argue that the Minister has too close a relationship with the Garda Commissioner', assuming that 'people' believed the Garda Commissioner and the Minister for Justice should be in a state of ongoing conflict. Like Collins, he called for an independent inquiry. We didn't yet embrace JATH territory but Independent Deputy Claire Daly ventured into physiological and psychological attachment theory. Accusing me of having an 'unsuitable relationship' with the commissioner, she asserted that 'there is a perception that the Minister and the Commissioner work very closely and they are, in many ways, hand in glove.' For Lucinda Creighton, a former Fine Gael colleague, who later formed and became leader of the ill-fated Renua Party, public comments made by the Taoiseach critical of GSOC for not complying with their reporting obligations were yet another 'flagrant public attack' on an 'independent institution' and 'an abuse of power'. Her wrath was unqualified.

The Dáil debate followed a sadly predictable route, generating more heat than light and was used as a platform to dredge up a variety of other garda-related controversies. By its conclusion, a number of journalists had reluctantly decided that by Wednesday the GSOC controversy could be over. They had not factored in the GSOC Commissioners' capacity to obfuscate and confuse.

The Dáil debate concluded at 7.30pm. Two hours later one of the GSOC Commissioners, Kieran Fitzgerald, appeared on *Prime Time*, the current affairs programme to which he had been attached as a reporter years earlier. By the time he had answered Miriam O'Callaghan's first question the entire issue had descended into confusion.

'So, Kieran Fitzgerald,' she asked, 'the Minister today seems pretty clear there's no evidence at all that you were bugged. So, were you bugged?'

He responded:

Miriam, it would be very very good if we were able to say definitively yes or definitively no. Unfortunately, the reality of modern surveillance and intrusive surveillance mechanisms, is that it's very often an inconclusive result. So, what we got were credible threats to our own security, we hired consultants, experts, international experts to consider those for us, examine those and test them. At the conclusion of their testing and their sweeps, their security sweeps, they are able to tell us that certain things did not look likely and other things they could not be definitively sure.

I felt a sense of unease and was concerned that, somewhere between GSOC's office and RTÉ's *Prime Time* studio in Donnybrook, three unexplained 'anomalies', 'vulnerabilities' or 'potential threats' had evolved into 'credible threats' and the report furnished by GSOC to me the previous evening had somehow slipped Fitzgerald's mind.

As the interview continued, some of his responses to Miriam's questions appeared to diverge from GSOC's public statement and to verify the *Sunday Times* story.

'You still believe there could have been bugging of your building and your equipment. And that is not what the Minister is saying, today,' she asserted. Fitzgerald responded, protesting that 'we have no disagreement at all with the Minister and we ...' Before he could finish the sentence, Miriam interrupted saying, 'Well, you clearly have.'

The confusion continued as Miriam quoted my saying in the Dáil that what was identified were 'potential threats and vulnerabilities', phraseology directly out of GSOC's own report and press release, 'but that there was no evidence that any surveillance had, in fact, taken place'.

Fitzgerald responded, 'There is no evidence to sugg– to confirm that surveillance has taken place. The Minister is absolutely right and we have no, as a result of our briefing to him, we have no disagreement on that topic.' [*sic*]

'But on the balance of probability, Kieran Fitzgerald, do you believe you were bugged?' Miriam asked.

Fitzgerald replied, 'It is difficult to say.'

Unfortunately, Fitzgerald's responses were readily interpretable as indicating that GSOC suspected but was unable to confirm that it had been bugged.

Miriam was persistent: 'In your statement last night, you said there was no evidence of Garda misconduct. Why would you say that in the first place if you weren't thinking that?'

He answered:

Because the reason we said that last night – and I am happy to repeat it here now – is that it's part of the public discussion in Dáil Eireann this evening and all over the airwaves for the last couple of days. People are pointing fingers, and may I say it is unfair of people to point fingers at An Garda Síochána on the basis of anything we have said or done.

The presenter continued, 'But your statement last night did that.'

Kieran Fitzgerald replied:

No. Our statement last night was meant to try to clear that up and say we did not find evidence of Garda misconduct, because the public discourse seems to be pointing in the direction of finding the Guards guilty of this thing, when we are saying, quite clearly and categorically and in no uncertain terms, we found no evidence to point to that direction, and for people to suggest that, you know, they were up to something – we're the people who did the examination, we're the people with the evidence. We do not have any evidence to point in that direction.

In a sane world, Fitzgerald's last response should have taken the Garda Síochána out of any controversy. Unfortunately, instead of doing so and providing clarity, his earlier replies to some of Miriam's questions merely sowed confusion and facilitated both Opposition TDs, media reporters and commentators to opportunistically cherry pick their preferred narrative. His responding that GSOC could not 'say definitively yes or definitively no' when asked was GSOC bugged and later responding 'it is difficult to say' when asked did he believe GSOC was bugged, facilitated conspiracy theorists to categorically assert bugging had occurred. His statement that GSOC 'did not find evidence of Garda misconduct' contributed to the narrative that the gardaí were the buggers but proving it was difficult. The perception was created of a GSOC Commissioner who believed GSOC had been bugged but could not explicitly say so. For those both in politics and in the media opportunistically attached to a conspiracy and cover-up narrative, neither GSOC's press release nor Fitzgerald's interview credibly absolved the gardaí of guilt and ruled them out as having engaged in domestic espionage. Both interventions simply fuelled the story. We were deeply into alternative facts territory and an alternative reality.

Watching a recording of *Prime Time* late that night at home my original optimism of Monday evening that the whole episode would be a storm in a teacup, evaporated. Having received Simon O'Brien's verbal briefing, the subsequent GSOC press release and their later report, I regarded some of Fitzgerald's replies to Miriam O'Callaghan's questions as inexplicable. I could not attribute it to inexperience due to his previous communication and broadcasting background. I concluded that either Fitzgerald was confused or unknown to me there was some internal disagreement between the commissioners or I had not been told the full truth. I regarded it as fortunate that I had insisted on a written report from O'Brien. Knowing the Opposition's determination to target me, and the media's appetite for controversy, I realised that 'the GSOC bugging scandal', as it had now been framed, still had mileage.

CHAPTER 5

Confusion Confounded and a Wandering Definitive

Confusion worse confounded –John Milton, *Paradise Lost*

As anticipated, the controversy and confusion continued into Wednesday morning. It filled hours of current affairs broadcasting time on the national airwaves. It resulted in a tsunami of opinions and abuse on social media and wall-to-wall print media coverage. Those addicted to conspiracy theories were firmly convinced GSOC had been under surveillance and that the gardaí were the culprits. Others took the view that GSOC had scored an own goal and that its credibility had been damaged. The *Irish Independent* in its editorial wondered 'why GSOC let this run, unfettered for 48 hours once it came into the public domain?' The editorial continued, 'clearly Mr. Shatter has laid his reputation on the line with his speech in the Dáil last night. Should anybody pick a hole in his comprehensive explanation his position will be untenable.'

Shortly after midday in the Dáil during Leaders' Questions, both the Fianna Fáil leader Micheál Martin, and Sinn Féin leader Gerry Adams, beat up on Enda Kenny for, as Adams put it, his 'insistence that GSOC was obliged or compelled to report to the Minister and his repeated misquoting of the Garda Síochána Act 2005'. The Taoiseach had referenced section 80(5) of the Act stating 'there is a clear provision in the law for GSOC to report major issues to the Minister' and GSOC knew they should have done so. He had done this based on our Sunday discussion when I was unaware that GSOC had formally undertaken its own 'public interest' investigation. Put under political pressure, Kenny partially apologised for criticising GSOC saying 'any excessive meaning attributed to my words is regretted'. Ignoring the express reporting obligation imposed on GSOC by section 103 of the 2005 Act, Adams in response wrongly asserted 'There is no provision in the law which insists that GSOC must report to the Minister.' This fake issue would trundle on for a further four months.

In the days that followed, the objective of picking a hole in what I informed the Dáil on the Tuesday evening moved to the centre of the political stage. Ascertaining what, if anything, occurred in GSOC's offices and the reason for the organisation's conduct became of secondary importance. The story was largely presented in simple black and white terms – good versus evil. That is, GSOC good, gardaí evil, minister more evil! The manner in which GSOC's Commissioners presented their story and responded to questions before the Oireachtas Petitions Committee assisted in this process.

The Petitions Committee meeting commenced at 4 o'clock on that Wednesday afternoon. Unusually, not only were the committee's members in attendance, but so also were nine additional members of the Oireachtas. Members of the Oireachtas are generally able to attend and participate in meetings of Oireachtas committees of which they are not members (except the Public Accounts Committee), but do not have voting rights.

The meeting opened with Padraig MacLochlainn, as chairperson, inviting Simon O'Brien, who was present with both Kieran Fitzgerald and Carmel Foley, to make an initial statement on behalf of GSOC. O'Brien expressed GSOC's 'unhappiness' at the contents of a secret document being released and confirmed he had apologised to me for my being 'blindsided'. He went on to describe, somewhat mysteriously, as 'inaccurate' concerns expressed in the document he believed leaked, but did not identify the inaccurate concerns he was referencing. He confirmed that initially two 'potential' not 'credible' threats had been identified and continued then to largely repeat the information originally furnished by him and GSOC to me on the Monday evening. It was a case of so far so good.

Explaining why I had not received a report from GSOC much earlier, O'Brien said 'the report was in my possession only just prior to the Christmas break ... At the time I made a strategic decision not to report what could be described as suspicious activity that did not meet the threshold of an offence.' He made no reference to the reporting provisions contained in sections 80 or 103 of the Garda Síochána Act under which GSOC operated. He did, however, acknowledge that 'now' he regretted that decision.

There was little new in what Simon O'Brien had to say until he responded to Labour Senator Susan O'Keeffe's second question. She was the first Oireachtas member out of the blocks. She asked whether O'Brien knew of other police ombudsman offices being bugged. He replied that he did not and that he also did 'not concur' with terminology such as 'bugged'. He continued: 'I certainly suspect or potentially suspect we may have been under some form of surveillance.'

He did not say this in his Monday afternoon meeting with me; in GSOC's Monday evening press release; or in GSOC's written report to me. This was very different territory to 'vulnerabilities', 'anomalies' or 'potential threats'. However, O'Keeffe swiftly moved on and missed the bombshell.

Viewing the proceedings in my office on the Oireachtas in-house television, I puzzled over how someone could 'potentially suspect' something. Despite the linguistic imprecision and ambiguity, the moment I heard O'Brien's response to Susan O'Keeffe, I correctly predicted the inevitable resultant media frenzy interpreting his words into 'GSOC believes it was bugged.' We were now deeply into espionage territory. The 'potential threats' spoken of by O'Brien in his opening statement had, by the time he answered O'Keeffe's second question, become a belief or a suspicion that GSOC was under surveillance and differed from the information given by me to the Dáil in reliance on GSOC's report. It also varied from my briefing to both the Taoiseach and Cabinet colleagues.

For a media eager to promote and substantiate the narrative that the gardaí bugged GSOC, O'Brien's response to O'Keeffe was gold dust. The fact that what O'Brien said differed from the information given by me to the Dáil in reliance on GSOC's own report brought added value. Then, later on in the meeting in response to a question from People Before Profit, Deputy Richard Boyd Barrett, O'Brien responded 'the Deputy is seeking clarity on whether we are now under surveillance. I have no idea'. It was, for those dedicated to conspiracy theories, the icing on the GSOC cake!

O'Brien having firmly planted his suspicion of surveillance, O'Keeffe asked him about a meeting he had with the Garda Commissioner the previous afternoon. O'Brien asserted that their conversation was confidential but explained that they had agreed to 'try to get past this particular difficulty'. When O'Keeffe asked whether the commissioner had a sense of grievance, O'Brien acknowledged 'had I been the Commissioner I would have had a sense of grievance'. I suspected that when Martin Callinan learned of O'Brien's contribution to the committee's proceedings, any feelings of grievance would be aggravated.

Replying to questions from Independent Deputy Michael Healy-Rae, O'Brien admitted that 'I think the people of the State are and should be horrified to think one State agency would in any way be surveilling another State agency. At present, we have no evidence that An Garda Síochána was surveilling my organisation. As was picked up earlier, any language around this can be injurious to the men and women of An Garda Síochána.' This acknowledgement by O'Brien clearly illustrated the extent to which he was oblivious to the impact of his own language as he delivered varied and imprecise commentary and responses.

Not only O'Brien but also those present at the committee meeting missed the irony. His public statement of Monday night on which I had relied when addressing the Dáil and briefing Cabinet asserted there was no evidence of garda misconduct. In responding to Healy-Rae's question, O'Brien qualified this by use of the words 'at present' lending further credibility to the belief of some that he and the other GSOC Commissioners not only suspected GSOC had been under surveillance but also that they knew the gardaí were guilty but there was a difficulty in proving it. As those present at the meeting asked further questions, the GSOC Commissioners continued to breed and feed suspicion.

When asked by Labour Deputy Derek Nolan about the commencement of GSOC's public interest investigation on 8 October 2013, O'Brien pronounced it a 'proportionate and justifiable action'. He revealed that, in the autumn of 2013, the commissioners stopped meeting together in their offices or texting or talking on their phones about their surveillance concerns and met in cafés in Capel Street near their offices. This was more fodder for conspiracy theorists and the next day provided great media copy. Unfortunately, the commissioners were never asked to reveal in which cafés they met.

Kieran Fitzgerald added to the confusion. When asked by Fine Gael Deputy, Patrick O'Donovan whether he accepted 'the statement of the Minister that there is no evidence to suggest unauthorised surveillance of [GSOC's] offices by An Garda Síochána', he delivered a qualified reply at variance with GSOC's own previous public statement. 'There is no definitive evidence rather than there being absolutely none. The Minister's statement, which may have been based on a briefing we provided to him, indicated there was no *definitive* evidence.'

The statement that there was 'no evidence of Garda misconduct' as contained in GSOC's own public statement of the Monday evening was unqualified. The word 'definitive' did not occur in that context. Unfortunately, the question asked had conflated the issue of 'surveillance' and 'garda misconduct'. I thought at that point that Fitzgerald's answer may have solely derived from GSOC's acknowledgement that 'no definitive evidence' of surveillance was found and that this might have been what he intended but failed to clearly portray. Unfortunately, he essentially asserted that there was no 'definitive' evidence of surveillance of GSOC by the gardaí, again leaving room for believing the gardai may have engaged in such surveillance.

As I watched the unfolding proceedings, I considered the commissioners' casual use of language raised a serious question mark over the extent to which I could rely on any reports provided to me or published by GSOC under the leadership of the three commissioners. Words matter, but it seemed to me the importance of words used entirely escaped them.

Kieran Fitzgerald ploughed on, responding to Patrick O'Donovan and trying to provide his own version of clarity. But he was only adding to the confusion. Unsurprisingly, Patrick O'Donovan interrupted to try and pin him down. 'Do you accept that the fact you are now introducing the word "definitive" cuts to the heart of the reason we are here? Does the GSOC still suspect that authorised or unauthorised surveillance was conducted on its premises or equipment by members of An Garda Síochána?' he asked.

'We have carried out a very thorough investigation and hired the best experts one could find. At the close of that investigation, we have no evidence to proceed on that basis,' replied Fitzgerald, believing clarity had now been achieved. O'Donovan persisted 'can I take it that there was at no point any surveillance, authorised or otherwise, by An Garda Síochána of the GSOC's premises or equipment?'

Fitzgerald immediately contradicted himself saying 'the Deputy can take it there is no *definitive* evidence to point towards Garda misconduct. That was the outcome of the investigation.'

Those watching the proceedings could, from the commissioner's responses, legitimately conclude that despite the absence of the required evidence, Fitzgerald, as when on *Prime Time*, was putting down a marker that he suspected the gardaí of wrongdoing. The reintroduction by him of the wandering 'definitive' when answering Patrick O'Donovan's laudable search for some precision amongst the verbal incoherence aided that perception.

Despite his best efforts, his Fine Gael colleague, Deputy Noel Harrington, was no more successful than the persistent Patrick O'Donovan. During the course of questioning Simon O'Brien, Harrington pointed out to O'Brien that GSOC's press release earlier in the week 'went to great lengths to exonerate An Garda Síochána'.

Before O'Brien could respond, Fitzgerald jumped in saying he 'would not use the word exoneration because it has specific connotations. What we did say was that no such evidence to point to the Garda was disclosed. The Deputy can call that exoneration if he wishes but it is not the same as categorically ruling in or categorically ruling out' garda involvement. With that, I anticipated the next day's news headlines would also include 'GSOC Commissioners Refuse to Exonerate Gardai'.

The hearing before the Petitions Committee took almost four hours. Deputies and senators present extensively questioned the commissioners. Many just wanted to know the truth of what, if anything, had happened. A small number only wanted to use the hearing to play politics. The questioning was searching, legitimate and considered and the longer the hearing lasted, the greater was the confusion created by the commisisoners' responses. Fianna Fáil's Niall Collins fairly asked Simon O'Brien whether it is 'custom and practice to inform the Minister of all public interest investigations the Commission initiates under section 102(4) of the Garda Síochána Act 2005 but which it did not do in this case?' O'Brien simply responded 'Yes' without expressly referencing the statutory obligation to report under section 103 of the Act. Nevertheless, his response should have put that issue to bed. It did not and even Collins ignored O'Brien's response. The next day in the Dáil he alleged that the Taoiseach had 'publicly' damaged GSOC's independent office when referencing the commissioners' reporting duties. Despite the media's blanket coverage of the controversy, not a single commentator ever referenced the inherent contradictions contained in Collins's approach to that issue. It did not suit the preferred narrative.

During the course of GSOC's hearing before the Petitions Committee, there were some interesting exchanges in relation to the 'potential threat' posed by the Wi-Fi device in GSOC's boardroom or conference room, as it was variously described.

'The first threat was a piece of existing technology that the staff of GSOC had both purchased and installed. It was not the device that was suspicious but the activity that it was undertaking', Simon O'Brien mysteriously explained.

Since the appointment of the current commission, they had rarely used the boardroom or conference room, according to O'Brien, although he believed it was used by their predecessors. 'When the electronic device was examined over a lengthy period by another piece of electronic kit, it was found to be exhibiting randomness in the way it was being activated.'

The explanation was becoming linguistically and technically more and more obtuse about a Wi-Fi device GSOC purchased but never used nor which was ever connected to any of their communication or data retaining systems or network and which was located in a room that the commissioners rarely, if ever, visited. It also all sounded increasingly sinister. While the 'Wi-Fi router' had been acquired by GSOC years earlier, O'Brien further explained 'its activity was apparently connecting outside'. 'Maybe,' he speculated 'something was calling upon it to connect?' At this stage all that was missing from the committee's meeting was a cameo appearance by ET, the extra-terrestrial from Steven Spielberg's famous movie, or an allegation of repetitive rogue broadcasts to the world beyond GSOC's headquarters commencing 'GSOC Calling GSOC Calling …'.

My difficulty was the use by O'Brien of odd terminology to talk about a Wi-Fi device purchased and installed by GSOC but never used, connected to no GSOC data, languishing in an unused room from which no information of any nature of value could be obtained which posed a threat to GSOC's security. Moreover, as far as I knew, the device was still retained by GSOC in their offices. If it truly posed a security threat it was blindingly obvious the GSOC Commissioners could have had it removed. It did not occur to any member of the Petitions Committee to ask why they had not done so. None of this made any sense whatsoever until Carmel Foley intervened to inform those present that, while GSOC occupied a building on the corner of Abbey Street and Capel Street in Dublin, they did not occupy the entire building. While the entrance was on Abbey Street, a convenience store was situated on the ground floor and had a separate entrance in Capel Street.

I was not familiar with GSOC's building having only met Simon O'Brien in the Department of Justice. It occurred to me that, if the convenience store had a café or coffee area with free Wi-Fi, as many do, this might have some relationship to whatever was stimulating random activity by GSOC's Wi-Fi device. Listening to the exchanges, I wondered whether this could possibly provide an explanation for one of the so-called 'potential' or 'credible' threats that had resulted in GSOC instigating a public interest investigation. Well, if it did, Simon O'Brien was not spilling the beans. As the meeting was ending, Independent Deputy Thomas Pringle returned to the Wi-Fi device, asking whether it was compromised by a connection traced to an IP address located in the UK. O'Brien said

'I will check this' but as far as he was concerned GSOC's enquiries on what the Wi-Fi device was connecting to were inconclusive and it had behaved 'in a very strange way'. I was subsequently to discover that insofar as anything was strange, it was the information furnished by the GSOC Commissioners to the Oireachtas Petitions Committee members about the 'threat' posed by the conduct of their allegedly rogue Wi-Fi device.

CHAPTER 6

GSOC Unchained and Post-Truths

If you want to be thought a liar, always tell the truth
–Logan Pearsall Smith

We live in a time when, strange to say, many quite cultivated individuals consider truth to be unworthy of any particular respect
–Harry G. Frankfurt, *On Truth*

Relating to or denoting circumstances in which objective facts are less influential in shaping public opinion than appeals to emotion and personal belief –Definition of 'post-truth', *Oxford Living Dictionaries*

The next day (Thursday, 13 February) the media went into overdrive. There was almost a unanimous view that the GSOC Commissioners knew their offices had been under surveillance and that I was spinning a yarn to protect the gardaí. There was a growing perception that I might have misled the Taoiseach and the Dáil. The Taoiseach, referenced as stating he was mistaken in his belief that GSOC had a reporting duty or that he had given 'an excessive meaning' to section 80(5) of the Garda Síochána Act, fed into this perception. The response given by Simon O'Brien at the Petitions Committee meeting to Niall Collins's direct question on GSOC's reporting duty was entirely ignored not only by Collins but also by Fianna Fáil's leader Micheál Martin, and his party colleagues. We had truly plunged into the era of post-truth politics.

The media's approach and eagerly adopted narrative that GSOC had given a sterling performance before the Petitions Committee and that I was out to mislead was neatly summarised by Miriam Lord in her satirical column in Thursday's *Irish Times*. Referencing my Tuesday's evening's speech to the Dáil which was entirely based on GSOC's supplied information, she wrote: 'The chairman of GSOC, Simon O'Brien totally contradicted his [that is, my] Dáil version of the story.'

She complained that 'no Government members on the Oireachtas committee to look into this affair seemed bothered to ask why the Minister seemed to have gotten his information so wrong when speaking to the Dáil'.

It did not occur to Lord, or any other journalist, that the story GSOC Commissioners told the Joint Oireachtas Committee may have differed from the verbal briefing and written report received by me. Not a single journalist stood back and analysed the inherent contradictions between the presentation made by the GSOC Commissioners to the Petitions Committee and their Monday evening press release.

That evening I personally drafted and sent a detailed letter to GSOC's chairperson asking about responses given at the Petitions Committee meeting which differed from GSOC's briefing to me the previous Monday. The letter also addressed issues that arose from the section 103 Report GSOC were obliged to furnish, which had finally been received at 6.45pm on Thursday in the Department of Justice, one day after the commissioners' appearance before the Petitions Committee. The report was more exact and careful in its language than the commissioners were in their presentations to the committee and revealed additional interesting information.

The report clearly referenced 'two potential operational surveillance threats' or 'vulnerabilities' being identified during the Verrimus September security checks. The threats or 'vulnerabilities' were not elevated to the status of the 'credible' threats referenced by Kieran Fitzgerald less than forty-eight hours earlier on *Prime Time*. With regard to the 'vulnerable wireless [Wi-Fi] device' identified in September 2013, it stated that GSOC 'has a wireless network capability but no wireless network operating in its offices'. Essentially, the report confirmed that GSOC's concerns that its office wireless network had been infiltrated were baseless as it had not been activated. In September 2013 'a wireless device was detected' which I had initially been informed on the Monday was subsequently identified as a component part of an AMX brand audiovisual system located in GSOC's conference room/boardroom area. The report explained that 'every device that can wirelessly communicate to a computer network has a unique 12-digit identifier known as a Media Access Control address or MAC address for short. The wireless device detected had a MAC address ending in 4B and for the purposes of this report' it was called 'device 4B'. However, the report stated 'device 4B could not be physically located at that time'. Their survey, did, however, indicate that 'it had been connected to the AMX audio-visual system and a network named Bitbuzz'.

Accordingly, the report explained, in September 2013 a 'potential security threat' had been identified from the wireless device, the exact location of which was unknown. It was clear that Verrimus were uncertain about the activity, if any, of the device. The survey 'indicated' but did not establish that the device had been connected to the unused audiovisual system in GSOC's unused boardroom/conference room and to the Bitbuzz network. Reading the report, I realised that in September 2013 'the device' had been labelled as a 'potential threat' without Verrimus taking whatever time was required to even locate its whereabouts and without the 'expert consultants' fully examining the AMX audiovisual system or attempting to detect the origin of the Bitbuzz connection.

The report continued 'on the weekend of Saturday, 19 October 2013, the security specialists returned for the purposes of identifying and physically locating device 4B, to fully inspect the AMX audiovisual system and to establish if it had a link to the Ombudsman Commission's service'. These were all tasks I would have expected to have been undertaken during the September security check and prior to GSOC's making any decision to launch a public interest investigation.

As I read on, I was increasingly astonished at the incompetence of this garda oversight body, which had its own independent investigative remit. I learned that it was only on Saturday, 19 October, that device 4B was identified as GSOC's own AMX control pad for the audiovisual system located, not in their conference room as O'Brien had that week wrongly informed me and then the Petitions Committee, but in the media room next door and was used to 'control the projector screen and other equipment in the media room'. A second control pad or console was located in the boardroom/conference room to control the equipment in that room. While the one in the media room seemed to be randomly connecting to the Bitbuzz network, the control pad in the conference room did not. The Wi-Fi located there did not 'at any point display any suspicious behaviour'. So contrary to the information given by the GSOC Commissioners to me three days earlier and to the Petitions Committee the previous day, there was never any question of any 'anomalous' behaviour by a Wi-Fi device in the conference room which could give rise to any suspicion of a third party accessing or overhearing private meetings held or any conversation in that room. My original suspicion, at our Monday afternoon meeting, that Simon O'Brien did not fully understand the technology we discussed was obviously correct and information given not only to me but also to the Petitions Committee was clearly inaccurate.

According to the report, on Sunday 20 October, the Verrimus 'security specialists' observed device 4B establishing a connection to the Bitbuzz network 'on numerous occasions'. However, it was also established that the AMX audiovisual system in the media room, incorporating device 4B, did not communicate with any of GSOC's databases or electronic equipment. Consequently, to advocate that this scenario supported the proposition that GSOC was 'potentially' or 'credibly' under surveillance was a leap of staggeringly inaccurate proportions. The report also revealed that the security experts discovered that the Wi-Fi system to which device 4B was communicating was 'located in a business premises' disingenuously described as 'close to the Ombudsman Commission's offices', which utilised the Bitbuzz network. I was not informed of the address or name of the 'business premises'.

At that point, the report detailed that the security specialists took the blindingly obvious action that should have been taken on their initial September visit to GSOC's offices or by GSOC's own personnel. They arranged to meet a Bitbuzz employee and learned, on Friday, 25 October, that Bitbuzz equipment establishing a Bitbuzz hotspot had been installed in the 'business premises' concerned as recently as August 2013, so that device 4B 'could only have been connecting to the Bitbuzz network' from that date.

The repetitive references in the report to an unidentified 'business premises near' GSOC's offices fuelled my suspicion that, not only was I still not being told the full truth, but that some aspect of the story of the 'potential threat posed by the Wi-Fi system' was being deliberately concealed. I was determined to get to the bottom of it.

The major portion of GSOC's section 103 report was taken up with the Wi-Fi 'anomaly'. The second 'potential threat' it addressed was described as 'evidence that a telephone device was potentially being monitored by unauthorised means'. The information contained in the report on this was a good deal briefer than that detailed in GSOC's Monday evening report to me. It referenced that the Polycom conference call unit located in the chairperson's office received a call of about three rings in duration at approximately 1am on the morning of 27 September 2013, almost immediately after an 'alerting test' had been conducted on it and that 'as the organisation's switchboard was an out-of-hours service, this call must have been made direct to the conference call unit'. The three rings, according to the report, were evidence of 'potential monitoring'. This also seemed to be an enormous leap of judgement. I did not regard the totality of the information given to me on how GSOC came to this conclusion as either adequate or persuasive.

The third 'threat' was said to derive from the detection on Sunday 20 October, during the course of the public interest investigation, of 'a non-standard GSM network' with a name 'consisting only of numbers' that did not identify a mobile service provider operating in Ireland. It continued 'subsequent enquiries indicated that the code was the identifier for a 3G telephone service provider in the UK. The security specialists attributed its detection ... to an interception device in the area.' This was described as good evidence of localised intelligence gathering. Subsequently, I was informed that GSOC conducted an operational test, which I was to later learn consisted of a conversation about a fabricated issue in which the GSOC commissioners participated, but the test yielded no results and provided 'no clarity to the threats identified'. In other words, nothing subsequently occurred to indicate that any individual other than those who attended the 'test conversation' knew what they discussed.

The report reiterated GSOC's original briefing to me that its investigation 'did not find any definitive evidence that GSOC was under technical or electronic surveillance'. It concluded stating 'it did, however uncover a number of technical and electronic anomalies that cannot be explained'. Nowhere contained in the section 103 report was there any reference of any nature to An Garda Síochána! I was left again wondering the extent to which GSOC understood their own technology and the reports furnished to them by Verrimus and to wonder about the true level of expertise of the Verrimus security specialists.

The controversy surrounding GSOC continued on Friday and on into the weekend. Commentaries appeared comparing and contrasting information given by me to the Dáil on the Tuesday evening with that given by the GSOC Commissioners to the Petitions Committee on the Wednesday afternoon. The presumption was that I had misled the Dáil and that favoured parts of the GSOC Commissioners' narrative could be relied on as accurate. Although Tánaiste Eamon Gilmore had categorically told the Dáil during Leaders' Questions on the Thursday that he was satisfied that 'no organ of state put the Garda Ombudsman Office under surveillance', there was continued speculation that An Garda Síochána had indeed done so. Opposition deputies exploited the controversy to the best of their ability and it dominated broadcast news and current affairs.

14 February – my birthday and St Valentine's Day – coincided with an event to celebrate the Fiftieth Anniversary of the Garda Training College in Templemore, Co. Tipperary. I attended together with the Garda Commissioner. The event afforded an opportunity for reporters to question each of us on the continuing 'bugging controversy'. Responding to journalists, the commissioner stated 'unequivocally' that 'at no stage was any member of the Garda Síochána Ombudsman Commission or any of its members under surveillance by An Garda Síochána'. I expressed concern that increasing credibility was being given to the narrative that GSOC had definitely been placed under surveillance. I continued to express my confidence in GSOC and its commissioners and kept to myself my growing misgivings about their professionalism and capacity to do their job.

The issue remained politically centre stage. Throughout the week John Mooney, the *Sunday Times* journalist whose report acted as the catalyst to the week's events, had become a permanent fixture on broadcast news and current affairs programmes promoting the 'GSOC were bugged by the Gardai' narrative. He was ably assisted by Mick Clifford of the *Irish Examiner*, who enthusiastically supported the theory together with a number of their media colleagues. On Saturday, 15 February, Conor Brady, former editor of *The Irish Times* and a GSOC Commissioner from 2006 to 2011 who, during the course of the week, had been commenting on the controversy, waded in with an article in *The Irish Times*. According to Brady, the GSOC Commissioner, Kieran Fitzgerald, had spoken 'with clarity and shining honesty' when addressing the Oireachtas Petitions Committee and there could be 'little doubt' that someone bugged or tried to bug GSOC's offices. Asking 'who are the suspects', he had no doubt that 'members of An Garda Síochána, must at the very least be potential suspects in any investigation that begins on the premise that an attempt has been made to penetrate GSOC security'.

Noting that the Garda Commissioner had said that no garda surveillance, authorised or unauthorised had occurred, Brady asserted that it was 'doubtful if the Commissioner knows everything that goes on in his force of more than 13,000 officers, as not a few of his predecessors in office found out to their cost over the years'. For Brady the most disturbing aspect of the whole affair was 'the rush by Kenny and Shatter to rubbish the GSOC's fears of having been bugged' which was 'consistent with a pattern since the establishment of the watchdog in 2005'. In his view, what we were witnessing was 'an intuitive effort by the State – by the political establishment – to roll back the declared objective of the Ombudsman sections of the 2005 Garda Síochána Act, to put in place an effective system of independent oversight, on behalf of the Oireachtas and the people, of the work of the national police force'. I marvelled at his absolute certainty and wondered how Brady, as both a former editor of *The Irish Times* and a former GSOC Commissioner, could in the absence of any substantive evidence, so easily rush to judgement. As I would shortly discover, when it came to garda related controversy, rushing to judgement was the chosen response of many from whom I expected a more considered, evidence-based and intellectually rigorous approach.

CHAPTER 7

Insomnia, the Pink Panther and Inspector Gadget

This is a very serious matter and everyone in this reum is under the suspicions –Inspector Jacques Clouseau (Peter Sellers) in *The Pink Panther Strikes Again*

Wowser –Inspector Gadget *The Movie*

I determined by the morning of Friday, 14 February, that I could not rely on GSOC or Verrimus to bring clarity to what, if anything, had occurred. I discussed with the Secretary General of the Department of Justice, Brian Purcell, our having the Verrimus reports peer reviewed and asked that a company or individual with the necessary expertise be identified. I also requested that GSOC be asked the exact address of the 'business premises' near their offices in which the Bitbuzz network had been installed in August 2013. Suspecting I already knew the answer, I arranged for a friend the next day, Saturday 15 February, to visit the convenience store located on the ground floor of the premises occupied by GSOC. If I had gone there myself and was spotted by a journalist or photographer or any member of GSOC, it would have further fed the media frenzy.

By lunchtime on Saturday, my suspicions were confirmed. There was a Spar convenience store on the ground floor of GSOC's premises that incorporated within it an Insomnia Coffee Shop. A Bitbuzz Wi-Fi connection was offered free of charge to its on-premises customers. It had to be the case that not only GSOC employees but also the Commissioners themselves on some occasions frequented the store and, as described to me, the Bitbuzz signage was unmissable.

In the context of the original September 2013 visit of the Verrimus operatives, it was beyond belief that they had neither visited the ground floor store before nor shortly after the discovery of the alleged Wi-Fi 'anomaly'. This was all worthy of Inspector Clouseau and the Pink Panther. The fact that some of the random attempted connectivity to the Bitbuzz network of the console in the GSOC media room had occurred and been detected in the small hours of the morning seemed entirely appropriate in the context of the 'Insomnia' linkage. Clearly the console late at night had difficulty sleeping and was bored!

GSOC could have fully explained in straightforward and simple language the origin of the so-called Wi-Fi anomaly, the exact location and business of the store, the extent to which it posed any real threat to GSOC's security and could have publicly confirmed that GSOC was not nor never had been under surveillance from this location by the gardai or anyone else. Instead the existence of the Bitbuzz network installed by the Insomnia Coffee Company for the benefit of its customers had continued to be referenced in sinister terms by GSOC's Commissioners throughout the week in both the reports they provided to me and in their public utterances. They had let the whole controversy intensify, occupy both substantial Government and Dáil time and spiral out of control. Moreover, after the Wednesday appearance before the Petitions Committee, they had maintained their silence and sat back while the Taoiseach and I and other Government ministers were engulfed by a flood of media criticism and allegations. I believed their conduct to be both deplorable and indefensible.

On Tuesday 18 February there was to be another Cabinet meeting and it was inevitable that I would have to update Cabinet colleagues on the continuing GSOC controversy. Sinn Féin had also tabled a Dáil motion for debate in Private Members time for that evening and for Wednesday, 19 February, calling for a public inquiry. It was also inevitable that the issue would again be revisited by Opposition leaders in the Dáil with the Taoiseach on Leaders' Questions. I believed it important to ensure the Taoiseach was up to date on where matters stood in case he was doorstepped by journalists over the weekend. On the Saturday morning I sent him the following text:

Good morning. Thought a summary of GSOC issue may be helpful. THE STORY SO FAR – media and opposition narrative GSOC bugged: Who dunnit? Must be Gardai. Shatter covering up! And now Labour narrative GSOC were bugged and possibly by Rogue Gardai. GSOC saying security check generated concerns/suspect or potentially suspect MAY have been under some form of surveillance or cannot rule out a suspicion they might have been but no definitive evidence of surveillance of any nature by anyone and GSOC state nothing compromised. No evidence that the Gardai have anything to do with the matter but GSOC's language in addressing stuff confusing and contributing to fuelling story. I tell Dail what GSOC tell me and next day GSOC in Petitions Committee decorate and add to the account I received from them prior to Dail statement and additions still continuing from GSOC. Gardai caught in cross-fire without a scintilla of evidence of any Garda involvement and I am pilloried for pointing that out on ground am taking the Garda side. I repetitively say if GSOC bugged it would be very serious but GSOC itself concluded it cannot say it was bugged by Gardai or anyone else. This is a conclusion largely ignored by media, opposition and now Labour ministers. Meantime, GSOC acknowledged leak from its own organisation for which it accepts only a member/employee of GSOC could be responsible and predicts further *Sunday Times* revelation of something it pre-warns is not accurate. Its all starting to lose its entertainment value but would possibly make a great novel or movie! Enjoy your weekend. A

The days leading up to the Cabinet meeting of Tuesday 18 February, even by current media standards, were remarkable for the level of hysteria, venom and accusation. Print and online media fed into broadcast media, which in turn fed back into online and print media. Any factual analysis ceased to be relevant. The only game in town was to repetitively validate the 'Gardai Bugged GSOC' narrative and the accusation that the Garda Commissioner and I were too close and joined at the hip. Vituperative online commentary reflected abusive and critical emails received attacking my role in the 'GSOC scandal' and assumed I was engaged in some form of 'cover-up'. Opposition spokespeople and independent deputies were in their element and, to maintain the narrative, the media valued their every word. In a political world where everyone wants to be loved on a daily basis and where there is an anxiety to avoid being sucked into other peoples' controversies, Cabinet colleagues started to get restless, as did some of the Fine Gael and Labour parliamentary party members. Attending the Labour Party's weekend annual conference in Enfield, Pat Rabbitte, the Minister for Communications, Energy and Natural Resources, was reported as being critical of the Garda Commissioner and speculated that GSOC could have been under surveillance by rogue members of An Garda Síochána. As Minister for Justice I knew of no evidence to substantiate any such claim.

The weekend papers reached a crescendo. The *Irish Independent's* Colette Browne asserted that 'despite all of the guff about accountability, transparency and openness when Fine Gael and Labour entered government, they have acted with depressing predictability to this scandal. Instead of giving any credence to GSOC's serious concerns that its offices had been compromised, they have opted to shoot the messenger and are now engaged in a witch-hunt to find the whistle-blower.' I had appeared on RTÉ's *Prime Time* on the previous Thursday evening and expressed concern over the inconsistent accounts of what had occurred given by the GSOC Commissioners to the Petitions Committee and the discrepancies between information given by them to the committee and to me. This fed into the 'GSOC good, Minister bad' paradigm. The fact that Simon O'Brien had announced GSOC was undertaking an internal investigation into the leaking of a document to *The Sunday Times* had, in Browne's critical analysis, morphed into being a Government 'witch-hunt to find the whistle-blower'. This theme would be revisited a week later by *The Sunday Times*' columnist Justine McCarthy who imaginatively claimed it was 'a common refrain from government quarters' that 'the leaker had to be hunted down!'

According to Colette Browne 'no duty exists' which required GSOC to report to me as minister on their public interest inquiry and at the very minimum there had been an attempt to bug their offices. She stated that 'the truth is, nobody – not the Garda Commissioner, the AGSI [Association of Garda Sergeants and Inspectors] or members of the Government know who attempted to bug GSOC's offices. The only way to move on now with everybody's reputation attached [*sic*] is to conduct an independent inquiry.' As for my efforts to get at the truth, she was colourfully withering: 'Mr. Shatter, who appears to have researched contemporary surveillance techniques by watching episodes of *Inspector Gadget*, is demanding incontrovertible evidence before deigning to lift a finger.'

In *Inspector Gadget*-speak this merited a 'wowser'! It entirely eluded Colette Browne that, as Minister for Justice, I was simply trying to establish whether any credible evidence existed to give rise to a legitimate suspicion that GSOC may have been under any form of surveillance or whether GSOC's dealings with the issue might actually reflect *Inspector Gadget*'s investigative expertise!

Dearbhail McDonald, the *Irish Independent*'s legal affairs correspondent, continued the theme. For her 'the fact that GSOC discontinued its investigation because there was no definitive evidence of unauthorised surveillance provides no comfort either way: it is the fact that it had cause to believe it was under surveillance that matters. But instead of acknowledging the potentially enormous consequences of GSOC being bugged, Mr. Shatter conducted an instant trial that found GSOC in the dock and summarily convicted, it seems, of bruising Shatter's ego'.

In her anxiety to be both critical and controversial, McDonald, together with other media commentators, conveniently ignored the fact that the information on the issue given by me to both the Dáil and Cabinet was entirely dependent on information I received from GSOC. Like her Independent Newspapers colleague, Colette Browne, she avoided analysing or trying to make sense of the contradictions between the statements made by GSOC's Commissioners to the Petitions Committee when compared to GSOC's original Monday night public statement.

Having got my bruised ego off her chest, she then acknowledged GSOC's reporting obligations under section 103 of the Act and excused their failure to report. My 'perceived undermining of GSOC' she asserted 'and unflinching support of the Gardai is deeply damaging to public confidence in all three parties'. It is unclear how being supportive of the Gardaí was 'deeply damaging' in circumstances in which GSOC itself had acknowledged there was 'no evidence of Garda misconduct' (ignoring the subsequent introduction of the wandering 'definitive') and where the GSOC chairman had acknowledged the Garda Commissioner was justified in being 'aggrieved'. However, her hyperbole knew no boundaries. Readers were informed that with regard to 'the promise of a new era in policing … the bright new dawn has turned into a murky long night of the knives, where the biggest victim, once again, is the public interest'.

The 'GSOC scandal' was the dominant story in that weekend's Sunday papers. John Mooney, the *Sunday Times* journalist who broke the story the previous Sunday, having participated in a week-long current affairs television and radio broadcast media fest and having temporarily become something of a celebrity, returned to home base to further develop the 'Gardai bugged GSOC' narrative. The new *Sunday Times* revelation was that GSOC had 'organised a counter-surveillance sweep of its headquarters after a senior Garda inadvertently revealed he was in possession of information about a secret report it was working on last summer. The level of detail known to the officer caused disquiet in GSOC' he claimed 'and this was one reason it hired Verrimus, a British firm, to advise on internal security'. According to Mooney, the garda at a meeting 'appeared to have specific information' contained in the text of a draft report that was omitted from the report when completed by GSOC.

This was the inaccurate story that Simon O'Brien had mysteriously predicted might appear that Sunday during his presentation to the Petitions Committee. O'Brien saying the story was inaccurate did not inhibit *The Sunday Times* presenting it as fact on its front page. Mooney could not entirely ignore what O'Brien had told the Petitions Committee, so he referenced later on in the story that O'Brien had said 'the final investigation report and the Verrimus documentation makes reference to reasons for the [security] sweep that do not accord with my recollection of these reasons'. However, Mooney did not relate this statement as being in any way directly relevant to his opening unqualified sensational assertion as to why what he referenced as a 'counter surveillance sweep' occurred.

Addressing the Petitions Committee, O'Brien had been unequivocal, telling the Committee:

> there is an inaccuracy referenced in three separate places in a report that may come into the public domain. I pointed out the presence of inaccuracies to the Minister. [He had done so at our meeting on Monday 10 February]. I laid out to him that, in view of the amount of detail in the public domain last Sunday, the Commission strongly suspects that a copy of a section of a report which is marked 'secret' was possibly in the hands of a journalist.

O'Brien continued, 'the final investigation report and the Verrimus documentation makes reference to reasons for the sweep that do not accord with my recollection of those reasons'. He then explained the security check had been arranged as none had been undertaken since 2007. No reference of any nature was made by him at the Petitions Committee meeting to a 'senior Garda' inadvertently revealing anything.

Having discounted the relevance of O'Brien's warning, Mooney could not resist a little self-praise and moved on to inform any *Sunday Times* reader who had spent the entire week on the planet Zog that 'the affair has dominated the political agenda since *The Sunday Times* revealed that "Government-level technology" was used to mount surveillance on the Garda Watchdog's Dublin Offices'. Having patted himself on the back, Mooney then decorated his story with journalistically useful quotes, which enabled him to 'move' the story on and up a notch. Labour Minister of

State, Joe Costello TD, was quoted as being critical of my Dáil statement about the controversy and stating his belief, 'that the Garda Ombudsman was placed under surveillance'. He asserted that he had no doubt that it was the Boylan case that was 'at the heart of this. Everything I know would lead me to believe this.'

In total that weekend's *Sunday Times* carried four separate GSOC stories authored by John Mooney based on the same theme, summarised in the headline of one 'Who was watching the Watchdog?' All led to the inevitable answer – An Garda Síochána. It seemed Mooney's personal investigative skills greatly exceeded those of GSOC, the independent investigative body that he was convinced had been bugged!

The *Sunday Times* coverage was replicated in all of the Sundays. The headline in the *Irish Mail on Sunday* above an article by veteran political columnist Sam Smyth 'A Probe won't clear up this mess and Shatter knows it' reflected Smyth's views. Referencing 'a pearl of Irish wisdom from the 1970s' Smyth thundered that 'if Watergate had happened here, Nixon would still be President but everyone would know who Deep Throat was'. As for GSOC's 'legal duty to inform the Minister' of their public interest investigation, he was in no doubt that 'they were wrong about the law but Enda Kenny, Alan Shatter, the Garda Commissioner and Garda Representative bodies pressed on and cast the apparent victims as suspect villains'. GSOC according to Smyth deserved 'better than the political chicanery and questionable leadership that directed the GSOC debacle last week'.

In both volume and noise the *Sunday Independent*'s wall-to-wall coverage which extended to sixteen separate articles overwhelmed the coverage of its competitors. Clearly, the paper's editor, Anne Harris, had determined to outgun *The Sunday Times* scoop of the previous Sunday, to acquire possession of the story and to target my competence and honesty. Fianna Fáil's Niall Collins was among the contributors in an article entitled 'No Amount of Shatter Spin will Kill off this Controversy', accusing me in the Dáil of having 'tried to snuff out the kindling story by vehemently suggesting the non-existence of any surveillance'. Journalist Brendan O'Connor warned *Sunday Independent* readers: 'Don't rely on our Leaders to cut through the Fog.' Commenting on the week's events, he had no doubt who was at fault: 'We can't clearly trust the government on this. We can't trust the Taoiseach to know about the law. We can't even trust the Minister to get out of Simon O'Brien what Simon O'Brien thinks happened. The only place we have seen any openness and transparency is in the media and at the [Petitions] Committee.'

The *Sunday Independent*'s political correspondents Fionnan Sheehan and John Drennan travelled a similar route. 'Shatter Told to Clear Up Watchdog Bug Scandal' was the title above their story. As it was the weekend of the Labour Party's annual conference there were plentiful quotes from Labour Cabinet colleagues. Clearly, each had been asked about the holding of a public inquiry into the issue and all rejected the suggestion while emphasising the importance of resolving the issue as speedily as possible. Ruairi Quinn was quoted as saying that 'the Petitions Committee should explore the process and come back with a report: it would be more effective and speedy and they have been quite effective to-date'. As is usual in the *Sunday Independent*, there was also a quote from an unidentified minister, the identity of whom, if the quote was real and not manufactured, likely came from one of the two regular anonymous Cabinet Sindo contributors whose identity was believed to be known by some members of Cabinet. The anonymous minister described the 'current dispute' as a 'real test' of my 'diplomatic skills', saying it is the Minister for Justice's job to negotiate a satisfactory outcome and that he 'will be on a sticky wicket, if he doesn't'.

CHAPTER 8

Sticky Wickets and Rits Crackers!

When the quality of myth invades the realm of reason, it becomes almost impossible to detach actual events from the overlay of projections streaming from the unconscious
–Peter Charleton, *Lies in a Mirror*

By Monday morning, 17 February, the wicket had become a good deal stickier. Labour Cabinet members were reported in the morning papers as getting angsty that the controversy had carried over through the weekend and negatively impacted on coverage of their weekend party conference. To make things worse, it looked as if the controversy was going to dominate Dáil proceedings for another week; inevitably at Leaders' Questions; Sinn Féin's Private Members Motion on Tuesday and Wednesday; and I was also appearing before the Petitions Committee on the Wednesday afternoon.

On Monday afternoon I read a report received from Rits, an independent Irish security firm that had previously undertaken work for the Defence Forces. Rits had been provided with all the documentation and correspondence I had by then received from GSOC, including three Verrimus reports given by GSOC to the Department of Justice. Rits were asked to clarify technical details contained in the reports and to provide opinions on the security risks (i.e. the three 'anomalies'/'vulnerabilities'/'potential threats'/'credible threats') to GSOC. In response to requests for clarifications, GSOC had also provided Rits with technical infrastructural information relating to its offices.

The Rits report contained a detailed analysis of all the material and concluded that 'Based on the reports provided there is no evidence of any technical or electronic surveillance operation against GSOC.' This opinion, Rits stated, derived solely from the information provided in the reports furnished to them together with GSOC's response to requested clarifications. Rits continued 'it is probable and it is our opinion that there are explanations for all the anomalies or items identified as threats in the reports provided and there was no evidence [of] technical or electronic surveillance of GSOC or any attack against it'.

Rits asserted that 'GSOC when presented with the [Verrimus] reports do not appear to have had the reports analysed by experts on their behalf to determine the real exposure of GSOC to the various items outlined in the reports.'

Rits chronicled in comprehensive detail the background facts and technical information on which its conclusions were based. The security firm was particularly critical of the limited, if any, information provided by GSOC to Verrimus concerning the technology systems or infrastructure within GSOC on the basis of which Verrimus had made their findings.

In addressing GSOC's Wi-Fi security issues, the report provided absolute clarity. It asserted that there was no possibility of a hypothetical unauthorised user on the Wi-Fi networks getting access to the GSOC internal network, as there was no connection between them. Further on Rits noted that 'detailed analysis of any network traffic between the AMX device and the Bitbuzz network would have indicated if there was any suspicious traffic. This does not appear to have been done'. As for the Polycom conference call unit in the chairperson's office and the three-second ring back, Rits noted that it was connected solely to GSOC's Internal Private Exchange (BPX). There was no circuit that connected the Polycon directly to an external communications carrier network so it could not have been subject to call-back. There was also no record of any such call-back. It was possible that the three-second call-back had resulted from the test undertaken by Verrimus causing unusual behaviour by the BPX which may have reconfigured, reinitialised or reset the analogue port.

As for the IMSI Catcher, so beloved and identified by *The Sunday Times'* John Mooney as confirming GSOC was under surveillance by 'Government-level technology', Rits advised, 'there are many examples available on the internet today of how to build what is referred to as an IMSI Catcher – the Government agency level device referred to in the (Verrimus) report. These examples outline the software and hardware, all off the shelf and legal needed for this' and estimated the cost to be in the region of €5,000. Rits continued, the 'range of these IMSI Catcher devices can be up to several kilometres depending on the type of system and the level of power applied to the antennae. There is no evidence in the (Verrimus) report to state that, even if there was an IMSI Catcher detected during the review, it was intended to intercept calls within GSOC'. Moreover, according to Rits, the Verrimus reports on this issue contained conflicting information. A second Verrimus report referenced the finding of a Hutchison 3G Network and stated that 'Three', the mobile operator brand in the UK, that is Hutchison 3G UK Limited, provides devices to its clients for mobile coverage in areas of poor coverage. It was possible according to Rits that 'Three' customers had utilised such a device or devices to connect them to the internet and avoid roaming charges. Alternatively, Rits postulated that there may have been an incorrectly configured GSM test device in the area. Rits also reported that:

'There are a number of Wi-Fi networks in the vicinity of GSOC that would indicate a workshop or laboratory where GSM-related technologies are worked on. These include Wi-Fi network names (SSIDs) such as GSM, GSM Solutions, GSM Free Wi-Fi, All Com Group. These are likely related to the company GSM Solutions Limited.'

Rits speculated also that it was possible that a customer had brought a 3G UK Femto cell for support/repair that 'would display the 3G network if powered on and connected to the internet'. It continued asking 'was there any attempt to validate that this was actually an IMSI Catcher as opposed to a Femto-cell from Hutchison?' Moreover, Rits critically noted that 'the information in the report on the presence of this suspicious cell is a screen shot from an Apple iPhone, a consumer device. There does not appear to have been any more rigorous or technical investigation on this seemingly significant finding'.

Rits's analysis was interesting and seriously undermined the credibility of any suggestion that an IMSI catcher had been used for covert purposes to detect goings-on in GSOC. Of course, this particular alleged threat or 'vulnerability', as described by Verrimus, should have given rise to no concerns for an organisation that asserted that neither its commissioners nor its employees used English-registered mobile phones for work purposes.

The job of Rits was to furnish me with as detailed and informative a report as was possible, based on the available information. I did not know whether the report would validate the legitimacy of GSOC's original concerns or dismiss them. Reflecting on the Rits conclusions, the extent to which they documented GSOC's failings and the absence of any evidence of GSOC being under any form of surveillance, I realised I had another problem. Opposition deputies and large sections of the media now had a vested interest in their 'Gardai Bugged GSOC' story. A number of print and broadcast journalists' reputations were now on the line as a result of the week-long over-the-top hysterical commentary. I did not believe that anything I had to say would be given any credibility. I did not have the technical expertise to adjudicate between them, where Rits had reached conclusions different to Verrimus. If I publicly advocated and expressed a preference for the Rits analysis, I would simply be accused again of covering up Garda misconduct and the Taoiseach and the whole Government would be embroiled in a continuing controversy. Moreover, I could not be certain that Rits were entirely right in their analysis as they had limited time to complete their work and it was essentially a peer review. No opportunity had been afforded to them to directly examine GSOC equipment or to interview GSOC Commissioners and investigators; employees of relevant commercial enterprises such as Bitbuzz; or any mobile phone network company. One way out would be to hold the public inquiry that some, including Sinn Féin, were seeking but that would be long drawn out, very expensive and the shadow cast by the controversy and public uncertainty would linger and inflict further damage on the gardaí and GSOC. The alternative was a preliminary informal inquiry into all that had occurred by a respected member of the judiciary who could recommend, if necessary, that a sworn statutory investigation or inquiry subsequently take place. It seemed to me that there might be no alternative but to follow that route.

I drafted a further detailed letter that evening and sent it to GSOC seeking detailed clarification on a range of concerns and specific direct replies from them. I emphasised the importance of my receiving a response in sufficient time to enable me to brief the Cabinet the following morning (Tuesday) and made no mention in the letter of the Rits report. No reply had been received by the Tuesday morning when the *Irish Independent* carried a story on its front page written by investigative crime reporter Paul Williams, revealing that GSOC 'has known for months that a Wi-Fi network in a coffee shop was the innocent explanation for one of the "anomalies" identified in a security sweep of its offices'. As a result the Insomnia Coffee Shop benefited from substantial free publicity and extra business throughout that day!

Williams had clearly experienced the same difficulty in obtaining information from GSOC as I had, reporting that 'a spokesperson for GSOC failed to respond when asked about the development last night'. The lack of response by GSOC to my letter resulted in Michael Flahive, the Assistant Secretary in charge of the Justice Department's Garda Division, at my request at approximately 9am on the morning of the Cabinet meeting, emailing GSOC. He asked, 'Is the Bitbuzz network that your Wi-Fi apparently connected to a network operating in the Spar/Insomnia branch in your building (or, if not, do you know its location?)'

While I was certain of this since Saturday, I wanted confirmation from GSOC for Cabinet. The reply arrived at 11.16am, after the Cabinet meeting had commenced. In it GSOC stated:

> The device in our conference room was connecting to the Bitbuzz network in Spar/Insomnia. The Bitbuzz router in Spar/Insomnia showed no record of a connection to GSOC's device. However, it was not the fact that the wireless device was able to connect to Bitbuzz in Spar/Insomnia that caused concern, it was the fact that the wireless device was able to connect to another network outside its own secure network.

For me and for GSOC, the key issue should have been whether the device was or was not connecting to the Bitbuzz network in the coffee shop. There was no question of it connecting anywhere else. No apology was offered for concealing this information from me or for misleading members of the Petitions Committee the previous Wednesday. Incredibly, despite GSOC's own section 103 report revealing that what was described as device 4B, based in their media room and not their conference room, was randomly connecting to the Bitbuzz network, the response incorrectly again repeated that it was the device in the conference room that had been making the connection. Despite a week of controversy and turmoil, the GSOC commissioners still could not get right the location of the allegedly troublesome device and obviously did not either understand or know what information was contained in their own section 103 report.

The reply was not only inaccurate and contradicted their reports to me, it attempted to justify their actions to date. In informing Michael Flahive that for them 'the key issue is that the device was connecting to another network and not specifically to Bitbuzz in the Spar/Insomnia', GSOC lost sight of the fact that the 'device' or the console concerned was installed by GSOC itself and that the connectivity or attempted connectivity had absolutely nothing to do with any covert action taken by any third party. The 'device' had not been planted in a secret location by any unidentified person engaged in espionage or surveillance. The reason given for concealing from me, the Cabinet, the Dáil and the Petitions

Committee the true and full details of the Bitbuzz connection was lamely attributed to GSOC's 'trying to maintain confidentiality and any adverse impact on local business premises'. [*sic*] Any adverse impact of their conduct on their own credibility, on that of An Garda Síochána, on me as Minister for Justice and on that of the Government was apparently of no concern! The whole thing was totally crackers and Rits peer review had exposed how crackers it was.

CHAPTER 9

Flying Empty Planes, Severed Hips and Rotting Fish

They say in films about the mafia that the fish rots from the head and I agree with that. There is a strong stench coming from the Minister's direction –Luke Ming Flanagan TD, sharing a personal insight when speaking in the Dáil on 19 February 2014

No one has ever doubted that truth and politics are on rather bad terms with each other, and no one, as far as I know, has ever counted truthfulness among the political virtues
–Hannah Arendt, 'Truth and Politics', *The New Yorker*, 25 February 1967

No man spreads a lie with so good a grace as he that believes it –Jonathan Swift, *The Art of Political Lying*, in which Swift deploys his wit to review a non-existent book proposed by his friend, Dr John Arbuthnot. With thanks to Gilbert Wesly Purdy's *Eclectica* magazine, eclectica.org, 2015 online publication

The Taoiseach had in place an arrangement whereby all requests for use of the Government jet were vetted by Mark Kennelly, one of his special advisers. As a result of the media's focus on the use of the jet, ministers were required to travel on commercial flights whenever possible. Time lost hanging around airports and ministerial work pressures were largely ignored to avoid media criticism that ministers were spending their time junketing in a luxurious plane around the globe at taxpayers' expense. In my case, because I was in charge of two ministries and there were extraordinary demands on my time, this was a particular problem. Apart from public and parliamentary engagements, substantial time was spent on work for which there was no public visibility and I believed very little understanding on either Kenny's or Kennelly's part. I was essentially working a six-day week and, on occasions, entire weekends. To some extent I was my own worst enemy as I was pushing to implement a broad range of reforms relevant to both departments in which I was working. In particular, I was anxious to substantially advance the legislative reform agenda within the Department of Justice. By the start of 2014, an unprecedented amount of reforming legislation had been enacted, some published bills were awaiting processing before the Houses of the Oireachtas and a variety of draft bills, called Heads of Bills, had been published for consultative purposes. I reckoned I had only five years in Government to address long-ignored issues and I was determined to complete an enormous legislative agenda. I hugely enjoyed the work and found it exciting but enormously time-consuming and had little patience for wasting time hanging around airports.

When flying to Brussels for European Union Justice or Defence ministerial meetings, I usually took the early morning Aer Lingus direct flight. However, when flights were lengthy or when destinations could only be reached through connecting flights, the Government jet was much more efficient.

I regarded the approach taken to use of the Government jets as farcical. The Air Corps' aircraft were being used so infrequently by ministers that air corps pilots, to clock up the annual mileage required for their international flying licences, were regularly flying empty planes. As a cost-saving mechanism, the whole thing was total nonsense. It was all about appearance, Kenny's and Kennelly's anxiety to avoid media criticism, and their desire for public applause.

In my experience, permission to use a Government jet would often be given or denied only two or three days before a flight. In case it was denied, commercial flights had to be reserved and, on occasion, paid for on behalf of the minister and accompanying officials.

As was usual, I started work at home around 5.15am on Tuesday, 18 February 2014, the morning of that week's Cabinet meeting. In the midst of all the lunacy a variety of other issues had to be dealt with and I worked on both Justice and Defence files and reviewed that day's Cabinet papers. A number of Justice and Defence issues were on the agenda.

Throughout the previous week and over the weekend while the GSOC controversy raged, I had continued to deal with a variety of important and substantial issues and read papers relevant to a forthcoming meeting of European Union Defence Ministers. The Greek Government held the presidency of the European Union and a meeting of EU Defence Ministers was scheduled for Thursday afternoon and Friday morning of that week in Athens. During Ireland's EU Presidency in the first half of 2013, we had held and chaired a succession of important meetings in the defence area and I was anxious to maintain that engagement. I did not want to miss the Defence Ministers meeting in Athens.

I knew if I flew commercially to Greece I had to depart from Dublin shortly after lunch on Wednesday and pick up a connecting flight to Athens, arriving late that evening. However, on the Wednesday I was not only taking Report Stage of the Fines Bill in the Dáil Chamber, I was also scheduled to appear that afternoon at 4pm before the Petitions Committee. If I postponed my departure until Thursday and travelled on commercial flights, I would miss part of that day's meeting of Defence Ministers, something I wished to avoid. Only a Thursday morning flight on one of the Government jets could get me to Athens in time for the start of the ministerial meeting.

Due to my hectic schedule and the enormous amount of Justice and Defence paperwork involved, Vincent Lowe, my private secretary in Defence, had requested use of the Government jet for the Athens trip, at least two weeks earlier, before the GSOC controversy erupted. Not only would this save time, but I could work on papers in privacy and have confidential discussions with department officials inflight.

I had, the previous week, spoken to Enda Kenny about my concerns but he had not reverted to me. I believed that involving the Taoiseach in micro-managing use of the Government jet was totally ridiculous but as my flight request remained on Kennelly's desk, I felt I had no choice. So around 4pm on Monday, I had texted Kenny about the Greek meeting and the 'unanswered request' for use of the Government jet, stating that I 'would greatly appreciate' if my request was 'dealt with' as there 'is enough to deal with in normal throughput both from Defence and Justice while dealing with the GSOC issue without getting to Greece adding an additional layer of complexity'. Also, officials attending the EU Defence meeting 'need to know arrangements'. That Tuesday morning, despite the GSOC controversy raging, I was going to have to discuss the flight issue with the Taoiseach. It was bonkers.

Prior to the Tuesday Cabinet meeting, two separate meetings were regularly held. Enda Kenny met with Fine Gael Ministers and Tánaiste Eamon Gilmore met with Labour Ministers. I briefed my Fine Gael ministerial colleagues on the GSOC developments and discussed them privately in advance of Cabinet with Kenny and Gilmore. I had texted Kenny at 7am that morning suggesting such discussion.

It was agreed that the sensible approach to diffuse the GSOC controversy would be to appoint a retired High Court judge to conduct a preliminary inquiry and, if the judge recommended it, establish a formal Commission of Investigation under the Commission of Investigations Act 2004. In a pre-Cabinet discussion, Attorney General Máire Whelan SC, suggested that recently retired High Court Judge John Cooke conduct the inquiry and he agreed to do so. He had been an excellent judge, was a former member of the European Court and his independence could not be credibly questioned. For the second time in eight days, I briefed the full Cabinet on the GSOC issue and all developments of relevance, factual, technical and political, since our previous meeting. The holding of an informal inquiry was agreed and the decision later publicised. Comprehensive terms of reference for the inquiry were drafted by the Attorney General's office and agreed on the Wednesday evening. They were published and John Cooke's appointment announced.

Sinn Féin had the previous Friday tabled a Private Members Motion scheduled to come before the Dáil at 7.30 that Tuesday evening in which they called for the establishment of an independent inquiry under the Commission of Investigation Act 2004 'into reports that GSOC may have been subjected to covert surveillance'.

Before the debate commenced, GSOC again featured in Leaders' Questions. Micheál Martin accused the Taoiseach of telling 'an untruth, deliberately or otherwise, about GSOC's reporting obligations', accused me of withholding information from the Dáil and wanted to know whether the Taoiseach was 'satisfied' with my behaviour 'in this entire episode'. He also stated that it required members of the Commission to go on *Prime Time* to 'bury the notion' that 'the whole thing was a bottle of smoke'. Sinn Féin's Deputy Leader, Mary Lou McDonald, joined the fray. As accusations swirled around the Dáil chamber and the Taoiseach engaged in a robust defence of my role and again explained the reporting obligations of GSOC, it was clear that despite the announced inquiry the controversy was going to rumble on.

The debate commenced at 7.30pm and it followed a predictable pattern. Jonathan O'Brien TD, Sinn Féin's former Justice spokesperson, kicked off, lamenting that 'the institutions of the State have been severely undermined' by 'the profoundly serious suspicions of bugging and intelligence gathering at the independent office' of GSOC and by 'the response of the minister, the Government and the Garda Commissioner to the mishandling of this affair'. No mention was made of any possible GSOC 'mishandling'. Stating that 'we are dealing with an allegation that

An Garda Síochána in some way had the Garda Ombudsman's office under covert surveillance', O'Brien rejected the establishment of the announced preliminary inquiry stating 'I, and many outside this chamber see this as the Government trying to wish away the issue, just as the Minister has been doing over the past ten days.' His Sinn Féin colleague, Martin Ferris, expressed the opinion that 'the people of the State suspect this scandal stinks to high heaven'. Another Sinn Féin Deputy, Michael Colreavy, announced that 'everybody, with the exception of the Minister, the Taoiseach and the rest of the Government accepts that GSOC's offices were bugged and that classified or sensitive information may have been compromised'. Sinn Féin, it seemed, had even prejudged the outcome of the work to be undertaken by its own proposed Commission of Investigation.

I responded to the Sinn Féin motion reiterating some of the content of my statement of the previous Tuesday, providing additional information obtained or discovered during the subsequent seven-day period and referencing statements made by the GSOC commissioners. I remarked that 'while I do not doubt the general legitimacy of concerns that have been expressed by various persons at reports of potential threats of surveillance, it is a pity that we could not have a more rational and balanced debate on these matters'.

I again travelled through the three 'anomalies' and included the role of the Insomnia coffee shop's Bitbuzz Wi-Fi hotspot in the whole affair. As for the alleged IMSI Catcher, I referenced that GSOC's Chairman Simon O'Brien, despite *The Sunday Times*' assertions', had 'clearly placed no reliance' on Verrimus's advice that such technology could only be acquired by Government agencies. I also detailed the Rits conclusion that there was no evidence at all of any technical or electronic surveillance against GSOC, 'not merely no definitive evidence'. With regard to the holding of an inquiry, I stated:

Up to Friday, it was my view that GSOC had inquired into these matters and reached a conclusion and that calls for an inquiry could be seen as undermining public credibility in GSOC and a rejection of the conclusion it had reached in the investigation it had undertaken. No such inquiry calls have in the past been made when, following an investigation, GSOC concluded that there had been instances of Garda misconduct. It seemed highly inappropriate to hold an inquiry in circumstances where GSOC had concluded there was no evidence of Garda misconduct. However, the manner in which this controversy has continued, the new information I have received and the need to bring absolute clarity, insofar as that is possible, to all of these matters, led me to the view that it is in the public interest that a retired High Court judge undertake the task agreed by the Cabinet. It is of the utmost importance that the full truth is established beyond dispute.

I then expressed the hope that 'all sides of the House' would welcome the inquiry, that GSOC would be able 'to proceed with its work unhindered by controversy', and concluded: 'It is important that no further comment be made leaving any cloud of suspicion hanging over anybody in circumstances in which there is no evidence for such a cloud. That is not in the public interest ... I plead with those contributing further to the debate that we have a discussion based on facts not fiction, based on reality not hyperbole.'

This was more in hope than expectation! For the rest of the evening and on Wednesday evening the debate travelled a predictable route, including some Opposition Deputies denying that GSOC had any legal obligation to report its surveillance concerns or the outcome of its internal investigation to me and accusing me of misleading the Dáil. These had become fairly standard charges repetitively made by Niall Collins and other TDs in the preceding days. I expected that Collins would return to that theme the next day when I was to answer questions before the Petitions Committee. I looked forward to an opportunity to respond directly to him.

My constituency colleague and rival, Independent Deputy Shane Ross complained that 'the instinct of the Government is all wrong in respect of these matters. Instead of taking an independent view of GSOC and the Garda or anything else in the area of justice, its immediate instinct is to rally to the Force, right or wrong'.

Reflecting Padraig MacLochlainn's by now well-used phrase, Ross identified 'the fundamental problem' as 'the joining at the hip of the Minister for Justice and Equality and the Garda Commissioner', stating somewhat severely that our connection 'should be severed'. No sensitivity was shown to recently hospitalised patients who had undergone painful hip replacement operations!

Deputy Luke Ming Flanagan then delicately ratcheted the debate up a notch. 'They say in films', he recalled, 'about the mafia that the fish rots from the head and I agree with that. There is a strong stench coming from the Minister's direction. When I stated on television that I believed there was corruption in the Garda Síochána over a year ago, I believed that to be true but I could not in a million years have thought it to be true to the extent that it is turning out to be the case.' This was a Dáil first. No one had previously sniffed the air and challenged my personal hygiene.

The Dáil chamber was now in full kangaroo court mode and facts had ceased to be relevant. However, Labour's Minister for State Kathleen Lynch, and some Fine Gael deputies tried to bring a touch of reality to the exchanges. Fine Gael's Michelle Mulherin got to the nub of it stating:

> The rule of law, which is the cornerstone of our democracy and which gives some certainty to the parameters of our behaviour and also the protections we experience in society, cannot be ignored and should not be undermined. We are a parliament. We pass laws. We are the legislature. Are we now going to suggest that there is no need for evidence and there is no need for anything substantial?

Looking back on it all now, Michelle Mulherin eloquently referenced the new world inhabited by both Opposition TDs and too many journalists and commentators. Facts, evidence and the rule of law had ceased to matter in the competitive scramble to sensationalise and rush to judgement.

By the time the debate recommenced on the Wednesday evening, much of the ground had already been fully travelled as, for three and a half hours, I had been answering questions before the Petitions Committee and continued to do so for a further thirty minutes as the committee meeting overlapped with the proceedings in the Dáil chamber.

There had been twenty-two Oireachtas members present for GSOC's session before the Petitions Committee the previous week. On Wednesday, 19 February there were twenty-five. Like a week earlier, there were serious and relevant questions to which I provided as much detail as possible in reply. When asked by Fine Gael Deputy, Helen McEntee, were the offices of GSOC bugged, I replied that while what were termed 'anomalies', 'potential threats' and 'vulnerabilities' were identified, there was no evidence that the offices were under surveillance at all. I continued:

> I have not been given information that says they were ... I have no evidence that GSOC was bugged. People have been disappointed that I am not talking about GSOC having been bugged. I hope the

judge dealing with this matter will address that issue in a manner in which there is full public confidence and that no one can suggest any particular presentation is being made for any political reasons.

Responding to Fianna Fáil Deputy Seamus Kirk, I assured him that the terms of reference for the inquiry to be held 'are designed as far as is possible to get at the full truth of all of this'. Fine Gael Deputy Patrick O'Donovan questioned why I did not agree the previous week to the holding of an inquiry. I responded to him in similar terms to my response the previous night in the Dáil chamber. Independent Deputy John Halligan made it clear that regardless of the facts, he was convinced GSOC had been under surveillance 'if one looks at exactly what Verrimus said'. He stated that 'the vast majority of people believed something happened in GSOC. I do not care if it [GSOC] has changed its mind. I believe, based on this security analysis that something has happened.'

In answer to various questions, I emphasised that it was for the judge appointed to undertake the inquiry to clarify any issues of conflict. As the meeting ended, I realised that Fianna Fáil's Justice Spokesperson Niall Collins, who was present at the start of the meeting, had disappeared during it and had not returned to ask a single question. I thought this surprising, considering his statements during the preceding week and his continuous critical commentary, including his article published in the *Sunday Independent*. I had expected he would be one of my earlier inquisitors and wondered whether, having used the issue to garner personal publicity and media attention, he might have realised that I was telling the truth and did not want to challenge me at the Petitions Committee. What I did not know was that, as I was answering committee members' questions, I was being ambushed on the Leinster House plinth by the Fianna Fáil leader Micheál Martin, together with Niall Collins, on an entirely different garda-related issue. The sticky wicket was about to get a lot stickier!

CHAPTER 10

Political Tsunami

You can imagine my frustration with the ongoing GSOC bugging saga. How many hours have been wasted debating this topic in the Dáil? How many column inches have been wasted writing about this allegation? How much money will be wasted in having a retired judge write a report (just what Ireland needs!) rather than helping my patients. May I respectfully suggest that our politicians, journalists, the Garda Síochána and GSOC learn a little common sense. I feel they have an over-inflated view of themselves. Sure who would want to infiltrate GSOC? This isn't Edward Snowden and the CIA! –From a letter in *The Irish Times*, 21 February 2014, by Gareth T. Clifford, 'a frontline healthcare professional in a large acute Dublin hospital struggling daily with limited (and ever-reducing) resources to provide high quality healthcare'

During the two days when the Sinn Féin Private Members Motion was being debated in the Dáil, and ultimately defeated, the media and online torrent of criticism and condemnation continued. The media pack were united in their criticism of how I dealt with the 'GSOC bugging scandal' and despite the evidence to the contrary, broadcasters, journalists and commentators were enthusiastically promoting the 'Garda Bugged GSOC' narrative. Any Government deputy or senator who had the courage to stick their head above the parapet and attempt to discuss the issue factually and calmly was subjected to a hostile cross-examination, heavily laced with sarcasm. Journalistic double-jobbing gave an interesting insight into the supposed objectivity of those who straddle the world of 'objective' broadcast interviewer and opinionated columnist and commentator.

Shane Coleman, presenter of the *Sunday Show* on Newstalk, writing in the *Irish Independent* on 18 February 2014, was in no doubt that the Taoiseach had got the law wrong, I had misled the Dáil and that the Government was guilty of 'consistent undermining of GSOC'. As for the Labour Party, according to Coleman 'it needed to make it clear behind the scenes that Shatter and Fine Gael's take on this story was, and remains, all wrong'.

The legendary and pugnacious Vincent Browne, writing the next day in *The Irish Times*, accused both the Fine Gael and Labour parties of being complicit in undermining GSOC. His article replicated his regular displays of apoplexy on his late night TV3 talk show. In that morning's *Irish Times*, Browne unexpectedly seemed to enter a perverse politico sub/dom world. He asserted: 'The impertinence of Alan Shatter in carpeting the chairman of the Commission, Simon O'Brien, undermined its independence. The dismissal of the bugging concerns on the part of the Commission belittled it. The submissive conduct of Simon O'Brien, his acquiescence in his humiliation and then his shrinking apology has not done much for the Commission's independence.'

He concluded that 'Alan Shatter would seem to be immune from accountability.' He seemed to miss the fact that as a minister accountable to Dáil Eireann, I had, within an eight-day period, made two detailed statements to the Dáil on the issue and participated in a four-hour question and answer session before the Petitions Committee. The only thing missing from Browne's *Irish Times* commentary was an accompanying cartoon of me with a leery smile, wearing lederhosen, whip raised, standing over a prostrate and terrified Simon O'Brien. The TV3 show host, like many of his broadcast media and newspaper journalists, was unwilling even to consider that maybe GSOC had not been bugged!

In the political and media tsunami in which I was enveloped, it seemed that for some it had even ceased to matter whether GSOC had or had not been bugged. *The Irish Times*' award-winning journalist, Miriam Lord, in her satirical column on 20 February 2014, caricatured the 'bizarre story' of GSOC's bugging as defying my 'drone attack' at the Petition Committee's hearing. For the *Irish Independent*'s legal correspondant Dearbhail McDonald, while it remained 'to be seen what facts may ultimately emerge out of the suspected bugging' of GSOC, she opined that 'in one sense, it doesn't matter if its fears turn out to be groundless'. What mattered was what she described as my 'derision' and my 'dismissal, bordering on contempt of the Ombudsman's concerns'. This was little more than a complaint that I had not simply adopted or opted into the narrative desired by her and an overwhelming majority of broadcasters and journalists commenting and reporting on the issue.

For some years it had become clear that most of the political journalists based in Leinster House operated with a pack mentality that influenced the perspective of other journalists and commentators throughout the country. As the story had developed in the days following publication of the *Sunday Times* article on 9 February, I believed it was becoming increasingly difficult for any journalist to report that GSOC may have got it all wrong and that I was simply telling the truth instead of playing to the media gallery and serving up the narrative many desired. While the rest of the population got on with their lives, the daily newspapers and their online relations did their best to out-sensationalise each other.

On 19 February, the *Irish Independent*, under the headline 'Days of Crisis: 11', published a summary of each day's GSOC-related events, carefully avoiding any complicated factual information that could be relevant. Ironically, the same day, the same paper carried an inside article by Paul Williams entitled 'PC Brigade Dragged me Through Mud – Imagine if I'd been Wrong!'. Independent Newspapers always like to have some marker down on both sides of a major controversy or alleged scandal. It adds to the entertainment value of a story and is particularly useful as a defamation prophylactic!

Referring to his previous day's story on GSOC's Bitbuzz Wi-Fi connectivity to the Insomnia Coffee Shop, Williams wrote of being attacked on social media 'by journalists barely out of college – essentially for not following the accepted PC agenda'. He said it reminded him 'that to challenge the media consensus is to risk the ire of liberal commentators, their militant wing on social media and inevitably, of course, Sinn Fein'. He told readers of his amusement 'listening to RTÉ's politically correct pundits and commentators having a pop off me for daring to suggest GSOC may have been less than forthcoming about all the facts around this affair … some have accused those who have been sceptical of GSOC's claims of being pro-Alan Shatter and the gardaí. That's the kind of abuse that's thrown around like confetti if you don't follow the accepted wisdom of the media mob'.

Williams's article gave an interesting insight into the world of Irish journalism generally and political journalism in particular. He also unconsciously revealed the prevailing personal and contaminating nature of journalistic prejudice – it was apparently viewed as a term of abuse to be accused of being pro-Shatter.

Anyone who wishes to engage in politics and survive requires a thick neck and an ability to turn the other cheek. It is also important to understand the symbiotic relationship between politicians and journalists and the critical role that a free media and journalism plays in a democracy, holding governments, politicians and people in positions of power to account, bringing information to public attention and in stimulating debate and the exchange of ideas. No one in public life gets everything right all of the time and no journalist or commentator can be expected to do so. However, difficulties arise when people are blinded by bias or prejudice or when competitive commercial demands distort stories in order to attract potential readers and advertisers or where greater value is given to speed over accuracy.

Most politicians are obsessed with their personal image and not a little paranoid, sometimes with justification – that either the media, political opponents or those who perceive them as rivals in their own party are out to get them. You have to be able to take and survive as good as you give but there are occasions when the level of collective media vitriol and vilification is so disproportionate as to be unfathomable. The media's attitude to people in public life ebbs and flows with events. It is also influenced by the extent to which those in public life leak confidential information to journalists and commentators, gossip about colleagues or co-operate in the validation or development of stories.

Throughout my time as a Cabinet minister I refrained from sharing a single criticism of a Cabinet colleague with any reporter and avoided being seduced into doing so by a leading question. In the early days of the Government formed in March 2011, reporters discovered that I would not leak Cabinet documents, reveal or criticise anything said at cabinet meetings or engage in tittle tattle about Cabinet colleagues. I genuinely valued Cabinet confidentiality and believed members of Cabinet should be able to fully trust each other. Even on those occasions when a Cabinet colleague publicly made an unhelpful, ill-informed or critical comment about a matter that fell within my brief, I refrained from any public response. I saw no good in publicly rowing with colleagues in Cabinet and I had no interest in endearing myself to a select group of reporters in return for the expected media favours.

This is not an ideal approach for those who desire good press. Vincent Browne, in more reflective mood in 2013 in the TV 3 broadcast series *Print and be Damned*, talking about Irish journalists, acknowledged that two of the most compromising features of Irish journalism are sources and friendships. He freely admitted that 'when someone is leaking information to us we tend, at the very least, to avoid critical commentary on them'. It seems my not being a source for headline-making leaks rendered me more vulnerable than some to critical commentary.

I could handle criticism and like everyone in life I did not get everything right all of the time. No one does. However, the extent of the unrelenting media venom to which I was subjected during the first ten days of the GSOC saga was extraordinary and went far beyond anything I had ever experienced. It was as if almost three years of collective bile suddenly rushed to the surface and the so-called 'GSOC bugging scandal' caused it to erupt in volcanic proportions. I maintained an external presentation of calm but it brought me back to when, at fifteen, I had been bullied in school. The bullying lasted about two months. Then one day in the schoolyard, I ceased to be a docile victim, decided I would not take it any longer and much to the bully's surprise, punched him in the face. It is the only time in my life I have physically assaulted someone and in my defence I would plead provocation. The bullying stopped instantly.

The GSOC affair, the personalised ferocity of the media frenzy, the unrelenting criticism, the questioning of my veracity, the deliberate ignoring of irrefutable fact and repetitive allegations that I had misled the Dáil in simply telling the truth as I knew it, based entirely on information supplied by GSOC to me, was deeply unsettling. I had no agenda other than to get at the truth. My saying that had no credibility in the eyes of dedicated media conspiracy theorists and those who regarded 'GSOC under surveillance by Gardai' and 'Shatter covers up Garda misconduct' as a far better storyline. I was surprised to discover from Paul Williams's article that he had experienced on one day a microcosm of the ten days I had lived through.

I assumed that, after my experience before the Petitions Committee and following the appointment of Judge Cooke to conduct a preliminary inquiry, I would have some breathing space to get on with my work. The assumption was mistaken. As the tide went out on the GSOC political tsunami, another gigantic wave came ashore on the Leinster House plinth as I was obliviously answering questions at the meeting of the Petitions Committee. This wave would ultimately have for me catastrophic political consequences. However, before we get to that, I think it appropriate that we first complete the GSOC story.

CHAPTER 11

GSOC Cooked

It was never right to attack GSOC on the basis of legislation that didn't exist –Gene Kerrigan, *Sunday Independent*, 23 February 2014, denouncing Alan Shatter's publicly detailing of GSOC's statutory reporting obligations, replicating the narrative of most media commentators at that time

This investigation is now closed. I need to think about reporting. This will be difficult, we have found nothing –Note recorded on 25 November 2013 in the personal log of Simon O'Brien, Chairperson of GSOC, quoted by Judge John Cooke in the *Cooke Report*

Having commenced, conducted and then closed an investigation in the public interest pursuant to section 102 (4) of the (2005) Act there was an obligation upon the Commission to furnish information in relation to its results to both the Minister and the Commissioner –Judge John Cooke, *Cooke Report*, June 2014

It was around 8.40pm on Tuesday, 10 June 2014. I had just signed off some post and emails in my Dáil office. Drinking a cup of tea and surfing Journal.ie's online news site, I discovered that Judge John Cooke had completed his inquiry and that his report had been published that evening. I had resigned from Government approximately one month earlier. Neither the Taoiseach nor Frances Fitzgerald my successor as Minister for Justice, or any former ministerial colleague had bothered to either inform me of the report's pending publication or to give me a copy of it. I would later learn that its publication had been authorised at a Cabinet meeting held around 7.45 that evening but the speed of its online publication after the meeting confirmed that advanced preparation had gone into its public release. At the very least, I believed I should have been alerted.

My immediate reaction to the online news report was relief – from a cursory reading it seemed that Cooke had independently established that there was no evidence to support the *Sunday Times* story that GSOC had been under surveillance or that surveillance on GSOC had been undertaken by members of An Garda Síochána. Perhaps, now, I thought it will be acknowledged that the political and media hysteria around the issue was entirely baseless. I discovered the report on the Government's website, downloaded it and drove home to read it.

The report, entitled *Inquiry into Reports of Unlawful Surveillance of Garda Síochána Ombudsman Commission*, had been furnished to the Taoiseach six days earlier on 4 June. Judge Cooke recorded that he had considered the Verrimus and Rits reports, interviewed their authors, engaged directly with GSOC, its solicitors and counsel, interviewed GSOC's commissioners and visited their offices, accessed all additional documentation of relevance in GSOC's possession, obtained information directly from Bitbuzz and from the mobile phone service provider whose UK country/network code featured in the Verrimus analysis. He also had a discussion with the principal of the firm that carried out servicing and repairs on GSOC's AMX audio/visual system and accessed relevant works and service records of its WiFi devices. BHC Consultants, an Irish consultancy firm that specialised in information and communications security had provided technical advice.

In addition to meeting the GSOC commissioners and giving them an opportunity to comment on his draft report, Cooke has also met the three designated GSOC officers who were mainly responsible for the decision to commence the public interest inquiry. Cooke found that while GSOC's Chairperson, Simon O'Brien, had been briefed, the formal decision that GSOC conduct an inquiry was not taken, as I understood, by the commission members themselves but by the acting director of investigations pursuant to a function delegated to him in 2007. This had not been explained to me or to the Petitions Committee members.

The *Cooke Report* revealed that, by 20 October 2013, Verrimus had established that the Bitbuzz network, which had received so much attention and had been labelled as a 'potential' or 'credible' threat was located as a Wi-Fi hotspot in the Insomnia Coffee Shop. This confirmed the accuracy of the information given by me to the Dáil four months earlier and of Paul Williams's article that had upset his media colleagues. It also emerged that the Verrimus operatives believed that a microphone was built into the console device in the GSOC conference room that could be used 'by an attacker to eavesdrop on conversations' and this resulted in it being presented as a 'potential threat'. However, when Cooke had the device fully examined, it was established that it possessed no microphone or audio eavesdropping capacity of any nature.

Cooke learned from the service and maintenance records relating to the two consoles and the audiovisual system, that work had been undertaken servicing, repairing, rebooting and reconfiguring them between 2007 and 2013. Neither Verrimus nor GSOC had properly examined either prior to or during GSOC's public interest investigation. The device labelled 4B located in GSOC's media room, not in its conference room, Cooke reported, had in April 2012 been found to be faulty, in that 'it was powering up but no signal from it was being picked up by the receiver in the communications console'. It was established that the console in the conference room had at no stage been powering up. The maintenance firm had provided quotations 'for a number of options to remedy the situation, including repairing the existing system or installing a new replacement'. None of the options had been taken up and there was no explanation for GSOC's inaction.

Cooke discovered that, on a call-out on 19 February 2013, 'the service engineer's report on the two touch panels of the audiovisual equipment recording' noted 'AV system controller failures in Boardroom and Media Room'. A report of a subsequent visit on 4 March 2013 recorded 'Boardroom unit faulty, Media Room ok'. Bizarrely, neither GSOC nor Verrimus had considered these records of relevance to the security assessment and public interest investigation undertaken. Cooke also established that there 'does not appear to be any concrete proof that device 4B at any stage subsequent to the installation of the hotspot' in the Insomnia Coffee Shop in August 2013, 'actually authenticated and registered in the Bitbuzz network so as to open up an internet connection between 4B and any third-party internet user'. Bitbuzz maintained records of all such connectivity, which included the Mac address of devices. Bitbuzz database records did not contain the identifying particulars of device 4B. Cooke concluded that:

It seems highly improbable that the haphazard performance of such a remote control device constituted the planned means of covert eavesdropping on GSOC in a sophisticated surveillance exercise by any agency equipped with the capability of 'intelligence service level'. Furthermore, having regard to the technical limitations of gaining access to the device over the internet by an external third party … it seems implausible that such a mechanism would have been used and that steps had been taken to 'wipe' all traces of the connection and to circumvent the statutory data retention records of the database of the network in connection.

Verrimus had contended to Cooke that their analysis was correct and alleged that records could have been 'wiped'. This contention he firmly rejected.

As for the IMSI Catcher, Cooke rejected both the conclusions of Verrimus and Rits. As a result of enquiries made by him, he learned that the Irish sister company of a UK mobile phone company 'in common with other mobile phone service providers had been' allocated the new 4G/LTE spectrum in 2012. In September and October 2013 it was in the process of rolling out and testing the equipment for that new service in a number of locations in Dublin, including one close to Upper Abbey Street. The core network for the 4G service in Ireland was not yet in place. As a result 'these tests involved connecting to the group's test bed' located in the UK. The particular network code, identified by Verrimus which had caused it to suspect surveillance had, in fact, been 'allocated exclusively to that test bed and would have been generated only by communications with the test bed'.

The 4G network tests had started on 5 September 2013 and ceased on 31 October 2013 when Verrimus was undertaking its first two engagements on behalf of GSOC. The mobile phone company believed these tests may have resulted in Verrimus mistakenly detecting a 'potential threat' posed by an IMSI Catcher and Cooke accepted this as 'the more probable' explanation for one of the so-called 'anomalies'. The tests clearly posed no threat of any nature to GSOC's security nor were they evidence of any nature of anyone engaging in espionage or surveillance.

As for the 'ring back' reaction to the alert test of the Polycom conference call unit in the chairman's office, Cooke concluded that it 'remains unexplained as a technical or scientific anomaly'. In the judge's view 'whatever the explanation may be, there is no evidence that the ring back reaction was necessarily attributed to an offence or misbehaviour on the part of a member of the Garda Síochána'.

Cooke detailed that in order to determine whether GSOC was under surveillance, Verrimus mounted a special counter-surveillance operation on 19 November 2013. A 'legend' was prepared of deliberately false and misleading information expected to be 'of particular interest to the suspected eavesdroppers'. Subsequently it was discussed at a meeting held in Simon O'Brien's office by two GSOC Commissioners and investigating officers with O'Brien, who was in the UK, participating by a conference call conducted over his office Polycom. No surveillance activity was detected. Cooke recounted that on 25 November, the investigating officers briefed Chairperson O'Brien and Commissioner Fitzgerald that there was no 'positive result'. Cooke notes that O'Brien then made a note in his personal log stating: 'This investigation is now closed. I need to think about reporting. This will be difficult, we have found nothing.'

Thus, while O'Brien did not receive the final Verrimus report until 16 December, as Cooke also confirmed, it was clear to me that he knew the outcome of the public interest investigation initiated on 8 October 2013 by 25 November 2013 at the latest and knew he was obliged to report it to me. His stated excuse for not doing so was the proximity of the final report to Christmas. In fact, he knew a full calendar month before Christmas that the investigation had been concluded and that nothing had been found.

Judge Cooke concluded that 'it is clear the evidence does not support the proposition that actual surveillance of the kind asserted in *The Sunday Times* article took place and much less that it was carried out by members of the Garda Síochána'.

Cooke detailed some of the 'misinformation' contained in the original article of 9 February 2014. He stated 'GSOC's Wi-Fi network was not compromised to "steal emails, data and confidential reports"'.

He found that the security sweep insofar as it 'examined a "Wi-Fi network" ... was confined to the wireless device of the audio/visual equipment and was unconnected to any data storage ... There was no "second Wi-Fi system" which had been created using an "IP address in Britain" ... No Government-owned technology had in fact been used to hack emails.'

While the information 'revealed' in John Mooney's article which originated the 'Garda Bugged GSOC' narrative and the political and media frenzy that followed was 'seriously inaccurate', its publication according to Cooke was 'evidence of a serious breach of security of GSOC's confidential information'. This was so 'as it appears to have its source in information known only to those who are privy to the conduct and outcome of the public interest investigation'. While Cooke recorded that the security breach was 'the subject of an internal inquiry by GSOC' he stated 'Having regard to the character of that breach, its investigation is not in any event suitable for an ad hoc non-statutory inquiry.' It was clearly his view that for any such inquiry to be properly conducted, it would have to be empowered to legally compel the provision of information and witnesses to attend before it.

A statutory sworn inquiry as envisaged by Judge Cooke was never undertaken into GSOC's internal breach of security. Following publication of the *Cooke Report* it became clear that neither the Government nor the Opposition had any interest in it. Nor did the media, which had been fixated by the wildly inaccurate fake narrative it had enthusiastically promoted.

Prior to Cooke reporting, GSOC had arranged in May 2014 for Mark Connaughton SC, to 'investigate' what occurred. When he reported, the GSOC Commissioners attempted to cover up his report. I had no doubt that Connaughton would do his very best to identify the individual responsible for *The Sunday Times* leak. It was, however, extraordinary that following publication of the *Cooke Report*, no calls were made to have the issue of the leak independently investigated by a statutory inquiry and it was regarded as acceptable that the nature and format of the investigation undertaken be determined by GSOC alone. It was to become clear in the days that followed that the impunity extended to GSOC, in particular its commissioners, was to continue even following publication of the *Cooke Report*. The Government's objective was to move on and to avoid controversy at all costs. The objective of Opposition politicians and those engaged in the February media frenzy was, except for a few, to save face, look away and hope that the whole thing would be forgotten.

Cooke also addressed GSOC's statutory reporting obligations which many Opposition TDs and media commentators denied existed and which had been the subject of heated Dail exchanges. He concluded that 'having commenced, conducted and then closed an investigation in the public interest' there was

> an obligation upon the Commission to furnish information in relation to its results to both the Minister and the [Garda] Commissioner. This was the 'mandatory obligation that arises under Section 103 (1) (b) of the 2005 Act and not the discretion which the Commission has under Section 80(5) of the Act to make a special report to the Minister drawing attention to matters of gravity or exceptional circumstances that have come to its notice.'

He noted that 'although the Commission appears to have been conscious of this obligation to report, it was not until after the publication of *The Sunday Times* article that the non-compliance was remedied on 13 February 2014'. This was the Thursday when I was furnished with GSOC's statutory report.

Cooke acknowledged that it was 'difficult to avoid the impression' that GSOC's concerns were 'heavily influenced by the atmosphere of frustration and tension that had arisen in relations between GSOC personnel and the senior ranks of the Garda Síochána, thus leading to the raising of suspicions which might not otherwise have been acted upon'. Of course, as a consequence of the new agreed protocols between GSOC and An Garda Siochana, concluded on 23 September 2013, any such frustrations and tensions should have been resolved.

I had concerns that the technical information contained in the first Verrimus report which resulted in the commencement of the public interest investigation had not been fully understood by the GSOC Commissioners and investigating officers. While Cooke concluded that members of the Commission and the GSOC investigating officers 'acted in good faith' in commencing a public interest investigation on 8 October 2013, he expressed the view that 'they were possibly unduly alarmed by the language used and perfunctory exposé of the findings presented' in the Verrimus September report and that it was 'unfortunate that further elucidation and advice from Verrimus or a second opinion was not sought before the public interest investigation was commenced'. Had GSOC so acted, and had there been further tests and enquiries, including those subsequently undertaken by Verrimus, he believed some of GSOC's concerns could have been allayed. Cooke concluded that GSOC's public interest investigation when commenced 'was not ... immediately necessary and was possibly a premature recourse' to its statutory powers to conduct such investigation. The judge did not comment on whether GSOC had acted 'in good faith' during the course of the controversy which had dominated so much Government and Dáil time in February 2014 or in failing to comply with its statutory reporting obligations. However, as I would discover, this 'good faith' reference would subsequently be relied upon to avoid all discussion of GSOC's incompetence and failings and to misrepresent Cooke as asserting that GSOC had throughout acted in 'good faith'.

There could be no doubt, following publication of the Cooke report, that conduct by someone within GSOC had resulted in the seriously inaccurate *Sunday Times* story. The question was who? It was also unknown whether accurate information revealed from within GSOC had been embellished by John Mooney or inaccurate information had been fed to him deliberately or accidently by an individual who was technologically deficient and did not fully understand the Verrimus reports. Even taking account of information in the Verrimus reports that was ultimately discounted by Cooke, *The Sunday Times* story simply did not hold up.

The *Cooke Report* was published approximately one month after I had resigned as Minister for Justice. What Mark Connaughton SC would have to say about the breach of GSOC's security I believed would be interesting.

I was curious to know how John Mooney and *The Sunday Times* would respond to the *Cooke Report*. There was no need for curiosity over the reaction of my successor in the Department of Justice and Equality, Minister Frances Fitzgerald. On the day that the report was published she gave GSOC a free pass and reiterated the promise made by me approximately two weeks before the controversy broke, to increase and strengthen GSOC's investigative remit.

No other government elsewhere, immediately following publication of such a report, would strengthen and extend the investigative powers of a police oversight body that behaved as GSOC did, or tolerate that the leadership of that body, which presided over such a debacle, remain in place. But Government policy was to avoid controversy at all costs. I had been set upon by the media for daring to ask GSOC questions, for questioning what was said by GSOC's Commissioners at the Petitions Committee meeting and for expressing concern about the contradictions in their narrative of what had occurred. There was no way my successor was going to criticise the commissioners publicly and risk the wrath of the Fourth Estate and the political opposition. Instead that night on RTÉ's *Prime Time* she expressed her full confidence in GSOC, as did Sinn Féin's Padraig MacLochlainn. When questioned by *Prime Time*'s Claire Byrne on whether during the GSOC controversy I had been treated unfairly, she evasively responded 'There is certainly room for people who made very shrill criticism at the time ... to read this report and reflect on some of the comments that were made in relation to Minister Shatter at the time.'

Claire Byrne persisted: 'Do you think he is vindicated tonight?'

Fitzgerald found it impossible to simply say 'Yes'. Instead she gave a half-answer:

Well this report is not about vindicating individuals, it is about finding the truth of what happened. And I believe in the truth of the situation. But certainly I would say that Minister Shatter told the truth at the time. And this report clearly says that there was, there is no evidence of surveillance taking place, much less that it was carried out by Gardai, An Garda Síochána.

The interview ended. While Fitzgerald confirmed I had told the truth, she avoided the 'vindication' word. By doing so, she kept herself out of the firing line.

CHAPTER 12

The Presumption of Guilt and Chasing Geese!

There is nothing to report here. Please move on –Micheál Martin TD, leader of Fianna Fáil, Dáil Éireann, 18 February 2014

It appears that the entire controversy was a bottle of smoke … The only conclusion to be drawn from the (Cooke) Report is that the political system and the media spent three months engaging in a wild goose chase –Stephen Collins, *Irish Times*, 14 June 2014

The story is becoming more Austen Power than James Bond –Paul Williams, *Irish Independent*, 14 June 2014

'Move on, nothing to see or report here,' was the taunt of Opposition leaders and deputies in the Dáil during the GSOC controversy, accusing me of covering up Garda surveillance of GSOC. Ironically, it neatly summarised Judge John Cooke's conclusions. Those who had deployed it as a political weapon were not best pleased. Neither were some journalists and commentators who were devotees of the false 'Garda Bugged GSOC' narrative. They extracted from the *Cooke Report* selective morsels of content that facilitated maintaining the story and saving face, while substantially ignoring Cooke's major conclusions.

In response to the Cooke Report, GSOC's Commissioners, instead of honourably departing the stage and apologising for the debacle, in their responding statement gave themselves a congratulatory pat on the back and adopted a similar approach. The Commissioners agreed with Judge Cooke's finding that *The Sunday Times* had got it wrong (what else could they have done?). They simply claimed that Cooke's conclusions mirrored 'key findings of their own investigation' which found that GSOC's 'databases were not compromised' and that 'there was no evidence of Garda misconduct'. It was as if the wandering 'definitive', 'potential' and 'credible' threats and the withholding of 'exoneration' from the gardaí had never been put on public display and the Petitions Committee meeting had never happened.

Their statement contained a selective and edited extract from the *Cooke Report*, quoting it as stating that 'in the world of covert surveillance and counter-surveillance techniques, it is ultimately extremely difficult to determine with complete certainty whether unexplained anomalies of the kinds identified were or were not attributable to unlawful intrusion'. This quotation was clearly seen by GSOC as some sort of defence or justification of its conduct. What Cooke in the passage quoted had actually said was determining such matters 'with complete certainty' is 'extremely difficult' in 'the somewhat febrile world of covert surveillance'. However, the phrase 'somewhat febrile', consistent with the GSOC Commissioners' prior verbal inexactitudes, had gone missing from the passage cited. As GSOC's Commissioners no doubt hoped, it was this edited extract from Cooke which, in the following days, was substantially reproduced as a sort of explanation, if not vindication, of GSOC's conduct by many of those who had enthusiastically embraced and promoted the 'Gardai Bugged GSOC' narrative. It was also used by some, including *The Sunday Times*, to suggest that there could still be some outstanding skulduggery to be uncovered.

'Febrile' is not a commonly used word and the significance of its omission by GSOC went entirely unnoticed. However, the 'febrile' reference in the *Cooke Report* was important and was, no doubt, a word chosen by Judge John Cooke with some care. Febrile is an adjective with origins in the Latin word 'febris' meaning 'fever'. In seventeenth-century French it evolved into 'febrile' meaning 'having or showing the symptoms of a fever or someone being characterised by a great deal of nervous excitement'. Essentially, what Judge Cooke referenced was the 'fevered' or 'nervous' world GSOC occupied when addressing the issue of possible covert surveillance and how events can be viewed through a 'fevered lens'.

As the State's garda watchdog body, I believe we are entitled to expect from GSOC a rational and evidence-based approach to issues and not a fevered and nervously excitable approach. It seemed, subsequent to publication of the *Cooke Report*, GSOC's wandering and now disappeared 'definitive' had been joined by Judge Cooke's 'febrile' also disappearing into the ether.

Of course, GSOC were not the only ones who selectively quoted and attempted to reframe the *Cooke Report*. John Mooney, having initiated the whole controversy, travelled this route in *The Sunday Times*, after the Cooke Report was published. While acknowledging that the report had criticised the *Sunday Times* story, he and the newspaper substantially ignored what Judge Cooke had detailed as being 'misinformation' in Mooney's original article. Instead, he brought a new absolutist 'definitive' into the narrative. Mooney asserted that Cooke 'stopped short of reaching an absolutely definitive conclusion' and continued 'While finding no evidence to support claims that GSOC was in fact snooped on, Cooke also said it was impossible on the basis of the technical opinions to categorically rule out that covert surveillance had taken place'. The extract quoted by GSOC was clearly continuing to evolve and not a 'febrile' in sight.

For *The Sunday Times*, the existence of no evidence of surveillance was sufficient to suspect at the very least that there was a possibility of GSOC being under surveillance because it could not be categorically (or 'definitively') proved that nothing happened. Such an approach, if applied to our criminal justice system generally, would result in all of us being presumed guilty of something and, perversely, the absence of evidence to substantiate guilt would be relied upon as proof of guilt. It is a concept of jurisprudence portrayed in Franz Kafka's famous novel *The Trial* in which the main protagonist is entirely preoccupied in attempting to defend himself against unspecified criminal charges levelled against him and is ultimately pronounced guilty.

Conor Brady, the former *Irish Times* editor and GSOC Commissioner who, the previous February, was certain GSOC had been a victim of surveillance, writing in the same edition of *The Sunday Times*, asserted that 'it was always likely' that Cooke 'would find no evidence to support the alleged surveillance of GSOC's offices'. Moderating his earlier views, he acknowledged that An Garda Síochána were 'officially in the clear on this issue' and that 'GSOC has sustained reputational damage'. Unlike Mooney, he recognised that the information secured by *The Sunday Times* 'represented a failure of [GSOC's] internal controls' and referenced Cooke's criticism in concluding that GSOC had insufficient grounds for initiating its public interest investigation in the first place. He had nothing to say about the lack of any regular security checks being undertaken on GSOC's offices and communications equipment during his time as a GSOC Commissioner or GSOC's failure to have repairs undertaken on equipment identified as defective.

Michael Clifford of the *Irish Examiner* had difficulty in acknowledging that media commentators who in February 2014, most enthusiastically promoted the narrative that the gardaí had bugged GSOC were mistaken and should not have rushed to judgement. He also found it impossible to acknowledge that I had properly dealt with the issue. In his book *A Force for Justice* published in September 2017 referencing 'the GSOC bugging matter', he wrote:

> In time, a report from retired Judge John Cooke would conclude there was no evidence that the offices of GSOC had been bugged. But Shatter's problem was that he leapt in immediately once the story broke to accuse GSOC of behaving unprofessionally. This was an astonishing reaction to the possibility that the confidentiality of the body overseeing the Gardai may have been compromised.

This intended continuing criticism of how I dealt with the issue conveniently ignored the fact that the single overall conclusion that can be derived from the *Cooke Report* is that GSOC's behaviour in dealing with the issue was grossly unprofessional. Clifford's real problem is that I called it correctly, told the truth and did not surf on the tide of his and nearly all of the media's frenzied preferred false narrative.

Subsequent to publication of the *Cooke Report*, no attempt was made by Mooney or *The Sunday Times* to address Cooke's criticism of the papers' inaccuracies or to apologise. In a tired and evasive editorial, the paper acknowledged that the last throw of Opposition party TDs who want to keep a wilting controversy alive is to imply that 'there are still questions to be answered'. The *Sunday Times* editor threw that very ball in the air and caught it himself. The paper protested that it had never used the phrase 'government owned technology' but had referred to 'government level technology' without reminding readers that this reference related to the activities of the non-existent IMSI Catcher which Cooke had, on specific factual evidence, discounted. While Cooke ultimately amended his report to reference government 'level technology' instead of government 'owned technology', *The Sunday Times* never printed any correction of any nature to their now discredited front-page headline 'GSOC under High-Tech Surveillance' of 9 February 2014 and the grossly inaccurate and misleading story it published. The editor also complained that *The Sunday Times* had not reported that 'surveillance was carried out by members of the Garda Síochána'. This was a last-ditch protest from a paper that had fallen over backwards in its reports to 'imply' that gardaí had bugged GSOC. It was particularly disingenuous having regard to John Mooney's numerous subsequent broadcast interviews. Rather than 'Gardai Bugged GSOC' being the paper's principal message on 9 February, it was now claiming that the important revelation was that the Department of Justice had not been informed of what had occurred. The paper essentially claimed that, without its publishing of misinformation, both I, as Minister for Justice, and the Department would have been kept in the dark. It was a strange defence of a fake and discredited story that had resulted in my being subject not merely to political criticism but also to personal vilification and abuse both inside and outside the Dáil, the Taoiseach's credibility being attacked, hours of Government, Dáil and some Seanad time being wasted, An Garda Síochána being publicly pilloried and its credibility being undermined over an issue for which it was blameless.

While *The Sunday Times* had initiated the GSOC story, all our print, broadcast and online media had both reported and stoked the ensuing controversy. Understandably, the report received extensive coverage the morning after its publication and it was generally accepted that Judge Cooke found that there was no evidence of GSOC being bugged or under surveillance and that GSOC was wrong not to have informed me or the Department of Justice of its public interest inquiry. There was some but very little speculation about the position of the three GSOC Commissioners. The *Irish Independent* reprinted the timeline of events last seen in February, the former prominent reference to 'crisis' was omitted and the timeline ended with the following entry: 'June 10. Cooke Report into alleged bugging of Garda Ombudsman Office finds GSOC overstepped the mark in setting up a special investigation into their suspicions of surveillance. However, it has "no evidence" to back up the claim that surveillance was carried out.'

In the forty-eight hours following the report's publication, serious questions remained over whether GSOC had learned any lessons from these events. Journalists were being briefed that questions remained to be answered over its bugging fears and these briefings were referenced in media reports by journalists who displayed a good deal more scepticism for GSOC's claims than they had done in the preceding months. There was little criticism or media soul searching over the political and media frenzy surrounding the issue or any substantial examination of the extent to which experienced broadcasters and journalists had opted into the Opposition's false narrative and willingly assumed I was lying.

The *Irish Independent* took some delight in what its political editor Fionnan Sheehan described as Cooke's 'damning indictment' of *The Sunday Times* story but no one in Independent Newspapers took the trouble to publicly reflect on the sixteen articles relating to the 'GSOC Bugging Scandal' that had dominated the edition of its own *Sunday Independent* published at the height of the controversy. However, Eamon Delaney, writing in the *Irish Independent*, two days after the *Cooke Report*, rightly praised RTÉ's crime reporter, Paul Reynolds, and the *Irish Independent*'s Paul Williams, for not being seduced in February by the prevailing media consensus. He commented that Cooke's conclusion that 'there was no evidence of surveillance … wasn't the message some people wanted to hear'. He also noted that 'the same media who had invested so much energy in alleging a Garda Watergate continue to dismiss the sceptics and feel compelled to keep the allegations going, saying there is still not "total conclusive proof" that there was no bugging of GSOC. It is hard to upset a consensus'. Paul Williams, giving his own unique perspective, succinctly described the GSOC bugging story as 'more Austin Powers than James Bond'.

Publication of the *Cooke Report*, as could be expected, generated a string of interviews on various television and radio current affairs shows. Some of the Opposition TDs and commentators, who had in February 2014 excitedly promoted the 'Gardai Bugged GSOC' narrative, reappeared selectively quoting extracts from the *Cooke Report* in an attempt save face. I thought Eamon Delaney's and Paul Williams's articles put it all in context, journalistically, from the inside looking out. They also reassured me that I was not disconnected from reality and occupying some parallel universe. Stephen Collins, the political editor of *The Irish Times*, perfectly summed it all up at the end of that week in his Saturday column. Referencing the whole controversy as 'a puff of smoke' he wrote 'the only conclusion to be drawn from the Report is that the political system and the media spent three months engaging in a wild goose chase'.

Sitting at home that Saturday morning, I doubted whether the insights of Delaney, Williams or Collins would influence in any way the Opposition's contribution to the Dáil debate scheduled to take place on the *Cooke Report* the following Thursday.

CHAPTER 13

Cooking Cooke and the Invisible Leak

With regard to the possibility of bugging, I would observe in response to the Report, that absence of evidence is not evidence of absence
–Niall Collins TD, Dáil Debates, 19 June 2014

Protecting sources is vital for good journalism
–Headline, *Sunday Times* (Irish edition), 14 September 2014

If [the Sunday Times journalist] had recent accurate 'source' information, around the date of publication, from someone then closely connected with the security sweep and investigation, his article does not reflect this –Mark Connaughton SC's report to GSOC on possible disclosure of confidential information, quoted in GSOC's statement of 24 September 2014

The Dáil debate on the *Cooke Report* took place on Thursday, 19 June 2014. It was a predictable and depressing affair. Frances Fitzgerald reprised Cooke's conclusions and recited his recommendations, which included that GSOC should more frequently have 'a thorough and suitable counter-surveillance examination' undertaken on its offices, equipment and facilities and that appropriate staff security training should be provided. Reference was also made to the need for legislative change to clarify 'the precise scope' of the competence afforded to GSOC to initiate public interest investigations. She expressed support for these and other recommendations and rightly emphasised the importance of An Garda Síochána and GSOC fully co-operating with each other in the exercise of their individual roles.

Validating the February media frenzy, she asserted that it was 'entirely understandable that these claims (that GSOC was under surveillance) led to serious disquiet, which in turn had the potential to, and indeed did, undermine the continued public confidence in policing and the oversight in policing'. She voiced no criticism of *The Sunday Times* for the publication of its 'grossly inaccurate' article, or of any media organisation, broadcaster, or journalist for assuming or advocating the truth of its content. Voicing any such criticism could have damaged her popularity as political flavour of the month with the media ensemble. Fitzgerald did, however, delicately invite members of the Opposition to reflect on their February rhetoric, saying:

> At that time, the former Minister, Deputy Shatter, made statements to the House and to the Joint Committee outlining the facts as he had been given them. Now that we have the Cooke Report, I believe members of this House should reflect on the responses they gave to the then Minister in light of how significantly ad idem the results of the Cooke Report are with what the then Minister told this House. We must all consider the advantage of developing a measured and reflective response to significant issues such as these, rather than making an immediate judgement.

Again she avoided the 'vindication' word. She concluded saying she was 'looking forward' to hearing the views of members of the House. Predictably, there was to be no measured and reflective Opposition response.

The unfortunate truth is that the 'GSOC bugging scandal' had become nothing other than a political game and the main tactic was to keep the ball in play, even if your heart was no longer in it. Opposition TDs gave it their last throw.

Fianna Fáil's Niall Collins's contribution starkly illustrated the 'questions still to be answered' approach caricatured a few days earlier in the *Sunday Times* evasive editorial. Intent on saving face, he asserted, 'With regard to the possibility of bugging, I would observe in response to the Report that absence of evidence is not evidence of absence.'

This tantalising tautological linguistic conundrum was as good as it got. The speeches were a mixture of disparaging inconvenient conclusions contained in the *Cooke Report* and selecting sometimes edited Cooke commentary to breathe life into the 'Garda Bugged GSOC' saga but their hearts were clearly not in it. Despite the report being forwarded by Frances Fitzgerald to the Justice Committee, no meeting of that committee to discuss 'all the issues' it raised, as envisaged by her, was ever held.

I had not spoken in the Dáil since my resignation and had little appetite for doing so. The truth is, I was both traumatised and stressed, not just as a consequence of being forced to resign but also due to the surreal circumstances of my resignation and the ferocious media onslaught and public and online abuse to which I had been subjected. This had included

Independent Newspapers journalists and photographers staking out my house for the entire day on two successive Saturdays, as well as tabloid and freelance photographers pursuing me at every opportunity. The obsessive attention of the photographers had continued in the weeks following my resignation. It included both a car chase and one photographer staking out the Pasta Fresca restaurant in Chatham Street off Grafton Street in Dublin, one lunchtime when I was having a quiet lunch there with Jane Lehane and my daughter, Kelly. He then pursued us down Grafton Street obsessively taking photographs, as if I were some axe-murderer on day release from prison. Finally, in exasperation, I told him to 'fuck off' as Kelly got increasingly distressed, but that had no impact.

I did not believe anything positive would result from my speaking in the Dáil. However, I believed it important to participate in the debate on the *Cooke Report*, anticipating correctly that for political reasons neither Frances Fitzgerald nor any Opposition TD would critically address GSOC's failings. I believed it was in the public interest that I did so.

Referencing RTÉ's *Morning Ireland* interview with Simon O'Brien, the morning after publication of the *Cooke Report*, in which he explained GSOC's failure to inform me as Minister of Justice about its public interest investigation on the basis that 'events overtook us', I noted that Cooke recorded that O'Brien's personal log detailed that on 25 November 2014, the investigation was closed and that reporting 'will be difficult, we have found nothing'. I continued:

> I do not regard the explanation of Mr. O'Brien given on RTÉ as credible and I believe the only reasonable conclusion to be drawn from the fact that no report was furnished to me was that the finding of 'nothing' in the public interest investigation was an embarrassment. What was said on RTÉ is sadly an indicator that GSOC has not learned from these events.

Later on, I said:

> The work GSOC does is of crucial public importance and it is essential there is public confidence in the leadership provided by GSOC commissioners, that they comply with and respect their statutory obligations, that when conducting an investigation they assume those subject to the investigation are innocent until proven guilty and that

they truthfully present to the Minister of the day, as well as to the public, actions taken by them. In this context, I believe the conduct of GSOC's commissioners and the narrative and conclusions of Mr. Justice Cooke raise genuine concerns as to GSOC's capacity to undertake and comply with its statutory duties under its present leadership. This is an issue that must be addressed before any additional statutory powers are extended to that body by new legislation.

Responding to the debate, Frances Fitzgerald entirely ignored my contribution to it. She would subsequently steer through the Dáil the legislation promised to extend GSOC's remit. Simon O'Brien continued as GSOC's Chairperson until he announced his resignation in January 2015 and on 2 February became Chief Executive of the Pensions Ombudsman Service in England. High Court Judge Mary Ellen Ring was subsequently appointed Chairperson and took up that position in September 2015. In December 2016, Kieran Fitzgerald was reappointed upon his term expiring and Carmel Foley retired from GSOC.

During the Dáil debate on the *Cook Report*, no questions were asked about the security lapse in GSOC which resulted in the *Sunday Times* article and no reference was made to the decision of GSOC that Mark Connaughton SC conduct, on its behalf, an investigation into the leaking of confidential information about the security sweep. The issue of the leak was important. It is crucial that when conducting investigations, GSOC's confidentiality is maintained to ensure that no member of An Garda Síochána is adversely affected by a false or malicious allegation of misconduct being publicised, that no prosecution is in any way prejudiced and to maintain public confidence in the organisation. Unfortunately, no value is attached to these principles by the media who regard all leaks from every State body and organisation as a valuable commodity to feed the news cycle and who present all 'whistle-blowers' in heroic guise, even when it is established that information provided is seriously inaccurate. The same applies to Opposition TDs who perceive information leaked to them as potential political capital and ammunition to be used on the political battlefield.

There is, of course, in every democracy a delicate balance between people's right to know, the right to individual privacy and the importance of information being kept confidential to ensure that the capacity of a public body to properly and ethically undertake duties in the public interest is not undermined. Achieving the correct balance can be difficult and there will always be shades of grey but a more limited variation on the shades than in the famous book of that title!

There was minimal media interest in the outcome of the Connaughton investigation and no Dáil Opposition interest in pursuing the issue. On10 September 2014, GSOC issued a one-page press release announcing it had received the *Connaughton Report* which it described as 'a fact-finding investigation' into the circumstances in which 'confidential information' relating to GSOC's security sweep 'may have been disclosed to a third party'. The statement said that 'the Report was unable to establish individual responsibility for any disclosure, either on the part of an employee of GSOC or any other party. It concludes that it is difficult to identify what additional information could usefully advance matters, short of obtaining the co-operation of the journalist in question who declined the invitation.'

GSOC said, in its view, 'proportionate measures to try to ascertain the facts' had been taken and no further action was intended. It also announced several internal measures had been taken to enhance its security. Stating it had furnished a copy of the *Connaughton Report* to the Minister for Justice, GSOC said it did not intend to publish it because it 'contains personal data which is impossible to redact effectively'.

The 'third party' and the 'journalist in question' referenced in the statement was obviously *The Sunday Times* journalist John Mooney and, relying on journalistic privilege, he was clearly not going to reveal his source or sources. It seemed to me that GSOC had now adopted the 'nothing to see here, move on' approach.

I had understood that GSOC would publish a full report of their internal investigation and regarded this brief dismissive statement as grossly inadequate. In a breathtaking display of double standards, Sinn Féin's Padraig MacLochlainn, who had as Chairperson of the Petitions Committee been an enthusiastic advocate of full transparency when promoting the 'Garda Bugged GSOC' narrative, announced that he believed the GSOC Commissioners were 'highly motivated' to find the source of the leak and he 'accepted' their statement that they were unable to do so. Neither he nor the previously loquacious Niall Collins of Fianna Fáil sought any additional detail of the *Connaughton Report*.

There is, of course, never any media interest or enthusiasm for the identity of an individual who leaks information being disclosed, even if the information leaked is seriously inaccurate. It was no surprise that the media showed minimal interest in the *Connaughton Report*. It also became clear that neither the Government nor the Opposition were interested in having a Dáil debate on the report nor would anyone question in the Dáil the failure of GSOC to publish it. No substantive information of any value was contained in GSOC's one-page statement so I decided to pursue the issue by use of the only practical Dáil procedure available to me – a Topical Issues Debate.

Each day of regular Dáil sittings, members can propose a subject for a Topical Issues Debate to the Ceann Comhairle. The selected TDs are granted six minutes of speaking time, four initially and a further two after the relevant minister has spoken. My application to the Ceann Comhairle to make a topical issues contribution was granted on Wednesday, 17 September. In it, I said that 'From the start of this affair, GSOC has sought to cover up and keep secret a disturbing level of incompetence and failure to comply with its statutory obligations.'

I called for publication of the *Connaughton Report* in full and the resignation of the GSOC Commissioners. In response, Frances Fitzgerald acknowledged that 'there is a major public interest in ensuring that as much information as possible is made available'. She informed the Dáil that she had asked GSOC to publish the report subject to 'what level of redaction might be necessary' to protect 'the rights of those involved'. Predictably she avoided again any criticism of the GSOC Commissioners and ignored my call for their resignation. It was clear that her request that GSOC publish the report would not have been made had I not sought the Dáil debate and publicly pursued the issue.

A week later, on 24 September 2014, GSOC published a redacted fifteen-page version of the *Connaughton Report*, a task it had described as 'impossible' just two weeks earlier. It made interesting reading.

Like Cooke, Connaughton commented on the *Sunday Times* article, having examined all the background material relevant to GSOC's security investigation. He concluded that the article 'is not a commentary or an opinion piece grounded on established facts. Rather, it boldly asserts alleged facts.' Referencing the GSOC report prepared following the conclusion of its security investigation, Connaughton concluded that John Mooney, the *Sunday Times* journalist, 'did not have a copy of the [GSOC] Report when writing the article. Indeed I might observe that had its content informed the said article, the exaggerated and incorrect claims made therein, could not have been made.'

According to Connaughton the article contained, 'both inaccurate and confused passages' and if informed by sources 'as the author contends' and 'if, assuming he has accurately transcribed the information provided by the source or sources indicated, then they were very poor factual historians'. Of course, whether the information reported was accurately transcribed from the source or sources is only known to John Mooney and the individual who furnished information to him and neither were talking to Mark Connaughton SC. Connaughton did, however, acknowledge that the article contained some accurate details 'however confused their expression'.

GSOC reported that Connaughton concluded that:

Certain of the content of the article, to which I shall turn in a moment, is so inaccurate that one must surmise that either the factual findings of that [security sweep] were deliberately exaggerated and conveyed that way to [the *Sunday Times* journalist] or there was a lack of understanding on the part of the source or sources [and the *Sunday Times* journalist] simply reported what had been revealed.

Mr Connaughton, perhaps somewhat charitably, concluded that:

I believe the latter to be much closer to the truth of the matter and while I have not had the opportunity of meeting with [the *Sunday Times* journalist] for the reason stated, I would expect that such an experienced journalist would be slow to paraphrase apparent technical information that might have been conveyed to him for fear of inaccurately reflecting the position.

Connaughton went on to state:

It follows that it is unlikely that the source or sources were persons who would have been technically competent or indeed at the very heart of the investigation. It is difficult to conceive of the possibility that someone who was directly concerned with the investigation and aware by no later than the 25th November 2013 that there was no conclusive evidence of bugging would have contributed to such an inaccurate article. To this must be added the important qualification … that some of the information contained in the article certainly comes close to identifying concerns that did exist, however inaccurate their expression in the article, at an earlier stage in the investigation.

Having referenced some inaccurate allegations detailed by Connaughton as being contained in *The Sunday Times* article, GSOC recorded Connaughton's conclusion that 'the detail disclosed in the article is such that I am satisfied, on the balance of probabilities, that its content, however inaccurate it may be as to the facts on the date of publication, was prepared with some assistance from some person or persons connected with the [security sweep/investigation]'.

It was a reasonable conclusion that in circumstances in which John Mooney would not disclose his source or sources, little more in reality could be done. Connaughton stated himself to be satisfied that at some juncture after the commencement of the security sweep, Mooney had received confidential information from 'some person or persons associated with the security sweep/investigation that assisted in the preparation of the article published on the 9th February 2014'. It was clear that in the absence of a confession, the identity of the individual concerned would never be known nor would their motive in leaking a mix of partially accurate and substantially inaccurate information.

The fuller version of the *Connaughton Report* documented in the GSOC statement of 24 September 2014 excited no greater level of media interest than did the original one-page statement of two weeks earlier. However, there was now in the public domain conclusions of two separate investigations into *The Sunday Times* report, both of which documented in detail major inaccuracies contained in it or to use the words of Connaughton 'exaggerated and incorrect claims'. As *The Sunday Times* perceives itself as a newspaper that deserves to be taken seriously, I was curious to see whether it would the following Sunday finally acknowledge and apologise for the inaccuracies and the consequences of its story. I assumed the paper's editor regarded factual and accurate reporting, insofar as that is possible, a vital ingredient to maintain the paper's credibility and attraction to its readers. I was incorrect in that assumption.

The Sunday Times entirely ignored the fifteen-page redacted version of the *Connaughton Report* GSOC had been reluctantly forced to publish and at no stage clarified whether John Mooney was misled by his 'source' of information or whether the paper's GSOC surveillance story was deliberately exaggerated. The paper's final reflections were contained in an editorial of 14 September 2014.

In an editorial entitled 'Protecting Sources is Vital for Good Journalism' the paper gleefully boasted of its GSOC bugging story 'taking off in all directions, leading to a crisis at the heart of Government that, with a couple of detours, eventually engulfed Martin Callinan, the former Justice Minister and Brian Purcell, the most senior civil servant in the Department of Justice'. No explanation or apology was offered for the 'misinformation', the 'serious inaccuracies' and 'the exaggerated and incorrect claims' for which the paper and its report were responsible. It was for the paper a matter of celebration and pride that the 'internal investigation overseen by Mark Connaughton, a Senior Counsel, designed to uncover the identity of *The Sunday Times* source, ended in failure'. Having taken a pot shot at the 'failure' of the *Cooke Report* to uphold the paper's fabricated narrative and exhibiting no remorse for its conduct, the editorial then targeted for criticism unnamed 'media outlets which have been on the wrong side of this important story' for being 'furious that our source was not uncovered'.

Asserting its moral superiority, the editorial proclaimed, 'In a previous era when Ireland enjoyed a more robust media than the compromised shell that exists today, a newspaper protecting its sources and beating the system would be a cause for celebration, not criticism.'

The truth, of course, was that all 'media outlets' had run with the Garda Bugged GSOC story initiated by *The Sunday Times* and none were in a position to credibly criticise *The Sunday Times's* reporting. In a previous era in which reporters took pride in their accuracy and when newspapers attached a value to the truth and public credibility, publication of the Cooke and Connaughton Reports would have resulted in a published apology and correction by both reporter and newspaper for a story which proved to be grossly inaccurate. The story was simply 'fake news' published before that phrase was adopted by Donald Trump, ironically one of the greatest contemporary originators and promoters of fake news on the planet.

The Sunday Times' response to both the Cooke and Connaughton Reports established that, as a paper, it had entirely lost its moral compass. John Mooney, or the *Sunday Times* editor, could have acknowledged the paper's serious inaccuracies while still protecting its source and clarified whether the inaccuracies derived from 'the source' or its own reporter's exaggeration. It chose not to do so. While it understandably asserted that 'protecting sources is vital for good journalism', it entirely ignored that verifying information received from sources and accurate and truthful reporting is of greater or, at the very least, equal importance. Regrettably, for *The Sunday Times* it seems that bluster, entertainment and fabricated sensationalism is a higher priority.

Postscript: on 6 December 2015 *The Sunday Times* triumphantly disinterred the GSOC Bugging story proclaiming in a headline that 'Garda Watchdog wasted €400,000 to find media leak'. In a report attributed to John Mooney and Colin Coyle it again publicly celebrated Connaughton's failure 'to identify the source' of the *Sunday Times* story. The actual report exposed the falsity of its headline as it emerged that the spend of €382,693 it referenced also included the legal costs associated with GSOC's interaction with Judge Cooke and with Sean Guerin SC who was conducting a different inquiry. Space was found in the article to carry quotes from Opposition Oireachtas members condemning the spend, ironically on inquiries they had demanded. However, it contained no reference of any nature to Cooke's or Connaughton's criticism of *The Sunday Times*. The truth is, had *The Sunday Times* never published its grossly inaccurate story, a substantial portion of the public expenditure it labelled as 'wasted' would never have been incurred.

CHAPTER 14

Along Comes Olly!

Well, here's another nice mess you've gotten me into
–Famous catchphrase of Laurel and Hardy

Two weeks before *The Sunday Times* reported the fake 'GSOC under Surveillance' story, I announced that, having reviewed the legislation applicable to GSOC, I intended to bring some proposals for reform before Government. Michael McDowell, when Minister for Justice in the 2002–2007 Fianna Fáil/Progressive Democrat coalition, had created the existing Garda and GSOC legal structures and regulations. They derived from the Garda Síochána Act 2005 that he had steered through the Houses of the Oireachtas. Having overseen their workings for almost three years, I believed they were unnecessarily complicated and deeply flawed. The provisions did not allow serving members of An Garda Síochána to make complaints of garda misconduct directly to GSOC. Instead, they had to be addressed to a 'Confidential Recipient'. I believed this needed to be changed. I intended to abolish the office of the Confidential Recipient and simplify the statutory structure. I also intended to end the prohibition on GSOC investigating allegations of misconduct made against a Garda Commissioner.

The provisions surrounding the operation of the Confidential Recipient system were unwieldy. To be appointed a Confidential Recipient, a person had to be a judge or former judge, a barrister, a solicitor or a serving or former senior public servant. A garda's confidential report had to be made in good faith and could not be made anonymously. However, when passing on a report, the Confidential Recipient was generally obliged to take 'all practical steps to ensure the identity of the confidential reporter' was not disclosed. The recipient was required to furnish the report to the Garda Commissioner. The commissioner was obliged to give a copy of any report received to the Chairperson of GSOC, together with details of the garda action being taken. Ultimately GSOC had to be told the outcome of any garda investigation conducted. This enabled GSOC to consider whether to invoke its own independent investigative powers.

In addition, with the consent of the Confidential Reporter, the Garda Commissioner could notify the Chief Inspector of the Garda Inspectorate of confidential reports received so the inspectorate could consider whether it should conduct an investigation of its own.

On receipt of a confidential report, the Garda Commissioner was required to 'investigate the allegation or cause it to be investigated' and to take any other action necessary as a result of the investigation.

Where a confidential report contained an allegation of misconduct against the Garda Commissioner, the Confidential Recipient was required to furnish the report not to the Garda Commissioner but to the Minister for Justice.

Neither a Garda Commissioner nor a Minister for Justice was required to act on any such report, if he or she had 'reason to believe' an allegation was 'not made in good faith' or was 'false, frivolous or vexatious'.

A minister in receipt of a report from the Confidential Recipient containing an allegation against a Garda Commissioner, which he or she believed was made in good faith, and not 'false, frivolous or vexatious', was required 'to cause the allegation to be investigated or to take such other action as he or she considers' appropriate in the circumstances'. However, no such report could be forwarded to GSOC for investigation as it could not investigate an allegation of misconduct made against a Garda Commissioner. Information regarding action taken following receipt of a confidential report was to be provided to the Confidential Recipient to be passed on to the Confidential Reporter.

The problem with the Confidential Recipient structure was ultimately that a complaint made by a serving garda furnished to the Garda Commissioner was essentially recycled back to An Garda Síochána for investigation. The nature of the complaint made could result in the identity of the anonymised complainant inevitably being revealed. I was also concerned that the preservation of anonymity could be unfair to those subject to a complaint under investigation. Additionally, where a complaint was not upheld, the fact that the investigation was internal to An Garda Síochána itself could give rise to a suspicion that any investigation conducted was not objective.

As Minister for Justice, I had no visibility as to how the structure was working in practice and how frequently and competently GSOC exercised its independent investigative powers. Although the regulations envisaged the Minister for Justice causing an allegation made against the Garda Commissioner to be investigated, the legislation conferred no investigative powers on the minister, on his or her departmental officials or on any third party appointed by the minister and no investigative unit existed within the Justice Department. So, on 27 January 2014, I announced I intended to abolish the office of the Confidential Recipient and extend GSOC's jurisdiction to enable it to directly receive complaints of alleged Garda misconduct from serving gardai. I had no inkling of the GSOC bugging controversy that was about to erupt.

The first person appointed as Confidential Recipient under the regulations, which became known as the Garda Whistleblower regulations, was Brian MacCarthy. He was a retired civil servant whose final post had been Secretary General to the President. The concept of the Confidential Recipient originated from a recommendation made by the Morris Tribunal, which had investigated allegations of garda corruption and misconduct in Donegal during the 1990s. It was intended to facilitate members of the force, and its civilian employees, report corruption and malpractice without fear of intimidation or of their careers being detrimentally affected. The system had first become operational in June 2008 when Fachtna Murphy was Garda Commissioner.

Shortly after my appointment to Cabinet, Brian MacCarthy's three-year term of office expired. Under the legislation, it was my responsibility to appoint his replacement. I believed it important that the post, which was part-time and modestly remunerated, was not seen as a sinecure for retired public servants. I also believed that it would enhance the status and independence of the office if the individual appointed was either a current or former member of the judiciary or an experienced lawyer with the people skills required to engage in a considered way with any garda making a report. I thought that Oliver Connolly would be an ideal choice. His appointment was agreed, on my recommendation, by Cabinet and announced on 14 June 2011. It was to have disastrous consequences.

I had first met Connolly (known as Olly to his friends) about eight years earlier. He had practised as an attorney in New York, at the English and Irish Bars and had been admitted to the Northern Ireland Bar. He specialised in civil and commercial arbitration and mediation and was an Alternative Dispute Resolution (ADR) member of the American Bar Association and the International Bar Association. He had also served on the Bar Council of Ireland's ADR and Arbitration Committee and on the Council of the Irish Commercial Mediation Association. He was the founder in Dublin of Friary Law, which specialised in mediation and the promotion of ADR as an alternative to contentious court litigation.

Originally Friary Law focused on civil and commercial mediation and it was one of the prescribed mediation bodies appointed by Michael McDowell, when Minister for Justice in April 2004, to mediate disputes under the Civil Liability and Courts Act 2004. Friary Law was similarly appointed, in early March 2011, by my immediate predecessor, Fianna Fáil's Brendan Smith TD, as a designated mediation body under the Multi-Unit Development Act, 2011. Friary Law, under Connolly's leadership, taught a qualified assessment programme for mediators seeking accreditation from the International Mediation Institute and provided courses for the New York Bar.

As a solicitor specialising in family law, I had for many years advocated the use of mediation instead of contentious litigation to assist estranged couples and parents resolve family conflicts. Connolly was aware of my writing and lecturing in this area and, in 2004, asked me to assist him in formulating a family mediation course for Friary Law. As a prelude to this project, he offered me a free place on Friary Law's Civil and Commercial Mediation course. I enjoyed the course, passed with flying colours and got an important positive insight into Friary Law's approach to teaching. I enthusiastically, for no remuneration, assisted in formulating the Family Mediation course and lectured at the first two courses.

I believed Connolly, while somewhat eccentric, to be independent-minded and principled. I thought him an ideal choice for the position of Confidential Recipient. When I called him to ask if he would take on the task, he expressed delight at what he described as 'the honour'. He knew nothing of and asked me nothing about the remuneration payable. When he accepted the post he merely understood from me that the position was part-time, the remuneration was modest and that I would be forwarding him a detailed letter offering him the position, subject to Cabinet approval. The remuneration for the position was, in fact a sum of €12,500 gross per annum, a sum Connolly could readily earn as counsel in a single case in the Circuit or High Court.

The downside in making the appointment was that Connolly was a Fine Gael supporter and had, over the years, attended the occasional Fine Gael fundraising event, including the annual President's Dinner (that is, the President of Fine Gael) organised by Fine Gael Headquarters. However, this was an appointment I was making on merit. I did not believe that a well-qualified individual should be excluded from appointment to a position simply because he was a Fine Gael supporter.

As the remuneration for the post was extremely modest when compared with Connolly's earning potential as a barrister, arbitrator and mediator, I did not anticipate his appointment becoming controversial. I could not have been more mistaken.

At the time of his appointment in 2011, I did not recall that in 2007 Connolly had contributed €1,000 to my general election campaign. This had been fully and properly declared and disclosed by me to the Standards in Public Office Commission and the information was published and freely available on its public register. Connolly had made no contribution to my 2011 general election campaign. Nevertheless, the 2007 contribution was seized upon both by sections of the media and Opposition TDs and presented as my doing a favour for a major personal donor by appointing him to a prestigious position for which he would be substantially remunerated. His capacity to undertake his duties 'independently' of me as minister was also unfairly queried. For me, it was the first major controversy to arise following my cabinet appointment. The media insinuated that the appointment, if not corrupt, was at least questionable. For Oliver Connolly, who was not used to being in the public limelight, it was something of a nightmare.

The nightmare continued throughout his period in office as some media outlets and members of the Fourth Estate decided that he was fair game for targeting on issues of no relevance to his part-time duties as Confidential Recipient. These included his attempt to expand Friary Law to a variety of countries, his temporarily renting out his Dalkey residence to the actor Timothy Dalton (who once played James Bond) and a rental dispute over the Friary Law premises between Connolly and the well-known businessman Harry Crosbie.

As Confidential Recipient, Connolly had an officially designated phone line for contact by members of An Garda Síochána. I was advised that his approach as a general rule, having spoken with a confidential reporter, was to invite the garda member to provide him with written details of the complaint being made and then meet with the garda at least once, or more often if necessary. Then it was a matter for Connolly, as Confidential Recipient, to furnish the complaint to the Garda Commissioner or, if the complaint was about the Commissioner, to me as Minister for Justice.

Connolly understood that his position was entirely independent and, as far as I knew, was dealing appropriately with all gardaí who contacted him.

On 2 February 2012, I received from Connolly a report on his first six months in office. It stated that he had to that date submitted two confidential reports for the Garda Commissioner's consideration and one for mine. He had met privately 'with each of the confidential reporters and with each of them on a number of occasions, prior to the submission of the three confidential reports'. He also informed me that he had met 'with other confidential reporters, whose reports are currently in preparation'. His report recorded that a total of six confidential reports had been furnished to the Garda Commissioner by his predecessor, Brian MacCarthy, during his three years as Confidential Recipient.

Connolly's report was brief, informative and appropriate, and properly preserved the anonymity of all who had confidentially reported to him and the confidentiality of his discussions with them. I was familiar with the content of the confidential report he had submitted to me. I had received it just a few days earlier, on 23 January 2012 and, by 2 February 2012, I already knew the Confidential Reporter to be a Sergeant Maurice McCabe, a member of An Garda Síochána then based in Mullingar Garda Station, Co Westmeath and formerly based in Bailieboro Garda Station in Co Cavan.

The allegations contained in the 23 January 2012 report and how I dealt with it are discussed in later chapters. Here I merely record that following its receipt, at my request, the very next day, Brian Purcell, the Justice Department's Secretary General, passed on the report to the Garda Commissioner for his response, to enable me to consider what further action, if any, was required. The Commissioner's response was received on 30 January 2012 and I replied to Connolly on 3 February 2012. Following receipt of that reply, it was for Connolly to further engage with Sergeant McCabe.

By February 2014, Sergeant Maurice McCabe had become a well-known public figure as a result of other complaints made by him alleging the wrongful cancellation by gardaí of Fixed Charge Notices and Penalty Points imposed on motorists for alleged road traffic offences. For approximately fifteen months the issue had given rise to substantial public controversy both inside and outside the Dáil and had become a lightening rod for media criticism of the Government, An Garda Síochána and of my role as Minister for Justice. I regarded McCabe's allegations as serious and had taken what I believed to be the correct steps to have them addressed. However, my political opponents and large sections of the media maintained that I had not. To this I return later on.

Four days prior to *The Sunday Times* first publishing its GSOC under Surveillance story, Mick Wallace, the Independent Wexford TD, briefly spoke in a Dáil debate on the Government's Protected Disclosures Bill being piloted through the Dáil by one of his Wexford rivals Brendan Howlin TD, the Labour Minister for the Department of Public Expenditure and Reform. The intent of the legislation, which I fully supported, was to give additional protection to whistle-blowers. During the course of his speech, amongst other matters Wallace mentioned the Fixed Ticket Charge/ Penalty Points issue and Sergeant Maurice McCabe. He then continued,

> A while back we were given a transcript of a conversation two years ago between Maurice McCabe and the Confidential Recipient. It is frightening. It includes the following:

> 'Well I'll tell you something Maurice, and this is just personal advice to you, if Shatter thinks you are screwing him, you're finished.' Here is another line:

> 'If Shatter thinks here's this guy again trying another route, trying to put you under pressure, he'll go after you.' Our Minister for Justice and Equality will 'go after you'. What is going on?

I was not present in the Dail for Wallace's speech and I knew nothing about it until the following morning.

The transcript next surfaced during Leaders' Questions in the Dáil on the following Tuesday, 11 February 2014, when it was mentioned by Fianna Fáil leader Micheál Martin, who was mainly focused on the *Sunday Times*-generated GSOC controversy. The Taoiseach confined his response to the GSOC issue but Martin was to return to the transcript the next day, which coincided with the dramatic appearance of the GSOC Commissioners before the Petitions Committee.

Speaking in the Dáil that Tuesday evening on the GSOC issue gave me an opportunity to mention the transcript from which Wallace and Martin quoted, the contents of which were a total mystery to me. Having said that I did not know anything about the meeting to which it related nor did I 'know how the transcript was created':

I do not know whether it was an agreed transcript of a conversation which allegedly took place between the Confidential Recipient and Sergeant McCabe. I do not know selectively what is being quoted from it. What I can say to Deputies is that there is no question in any circumstance of me threatening anyone or authorising anyone to threaten anyone and the suggestion is absolutely outrageous.

Asserting that I had never seen the transcript quoted, I continued:

The Confidential Recipient is supposed to be operating on a confidential basis. It is not appropriate that I start to access private conversations which allegedly took place between the Confidential Recipient and a member of the Garda Síochána but I would make it absolutely clear that no-one would have my approval or imprimatur, whether a Confidential Recipient or anyone else, to issue any threat to any individual, who, in good faith, was reporting on any issue. It is outrageous that Deputy Wallace should suggest that.

The next day, Wednesday, 12 February 2014, Micheál Martin in full flight returned to the issue on Leaders' Questions. The transcript, he said, made 'for serious and grave reading'. It revealed 'efforts, if not subtle threats, that if the material that the whistleblower had ever got to the media the Minister, Deputy Shatter, would come after the whistleblower'. After quoting the passage detailed in the Dáil the previous Thursday by Wallace, Martin referenced another extract which recorded Oliver Connolly telling Sergeant McCabe that his 'Complaints went to the Department of Justice and that annoyed the Commissioner greatly. I am sure it's going to be an embarrassment for the Gardai, a disaster for them. And, listen, if your complaints are exposed to the print media, it will make him an angry man.'

Martin alleged that the Confidential Recipient was 'protecting the Minister, the Department and the Commissioner but not the whistleblower' and questioned whether Connolly's position was 'now tenable?'

Enda Kenny, referencing what I had said in the Dáil the previous evening, stated that I had no knowledge of 'the alleged conversation, of a transcription of the conversation or of a tape of that conversation nor, indeed, is there any basis for implying that the Minister ever expressed the kind of views that are attributed to him in what has been alleged'. Saying that he regarded this as a matter of 'public concern' and it was important to know whether the conversation detailed in the transcript took place, he confirmed we had discussed the issue and he had sought a report from the Department of Justice.

I had first learned of Wallace's Dáil speech the day after it was delivered by him and was astonished by the quotations from the alleged transcript. Stating he had received the transcript 'a while back' and that it related to 'a conversation two years ago', Wallace had not revealed the exact date of the alleged conversation between Oliver Connolly and Sergeant McCabe. I could not fathom why Connolly would have made the reported remarks to McCabe which had no basis in fact and which were outrageous. I believed that if he had said what was allegedly transcribed, Connolly's continuation as Confidential Recipient was untenable, even pending abolition of the office.

Behind the scenes from that Thursday, Brian Purcell had, at my request, attempted to make phone contact with Connolly but was initially unsuccessful. It ultimately turned out that Connolly was on holidays with his family in Dubai. Subsequent to a conversation between him and Purcell on the Wednesday afternoon,12 February 2014, after Leaders' Questions in the Dáil had concluded, Purcell received an email from Connolly which he passed on to me. In it Connolly stated that, as a Confidential Recipient to An Garda, he was subject to the An Garda Síochána (Confidential Reporting of Corruption or Malpractice) Regulations 2007 and to the provisions of the Official Secrets Act 1963 and that he would not be responding to the alleged tape's contents. He complained that 'a Garda allegedly came to what is a statutorily confidential meeting for both parties and proceeded to allegedly tape our meeting without notice' and amongst other things asserted that his (Connolly's) constitutional right to privacy had been violated. As he was to repeat in subsequent conversations with Purcell and in a press statement he issued on 4 March 2014, he maintained that the law prevented him from publicly commenting on any confidential report or discussion.

While the media was obsessing on the GSOC surveillance story and it, together with a variety of other justice and defence issues fully occupied my time, on the days that followed Purcell unsuccessfully attempted to find out from Connolly exactly what occurred two years earlier at his meeting with McCabe. Like Connolly, I was both surprised and disturbed that McCabe had secretly recorded their meeting and made a transcript of the recording but it was the substance of the reported conversation that caused me the greatest concern. From Connolly's communication to Purcell, it was clear that he had no understanding of how his reported comments undermined his credibility as Confidential Recipient or of how damaging they were to me personally. At a time when I was being falsely accused of misleading the Dáil on the GSOC issue, of covering up Garda surveillance of GSOC and of undermining GSOC's independence by meeting with its Chairperson, Connolly's depiction of me as someone intent on 'going after' McCabe was a gift to Opposition Deputies and a frenzied media. If, as Wallace stated, he had first received the alleged transcript 'some time ago', it was an extraordinary coincidence that it had emerged into the daylight practically simultaneously with the GSOC controversy igniting and to coincide with my attempting to progress through the Justice Committee, on 12 February 2014, the Committee Stage of the controversial Legal Services Regulation Bill. (I would later discover that Wallace had made a passing incomprehensible reference to a quote from the transcript in the Dáil chamber on 4 December 2012.)

The Legal Services Regulation Bill sought to modernise the legal profession, end anti-competitive practices of the professional bodies and reduce legal costs. It had particularly attracted the wrath of the Bar Council – the Barristers' representative body – which had mounted a vigorous and sometimes vitriolic Opposition to many of its proposed reforms. There could be little doubt that some of those opposed to the Bill welcomed my being entangled in controversy.

On Wednesday, 18 February 2014, Broadsheet.ie published the full transcript of the alleged conversation between Connolly and McCabe. In its introduction the online news site noted that McCabe had given Connolly a report containing a number of allegations of garda wrongdoing and stated 'the follow-up meeting' detailed in the transcript took place on Thursday, 9 February 2012. My knowledge of its contents until then was confined to the extracts quoted by Wallace and Martin in the Dáil Chamber. I had not sought a copy of the transcript from either of them. I regarded it as improper that the Minister for Justice would seek to read a transcript of a confidential conversation between a Confidential Recipient and a member of An Garda Síochána. I also regarded it as wrong that any such conversation be recorded without the knowledge of one of the participants, transcribed and then distributed to third parties by a member of An Garda Síochána.

Clearly, the transcript had been furnished by someone to Broadsheet. ie for publication. The world had moved on, it could be generally accessed and read by anybody without restriction and it made no sense that I refrain from reading it. Upon my doing so, I discovered that it not only contained the outrageous extracts quoted in the Dáil Chamber but also other comments that were beyond astonishing and some not entirely coherent, if transcribed correctly. Having warned McCabe that if his complaints became public I would 'go after' him and after encouraging him to use 'the Courts' to address his issues, Connolly was quoted advising McCabe,

> if you're going to kill a King, if you're going to strike and I mean in the public forums of the Courts with the former Attorney General [Michael McDowell who was advising McCabe] they'll all be terribly interested. The broadcasting media will get a field day on your case, it's actually the only forum to speak to them. Then what will happen with the Minister, all's fair in love and war.

This was all deeply disturbing and particularly ironic if stated by Connolly within eight months of his appointment, considering the criticism voiced by some that I was appointing a pal who would not act independently. It appeared he was not only acting independently but, if the transcript was accurate, he had strayed way beyond his statutory role and entered into some delusional fantasy world.

Connolly was transcribed as then referencing my relationship with Martin Callinan. Stating I was only 'in the job a month' Connolly continued: 'And he had the Queen of England and the President of the United States [visiting] and he's Minister for Justice and Defence and he has to work very closely [with Callinan] because both their careers, everything is on the line, both of them, Shatter and the Commissioner. He's the new best friend for about 2 or 3 months.'

'The Commissioner?' asked McCabe.

'Had to be, had to be and I would say I am only speculating,' replied Connolly.

I regarded Connolly's engagement with McCabe as highly irregular and totally bizarre. His role was to facilitate McCabe as a member of An Garda Síochána make an anonymised complaint of Garda misconduct to be furnished to the Garda Commissioner or, in limited circumstances, to me as Minister for Justice. If McCabe was unhappy with my response to his complaints, as we shall see, I had left open the door to his reverting to me with additional evidence and information to substantiate his complaints and challenge the Commissioner's response to me. Yet Connolly seemed to be encouraging McCabe to address his concerns through the Courts and to be spinning a yarn about my relationship with the Commissioner which was damaging to my and the Commissioner's credibility. The narrative that we were 'best friends' or 'too close' had contaminated political discussion on various issues of Garda controversy for some time and became particularly prominent during the GSOC controversy in which I was still engulfed. It was being repetitively alleged that we were 'joined at the hip'. I wondered whether Connolly had unwittingly originated this pejorative public depiction by some of the relationship between Callinan and myself, a relationship he knew nothing about, and which I had never discussed with him.

Further on in the transcript Connolly appeared to give contradictory advice to McCabe. Having so unflatteringly depicted me and advised McCabe to pursue his complaints through the Courts, he then urged McCabe to give me 'some other ammunition' and asserted that because of his (Connolly's) 'close proximity to Alan, he's going to help us'. The conversation as transcribed then completely turned around with Connolly quoted assuring McCabe that 'Alan is not out to get you.' (A quote never referenced by any of my detractors in the Dáil nor by any media commentator!)

Later, Connolly is recorded telling McCabe that 'the Commissioner should be asked to stand aside, he's a vested interest', informing him that Martin Callinan had essentially been asked by me to investigate himself. This was total nonsense. The Commissioner had merely been requested to respond to McCabe's complaints. He had done so and, in his response, referred to the outcome of investigations in which other senior members of An Garda Síochána had been involved. However, Connolly's contention that the Commissioner had been asked to investigate himself was later to be repeated by McCabe as an accusation and given substantial credibility by others until publication in May 2016 of what became known as the *O'Higgins Report*, of which more later.

At various stages in the transcript Connolly is quoted warning McCabe against leaking information to the media and McCabe assures Connolly he will not do so as he had 'too much to lose' and that he 'would be destroyed'. At no stage does McCabe inform Connolly he is recording their conversation.

When asked by Connolly what he wants, McCabe replies 'I want somebody independent to have a look at all the allegations and I would not look for that only I can stand by everything I have said.' Later on, Connolly assures McCabe that he believes him, that he 'thinks the Commissioner has a case to answer' and acknowledges that McCabe was 'just standing up for what is right'.

Despite the Broadsheet.ie publication of the alleged full transcript of the Connolly/McCabe conversation, the GSOC controversy remained centre-stage within the media and in the Dáil Chamber. However, it was clearly inappropriate that Connolly remain the Confidential Recipient and the next day an email was sent to him terminating his position.

On Wednesday, 19 February 2014, during Leaders' Questions, Micheál Martin returned to McCabe's transcript of his 'confidential' conversation with Connolly. He informed the Dáil he had met McCabe and 'listened to the audio tape of that conversation and can confirm its existence'. He continued: 'It reveals the frustration of the whistleblower and also the desire of the Confidential Recipient that at all costs this must not get into the print media, that it must be kept out of the media.'

Martin described McCabe as a 'credible man' and so regarded by others he had met 'who had been in authority', presumably retired garda officers. Martin asserted that Sergeant McCabe 'has some story to tell' but that I had 'not allowed him to tell it'. (This allegation was false as would be clearly established over two years later following publication of the *O'Higgins Report*.) The 'story to tell' as referenced by Martin was contained in McCabe's allegations that I had received from Connolly on 23 January 2012. According to Martin, McCabe had received 'no response of any consequence' to his allegations. (The *O'Higgins Report* would later conclude that I dealt appropriately and reasonably with McCabe's allegations.) Martin referenced also the 'penalty points saga' and then asked whether the Taoiseach thought 'the position of the Confidential Recipient is tenable, given the existence of this transcript and the treatment of Mr Maurice McCabe?' In reciting extracts from the transcript, Martin omitted any reference contained in it to Connolly's inconvenient assurance to McCabe that I was not 'out to get' him.

Enda Kenny replied that the Secretary General of the Department of Justice had 'made a number of contacts with the Confidential Recipient in regard to the veracity or otherwise of the transcript' and informed the Dáil that I had that morning 'relieved Mr Connolly of his duties'.

Martin acknowledged that 'the decision was the inevitable outcome of the conversation that had taken place between the Confidential Recipient and McCabe'. He then demanded that I 'come into the House to answer serious questions about how' I dealt with the whistle-blower. Further on in his contribution, Martin informed the Dáil that 'material' had come into his possession concerning 'a more serious matter' which 'must be taken out of the Department of Justice and Equality to get to the truth of this'. He did not reveal that the 'material' referenced by him had been given to him two days earlier by Maurice McCabe when they had met and included McCabe's report that I had received from Connolly in January 2012.

The Taoiseach requested that 'the information of national importance' as mysteriously referenced by Martin be personally handed to him. He then reminded Martin that 'Deputy Shatter has said on a number of occasions that he is not happy with the operation of the Confidential Recipient' in the structure created by the Garda Síochána Act 2005 which 'has been around for a number of years, nor is it acceptable to the Minister that members of the Garda Síochána are a liaison between GSOC and the Garda Síochána'. Kenny confirmed it was my intention to propose to the Dáil changes to the 2005 Act.

The exchanges in the Dáil moved away from the Connolly/McCabe transcript and became enmeshed in the continuing GSOC surveillance controversy. Referencing both, Sinn Féin's Mary Lou McDonald accused me of being intent on 'burying any controversy arising in respect of malpractice by An Garda Síochána'.

I expected that the Connolly transcript would be a major issue for that day's Leaders' Questions and that the GSOC issue and the McCabe recording would become intertwined. However, by the time that part of Wednesday Dáil's business had concluded, it seemed that another layer of controversy was on the horizon in the guise of the 'material' of 'national importance' received by Micheál Martin from an unrevealed source that he was to give to the Taoiseach. I wrongly assumed it was some entirely new revelation or issue and did not know it had any connection with Maurice McCabe.

Later that evening I reflected on the Connolly/McCabe transcript. Initially I had been mystified by its contents. Mystification was now replaced by a mixture of dismay and anger. I did not know what motivated Connolly's conduct and clearly there was no explanation given or apology forthcoming from him.

The only subject about which there seemed to be political consensus was that Connolly's position was untenable. Yet on Leaders' Questions the next day in the Dáil (Thursday, 20 February 2014) Micheál Martin asked the Minister for Social Protection, Joan Burton (who was standing in for the Tánaiste, Eamon Gilmore, who usually took Leaders' Questions on a Thursday) that I make a comprehensive statement on the reasons why Oliver Connolly was relieved of his duties and both Fianna Fáil and Sinn Féin went to some lengths to depict Connolly as a victim of events. Sinn Féin's Pearse Doherty claimed that to protect both the Garda Commissioner and myself, Connolly's head 'had to roll'.

I was, that Thursday, then airborne on my way to Athens to attend a 4pm meeting of all my EU Defence Ministerial colleagues whose parties were members of the European People's Party. This meeting was to be held in advance of a meeting of EU Defence Ministers under the Greek EU Presidency, starting at 5pm.

During the flight, as I read the updated comprehensive brief provided by Defence officials for the Athens meeting, the Department of Justice press office issued a statement prepared the previous evening on the Confidential Recipient. Referencing that the previous day 'I found it necessary' to relieve Oliver Connolly of his position, it stated that 'The Confidential Recipient must adopt an approach that creates confidence for any member of An Garda Síochána communicating on an issue of concern'. It explained that I had asked 'my Department two weeks ago to contact Mr Connolly outlining my concerns' about the content of his alleged conversation with McCabe and stated that 'if the conversation as reported had taken place, then his actions had undermined the office of the Confidential Recipient'. It recorded my dissatisfaction with Connolly's response to the controversy and 'in the context of his failure to unequivocally repudiate the content of the alleged conversation or take the necessary action to restore public confidence' in the office 'I believed his position was untenable' and had relieved him of it.

It had been my hope that the termination of Connolly's position, my detailed response to the four hours of questioning within the Petitions Committee the previous day on the GSOC controversy and the announced appointment of Judge Cooke to conduct an independent inquiry into it would provide me with some respite. Landing in Rimini for refuelling, I was to discover this was an unduly optimistic view.

Connolly made no public comment on the transcript and his ceasing to be Confidential Recipient until 4 March 2014 when he issued a public statement. In it he criticised 'certain members of Dáil Eireann' for 'a naked political attempt to embarrass a Minister for Justice whom they oppose' by 'selectively' extracting 'lines from an unverified transcript of a confidential conversation between a serving member of An Garda Síochána and myself, acting in my former role of Confidential Recipient'. He also criticised 'the media' for reporting and commenting on the contents of the transcript. In his criticism he particularly focused on the confidential nature of discussions with Confidential Informants and his constitutional right to privacy.

Connolly claimed that the provisions applicable to his former office of Confidential Recipient precluded him from commenting on the content of the transcript and asserted he was 'satisfied' that he had properly discharged his statutory duties. Stating he understood 'the principal whistleblower's frustrations', he explained he regarded recording and publishing their conversation as 'a very serious breach of confidence' which resulted in his having 'a personal sense of betrayal'.

Connolly concluded his statement by expressing 'a particular understanding' for what he described as my 'reforming zeal' and continued:

> The Minister is often misunderstood and strange as it may seem to some, despite recent events, I remain an enthusiastic supporter of the Minister in his program of reform. However I would remind the Minister and, indeed, An Taoiseach, as I am bound to do, I shall continue to preserve the confidentiality of the outgoing office of the Confidential Recipient even if, as it now appears, I am the only one to do so.

Connolly unfortunately missed the point. Like him, I regarded the confidentiality of conversations between a Confidential Recipient and a Confidential Reporter of great importance. In the circumstances that had arisen, Connolly was entitled to regard the secret recording by Sergeant Maurice McCabe of his conversation with him as wrong. However, if the recording and transcript faithfully disclosed comments made by Connolly to McCabe, an explanation was clearly required from Connolly.

As a result of McCabe's actions the alleged conversation was now in the public domain and Connolly in his statement still seemed oblivious to the damage inflicted both on me personally and to the office of the Confidential Recipient by the content of some of the comments attributed to him in the transcript. He also seemed totally oblivious to the possible impact of his bizarre comments on Maurice McCabe and his perception of my conduct as Minister for Justice. I felt utterly betrayed by Connolly for whom, until the events of February 2014 unfolded, I had substantial personal regard. To this day his conduct remains to me a complete mystery.

Connolly's depiction of me as portrayed in McCabe's transcript was repetitively referenced in Dáil speeches and media articles for the remaining weeks of my being a minister and following my resignation from Government. It was enormously damaging. It continued to feature in retrospective references to my time both as a Government Minister and a TD after I lost my Dáil seat in February 2016, until publication of the *O'Higgins Report* in May 2016. One of the issues O'Higgins addressed was the Connolly/McCabe meeting as transcribed from McCabe's recording of it. I was afforded the opportunity of giving evidence on oath, of being cross-examined and to make submissions to the O'Higgins Commission, as were both McCabe and Connolly

In its report, the O'Higgins Commission acknowledges that 'it is clear' that McCabe recorded part of his meeting with Connolly on 9 February 2012 and that 'a purported transcript of this recording subsequently entered the public domain'. O'Higgins did not investigate how it entered the 'public domain' nor did he mention that McCabe provided either the transcript or extracts from it to Mick Wallace or to Micheál Martin or that he enabled Martin to listen to his recording. He also did not inquire into how many copies of the transcript were distributed and to whom or how it came to be published on Broadsheet.ie. O'Higgins detailed that Connolly 'stressed to the Commission' that he still 'regarded himself as bound by the confidentiality requirements of the office he held' and described McCabe's recording to the Commission 'as a betrayal of his expectation of confidentiality'. The *O'Higgins Report* offered no explanation for the remarks attributed to Connolly in the transcript.

O'Higgins detailed that:

In the recording certain inappropriate and unpleasant views, opinions, and attitudes were attributed to the former Minister which he adamantly repudiated in his evidence. His denials were unchallenged and uncontradicted and are unreservedly accepted by the Commission. In circumstances where the former Minister did not hold the views, opinions and attitudes wrongly attributed to him, the Commission appreciates the hurt and damage done to him.

Referring to evidence given to the Commission by McCabe, O'Higgins reported that 'Sergeant McCabe accepts that the recorded conversation was "absolutely" not evidence that any such views were ever held by Mr Shatter.'

The transcript of the recording had been relied upon in the Dáil as evidence that I was intent on going after or damaging McCabe and he was aware of it being publicly used as political ammunition to undermine my credibility and seriously damage my reputation. If, prior to giving sworn evidence to the O'Higgins Commission, McCabe accepted that his recorded conversation with Connolly was 'not evidence' that I would behave as Connolly allegedly depicted, an unanswered question is why did he furnish to others the transcript of his recording and facilitate my being targeted by political opponents and the media?

Unfortunately, this 'acceptance' by Maurice McCabe was far too late to undo the enormous reputational damage done to me as a consequence of his furnishing the transcript to Micheal Martin and Mick Wallace and it being published on Broadsheet.ie and widely quoted both in the Dáil and in the media.

As we shall see, throughout my period as Minister for Justice, McCabe was represented by solicitors who corresponded with the Department of Justice on his behalf about allegations of Garda misconduct. He was also for some, if not all, of my time as Minister for Justice receiving legal advice from Michael McDowell SC. If McCabe believed Connolly's threat that I would in some way 'go after' him, it is a mystery why, in the two years following his recorded meeting with Connolly in February 2012, no one on McCabe's behalf ever wrote to me or the Justice Department or the Taoiseach's Department to complain. There was no obstacle to doing so on a 'without prejudice' basis without fear of any adverse legal repercussions. But no such complaint was ever made. The threatening extracts from the transcript for the first time saw the full light of day in the Dáil chamber almost exactly two years from the day when McCabe recorded the conversation between himself and Connolly, as the GSOC controversy was erupting and, coincidentally, just shortly before the Legal Services Regulation Bill was to proceed through Committee Stage before the Joint Oireachtas Justice and Equality Committee.

Not only Micheál Martin and Mick Wallace but also other Opposition TDs regularly quoted extracts from the McCabe transcript during the first half of 2014. However, in the Dáil debate on the *O'Higgins Report*, on 25 May 2016, not a single speaker mentioned O'Higgins's conclusions on the issue. Neither did any TD withdraw the false charges repetitively made against me, accusing me of the views falsely attributed to me by Connolly. Media commentators who had also fed off the McCabe transcript to excoriate me largely ignored what O'Higgins had to say about the McCabe/Connolly recording. In his book dealing with this period, *A Force for Justice: The Maurice McCabe Story*, published in September 2017, *Irish Examiner* journalist and McCabe biographer Michael Clifford reproduced extracts from McCabe's recording of his 9 February 2012 conversation with Connolly and disingenuously omitted any reference to the O'Higgins Commission's conclusions. This approach was replicated in a RTÉ *Prime Time* special *Whistleblower: The Maurice McCabe Story* in November 2018 when RTÉ broadcast Micheál Martin in the Dáil pilloried me in February 2014, dramatically quoting an extract from McCabe's transcript of the Connolly recording. To have referenced O'Higgins's conclusions might have diluted the simple narrative of good and evil *Prime Time* was intent on portraying. The same programme also carefully omitted inconvenient facts, events and findings relevant to the story it told. As for the general public, I have little doubt that the image of me portrayed by McCabe's transcript as regularly referred to by Opposition politicians and media commentators and as disinterred in Clifford's book and by RTÉ, still colours some people's perception of my character.

CHAPTER 15

A Tangled Web and Armageddon

Alan Shatter had better buckle up tight. For he's not out of the turbulence yet, thanks to the whistleblower's smoking gun now sitting in Enda's office – not by a long shot
–Lise Hand, *Irish Independent*, 21 February 2014

With the scent of political blood in the water, the opposition is circling Shatter in the hope of inflicting a mortal wound that could do lasting damage to the Government
–Stephen Collins, *Irish Times*, 22 February 2014

Pugnacious Shatter picks the wrong fights and is too close to Garda Chief for his own good. Enda will show him the door shortly –Headline of article by Cormac Lucey, *Irish Mail on Sunday*, 23 February 2014

'Niall Collins was practically levitating off the plinth on a magic carpet of incredulity and indignation,' wrote Lise Hand in the *Irish Independent* on Thursday, 20 February 2014. She was colourfully describing Niall's demeanour the previous afternoon in the company of his party leader, Micheál Martin, at the press conference Fianna Fáil organised on the famous plinth in Leinster House while I was occupied appearing before the Oireachtas Petitions Committee discussing the GSOC bugging controversy.

Hand dutifully recorded, as did some of her other media colleagues present, Martin's description of my position as 'not tenable' while claiming that he (Martin) was 'in possession of documents that allege murders, abductions and serious assaults not investigated by the Gardai'. From that morning's newspaper reports it clearly did not strike Hand or others present on the plinth that the timing of the theatrical event was distinctly odd. It seemed, from the reports I read the next day that no journalist questioned why the press conference was organised to coincide with the meeting of the Petitions Committee if Martin and Collins were really interested in questioning me about the information I had given to the Dáil on the GSOC affair.

I first learned of Fianna Fáil's Wednesday afternoon press conference during our Thursday morning refuelling stopover at Rimini on the way to Athens. The Petitions Committee meeting had not finished until about 8pm the previous evening and after it I had gone straight to the Dáil chamber to listen to the remainder of Sinn Féin's Private Members Motion on GSOC. By the time the voting was over it was close to 9.30pm. It had been a long and gruelling day. I had started work around 5am on Justice and Defence papers, had lunchtime sandwiches with members of the Cabinteely Active Retirement Association, having arranged their visit to Leinster House, and had eaten only a banana since. Checking in with Chris Quattrociocchi, my Justice Private Secretary, I learnt that there had been no word from the Taoiseach's Department about Micheál Martin's material of 'national importance'. I collected Justice files and papers to work through over the next forty-eight hours during the trip to Greece and went home. Nothing was said to me about Martin's afternoon caper on the plinth.

It had been a smooth, uneventful flight but political turbulence hit big time when we landed at Rimini. A torrent of texts arrived when I switched on my phone. The officials who accompanied me on the flight, led by Assistant Secretary General Ciaran Murphy, were all from Defence. The texts all concerned Micheál Martin's issue of 'national importance'; the papers relevant to it he had given to the Taoiseach and that morning's Leaders' Questions being taken by Joan Burton, deputising for Eamon Gilmore.

We had landed at a semi-redundant air force base in Rimini and the terminal resembled an old Second World War aircraft hangar. Although I had received the texts, it proved difficult to get a phone signal. Eventually I succeeded in getting through to Brian Purcell. He told me that the documents referenced by Martin during Leaders' Questions in the Dáil the day before, which had been provided to the Taoiseach's Department, had originated from Sergeant Maurice McCabe. They comprised the allegations contained in the report of 23 January 2012 written by McCabe, which I had received from Oliver Connolly just over two years earlier. Headlined 'Wrong doing and Malpractice in Cavan/Monaghan Division', McCabe had accused Garda Commissioner Martin Callinan of corruption and Assistant Commissioner Derek Byrne of covering up serious corruption, as well as accusing both of them and other garda members of serious malpractice and gross dereliction of duty.

The allegations had been the subject matter of McCabe's recorded and transcribed meeting with Oliver Connolly. I was told that Martin was alleging that I had failed to respond to McCabe's allegations. It was anticipated that Martin would again raise this issue on Leaders' Questions with Joan Burton. I was also informed of Martin's press conference on the McCabe allegations the previous afternoon on the Leinster House plinth and Thursday morning's media coverage of it. (At the time of the press conference Purcell, like me, had been tied up at the Petitions Committee meeting.) A selection of that day's newspaper reports had been emailed to me and, with some difficulty, by roaming around the hangar, I was eventually able to download the reports and access various newspaper websites.

I got the impression from Purcell that general pandemonium had broken out and I considered aborting the flight to Athens and returning to Dublin once the plane was refuelled. I knew that I had treated McCabe's allegations seriously, that the background was a great deal more complicated than misrepresented by Micheál Martin and that McCabe had contributed to the complexity of addressing his allegations. However, McCabe was portrayed in heroic light by both Opposition deputies and the media, while I was depicted as the personification of evil. I knew there was no space for complex narratives.

The background to the issues raised by Martin could not be adequately addressed at Leaders' Questions. However, I knew this would not inhibit Martin from pursuing them. Getting at the truth was not the objective. The central objective was to portray and target me as an incompetent, insensitive and vindictive minister presiding over a justice system in a state of chaos. On the phone, I provided as much guidance and information as possible for the preparation of responses to assist Burton in the Dáil chamber and, following a series of phone discussions, decided I should continue the journey to Athens. There was little to be gained by returning to Dublin as Leaders' Questions would be long over. It was important that Ireland was properly represented at the Athens Defence Minister's meeting and I was determined not to be set off course.

Since becoming Minister for Defence, I had ensured that Ireland contributed more positively to EU defence issues than in the past. I attended as many meetings of EU Defence Ministers as possible. This engagement at political level was particularly welcomed by my EU colleagues who informed me that, for some time before my appointment, the appearance of the Irish Minister for Defence at EU Defence Ministers meetings was a rarity. Most times Ireland had been represented by the

Secretary General of the Department of Defence who some believed to be the Minister (then being the highly competent and professional Michael Howard).

During Ireland's EU presidency in the first half of 2013, I had hosted a series of innovative meetings to discuss current and emerging defence and security issues of importance, including the first ever EU joint defence and justice meeting for high-level EU officials on cyber security. I was determined to ensure that the work we had originated was continued. My presence at meetings of defence ministers signalled that, as a state, Ireland took its engagement and responsibilities seriously and had a positive contribution to make.

As we continued our journey from Rimini to Athens, Leaders' Questions went ahead in the Dáil chamber. I read the transcript before breakfast the next morning.

Micheál Martin at the start stated that:

> Yesterday I handed a series of shocking cases to the Taoiseach involving assault, sexual assault and a range [of] very profound, serious and shocking incidents. The Confidential Recipient would have had possession of all this material for approximately two years. It involves, in its entire detail the case of the abduction and assault of Mary Lynch, the subsequent abduction of a child in Tipperary by the same culprit and the subsequent murder of Sylvia Roche-Kelly.

He continued: 'The Minister knew about these very shocking and serious cases for two years. With knowledge of those cases, he comes into this House and actively accuses the whistleblower (McCabe) of not cooperating with the Gardai in its inquiry into the penalty points saga, undermining the man's credibility in the public domain. This was fundamentally wrong.'

Martin then sought the reasons for Oliver Connolly being 'relieved of his duties' (the previous day he had stated this was the inevitable outcome of the conversation contained in the transcript), wanted me to apologise for my allegation of non-cooperation and asked Joan Burton whether she retained confidence in me as Minister for Justice.

In her reply, Burton stated that the Taoiseach required time to consider the material he had received and she had not seen it. Exchanges followed about the GSOC controversy and Judge Cooke's appointment to conduct an inquiry. It seemed from the transcript I read that, as the exchanges got more heated, little emerged other than Burton stating that 'the Government has confidence in Minister Shatter' and Martin announcing that he had only that morning received another document of relevance and demanding a commission to inquire into 'these grave matters of public concern'. As Burton knew nothing about the latest document received by Martin and had not seen any of the other documents, she simply told him that she would read the material when she received it. Sinn Féin's Pearse Doherty then demanded the appointment of a statutory commission of investigation, alleging that I had not properly addressed the 2012 allegations, quoting from McCabe's transcript of his meeting with Oliver Connolly.

I later learned that Martin's allegations became the lead story on that Thursday's broadcast news and current affairs talk shows. They also received substantial coverage in Friday's newspapers. We were clearly in the territory of yet another garda-related crisis. It was clear from the coverage that Micheál Martin, during both his Wednesday afternoon Dáil plinth performance and in the Dáil chamber on the Thursday, neglected to mention when the alleged garda misconduct or failures had occurred. No doubt as intended, the various media reports assumed the incidents occurred on my watch as Minister for Justice and it seemed that no member of the Fourth Estate had queried Martin on this.

Consistent with her GSOC forays, Dearbhail McDonald, in that Friday morning's *Irish Independent*, entered the fray with all guns blazing. According to her, I stood 'accused' of protecting a powerful institution, in this case An Garda Síochána and 'its occasionally fractious Commissioner, Martin Callinan'. She analysed my political 'blindspot' as a 'near Messianic belief in his own opinions' which together with a 'dismissiveness towards anyone who challenges his consensus' [*sic*] could be my Achilles heel. I was, according to her, 'holding onto power at all costs'. The hyperbole was stunning.

I did not return from Athens until the Friday evening and it fell to Michael Noonan, the Minister for Finance, in my absence to attempt to put the latest controversy into context. In the same paper Fionnan Sheahan, the political editor, quoted Noonan as pointing out that the incidents alleged by Martin had occurred in the 2007/2008 period and that 'it's quite clear the Opposition parties have him targeted and they're trying to smear him'.

The ensuing weekend papers and broadcast media coverage presented events as if we were in the midst of some policing Armageddon. Oliver

Connolly's recorded comments to McCabe stating that I would 'go after' him if he publicised his concerns were recited as if true and I was pilloried for my alleged bad treatment of garda whistle-blowers and, in particular, McCabe. The penalty points saga, the 'GSOC bugging scandal' and the McCabe allegations of January 2012 'disclosed' by Micheál Martin were increasingly confused and intermingled into a single condemnatory narrative by my political opponents and by media commentators. The cacophony of misinformation, confusion and invective was mind-boggling. Michael Noonan was targeted for daring to point out that the documented allegations of garda misconduct produced by Micheál Martin concerned events that had allegedly occurred in 2007/2008 while Martin was part of the then Fianna Fáil-led Government. The Taoiseach was pilloried for stating simply that 'Minister Shatter, no more than any other Minister for Justice, is required to have a strong working relationship with the [Garda] Commissioner.' Anyone who simply told the truth or attempted to go beyond a simple sound bite supporting the Opposition and the media's desired narrative became fair game for ridicule or strident criticism.

Understandably, most of my Cabinet colleagues kept their heads down throughout the weekend, save for the couple who regularly and obsessively sought media acclaim and applause and who, as anonymous 'sources close to the Government', assisted in hyping the hysteria and sense of crisis. One well-known commentator, the *Sunday Independent*'s Gene Kerrigan, told the nation that 'the future of the Force hangs in the balance' while his columnist colleague, Brendan O'Connor, concluded that 'we live in quite a scary country'. Another *Sunday Independent* columnist, Eoghan Harris, continued the theme. According to Harris 'as a political drama, Shatter-gate recalls the Arms trial of 1970'. The only difference was when the then Taoiseach Jack Lynch learned that 'some of his Ministers were planning to smuggle arms into Ireland for the IRA ... he promptly sacked Charles Haughey and Niall Blaney as they would not resign' while Enda Kenny's reaction to 'Micheál Martin's toxic transcript has been to back Shatter to the hilt.' According to Harris I was a political reincarnation of a terrorist arms supplier and of Charles Haughey, a corrupt former Fianna Fáil Taoiseach. Despite his reputation as a commentator dedicated to criticising others for factual and historical inaccuracy, it did not occur to Harris that the toxicity in the McCabe generated transcript from which Micheál Martin quoted in the Dáil may have derived from its inaccurate depiction of my ministerial conduct. Sharing Dearbhail McDonald's certainty and wrath, Harris hit out at the 'hapless RTÉ reporting and the complicity of the Labour Party' as being partly responsible for my continuing political survival. According to him 'the big question' was 'how Shatter has lasted so long?' There are occasions in politics when you wonder about the origin of the bile that masquerades as objective comment or informed analysis.

In the same paper Maeve Sheehan recounted the story of 'the Gardai, the whistleblower and a tangled web' reporting that Sergeant Maurice McCabe was 'determined to have his day to tell exactly what happened'. It would take over two years before the revelation of how truly 'tangled' was the web of allegations woven by Maurice McCabe. When the entanglements became clear, those who assumed his every allegation to be true carefully overlooked those which were independently established by the O'Higgins Commission to be 'exaggerated', 'unfounded', made 'without a scintilla of evidence' or which he withdrew.

Monday and Tuesday's media outlets continued the weekend theme. The media pack, having in the previous weeks believed the gardaí had GSOC under surveillance, now generally assumed that all of the allegations made by McCabe were true, that I had entirely ignored them and was intent on going after him in some way. Worst of all, according to Shane Coleman, in the *Irish Independent* on Tuesday, 25 February, was my 'seeming dismissal of the serious questions surrounding the case of murdered mother of two, Sylvia Roche-Kelly, which had occurred in 2008'. The dreadful background circumstances relating to her murder, unknown to Coleman, had been fully investigated by GSOC, the very body he criticised me in the same article for disrespecting. I believe it was also unknown, at the time, that McCabe, who bore no responsibility for what had occurred, knew of GSOC's involvement before I received his confidential report of 23 January 2012, having been interviewed by GSOC on 1 September 2011. This interview was most recently mentioned in March 2018 during McCabe's evidence to a Tribunal of Inquiry (the Disclosures Tribunal) of which more later. No reference to GSOC investigating the alleged garda failures of relevance to the murder of Sylvia Roche-Kelly was contained in McCabe's January 2012 report to me. I do not know whether, when he first met Micheál Martin, McCabe informed him of it prior to Martin's 'revelations' and accusations on the Leinster House plinth.

Dearbhail McDonald in the same edition of the *Irish Independent* was in her element. 'Shatter omnishambles is bigger than one man – the Minister should go,' she railed, informing her readers that 'we cannot play politics with the constitutional integrity of the State'. The dramatic condemnation was reaching a crescendo.

Behind all the media and Opposition noise, the Taoiseach and Tánaiste had over the weekend discussed the Micheál Martin démarche and the McCabe-related allegations and concluded that there should be another non-statutory inquiry. The Taoiseach discussed this with me on the Tuesday morning before our Cabinet meeting. I was informed that the inquiry would be conducted by a Senior Counsel, Sean Guerin, whom the Taoiseach would that afternoon in the Dáil describe as 'an experienced and respected criminal lawyer'.

It was my understanding that Sean Guerin's name had been suggested by the Attorney General, Máire Whelan. However, Whelan, some weeks later, asked me how he came to be nominated to conduct the inquiry. She denied that she had suggested his appointment. About a week after my resignation from Cabinet, in May 2014, I learned that Guerin shared offices with Senior Counsel Frank Callanan who was chairman of the Fine Gael Board of Trustees. To this day I do not know whether Frank Callanan or someone else suggested Guerin's name to Enda Kenny as the person to conduct the inquiry.

I did not know Sean Guerin and was not greatly concerned who conducted the non-statutory inquiry. Although the holding of another inquiry looked bad, I had nothing to hide. As Micheál Martin's material of 'national importance' had been given by Martin to the Taoiseach's Department, the Taoiseach informed me that his department, rather than Justice would be the 'lead department' for the inquiry. This meant that the administrative and resourcing arrangements to facilitate the inquiry would be coordinated through the Taoiseach's Department with Sean Guerin and that his formal letter of appointment would issue from Martin Fraser, the Taoiseach's Secretary General. As the inquiry was into justice matters, it would have been more usual for the Justice Department and not the Taoiseach's Department to act as lead department but I had no difficulty with this arrangement.

If Justice were the lead department, it was inevitable that both the Opposition and media commentators would develop a narrative impugning the independence of the inquiry and alleging it would be wrongly influenced by me. I had no reason to anticipate anything untoward and regarded Kenny's proposed arrangements as helpful. As I believed it likely that following his reading of all relevant papers Guerin would wish to interview me on my approach to McCabe's allegations, I considered it important that there could be no suggestion, however spurious, of my attempting in any way to wrongly influence his conclusions and recommendations.

The Cabinet that morning agreed to the holding of a non-statutory inquiry to be conducted by Sean Guerin. Máire Whelan was asked to draft its terms of reference. I fully briefed Cabinet colleagues on the background and arrangements were agreed for a Dáil debate the next day, Wednesday, 26 February. Only a week had elapsed since the announcement of the Cooke inquiry and Guerin, like Cooke, was to be asked to report within eight weeks or 'as soon as may be thereafter'. While I believed it possible that Cooke could report within eight weeks, I expected Guerin would require far more time because of the likely volume of documentation he would have to read and also because of the number of people he would have to interview or otherwise communicate with during his inquiry.

Enda Kenny had originally informed me that he wanted Guerin to report within six weeks and I had argued that this would be impossible. As a result, the expressly designated time period was extended to eight weeks and, in case he needed more than eight weeks to properly complete his work, the 'as soon as may be thereafter' formula created time flexibility. I had little doubt that, if either Cooke or Guerin required additional time to fully and properly comply with their terms of reference, they would avail of it. This had happened with many inquiries, both statutory and non-statutory, in the past.

Caught up in the tsunami of controversies, I never stood back and reflected on the broader political horizon and why the Taoiseach wanted both inquiries to conclude before Easter 2014. The European and local Government elections were scheduled to be held on 23 May 2014 and the desirability of ensuring any continuing garda-related controversy was removed from the political agenda at least three weeks before polling day did not occur to me.

CHAPTER 16

The Truth, the Whole Truth and Nothing but the?

... some of these allegations have been investigated by the Garda Commissioner, by GSOC in part or in full, or by the DPP. That work has been done. It is now necessary, in the interests of truth and credibility, to have the truth established here
–Taoiseach Enda Kenny TD, responding during Leaders' Questions in Dáil Éireann to Fianna Fáil leader Micheál Martin, 25 February 2014

It is to be hoped that the decision not to launch a full inquiry at this stage has been taken for pragmatic reasons and is not an exercise in protecting the position of the Justice Minister, Mr. Shatter
–*Irish Independent* editorial, 26 February 2014

Leaders' Questions time in the Dáil on Tuesday, 25 February 2014, was again dominated by Sergeant Maurice McCabe's allegations and the accusation that I had ignored his report of 23 January 2012. Enda Kenny, responding to Micheál Martin and announcing Sean Guerin's appointment 'to conduct an assessment of the various issues and allegations', stated his anxiety to 'have the truth established'. Explaining that Guerin was to 'examine and assess all the relevant papers and recommend what further action might be taken', he assured Martin that Guerin's report would be published and debated in the Houses of the Oireachtas and, should he recommend the establishment of a Commission of Investigation, 'it will be done'. Martin in response complained that 'the material was with the Minister two years ago and was supplied to the Confidential Recipient two years ago'. His preference was for the immediate appointment of a Commission of Investigation under the Commission of Investigations Act 2004. However, he said the Taoiseach would have his support 'if the role and function of the Senior Counsel is to scope out the basis for the initiation of a Commission of Investigation and to meet the key people concerned and engage with them'.

I had no difficulty with what Martin was proposing which, at that moment, seemed also to be agreed by Kenny who reiterated the necessity 'to have the truth established here', comparing the task given to Guerin with the independent review conducted by Shane Murphy SC which preceded the Morris Tribunal of Inquiry into allegations of garda misconduct in Donegal initiated in 2002. (It was an erroneous comparison as Murphy's report was confidential to the Government, while Guerin's was to be published.)

It was not until approximately ten weeks later that I was to discover that, in undertaking his task, Guerin, in order to establish 'the truth' sought by the Taoiseach, did not regard it as necessary to either 'meet the key people concerned and engage with them' or to 'examine and assess all the relevant papers' as Enda Kenny had promised the Dáil. It would be another nineteen months before I learned, through a Freedom of Information Act request for documents, that Kenny likely knew two weeks before receipt of Guerin's report that, contrary to his Terms of Reference, Guerin decided to not read 'voluminous' papers of relevance to his inquiry that were in GSOC's possession – papers which GSOC advised he should read prior to completing his work. There can be little doubt that this decision, conveyed in an email forwarded to Martin Fraser, the extremely competent and efficient Secretary General in the Department of An Taoiseach, was communicated by Fraser to Kenny. Whether prior to receiving Guerin's report Kenny understood that the only key person Guerin would take time to interview would be Sergeant Maurice McCabe, or whether that was intended by him at the time of Guerin's appointment and concealed both from the Cabinet and myself will probably never be known. Neither I nor the Cabinet were informed, prior to the conclusion of Guerin's inquiry, of his intention to report without reading GSOC's papers as required by the Government's terms of reference. Kenny also concealed any advance knowledge of this following the *Guerin Report*'s publication.

Central to this particular controversy was the 'confidential report' received by me on the evening of 23 January 2012 from the then Confidential Recipient, Oliver Connolly. It contained, amongst other allegations, what Connolly described as 'a complaint against Commissioner Martin Callinan made under the Charter of the Garda Síochána [Confidential Reporting of Corruption or Malpractice] Regulations, 2007'. The applicable regulation required Connolly to protect the identity of the Confidential Reporter and he informed me that he had 'redacted the relevant personal details on the face of the report'. The 'report' alleged a litany of garda failures in Bailieboro Garda District for which it was alleged a Superintendent Clancy was responsible as the supervising officer in charge. It claimed that the 'incidents, along with many more relating to him, were investigated by Assistant Commissioner Derek Byrne and Byrne, despite upholding the serious ones, came to a decision that the complaints against Superintendent Clancy were not substantiated in any way and he made no adverse findings against Clancy'.

The report continued: 'alarmingly Commissioner Callinan and Deputy Commissioner Rice agreed with Byrne. However, it may be the case that Derek Byrne hid evidence, material and certain findings from his superiors because he was the Commissioner in charge of the region at the time of the wrongdoing and in receipt of a bonus.'

Finding it 'hard to understand that the Commissioner of An Garda Síochána has rewarded Superintendent Clancy and placed him on the promotion list for the rank of Chief Superintendent', the Confidential Reporter asserted that 'Commissioner Callinan should have known of the malpractice' alleged by him and had 'made a serious error of judgment by placing Superintendent Clancy on a promotion list'.

The complainant continued:

the evidence is clear and it is corruption as defined by An Garda Síochána's Charter on Confidential Reporting. Gardai engaged in falsifying records, erasing official records, erasing report incidents, destroying official records, altering official records, covering up serious investigations and in gross dereliction of duty on a massive scale and it appears that the Commissioner was or is aware of it all. It also questions the whole PULSE system when Gardai can erase, alter, destroy, etc any record or information without any accountability or sanction.

Assistant Commissioner Byrne was accused, amongst other things, of conducting an investigation which made 'findings which cover up serious corruption'. Having accused the Garda Commissioner of corruption, the unidentified complainant towards the end of his report then contradicted his allegation, asserting that 'Commissioner Callinan may not have been given all evidence in my complaints and he may have been misled by the investigation team. The evidence is shocking.'

'Corruption' is the most serious allegation that can be made against a Garda Commissioner or against the head of any police force and it was this allegation made against Martin Callinan that required the anonymised report of Sergeant McCabe to be sent to me. Had McCabe made no such allegation and had his allegations been confined to gardai of lesser rank, including the superintendent, the report would have been furnished directly to Callinan for action by him, which included his furnishing a copy of it to GSOC, and it would not have arrived on my desk.

The allegations against Callinan were both shocking and puzzling. I interpreted the letter as essentially alleging that the Garda Commissioner had corruptly placed Superintendent Clancy on a promotion list and corruptly concealed serious failures and malpractice by members of An Garda Síochána. The allegations against Assistant Commissioner Byrne were no less serious. The allegation of gardai erasing, altering and destroying PULSE records would be one destined to be repetitively made by McCabe and repetitively investigated in the four years that followed, despite it being technically impossible to do so.

Clearly a central issue was whether Superintendent Clancy was responsible for the garda failures alleged in the letter, if they had occurred. However, a separate issue related to how the Commissioner could have 'placed' the superintendent on a promotion list when under the statutory arrangements an independent board composed of two civilians (one of whom chaired the board) and one member of An Garda Síochána were responsible for deciding who was suitable for promotion. (I was later to learn the garda representative on the relevant board was Noirín O'Sullivan, then a Deputy Commissioner, who succeeded Martin Callinan as Garda Commissioner.)

Having reflected overnight on the confidential report I discussed it the next day with Brian Purcell. We agreed that initially it should be furnished to the Garda Commissioner for his comments and following his response I would decide what further action, if any, to take. I had various available options. The regulations relating to reports received from the Confidential Recipient alleging corruption by a Garda Commissioner stated that I could 'cause an investigation to be conducted' or take any other action I considered appropriate. However, the relevant regulations granted no investigative powers to any individual a Minister for Justice might appoint to conduct such an investigation and were seriously deficient. Clearly, An Garda Síochána could not be asked to investigate allegations of corruption made against the Garda Commissioner as any such investigation would not be seen to be independent of the Garda

Commissioner. Moreover, GSOC was legally excluded from investigating such allegations of misconduct. I knew that I also had the option of appointing an individual to conduct an inquiry under Section 42 of the Garda Síochána Act 2005 but that the section was also deficient. It did not provide for a sworn inquiry or specify crucial fair procedure protections or envisage members of the public giving evidence. All of these provisions were unfortunately fatally flawed and, ironically, the brainchild of one of my predecessors in Justice, Michael McDowell, who I was to later learn was instructed by Sergeant McCabe to represent and advise him as part of his legal team. The only real substantive credible option, if action was required, was the appointment of a current or retired member of the judiciary to conduct an investigation under the Commission of Investigations Act, 2004 or an inquiry through a specially created Tribunal of Inquiry. Either of these options required a Government decision and would result in substantial public expenditure. I believed they could not be properly proposed to Cabinet without my first giving the Garda Commissioner an opportunity to respond to the allegations and my considering his response. I regarded doing so as the appropriate, fair and rational route to follow.

I emphasised to Brian Purcell the importance of a speedy response from the Commissioner and, seven days later on 30 January 2012, it arrived. It described the complaints as bearing 'remarkable similarities' to previous complaints, made under the same scheme, which were extensively investigated by Assistant Commissioner Derek Byrne and Chief Superintendent Terry McGinn. I was informed that the Confidential Reporter was a Sergeant Maurice McCabe who 'exposed his position' and that files had been furnished to the Director of Public Prosecutions (DPP) 'who directed that no prosecutions take place'.

I learnt that a series of complaints had been made to the previous Confidential Recipient (Brian McCarthy) by McCabe during the 2008 and 2009 period which were 'thoroughly investigated' and that 'unsolicited and repeatedly Sergeant McCabe divulged' his identity. According to the Commissioner the 'extensive investigation and supporting documentation was presented in a 10 volume file' to the Director of Public Prosecutions 'who having considered the material directed no prosecution on the basis that no criminality was disclosed against any member' of An Garda Síochána. I was told that eleven out of the twelve cases which had formed the basis for McCabe's January

2012 allegation of corruption and malpractice against the Garda Commissioner, Assistant Commissioner Byrne and Superintendent Clancy were included in the Byrne/McGinn investigation and the files which were given to the DPP. I was also advised the investigation had been reviewed by Deputy Commissioner Nacie Rice who concluded it had been carried out 'professionally, impartially and with propriety'. As for the twelfth case detailed in McCabe's report, the Commissioner said it was 'a case of child pornography and rape of a minor in September 2007 where the offender was a priest in the District'. This investigation 'commenced in Bailieboro in September 2007 and centred on offensive and inappropriate behaviour with a 14-year-old boy. It is apparent that the investigation was efficiently and speedily carried out and resulted (November 2009) in the priest being sentenced to five-year concurrent sentences at Cavan District Court.' (It would later emerge upon publication of the *O'Higgins Report* that the information upon which Callinan relied to depict that investigation as efficient was not accurate, despite the successful outcome.)

The Commissioner's response also detailed that Byrne and McGinn had met with McCabe and a representative of the Association of Garda Sergeants and Inspectors at the Hillgrove Hotel in Monaghan in November 2010, to inform McCabe of the outcome of the investigation conducted into his allegations. McCabe, I was informed, brought to the meeting two file storage boxes containing Garda PULSE printouts which he 'generally alleged' were further evidence of malpractice by gardaí stationed in Bailieboro but 'made no specific allegations with regard to the documentation'. Assistant Commissioner Byrne had taken 'possession' of the storage boxes and following the meeting 'Sergeant McCabe made a complaint through his solicitor, alleging assault and false imprisonment during the meeting.' The letter explained 'his allegations were made against Assistant Commissioner Byrne, in the context of his [McCabe's] refusal to hand over the official documents to Assistant Commissioner Byrne who insisted he needed to have the official documents complained about before he left the room so that they could be examined'. Deputy Commissioner Rice had been appointed to investigate these allegations and, following completion of that investigation in February 2011, 'notification was received from the DPP directing no prosecution'. The Commissioner also detailed that there was no clarity as to the nature of the complaints intended by Sergeant McCabe with respect to 529 of the printouts contained in the two boxes retained by Commissioner Byrne and that as of 27 January 2012 'the Sergeant has declined to assist the investigation of these printouts (529) despite a number of items of correspondence from the Deputy Commissioner to Sergeant McCabe and his legal representatives'.

As for allegations made against Superintendent Michael Clancy, the Commissioner stated that he was 'satisfied that no adverse findings or no evidence of corruption or malpractice were discovered' and that the complaints made by Sergeant McCabe about Superintendent Clancy 'were not substantiated in any way'. Clancy had, according to the Commissioner 'continued to discharge his duties in an exemplary manner' and had been placed 'on a promotion list to Chief Superintendent following an independent competitive process'. Deputy Commissioner Rice, in addition to investigating McCabe's allegation of assault and false imprisonment by Assistant Commissioner Byrne, on the Garda Commissioner's direction had also reviewed 'all the modules of the investigation previously conducted by Byrne and McGinn' and the Commissioner stated Rice had 'concluded they were carried out professionally, impartially and with propriety'.

Following the Byrne/McGinn investigation the DPP had directed that no prosecutions were warranted. In that light and as the GSOC, upon notification of the allegations or following the outcome of the investigation, was empowered to undertake its own independent public interest investigation had it any suspicion of garda misconduct, I believed no further action by me at that stage was required. My view was reinforced by my understanding that the initial investigation had been reviewed by Deputy Commissioner Rice and by the findings relating to Superintendent Clancy.

I also concluded that there was nothing contained in the information received from McCabe that justified his accusation that the Garda Commissioner was guilty of corruption or malpractice. The linkage of the allegation of corruption to the Commissioner's 'placement' of Superintendent Clancy on a promotions list did not stand up. This could not have occurred, as there was a statutory promotion process. The allegation of assault made by McCabe against Assistant Commissioner Byrne, dismissed by the Director of Public Prosecutions, was an additional issue that I could not disregard when determining my approach. I concluded that the information available to me did not support a proposal to Cabinet for either a Tribunal of Inquiry or a Commission of Investigation.

In the context of the individual cases raised by Sergeant McCabe, the one which gave rise to most concern was the circumstances which led to the murder in 2007 of Sylvia Roche-Kelly by Gerry McGrath, a violent criminal who, at the time of her murder, was already on bail for two pending prosecutions. It was this dreadful case that two years later was to be highlighted on the Leinster House plinth and in the Dáil by Micheál Martin as a new revelation of garda misconduct made by Sergeant McCabe which I had ignored. In discussions with officials prior to responding to McCabe's allegations, I learned that alleged garda failures which had occurred prior to the murder of Sylvia Roche-Kelly were the subject of an independent investigation by GSOC. Their investigation was undertaken following a complaint made to GSOC by her bereaved husband, Lorcan. I did not know at that time that McCabe, who bore no responsibility for any garda failures that occurred, was one of those interviewed by GSOC in 2011 during its investigation into the background to her murder.

I did not ignore the complaints relating to the murder of Sylvia Roche-Kelly raised by Sergeant McCabe, as Micheál Martin alleged in the Dáil in February 2014. It was simply that I knew they were subject to an independent investigation by GSOC and I believed there was no reason for a duplicate investigation or inquiry. I also learned that in 2009, at a time when Micheál Martin was in Government, Lorcan Roche-Kelly had issued proceedings against the State arising out of the circumstances relating to her death, on which the previous Cabinet should have been briefed by the then Attorney General.

On 3 February 2012, I responded to Oliver Connolly, the Confidential Recipient. My letter recorded that 'the allegation made in the Confidential Report against the Garda Commissioner is that he made a serious error of judgement by placing a named Superintendent on a promotion list when he should have known and, indeed, did know, of malpractice on the part of the Superintendent. The Confidential Report contains details of the allegations of malpractice' and as a consequence the question of the 'Garda Commissioner having a case to answer arises only in the event that the Superintendent has been found to have committed the alleged malpractices'. I referenced the investigation previously carried out by Assistant Commissioner Byrne and the review by Deputy Commissioner Rice and recorded that the Garda Commissioner advises me that, having regard to the outcome of the investigation and review, he is of the view that no evidence was found of any wrongdoing (corruption or malpractice) on the part of the named Superintendent or Assistant Commissioner Byrne. On the basis of these findings there is no evidence to support any further action by me in relation to the allegation made in the Confidential Report against the Garda Commissioner.

The reply left it open to McCabe to furnish any additional evidence he had to substantiate his allegations and concerns.

In May 2012, I received a letter through Connolly from McCabe accusing me of having asked the Commissioner to 'investigate himself'. It was not until February 2014 that I would discover this allegation repeated a view attributed to Connolly in the transcript of the recording made by McCabe, unknown to Connolly, of their meeting on 9 February 2012 to discuss my response to McCabe's report. In his May 2012 letter McCabe asked, 'what level of wrongdoing, malpractice or corruption has to be alleged against an Assistant Commissioner or Commissioner before he [that is me] will take serious cognisance of it and not seek a report from the Commissioner. The corruption I reported is at the highest level and it has been covered up.' According to McCabe I, as the Minister, had behaved 'in an inappropriate way' and 'it was wrong' of me to request a report from the person he had complained about. Unknown to me, McCabe was destined over three years later to express an entirely different view to the O'Higgins Commission which would be referenced in its report.

The accusation that I had asked the Garda Commissioner to investigate himself and, additionally, that I had automatically accepted the result was to resurface, both inside and outside the Dáil in February 2014 during the course of the controversy initiated by Micheál Martin. In reality, what was sought from the Garda Commissioner were comments or observations on the allegations made to enable me to decide what action, if any, I should take. It would have been entirely wrong and inappropriate to propose to Cabinet that an inquiry be conducted based on McCabe's allegations without my first giving the Garda Commissioner an opportunity to respond and to furnish me with relevant background information.

McCabe's solicitors, Sean Costello & Co., in September 2012 wrote to me referencing the issues reported by McCabe as being 'of an extremely serious nature' and 'undoubtedly of public concern' and sought an inquiry pursuant to Section 42 of the Garda Síochána Act. They enclosed what they described as 'three booklets of documents provided by our client relating to Malpractice and Corruption within An Garda Síochána in the Cavan/Monaghan Division'. The incidents documented they asserted 'unquestionably involve corrupt practices'. (The O'Higgins Commission would in its report in 2016 entirely reject the 'corruption' allegations.)

While the documentation raised new issues and revisited issues referred to in McCabe's January 2012 letter, I was conscious that McCabe's original allegation of 'corruption' against the Garda Commissioner had no validity. I determined Martin Callinan was entitled to an opportunity to respond to the new material to enable me better assess what to do next. To obtain his response I had first to overcome an obstacle created by McCabe's solicitors.

The correspondence from Costello & Co., sent by registered post, was marked 'Strictly Private and Confidential: Addressee Only'. Consequently, I believed that I could not pass on the documentation to Martin Callinan without McCabe's solicitors' agreement. McCabe, at that time, was the plaintiff in two separate High Court cases. The Garda Commissioner was named as a defendant in both and the Minister for Justice in one. The cases related to events that had occurred before my appointment. I did not want to be at the receiving end, as Minister, of a writ resulting from an allegation made that I had violated McCabe's privacy by furnishing private correspondence to the Garda Commissioner without his permission or that of his solicitors. I was particularly sensitive to this due to the content of McCabe's May 2012 letter in which he had objected to my obtaining the Commissioner's response to his 'confidential' report of January 2012.

In October, my then Justice Private Secretary, Damien Brennan, wrote to Costello and Co. seeking confirmation that they had 'no objection' to the correspondence and documentation 'being forwarded to the Garda Commissioner for his views'. He also requested copies of PULSE records referenced by them but not enclosed with their letter. On my personal initiative, reminder letters (three of which I dictated), seeking a substantive response, were sent in November 2012, January 2013, March 2013 and in May 2013 but no substantive reply was ever received to the requests. (The *O'Higgins Report* confirms the lack of any substantive response to this correspondence.)

I was deeply frustrated by both McCabe's and Costello's failure to reply and, by May 2013, wondered whether McCabe no longer wished his complaints to be addressed. The lack of a substantive response was particularly puzzling when contrasted with McCabe's focussed engagement in the September 2012 to May 2013 period on other allegations made by him of corruption and malpractice concerning Fixed Charge Notices and the imposition of penalty points on motorists for alleged road traffic offences.

I made two attempts to end the impasse. In December 2012, I asked Brian Purcell to seek additional information from the Garda Commissioner on the original twelve issues raised by McCabe the previous January and in September 2013 I asked Justice officials to obtain advice from the Attorney General's office on the predicament in which we found ourselves. It was not until May 2014 that I was to learn, on publication of the *Guerin Report*, that advices from the Attorney's office had been received in the Garda division of the Department of Justice in December 2013 but had neither been given to me nor acted upon.

I had, on various occasions during 2013, asked whether any new information of relevance had emerged that shed further light on the issues raised by McCabe and had been informed there was none. On Wednesday, 26 February 2014, as I was finalising my speech for later that morning in the Dáil in response to Micheál Martin's accusation that I had ignored McCabe's various allegations, Brian Purcell arrived in my office in Government Buildings, looking embarrassed. He said, 'Minister you better look at this.' He handed me a letter sent to him by the Garda Commissioner exactly one year earlier, 26 February 2013, containing additional relevant information of importance. He apologised for failing to give it to me earlier but offered no explanation. The explanation ultimately given for the very long delay was simply that 'it fell through the cracks' within the Garda Division in the Justice Department to which a scanned copy of the letter had been forwarded by email from Purcell's office. Upon reading the letter I knew that had I received it earlier, I would have reverted to the Commissioner with additional questions and I assumed its content would assist Sean Guerin in his inquiry.

I regarded the failure to furnish the letter to me as a one-off bureaucratic cock-up resulting from work pressures. Ireland had held the Presidency of the European Union from January to June in 2013 and everybody in Justice had been working flat out on EU-related matters as well as progressing our enormous domestic agenda. Unfortunately, I was to be proved wrong. Unknown to me, the Garda Division in the Department of Justice was seriously dysfunctional and, less than two weeks later, in March 2014, another letter of enormous importance was to 'fall through the cracks' – with devastating consequences.

CHAPTER 17

Guilty Until Proven Innocent

In fairness to members of An Garda Síochána I cannot simply take at face value serious allegations made against them and assume they are guilty until proven innocent. This is not the approach of our legal system and nor is it compatible with concepts of constitutional justice and human rights –Alan Shatter, Dáil Éireann, 26 February 2014

What each of these scandals has demonstrated is an unhealthy close relationship between the Minister for Justice and the Garda Commissioner –Gerry Adams TD, leader of Sinn Féin, Dáil Éireann, 26 February 2014

If the Minister stays in power and the Commissioner remains in place, then this Parliament is a sham ... it is time for the Minister to go and to bring the Commissioner with him
–Mick Wallace TD, Dáil Éireann, 26 February 2014

The truth will set you free
–Feargal Purcell, Government Press Secretary, 26 February 2014

Dáil proceedings on Wednesday, 26 February 2014, were dominated by issues relating to Maurice McCabe. The primary focus was McCabe's report of 23 January 2012 and Micheál Martin's charge that I had ignored McCabe's allegations contained in it. Other issues of garda controversy also resurfaced. Extracts from the transcript of the Connolly/McCabe conversation were extensively quoted by various speakers to give further oxygen to the narrative that I was out to get McCabe and that the Garda Commissioner and I were in cahoots. The Fixed Charge Notice/Penalty Points issue which by then had both been referred to GSOC, and on which a report of the Garda Inspectorate was imminent, also featured.

Shortly before I went into the Dáil Chamber to commence the debate, Feargal Purcell, the Government Press Secretary, called into my office. I gave him a copy of my speech. He informed me that because of all the drama, the *Sean O'Rourke Show* on RTÉ Radio 1 intended to broadcast some of my Dáil speech live that morning. We discussed the perfect storm of garda-related controversies that had raged throughout February and the political downside of having two issues in which I had been engaged now subject to two different independent informal inquiries.

I had been under dreadful political pressure during the entire month. I usually managed to remain calm and analytical in a crisis but I knew that February's continuous political drama was taking its toll. I was having difficulty sleeping and capillaries in each of my eyes had burst on three separate occasions causing my eyes to become bloodshot. My resulting red eye, while not painful, made me look hungover or like someone recovering from a barroom brawl. I knew this only happened when I was very stressed.

I liked Feargal. Before we entered Government, he had been Fine Gael's Press Secretary. We had worked together on many issues, shared mutual frustrations, had many a good laugh and I regarded him as a friend. As a former officer in the Defence Forces, I also respected his judgement. Before we parted ways, referencing the two inquiries and confident that I had always been truthful about the issues to be examined, he tried to reassure me it would all work out fine. Turning philosophical he cheerfully asserted that 'the truth will set you free' as he left my office. As I walked across the bridge linking Government Buildings to Leinster House the words 'arbeit macht frei' jumped into my head, a German phrase meaning 'work sets you free'. It is a phrase made notorious by its presence at the entrance to the Auschwitz and other concentration camps. I was momentarily taken aback by the similarity between the two phrases, which would not have occurred to Feargal. Maybe I should have seen it as a warning that things were not as straightforward as they seemed?

I opened the Dáil debate and described the steps taken in response to McCabe's allegations and the difficulties I had experienced in obtaining a response from his solicitors to correspondence sent to them. Detailing the background to my approach I stated:

I intend to demonstrate to the House today that none of Deputy Martin's political charges are true. Deputy Martin has spoken much in recent days about the maladministration of justice. There are, of course, fundamental principles of justice that are crucial to this State. They concern fundamental constitutional and human rights and the rule of law, which is something to which I have been passionately committed throughout my adult life. As Minister, I cannot opt to respect the rights of one person and ignore the rights of others. Put simply, while of course any allegations of wrongdoing must be taken seriously, allegations are not facts. I cannot proceed on an assumption that allegations made by one member of An Garda Síochána against many of his colleagues are correct and ignore the rights of those against whom allegations are made. This basic principle holds whether we are talking about An Garda Síochána or any other organisation, group or individual.

Further on I continued:

What is crucial is that the evidence of allegations made is carefully and properly examined. Allegations ultimately may be proved to be true, partially true or false. Where false, the original allegation need not be malicious in any way but may derive from a mistaken perception or understanding of events. Life is complicated and not everything is simply black and white.

I informed the Dáil that in 2009 McCabe had written to the then Fianna Fáil Justice Minister Dermot Ahern TD 'alerting him to the fact that he had made a complaint about garda malpractice and corruption in the Bailieboro District' and that his private secretary had replied to McCabe on Ahern's behalf stating that:

The conduct of the investigation was a matter for the Garda Commissioner, in accordance with the Garda Síochána Act 2005, that the Minister had no role in directing the Commissioner in such operational matters and that, in the circumstances, the most appropriate action was to allow the Commissioner to complete his work and let due process take its course.

In referencing this, I stated expressly that I was not in any way criticising the response of one of my Fianna Fáil predecessors. I also detailed the role of GSOC, its investigation into garda failures which had occurred connected to the murder of the late Sylvia Roche-Kelly and the fact that her husband Lorcan Roche-Kelly had initiated High Court legal proceedings against the State in February 2009, so the State was aware of particular issues related to her murder when Micheál Martin was in Government.

I also explained that Dermot Ahern, when replying to correspondence received from Lorcan Roche-Kelly through his private secretary, had 'expressed his sympathy and explained how a complaint could be made to GSOC'. I speculated that had Martin been aware of this 'he might have taken a more considered approach'. I was to be disabused of this notion at an early stage in Martin's response.

Towards the end of my contribution I stated:

> My concern is, as always, that the full truth is known. From Deputy Martin's contribution in this House last Thursday and his dramatic appearance on the plinth last Wednesday, he raised these very important issues as if they were entirely new, had never arisen during his term in the previous Government and had never been addressed either by the Confidential Recipient, An Garda Síochána or GSOC. He falsely accused me of undermining the administration of justice, a charge which I entirely reject.

I asserted the importance of An Garda Síochána adhering to the highest standards, public confidence being maintained in the force and of it not operating 'under a cloud of suspicion'. Somewhat over-optimistically, I concluded, expressing the 'hope that the processes we have put in place will deal effectively with any wrongdoing and also avoid clouds of suspicion being allowed linger unfairly'. My hopeful expectations were to prove illusory.

In response, Micheál Martin did not allow facts to deflect him from his prepared script of vilification. He entirely ignored the difficulties I described caused by McCabe's solicitors' failure to respond to correspondence sent to them. Martin alleged that the announcement of the Guerin inquiry 'comes two years on from the issues being raised and after weeks of delay and denial'. According to him, on the evidence available, 'efforts have been made at various levels to dampen if not quash allegations that were made about some past activities within the Garda' and 'only the most gullible will accept, having listened to the Minister this morning, that he tried to give a balanced and fair view of the record'. 'Serious questions' had arisen 'on a number of fronts' and there was 'no faith that they have been handled properly'.

Sinn Féin leader Gerry Adams TD, took up the theme. Maintaining consistency with his party's narrative that the gardaí bugged GSOC, he charged that there was 'an unhealthy close relationship between the Minister for Justice and Equality and the Garda Commissioner'.

Acknowledging that Sergeant McCabe's 'allegations may be totally and absolutely unfounded', he continued:

> I do not know and we have refrained from making any comment on that. Some of us have been at the receiving end of totally unfounded allegations for a very long time. However, these allegations were not new to the Minister for Justice and Equality. Indeed the allegation is that he has known about them for two years.

Also entirely ignoring the information I gave to the Dáil, his charge was in essence that I had behaved badly and ignored McCabe's concerns. Clearly being on the receiving end of 'totally unfounded allegations' did not inhibit Adams from making totally unfounded allegations of his own!

Next came Mick Wallace TD. Alleging that 'for almost thirty years people have hidden behind a wall of silence, deceit, corruption and cover-up' he asserted 'if the Minister stays in power and the Garda Commissioner remains in place, then this Parliament is a sham'. Then to my surprise, he gave expression to a profound personal insight. 'People are right to be cynical about politics and politicians', he asserted. 'This place is a joke.' At that moment, for the very first time, Wallace and I were briefly on the same page. Then, denouncing the 'games' played in the Dáil, he roared at the top of his voice, 'It's time for the Minister to go and to bring the Commissioner with him.'

Wallace did not want an inquiry. He wanted a lynching! Based on his business engagements and tax history I was bemused by his self-righteous sermon about deceit and corruption. In October 2017, due to a €1.4 million under-declaration of VAT by his construction company MJWallace, over a two-year period 2008–2010, the TD was disqualified by the High Court for six years from acting as a company director for a 'fraud on the revenue', said to be 'deliberate and systemic' and 'entirely lacking in commercial probity'. Wallace's conduct was already known in 2014 and had been referenced by him in an apology to the Dáil in 2012. It did not, however, inhibit the media from regarding his version of events as being entirely reliable and his accusations against me as entirely credible.

As the debate wore on, denounciations from the Opposition benches increased both in volume and ferocity. They included a contribution from my constituency colleague and rival, independent Deputy Shane Ross who spoke of 'an utter crisis in the justice system' which he labelled 'toxic' and called for the Garda Commissioner 'to fall on his sword and resign'.

On the Government side impressive contributions in my defence were made by my Fine Gael colleagues Charlie Flanagan, Patrick O'Donovan, Seán Kyne and Noel Coonan. Coonan got to the heart of it: 'The tradition of Fianna Fáil has always been to berate a Fine Gael Minister for Justice. It did so with Mrs Nora Owen in terms of zero-tolerance. It tried to hound her out of office. It is now hoping that history will repeat itself.'

Seán Kyne remarked that 'for some people establishing the facts of what happened has become secondary to political point scoring'. He was right. Political point scoring substantially dominated the rest of the exchanges.

The next day, Wednesday's Dáil exchanges were comprehensively reported and commented upon. There was acceptance by some that the background to the issues raised by Micheál Martin was more complex than he originally presented. The controversy was not over but it seemed that it might have cooled down temporarily to await the outcome of the Guerin inquiry. It was my hope and expectation that, upon publication of Guerin's report, it would be acknowledged that I had dealt properly with McCabe's allegations and that they had not been ignored.

For the first time in almost three weeks a garda-related controversy did not feature in Leaders' Questions, taken that Thursday by Tánaiste Eamon Gilmore. The topics were health, flooding in Cork and mortgage arrears. Coincidentally, Oral Justice Questions were on the agenda. Oliver Connolly's ceasing to be Confidential Recipient, the GSOC controversy and other matters were the subject of questions but there was nothing new.

I attended a dinner that evening in the Shelbourne Hotel with members of the Advisory Committee on Garda Interviewing of Suspects. Martin Callinan was also there and after dinner we discussed the events of the previous two weeks. GSOC, the Guerin Inquiry and the controversies relating to Sergeant McCabe all featured but there was no mention or suggestion of any new or unexpected controversy on the horizon. The evening was a welcome oasis of calm and interesting discussion at the end of the most difficult and pressure-filled month of my three years as a Minister.

While all the garda controversies raged, I dealt with a myriad of other issues. As was my habit, throughout the month, I started work at around 5am every day and most days did not finish until between 9.30pm and 11.30pm. Friday evenings were the exception. I tried to ensure that I left work between 5pm and 7pm to have a quiet dinner at home with my wife, Carol.

Work inevitably spread into every weekend but I usually managed some real relaxation time on Saturday or Sunday. This proved difficult during the rollercoaster month of February 2014. An enormous amount of my time was taken up with the garda controversies and the need during the weekends to keep up with a broad range of other issues and the huge amount of paperwork from both Justice and Defence, as well as constituency issues. I was determined to ensure that the events I was engulfed in did not disrupt the substantial reform agenda I wished to implement.

Despite the controversies of February 2014, we had launched 'Tackling Youth Crime – A Youth Justice Action Plan 2014–2018', a very important new initiative in the youth justice area. I also completed, before the Select Committee on Justice, Equality and Defence, the Committee Stage of the mammoth Legal Services Regulation Bill 2011, which prescribed major legal reforms of the legal professions and the delivery of legal services. To my frustration, development of the Bill had been substantially delayed. It was essentially put on the backburner by the Attorney General's office until after the enactment of new insolvency legislation that I steered through both Houses of the Oireachtas, comprehensively reforming our insolvency and bankruptcy laws. The passage of the Fines Bill was also completed in the Dáil that month. Its objective was to allow fines imposed by a Court to be paid in instalments, or deducted from the earnings of those who failed to pay, as an alternative to imprisonment. Draft legislation for the establishment of a Court of Appeal, following a successful constitutional referendum held in October 2013, was also published. As a lawyer I had for many years believed a Court of Appeal was essential to reduce delays and improve efficiency in our court system. The success of the referendum and the publication of the draft Bill was the fulfilment of a major personal political objective. The draft Criminal Justice (Community Sanctions) Bill was also published to replace the Probation of Offenders Act 1907 with modern statutory provisions for community sanctions. This was of particular importance in relation to how the Probation Service engaged with offenders. It also provided for the abolition of the Court Poor Box, replacing it with a statutory Reparation Fund, which would be put towards financing victim support services and the Criminal Injuries Compensation Scheme. All in all, despite the difficulties of the month, real progress was made with important new legislative measures and other initiatives.

Well in advance, I had ensured that I would have some breathing space on Friday, 28 February. There were no events or meetings scheduled in my diary. Neither the Dáil nor the Seanad were sitting. The Fine Gael Ard Fheis was taking place in the RDS, Ballsbridge that weekend, and I had set aside the day to relax, go for a walk in Marlay Park near my home and prepare my speech for Saturday afternoon.

The Ard Fheis was to focus on the economy and on jobs growth and give a boost to Fine Gael candidates in the forthcoming European and local elections. It was to be opened that evening by the Taoiseach. I was concerned that if I attended the opening, I would inevitably be surrounded by a posse of journalists and broadcasters intent on reprising the garda controversies, and be a distraction from the theme of the Ard Fheis. I texted Enda Kenny to say that I would not be at the Ard Fheis opening, but would be there the next day. Going to bed that evening, I wondered what reception I would receive from the many Fine Gael members who would travel from all over the country to the Ard Fheis. Would they be friendly or hostile? Did they believe that, as depicted in the media, I was a mixture of evil incarnate and gross incompetence as Minister for Justice and intent on persecuting whistle-blowers or would they believe I was dealing competently, reasonably and objectively with the extraordinary series of issues that had become a lightning rod for substantial controversy? I had absolutely no idea.

CHAPTER 18

The Ides of March

Soothsayer: Beware the ides of March.
Caesar: What man is that?
Brutus: A soothsayer bids you beware the ides of March
–William Shakespeare, *Julius Caesar*

Julius Caesar, the Roman consul and dictator, appeared before the crowd in the streets to receive its acclaim. From out of the crowd the soothsayer's infamous warning is voiced. The Ides of March originally did not signify anything special. The notion of the Ides being a dangerous date in the scene depicted was an invention of William Shakespeare for dramatic effect. Strictly speaking, the Ides of March was a day on the Roman calendar that corresponds to 15 March today and became notorious as the date of the assassination of Julius Caesar in 44 BC. In popular parlance, it has evolved to depict that March can be a dangerous month.

March 2014 proved to be a dangerous month. In its early days I believed the storm had passed. In reality, the sun briefly appeared before dark clouds again gathered on the horizon and more garda-related troubles erupted.

Early on Saturday, 1 March, I did a run-through of my speech for the Fine Gael Ard Fheis that afternoon. I had put together a series of notes as a road map to follow rather than a set script. I wanted to speak about the core values and principles which I considered essential to my and the Fine Gael party's approach to the Justice and Defence brief, to detail the impact of the many reforms already implemented and to set out the Justice and Defence agenda for the next twelve months. I was also determined to address the garda controversies head on. While I knew they were the only issue of interest to the media, I did not want my time in Justice and Defence to be defined solely by them and the hysteria surrounding them. I was reasonably confident that when retired High Court Judge John Cooke and Senior Counsel Sean Guerin each completed their informal enquiries there would be no doubt I had addressed the difficulties that had arisen appropriately and that I had told the truth. I considered my Ard Fheis speech as a golden opportunity to lay to rest, at least in the minds of Fine Gael members, any doubts that I had taken the issues seriously, to establish that I had done no wrong and that the controversies were politically inspired by my political opponents.

As the February garda-related controversies multiplied and the media's hostilities escalated, I had felt increasingly under siege. The difficulties were exacerbated to some degree by critical media briefings allegedly given by an unidentified Fine Gael Cabinet colleague who poured oil on the fire and some spin from the Labour side. However, by and large, I received substantial support from most of my Fine Gael colleagues and most members of the Labour parliamentary party just kept their heads down. I knew that a month of controversy was not only damaging to the Government but also to both parties and was distracting from the steadily improving fiscal, economic and jobs outlook. I was concerned that the garda controversies had not only dominated Leaders' Questions in the Dáil and political debate throughout February but had also followed the Taoiseach both at home and abroad.

Enda had informed me that he was being privately asked questions by colleagues and clearly there was some concern, not voiced in public, that I was not telling the full truth. From my perspective, it seemed that it was my telling the truth about the issues that had arisen which was causing my greatest difficulty.

Throughout February I regarded Enda Kenny, on a personal level, as being both helpful and supportive. We maintained regular contact and I tried to ensure he was kept up-to-date with developments. At around 7.30 on that Saturday morning, I received a text that I regarded as typical of his concern and decency: 'Today an important day for you. While supporters may want to be very loud I think you should stay in exactly the space you are in! It's the bigger picture you are interested in, truth, transparency, accountability and both a police force and an oversight that people have faith in. Good luck and will see you there.'

I assured him in response that I 'intend to be terribly Ministerial and positive' and wished him 'good luck' with the speech he was to deliver at the Ard Fheis that night. I would later develop a more cynical perspective on Enda's interest in 'truth, transparency and accountability'.

My session entitled 'Transparency, Accountability and Justice' was at 2.45pm in the RDS concert hall. Satisfied with my preparation for the speech, I had my usual Saturday morning walk in Marlay Park, came home, showered, got into an appropriately ministerial suit and arrived in the Ard Fheis at around 12.15pm. Jane Lehane, my brilliant special adviser in Justice and Defence, who first commenced working with me as a Parliamentary Assistant in 2007, accompanied me on the drive to the RDS. Despite my many years in various positions on the Fine Gael Front Bench and my attending previous Ard Fheiseanna as a member of Cabinet, I usually maintained a relatively low profile at such events. This time it was dramatically different.

When I entered the exhibition hall, I was immediately engulfed by an excited crowd of Fine Gael members congratulating me on standing up in the Dáil to the month-long onslaught of Opposition TDs. I was surprised and taken aback by their enthusiasm, backslapping, hugs and fervent handshakes. 'Good on you, stand your ground, don't give in to the F F'ers [Fianna Fáil-ers] were some of the comments. Within a few minutes, journalists and media photographers attracted by the hubbub arrived on the scene. Staying away from serious questions, I engaged in some banter and stuck to my objective of keeping the serious stuff until my speech later in the afternoon.

I spent about two hours just mixing round and chatting with people and thoroughly enjoyed the experience. It seemed that briefly I had entered an entirely different and more supportive world entirely disconnected from the space I had inhabited since early in February.

The Justice session was usually scheduled for shortly after lunch and, on occasions, coincided with a rugby international that diverted delegates to televisions in the local bars. Because of the important focus on economic matters and jobs growth, Justice sessions were also relegated to a side hall and not particularly well attended. Journalists were more frequently noted for their absence than their presence and most, if reporting the Justice session, were happy to rely on whatever prepared script was given to them. On this occasion, due to the background controversies, I expected our session would be better attended and the absence of a prepared script required attendance if what I had to say was worthy of reporting. I did not anticipate the room would be completely full, with standing room only.

In the midst of all the controversies, I believed the Opposition, the media and the public had lost sight of the vitally important work done on a day-to-day basis by An Garda Síochána and that I had been misrepresented as being opposed to the important garda oversight work of GSOC. The approach suggested by Enda was exactly the approach I intended to take and was incorporated in the notes made the previous day.

I received a rapturous reception from the Fine Gael delegates. I acknowledged that it was a 'privilege to be a Minister in two great departments' and first dealt with the Defence brief. I detailed the duties undertaken by our Defence Forces both at home and abroad, the restructuring of the Defence Forces that had been undertaken and the fact, that despite the State's chronic financial and economic difficulties, we had continued to play a vital role in a variety of UN peacekeeping and humanitarian missions and maintained the strength of the Defence Forces at 9,500 through appropriate recruitment. I also referenced the investment of over €100 million in the important purchase of two new naval vessels. Without these vessels the Navy would have lacked the capacity, subsequent to my resignation, to undertake its mission in the Mediterranean, saving the lives of thousands of refugees. On the Justice side, I referred to the legislative agenda to be completed in the following twelve months, which included the final enactment of the Legal Services Regulation Bill and Bills on Victims' Rights and Immigration, Residence and Asylum. I detailed some of the ground-breaking reforms contained in my recently published draft Children and Family Relationships Bill, major portions of which I had personally drafted, and looked forward to the holding of the Marriage Equality Referendum I had proposed to cabinet be held in the Spring of 2015. I then said that there had been 'some controversy in recent weeks' and spoke of the vitally important role played both by An Garda Síochána and by GSOC. Acknowledging that every organisation, on occasion, gets something wrong, I emphasised that is 'why oversight and review procedures and transparency are so important. That is why lessons must be learned from errors made and corrective action taken. But we must never lose sight of the valuable contribution made by both agencies.'

Referencing An Garda Síochána, I stated that 'we should never forget that the brave men and women of An Garda Síochána, on a daily basis, can find themselves in harm's way when performing their duty to protect the community, prevent and investigate crime and facilitate those guilty of crime being dealt with and sentenced by our Courts'.

I continued:

I will take no lectures on policing from the Sinn Fein party which includes TDs who stood at the prison gates to meet and greet the killers of Detective Garda Jerry McCabe and to celebrate their release or which feigns concern over the conclusions of the Smithwick Tribunal while refusing to condemn the barbaric cold-blooded murder of two

RUC officers committed to protecting communities both North and South from the Provo's campaign of murder and mayhem.

Sinn Féin is anathema to most Fine Gael members and my reference to that party was enthusiastically applauded, as was my following reference to Fianna Fáil:

> I will also take no lectures on policing from Fianna Fáil who so bankrupted the country that recruiting to An Garda Síochána had to cease for five years and whose Justice spokesperson went AWOL for almost the entire four hours of the recent Oireachtas Petitions Committee hearings to which he made no contribution on an issue on which he had repetitively broadcast allegations, innuendo and criticism, while pretending to have a genuine interest and concern in the days leading into the Committee's meeting.

Here, of course, I was referencing Niall Collins's absence from the meeting of the Petitions Committee at which I was questioned on the alleged GSOC bugging issue. I wanted to leave the Fine Gael delegates in no doubt that I had the necessary backbone to stand firm and to confront my detractors. Bringing my speech to a close I said:

> One of the things I have done throughout my life is stand up to bullies and defend others against hate speech and prejudice ... let me quietly state clearly this afternoon that this Minister will not waiver or hesitate from taking the right path or succumb to the bullying and slanderous political opportunism and hate speech with which I am confronted on a daily basis. It is regrettable that the political discourse in our State has been so coarsened and degraded by those who choose to engage in such conduct.

I concluded urging all present to get behind and support the Fine Gael candidates standing for election in the May local Government and European elections. 'I am looking forward to the opportunity that these important elections give to all of us to continue our conversation with the people that we serve.'

There were rousing cheers and I was the happy recipient of a lengthy standing ovation. My speech brought the session to an end and I was surrounded by enthusiastic delegates anxious to shake hands, express their congratulations and whisper some word of advice or encouragement in my ear. While I knew I was addressing the staunchest group of Fine Gael supporters to be found anywhere in the country, it was an emotional and encouraging start to the month of March.

At 7.20pm I entered the main auditorium for the Taoiseach's address. When my name was announced I again received rousing cheers and applause. After I sat down, someone shouted 'three cheers for Alan Shatter' and cheers resounded around the auditorium. Enda Kenny, in his speech, briefly touched on the garda controversies and expressed support for me in my role as Minister for Justice and Defence. His comments were greeted with applause. He delivered a good speech that night and as he concluded, as usual, a group of parliamentary party members rushed up around him to feature in RTÉ's closing shots of the Ard Fheis preceding the *Nine O'Clock News*.

Over the years, I had always marvelled at the speed and determination of some of my colleagues to get in the picture with Enda after his speech, in particular Frances Fitzgerald and Michael Ring, and their obvious belief that it was good for votes. I regarded the frenetic scramble with some humour but had little interest in it and usually hung back. On this occasion, Enda spotted me. He gestured, grabbed my hand and pulled me into the centre of the crowd. He raised both our arms into the air and we stood there momentarily, arms raised in a victory salute to the crowd, like two prize boxers after winning their bouts. I understood, as did the crowd, that this was a very deliberate and exuberant public show of support for me by the Taoiseach at a time of political difficulty. A picture of us standing united, arms in the air, flashed across television screens throughout Ireland and appeared in Monday's print media reports of the Fine Gael Ard Fheis. Unfortunately, as I was to later learn, in politics such public displays of support should never be relied upon.

CHAPTER 19

Ticket Charges and Penalty Points

The Commissioner Martin Callinan has serious questions to answer and I feel his position is untenable as the Commissioner of An Garda Síochána –From document given by Sergeant Maurice McCabe to the Department of An Taoiseach, August 2012, and furnished to the Department of Justice, September 2012

The general public first became aware of the events resulting in the Cooke and Guerin Inquiries in February 2014 but they were not the only cause of garda-related controversy and political drama. In September 2012, correspondence originating directly from Sergeant Maurice McCabe had been received in the Department of Justice from both the Taoiseach's Department and the Department of Transport, Tourism and Sport, together with supporting documentation. In it McCabe alleged, amongst other things, 'ticket fixing', 'wrongdoing', 'shocking criminality', 'perversion of the course of justice on a massive scale' and 'serious fraud and corruption' by members of An Garda Síochána in the cancellation of Fixed Charge Notices or 'ticket charges' arising out of alleged traffic offences.

Ticket charges are issued for road traffic offences, such as excessive speeding, drink driving, breaking traffic lights, no motor tax/insurance, holding a mobile phone while driving and failure to wear a seatbelt. An offence may be detected in one of two ways: intercept or non-intercept. An intercept occurs when a garda stops a motorist at the time of the offence. At this point, a garda can exercise his or her discretion whether or not to issue a ticket charge. A non-intercept offence is captured on camera by a garda contracted 'Go Safe van', a garda robot van or a speed camera. A ticket charge is then automatically posted to the motorist. After the charge has been issued, a garda discretion can be lawfully exercised in appropriate circumstances to cancel the charge and not issue a Road Traffic Summons. During my time in Justice, a motorist who got a ticket charge had the option of either paying €80 and receiving two penalty points for breach of the Road Traffic Acts or being summonsed to attend before the District Court. Accumulating twelve penalty points automatically meant a six-month driving ban.

According to McCabe 'thousands of Gardai and family members' had traffic tickets wrongly terminated. Targeting Martin Callinan, he accused the Garda Commissioner 'of a serious lack of duty, lack of judgement and lack of standards'. He also alleged 'shocking criminality' by several garda officers of inspector and superintendent rank and that records contained on the garda PULSE system had been falsified, altered, destroyed and erased. Most shockingly, he claimed that 'numerous persons who had speeding tickets quashed were subsequently involved in fatal road traffic collisions'. The clear implication was that had speeding tickets not been quashed, lives would have been saved.

The accompanying documentation detailed the names of some individuals entered on the Garda PULSE system and listed a variety of incidents which he described as 'a very brief small sample of the corruption'. McCabe also referenced his Confidential Report of eight months earlier received by me from Oliver Connolly, the Confidential Recipient, in which he had alleged the Garda Commissioner was corrupt. He asserted that Assistant Commissioner Derek Byrne should consider his position for allegedly 'covering up the wrongdoing' and that 'Commissioner Martin Callinan has serious questions to answer'. Callinan's 'position' he stated was 'untenable as the Commissioner of An Garda Síochána'.

McCabe, I later learned, furnished the same or similar documents to the Comptroller and Auditor General and to the Road Safety Authority. Nevertheless, he insisted that his 'e-mail and attachments must remain highly confidential as if my name gets out I would be finished policing in An Garda Síochána and the backlash would be unbearable'. This insistence by McCabe on confidentiality and anonymity was consistent with the approach taken both by him in January 2012 and by his solicitors in September 2012 detailing other complaints he made. His wish for confidentiality was also reiterated in an email he sent to the Taoiseach's office on 5 November 2012, complaining that neither my office nor the Taoiseach's office had ordered 'a halt to the criminal and illegal terminations' of traffic tickets. Unfortunately, my respecting McCabe's demand that his anonymity be preserved sowed the seeds for my subsequently becoming entangled in toxic political controversy.

I do not know if McCabe's solicitor when writing to me in September 2012 was aware of his client's direct communication with Government Departments and Agencies in the summer of 2012 about the alleged 'Ticket Fixing' issue or why McCabe dealt with some issues through solicitors' correspondence and others by personal engagement.

I was first briefed on McCabe's and his solicitors' correspondence in October 2012, having been out of action for part of September due to a prostate operation. To address the ticket charge issue, I decided initially to furnish all the allegations made and documentation received to the Garda Commissioner while respecting McCabe's request for anonymity. A similar approach could not be taken to the correspondence and documentation received directly from McCabe's solicitors in September 2014, due to its being expressly designated as 'private and confidential' for the 'addressee only'.

Callinan appointed Assistant Commissioner John O'Mahoney to fully examine the allegations including, as they were to be later described by Callinan, the 'grave assertions citing criminality, corruption, deception and falsification committed by named and unnamed officers by virtue of their discretionary terminations of Fixed Charge Notices'.

Almost three weeks later, on 7 November 2012, I received a letter from Leo Varadkar, then Minister for Transport, Tourism and Sport, enclosing an email he had received from McCabe. In it McCabe repeated his ticket charge allegations already furnished to the Garda Commissioner, complaining that 'no one seems to want to deal with the issues I report' and repeated his request for confidentiality. In his letter to me, Varadkar acknowledged that McCabe had been in contact with his Department and the Road Safety Authority 'earlier in the year' and met with officials. He quite reasonably stated that he believed it was 'in everyone's interest that the matters referred to are investigated and that we are in a position to respond to these claims'. Like Varadkar, I regarded it as absolutely crucial that all of the issues raised by McCabe be fully and comprehensively addressed.

Following receipt of a detailed response from the Garda Commissioner, I intended to consider what further action, if any, was required. A central issue was whether McCabe's allegations were true and, more particularly, whether tens of thousands of ticket charges had been wrongly quashed, as alleged by him, with PULSE records deleted, falsified and destroyed to hide wrongdoing and road fatalities resulting from wrongful conduct by members of An Garda Síochána. The scenario painted by McCabe was not only one of 'criminality', 'serious fraud and corruption' but also of 'certain Garda Inspectors and certain Garda Superintendents perverting the course of justice on a massive scale'. Intent on establishing the truth, I recognised that following receipt of the Garda Commissioner's report it might prove necessary to involve either GSOC or the Garda Inspectorate. However, I was anxious to make no premature judgements.

I believed that, in January 2012, McCabe had made a spurious allegation of corruption against Callinan, as the *O'Higgins Report* published in May 2016 would later confirm, and I had substantial concerns and reservations resulting from the extreme nature of the allegations made and the language used by him. These were bolstered by the fact that the DPP had directed that no criminal prosecution be initiated against Assistant Commissioner Byrne following the completion of an investigation into McCabe's allegation that the Assistant Commissioner had both assaulted and falsely imprisoned him. I believed that caution was required in responding to McCabe's allegations.

Proper administration of the ticket charge system was important in the context of road safety, However, as the Garda Inspectorate would later state in 2014 following its own investigation, it was 'a relatively minor part of the law enforcement responsibilities' of An Garda Síochána compared with their crime prevention and investigative duties relating to terrorism and subversion, gangland crime, murder, rape, physical and sexual assaults, fraud, robberies, burglaries, kidnappings and the general preservation of law and order. I believed it was important to keep matters in proportion and that it was both fair and right that Martin Callinan be given an opportunity to provide a detailed response to the allegations that I could consider before making any judgements.

Assistant Garda Commissioner O'Mahoney, appointed by Callinan to investigate the allegations, led a twenty-eight member team dedicated to his investigation, including five Chief Superintendents, six Superintendents together with their respective staff and an incident room staff of seven. I received his interim report on 28 November 2012 and his final report on 28 March 2013. In addition, in April 2014, I received a detailed report from the Garda Professional Standards Unit (GPSU) on the processes and systems in place to deal with the cancellation of Ticket Charges and Penalty Points.

In the period November 2012 to April 2013, while I continued to preserve McCabe's anonymity, allegations of 'Ticket Fixing' and Garda corruption and misbehaviour in the quashing of Fixed Charge Notices and Penalty Points became a focal point of media and political controversy.

In late November 2012, the print media started to report allegations made in the Dáil of gardaí wrongly cancelling Penalty Points and this continued into the New Year. Alleged incidents reported replicated those referred to in the McCabe documentation received in the Department of

Justice and incidents under examination by O'Mahoney and his team. It was clear that the information originated from the Garda PULSE system, which I understood did not fully detail all the background information relevant to ticket charges cancelled.

PULSE is an acronym for 'Police Using Leading Systems Effectively'. Its main purpose, during my time as Minister for Justice, was to collect information in an electronic and confidential format. As an information collection system it facilitated easy and speedy access to information by members of the gardaí conducting investigations and prosecuting court proceedings. PULSE was not then a performance management system nor was it used to monitor the work of gardaí. Under Data Protection legislation, the Garda Commissioner is obliged, as 'data controller', to ensure the confidentiality of information held on PULSE and to ensure that the privacy of individuals is protected. The Garda Síochána Act 2005 obliges current and former members of An Garda Síochána not to disclose any information obtained in the course of their duties. This includes not disclosing information which prejudices 'the security of any system of communication of the Garda Síochána' or engaging in any action which 'results in the publication of personal information and constitutes an unwarranted and serious infringement of a person's right to privacy'. Included amongst the exemptions to this non-disclosure obligation is providing information to 'a Member of either House of the Oireachtas where relevant to the proper discharge of the [Garda] members' functions'.

I was greatly concerned, as was the Garda Commissioner, that some motorists, who had no opportunity to defend themselves, were being named and shamed in the Dáil Chamber. Dáil Privilege rendered TDs immune from defamation proceedings even where they caused damage to the reputations of the people they named by implying they were guilty of wrongdoing. Media outlets quoting what was said in the Dáil Chamber could not be sued for defamation either. As a result, motorists named in the Dáil were also identified in the print media in the words of People Before Profit TD Joan Collins as 'the beneficiaries' of 'malpractice and the systematic abuse of the system'. There appeared to be no concern of any nature about this abuse of Dáil Privilege. I regarded it as a gross violation of personal rights.

Much of the media commentary and some of the Dáil exchanges were based on an assumption that there was no legal basis for the gardaí exercising discretion to cancel Ticket Charges. This was entirely wrong. Since the inception of the Fixed Charge Notice System, the gardaí had a discretionary power to do so. Use of the discretion was informed by Guidelines for Prosecutors issued by the DPP and prescribed Garda Policy and Procedures contained in a Garda Manual and Directives. It was also based on advice from the Attorney General's Office, not all of which was being fully followed, as would become evident in 2014 upon publication of the Garda Inspectorate's report into the issue. In addition, there were explicit statutory grounds for cancellations such as medical conditions which exempted individuals from wearing a seatbelt, exemptions from speed limits for emergency vehicles, including fire engines, ambulances and vehicles used by a Garda in the performance of his or her duties or a person 'driving under the direction of a Garda, where such use does not endanger the safety of road users'. The major area of concern centred around whether there was compliance with the prescribed procedures and whether the discretion to cancel ticket charges was being abused.

While ticket charges could be cancelled by a Garda District Superintendent, or, in certain circumstances, an Inspector, the Fixed Charge Processing Office in Thurles, managed by a Superintendent, had a central role in the recording and processing of Fixed Charge Notices and the Superintendent-in-Charge in Thurles could also cancel them. TDs who were naming motorists in the Dáil had no knowledge of the background circumstances nor of the procedures applied in individual cases. Neither did the media outlets reporting what was said in the Dáil chamber. I was concerned that not only were they effectively prejudging the outcome of O'Mahoney's investigation and damaging the reputation of individuals named, but that they were also damaging the reputation of gardaí throughout the country who were, at all levels, being depicted as guilty of corruption, criminality and the alteration, erasure and destruction of garda records.

As Minister for Justice, I regarded it as important that public confidence and trust in the gardaí and in the Fixed Charge Notice Processing System be maintained. I also believed that, if there was wrongdoing, it should be properly exposed and addressed. I made no assumptions about the accuracy or not of McCabe's allegations and was intent on them being fully investigated. However, the actions of Opposition TDs and the media narrative were substantially focussed on validating all the allegations made and, for some, my failure to instantly do so was tantamount to a cover-up of garda wrongdoing. There was no room for a considered and careful response.

On 28 November 2012, an interim report I received from Assistant Commissioner O'Mahoney clearly indicated that while his investigation would likely validate a number of McCabe's serious concerns, there was no truth to allegations made of garda wrongdoing in a variety of incidents detailed by him.

Although this was an interim report, not for publication, I believed it would be helpful to share with Deputies some information contained in it. In response to Dáil Questions on 11 December 2012, I stated that the allegations were being taken seriously, thoroughly investigated and that I would publish the outcome of O'Mahoney's investigation. I cautioned that they should not assume all cancellations of ticket charges to be wrong. I explained that amongst the incidents of alleged 'ticket fixing' were cases where car registration numbers were wrongly recorded and of a motorist making an emergency trip with a child to hospital. I cautioned against 'any rush to judgment before all the facts are known' and asked Deputies 'to desist from naming individuals' in or outside the Dáil on the assumption that they had been guilty of wrongdoing.

Unfortunately, exercising caution and telling the truth does not attract the same media attention and praise as naming individuals under the protection of Dáil privilege. That afternoon, exchanges on the issue involving Deputies Mick Wallace and Clare Daly travelled from Justice Question Time to one of that day's Topical Issues where Daly and Wallace were joined by People Before Profit Deputy Joan Collins. She alleged 'malpractice and systemic abuse of the system' based on the 'information we have seen'. She named three well-known individuals who had been identified in the papers received from McCabe and, in doing so, generated the expected dramatic news headlines and media coverage.

Nine days later, on 20 December 2012, Wallace, Daly and Collins were joined by Independent Deputy Luke Ming Flanagan for a much-promoted press conference in the famous Buswells Hotel, adjacent to Leinster House. They intended to 'expose' a 'dossier of evidence' on people who had Penalty Points struck out by the gardaí. Following a last-minute intervention by Billy Hawkes, the Data Protection Commissioner, they desisted from generally distributing the dossier. Nor did they name names as some reporters eagerly anticipated. However, a dossier must have been available to be photographed as extracts appeared the next day on Journal.ie and some of the incidents 'exposed' clearly resembled those detailed in the documentation received by the Department of Justice. They included six alleged incidents of motorists who had ticket charges for speeding cancelled and who, it was alleged, were later involved in fatal road traffic incidents. Amongst the 'exposed' incidents, recorded in a photograph published online by Journal.ie was a motorist 'caught with a mobile phone' whose traffic ticket was allegedly fixed. This would prove particularly ironic a few months later when controversy erupted involving both Wallace and Flanagan.

Shortly before the Dáil exchanges the Garda Commissioner had issued a memo reminding all gardaí of the importance of preserving the confidentiality of the PULSE system and warning them not to release confidential information to external parties. Clare Daly, who had obviously been briefed on the contents of the memo, depicted it as 'trying to intimidate whistleblowers who are lawfully entitled to go to Members of the Oireachtas'.

Two months later, in February 2013, Daly rightly complained when media reports emerged of her arrest and removal to Kilmainham Garda station under suspicion of driving over the alcohol limit. She had mistakenly made an illegal right turn off the South Circular Road in Dublin. A test administered in the station established she was not over the limit. I was outraged by the leak of her arrest, believing it to be entirely wrong and the Garda Commissioner was informed of my view. I subsequently learnt that, within twenty-four hours of her arrest, details of the incident on the PULSE system had been accessed by over 130 gardaí across the country. It was never established who leaked the story to the media. Daly issued a statement demanding a full investigation into 'those who sought to damage' her. I doubt if she ever acknowledged the irony of this unfortunate incident occurring less than two months after she had criticised the Garda Commissioner in the Dáil for his memo to members of the garda force stressing the importance of information on PULSE remaining confidential and not being leaked to third parties.

Subsequent to the Dáil exchanges of 11 December 2012, I learnt that three days earlier a Garda John Wilson based in a station in Cavan, was seen printing off PULSE records. Questioned by a Sergeant, Wilson asserted that he was working with another Garda (later revealed to be Maurice McCabe) to give information to a public representative, later revealed to be Clare Daly. This resulted in the Garda Commissioner, on 14 December

2012, issuing a 'Direction' to both McCabe and Wilson 'to desist searching PULSE and dissemination to a third party of sensitive personal data regarding cancellation of Fixed Charge Notices'. A Chief Superintendent arranged a meeting with McCabe that day and read the 'Direction' to him, which they subsequently discussed. McCabe would later complain that he was not given a copy of the Direction and the reason for his not receiving one is difficult to understand. However, it did not greatly matter as, unknown to the Chief Superintendent, McCabe recorded their meeting and just over fourteen months later, on 24 February 2014, published the alleged transcript of the recording. He did so in support of his denial in a public statement that the Garda Commissioner had written to him in December 2012 'directing' him 'to cooperate with the investigation into the allegation that Penalty Points had been cancelled'. McCabe had not been interviewed by O'Mahoney prior to completing his investigation and this had, for a number of months, been a focal point for controversy, despite McCabe's many assertions and requests that his identity be not revealed to the garda authorities as the complainant.

An extract from McCabe's published transcript reads:

The Commissioner understands that you have been searching and printing out from PULSE documents that contain sensitive personal data regarding the cancellation of the fixed charge notices. The Commissioner further understands that it is your intention to provide a third party with that documentation. It is noted that sensitive personal data in relation to fixed charge cancelation(s) have already appeared in the public domain.

The Commissioner has sought the advices of the Attorney General and has consulted with the Data Protection Commissioner in respect of this matter. You are aware that there is power as set out in the Garda policy procedure and guidelines for cancelling these fixed charge notices in certain instances in such circumstances. Having consulted with the above mentioned authority the Commissioner is satisfied that you're [*sic*] continued access PULSE data and disclosure of such it [*sic*] and personal data to a third party is likely to be in breach of the Data Protection Act and other legislation, as well as being prejudicial to the current investigation being undertaken by Assistant Commissioner John O'Mahoney.

Ok, so that is the instructions to you in this direction.

The direction is as follows:

The Commissioner is now directing you to desist from the practice of accessing PULSE and or disclosing to third parties sensitive personal data regarding the cancellation of fixed charge notices by members of An Garda Síochána. If you have any further concerns and without prejudice of your rights under the Confidential Reporting Mechanism such matters can be brought to the attention of Assistant Commissioner John O'Mahoney, Crime and Security, who will fully investigate those matters.

McCabe, in his February 2014 public statement, protested that the Direction did not in December 2012, as he put it, direct him 'to cooperate with the investigation being carried out by the Assistant Commissioner' and 'direct' him to 'bring any information and concerns' he had to the inquiry team. To a degree he is right. The Direction was to 'desist from the practice of accessing PULSE and/or disclosing to third parties personal data regarding the cancellation of Fixed Charge Notices'. It did, however, 'direct' that if he had 'any further concerns … such matters can be brought to the attention of Assistant Commissioner John O'Mahoney' who 'will fully investigate these matters'. (If the word 'should' had been used instead of the word 'can', there could have been no subsequent dispute over the content or intent of the Commissioner's direction.)

If he had further concerns or additional information relevant to the O'Mahoney investigation, the Garda Commissioner's communication expressly invited McCabe to contact O'Mahoney. McCabe's protest essentially amounted to a complaint that the Commissioner issued an invitation not an order. Some would regard that as the more considerate approach, including the assurance given that his concerns would be 'fully investigated'. However, upon McCabe publishing the transcript, there was no possibility that media commentators and Opposition politicians dedicated to targeting both the Commissioner and myself would do so.

Other than Callinan's Direction, nothing further was done by gardaí at senior level to engage with McCabe on the Ticket Charge issue before O'Mahoney completed his report. O'Mahoney not interviewing McCabe and whether McCabe did or did not 'cooperate' with O'Mahoney, following publication of O'Mahoney's report, became a focus for ongoing political controversy and a distraction from the actual action taken following receipt of McCabe's allegations. It also distracted from unsubstantiated allegations made by McCabe of serious misconduct, including garda corruption, criminality and the alteration and destruction of garda records.

When later questioned before the Public Accounts Committee (PAC) in January 2014, O'Mahoney explained that he did not interview McCabe because the 'documentation provided to the Commissioner was unsigned and unattributed' and that he proceeded with his examination on the basis that the allegations he was investigating came from an anonymous source. However, later on, at the same meeting, O'Mahoney acknowledged that he had strongly suspected the identity of the source of the documentation and that 'during the course of his investigations' he became aware of the 8 December incident. He explained that he did not interview McCabe because he was doing 'his examination and finding that, in most cases, but not all, what was on PULSE did not accurately reflect what these people were alleging'. He further explained that 'bearing in mind the issue of Confidential Reporters and Confidential Recipients and honouring that system – I would have gone back to the Commissioner had I any reason to interview those people and asked him whether I could find out for definite who they were'. Although McCabe had not addressed the Ticket Charge/Penalty Points issue through the Confidential Recipient, as I had preserved McCabe's anonymity, his allegations had been treated by O'Mahoney as if made through the Confidential Recipient. O'Mahoney would four years later similarly explain his approach before what became known as the Disclosures Tribunal.

In 2014, when I read the transcript of O'Mahoney's comments to the PAC, I concluded that if the PULSE system truly 'did not accurately reflect' the allegations of McCabe (or Wilson) and as O'Mahoney strongly suspected he knew the identity of the complainant, had I been in his shoes I would have concluded that there was a good 'reason' to do what was possible to attempt to interview McCabe. The level of public controversy at the time clearly indicated the wisdom in doing so. However, prior to my reading the PAC transcript I had no knowledge of O'Mahoney's suspicions.

The day after the 11 December 2012 Dáil exchanges and prior to the Commissioner's 'Direction' issuing, I received an email from McCabe stating that he stood by all the allegations he had reported about 'ticket fixing' and 'thousands' of 'illegally and corruptly terminated' Ticket Charges/Penalty Points. This email clearly resulted from the media reporting some of the allegations made by him to be incorrect as a result of comments made both by the Commissioner and later by me on 11 December 2012 in the Dáil.

Five days later, a detailed response, which I approved, was emailed to McCabe from Michael Flahive, Assistant Secretary in charge of the Garda Division in the Justice Department. Addressing the 'allegations of improper cancellations of Fixed Charge Notices' Flahive stated 'at the outset' that the allegations 'are taken seriously', that the Garda Commissioner had given 'a public assurance that [the] investigation will be comprehensive and rigorous' and informed McCabe of receipt of O'Mahoney's Interim Report. The letter reflected my concerns that the 'names or identities of some private citizens' had been cited in media reports and that 'members of the public are entitled to expect that, in their dealings with the Garda Síochána, their privacy and, in particular their rights under the Data Protection legislation, will be respected'. The letter requested that there be no 'rush to judgment' pending the 'final outcome' of the 'thorough and objective investigation currently underway'. It continued stating that due to 'the strength and seriousness' of his 'assertions' I believed it 'necessary to point to a few specific examples as evidence of the desirability of awaiting the final outcome of the investigation'. The letter continued:

> as regards the allegations that hundreds of cases have been wiped from PULSE to hide malpractice, my understanding from the interim report is that PULSE records cannot be erased. They can be updated, but even then the detail of the previous versions is always available. In fact, any changes made to a PULSE record leave a technical audit trail which can be followed.

> Turning to a specific allegation, you allege that a member of the board of the Road Safety Authority had a speeding case quashed. In fact the interim report discloses the Fixed Charge Notice was issued for speeding to a different person who simply had the same name as the Board member. It would appear that you wrongly assumed that this person was a member of the RSA board (and I should also add that there appears to be a reasonable explanation as to why that person had the Fixed Charge Notice cancelled).

Another allegation is that a named woman from the Dublin area was issued with four fixed charge notices relating to speeding and that these were terminated by the same Garda Inspector. This is true, but the reason they were cancelled (by the Fixed Charge Processing Office) is that the car actually captured by the GoSafe speed camera was a Garda car (which as you know is exempt from speed limits), the registration number of which differed from the registration number of the woman's car by one digit. The Fixed Charge Notices were therefore issued in error and promptly cancelled.

Another allegation was that a named person was detected at excessive speed on four occasions in 2011 within six months and that all the Fixed Charge Notices were terminated by the same Garda Inspector. In fact, the vehicles in question (three notices were in respect of one vehicle and one in respect of a different vehicle) were ambulance response vehicles on urgent calls.

In conclusion, Flahive referenced the Garda Commissioner's 'absolute' commitment 'to the proper enforcement of road traffic laws', saying 'the Garda record on this is one of which every member can be proud'. He acknowledged that 'while the major reduction in road traffic fatalities and injuries is due to a number of factors, including the excellent work of the Road Safety Authority and the responsibility of the vast majority of motorists, the work of An Garda Síochána has played a major part'.

There had been a continuous decline in road traffic fatalities. For the year 2012 the number was 160, as compared to 396 fatalities in 2005. At the time of McCabe's allegations, road fatalities were historically low. The connection between garda enforcement of the road traffic laws and the effectiveness of the Fixed Charge Notice and Penalty Points system in bringing about the fatalities reduction was entirely ignored both in Leinster House and by the media. Unfortunately, road fatalities increased in 2013 to 190. Leo Varadkar having as Transport Minister acclaimed the reduced fatalities in 2012, looked the other way when iconic RTÉ broadcaster and television personality, then Chairman of the Road Safety Authority, Gay Byrne, publicly pilloried me for their increase in 2013. Byrne blamed the increase in fatalities on reduced garda numbers resulting from the financial stringencies imposed by the Troika and agreed by the Cabinet following the State's and all the major banks' financial collapse.

During the 2011–2014 period, I had fought a rearguard battle in Cabinet and with Brendan Howlin, the Minister for Public Service and Expenditure to ensure garda numbers did not fall below 13,000. This was despite pressure from the Troika to reduce the numbers from 14,500 when the Government assumed office in 2011, to 12,000 as had been agreed by the previous Fianna Fáil-led Government. No support was ever voiced by Varadkar either in private or in public for additional funds to be allocated to Justice to maintain garda numbers at 14,500 or to recommence garda recruitment, which had stopped in 2009. By 2012, it was clear that garda enforcement of the road traffic laws had substantially reduced the numbers of road fatalities. It would also later be understood that the 2013 increase in deaths did not directly result from reduced garda numbers or checkpoints but from pedestrian deaths, motorcyclists and what became known as driver distraction caused by the use of mobile phones. All of these issues were subsequently, in March 2014, the focus of a one-day conference held by the Road Safety Authority which generated new unexpected political drama.

Michael Flahive, on my behalf, assured McCabe that 'if the investigation discloses any improper practices in relation to the enforcement of road traffic laws' the Garda Commissioner will take 'any necessary steps'. Flahive, concluding, advised McCabe that if there was 'further information in your possession which would be helpful to the investigation, the proper approach would be to provide this to your authorities within the Force'. He also advised McCabe he could utilise the services of the Confidential Recipient.

Flahive's letter to McCabe could have left him in no doubt that I was taking his allegations seriously. To ensure that both the Taoiseach and Varadkar were kept informed and aware of our engagement with McCabe following receipt of O'Mahoney's interim report, the letter to McCabe was copied by Flahive to both the Taoiseach's office and the Department of Transport, Tourism and Sport and McCabe was so informed.

Despite our keeping his Department informed of action being taken in response to McCabe's allegations and correspondence, Varadkar, fifteen months later on 20 March 2014, used a one-day conference of the Road Safety Authority as a platform for a publicity-seeking piece of self promotion. He accused the Garda Commissioner, me and the Department, of preferring to turn a blind eye than face up to the truth with regard to McCabe's allegations.

Unfortunately, none of the action taken in response to McCabe's concerns inhibited Opposition Deputies or the media from alleging his claims were being entirely ignored and suggesting that there was some sort of cover-up. This reached a crescendo in February 2014 with Micheál Martin's political attack on me, both on the Dáil plinth and in the Dáil Chamber. Varadkar, in his March 2014 demarche, simply colourfully replicated the Opposition narrative and took a public stance that, coming from a Cabinet Minister, was guaranteed to attract media attention, approval and applause.

CHAPTER 20

Disgust

My position is very clear. Anyone who makes any report of wrongdoing to me, I will deal with it very seriously. I am sure I speak for my officers beside me and elsewhere when I say that is the case … I will not allow anyone reporting wrongdoing to be bullied, harassed, intimidated or whatever adverb or adjective the Deputy [Shane Ross] chooses to use.

That will not happen on my watch … Clearly here, however, we have two people out of a force of over 13,000, who are making extraordinary and serious allegations. There is not a whisper anywhere else or from any other member of the Garda Síochána, however, about this corruption, malpractice and other charges levelled against their fellow officers.

Frankly on a personal level, I think it is quite disgusting. That said, I've openly admitted here to this Committee that there were difficulties within the system [i.e. the Fixed Charge Processing System] and that we have addressed them –Former Garda Commissioner Martin Callinan responds to questions from Shane Ross TD at a meeting of the Public Accounts Committee, 23 January 2014, considering the issue of Fixed Charge Notices issued for alleged road traffic offences

Three days after Michael Flahive's letter to McCabe, just before Christmas 2012, I wrote to the Garda Commissioner requesting that 'in addition to the detailed allegations received, a further 1% of [traffic] tickets cancelled during the period, selected at random' be investigated by O'Mahoney and his team. I believed this would help to provide as much insight as possible into the true extent of any possible illegality or abuse of the discretionary power to cancel ticket charges and penalty points. I also publicly stated that should issues of concern arise out of the *O'Mahoney Report*, I would ask the independent Garda Inspectorate to report on the ticket charge issue. My doing so was briefly reported, largely ignored and quickly forgotten.

McCabe did not, in response to either the Garda Commissioner's invitation or Flahive's letter, make any contact with O'Mahoney or any member of his team. I received O'Mahoney's final report on 28 March 2013 and the report of the Garda Professional Standards Unit about four weeks later. On 21 April 2013, McCabe emailed the Taoiseach complaining that he had not been interviewed during the O'Mahoney investigation. The email contained no reference to his request for continuing anonymity in his previous correspondence to the Taoiseach and to Varadkar nor to the request for confidentiality contained in his solicitor's correspondence to me in September 2012. Three days later, McCabe in an email to the Taoiseach, informed him that he had contacted the Assistant Commissioner's office and that O'Mahoney had returned his call. No explanation was ever given by McCabe to me for not contacting O'Mahoney in December 2012, immediately following the Commissioner's invitation to do so, or on receipt of Michael Flahive's letter.

McCabe stated that in their phone conversation he had asked O'Mahoney why he had not been interviewed and if he could be interviewed. He informed Kenny that O'Mahoney replied that he had completed his investigation, that the report was with the Minister and that he (O'Mahoney) understood that the Commissioner had informed McCabe in December 2012 that if he had any concerns he was to contact him. McCabe continued that he informed O'Mahoney that this was not correct, that a Chief Superintendent had given him 'a gagging order' and that he was not allowed to avail of his rights under the Confidential Reporting Mechanism without first contacting O'Mahoney. McCabe told Kenny that he remarked to O'Mahoney that he was seriously concerned that he had not been contacted or interviewed, that 'in keeping with fair procedures and natural justice' he should have been and that 'alarmingly, he [O'Mahoney] then asked me if I wanted to speak to someone on his investigation team. I ended our call having expressed concern about him not interviewing me.'

McCabe did not explain what was 'alarming' about being asked did he want to speak to someone on O'Mahoney's investigation team or how he reconciled his repetitive requests for anonymity with his complaint that he was neither contacted nor interviewed. On 29 April 2013, McCabe in an email to me complained of having been 'totally excluded from the penalty points investigation' and attributed this to a 'fear I would come out and reveal the truth'. At that point I believed he had excluded himself from the investigation by continuously stressing that his identity should not be revealed and by not contacting O'Mahoney or any member of his team after receipt of Michael Flahive's letter.

McCabe followed up with other emails to the Taoiseach's office, including one of 1 July 2013 in which he asserted that: 'I repeat this in the strongest possible terms: Garda authorities produced a cover up report relating to the terminations of Fixed Charge Notices. The Transport Department knows it, the RSA knows it and the public knows it. I want to show An Taoiseach the evidence to contradict O'Mahoney's report and he won't meet me.'

Other emails were sent by McCabe in the final months of 2013 and, in particular, he engaged in a lengthy email exchange with Michael Flahive in the Department of Justice. During that exchange Flahive repeatedly sought from McCabe the basis on which he had rejected the *O'Mahoney Report* and labelled it a cover up. The following extract from one such email to McCabe in November 2013 is representative:

> as you know, and has been acknowledged, the inquiry did identify a failure to follow procedures in some instances, and those procedures have since been tightened up. Disciplinary inquiries were also undertaken in some cases. The Independent Garda Inspectorate is also reviewing the process of cancellation of Fixed Charge Notices to see if any further changes are necessary.

> However, in rejecting all of the findings of the inquiry, you appear to be insisting that, for example, in the cases cited involving road traffic fatalities, the notices concerned were indeed improperly cancelled and that there is indeed a causal connection between that and the deaths. To take another example, you appear to be insisting that many cases were indeed wrongly deleted from PULSE, rather than simply transferred to be dealt with as juvenile offender cases as the inquiry found. To take another example, you appear to be insisting that the inquiry was wrong to say that some of the cases identified by you in fact involved emergency vehicles which are exempt from speed limits. I could give other examples, but I am sure that you take my point. The point is to know why, on what basis, you are rejecting all of these findings. This is a matter of significant public interest, and once again, we await your final response.

I was advised that McCabe never provided an explanation to Flahive for the stance taken by him.

The *O'Mahoney Report* uncovered substantial procedural and administrative failures and dysfunction in respect of the discretionary cancellation of Fixed Charge Notices. It also established that required detailed garda records were not always properly maintained. (When investigating such garda failures, the *O'Higgins Report* would later be rightly critical of the manner in which gardaí retrospectively updated PULSE records to fill in recording gaps that should never have occurred.) Where the prescribed procedures were followed, there were instances in some cases of unduly lenient decisions being made to cancel traffic tickets and, in others, of decisions made which I described as defying 'logic and common sense'. They were further described by me in the Dáil as 'exotic'.

The *O'Mahoney Report* was a substantial document, which together with the report of the Garda Professional Standards Unit, comprehensively examined the workings of the Fixed Charge Notice Processing System. It detailed each allegation made by McCabe and the outcome of the investigation concluded into each. It recommended that inquiries be conducted into the conduct of three senior members of An Garda Síochána to ascertain whether they were responsible for some ticket charges being terminated contrary to administrative policy and procedures. Ultimately, two were found in breach of discipline. One was reprimanded and the other had a temporary reduction in pay imposed. Sixty-two senior members of the force (Superintendents and Inspectors), found to have breached garda procedures on ticket charge cancellations, were issued with letters instructing them to adhere to prescribed procedures. Detailed recommendations for reform and change were made.

I considered both reports and was determined to ensure that the serious dysfunction disclosed did not reoccur. I was concerned that, while the *O'Mahoney Report* set out in detail the deficiencies in the decision-making process and the failures to abide by the prescribed rules and procedures, it refrained from criticising some questionable substantive decisions. Some of the decisions made cancelling traffic tickets I regarded as indefensible. I believed it was crucial and in the public interest to obtain the views of the independent Garda Inspectorate and on publication of the *O'Mahoney Report* in May 2013, I announced I was doing so.

Before publishing the *O'Mahoney Report*, I personally drafted what I described as 'The Seven Essential Principles relating to Fixed Charge

Notices' to ensure the discretionary powers to cancel such notices were exercised in a fair, impartial and transparent manner. They are as follows:

1. There must be no question mark hanging over the integrity of the Fixed Charge Notice system and in the application of penalty points.
2. No individual should receive preferential treatment because of their perceived status, relationship or celebrity.
3. The law and any discretionary application of it to individuals must be administered fairly, with compassion and common sense.
4. No member of the Garda Force should feel compelled by a person's position, relationship or celebrity status to treat that person any more or less favourably than any other person.
5. There must be proper oversight and transparency to the discretionary decision making process and the applicable rules and procedures must be fully complied with.
6. All statutory provisions, regulations, rules, protocols and procedures applicable to the termination of Fixed Charge Notices must be readily accessible to all members of the Garda Force and the circumstances, factors and procedures applicable to the termination of Fixed Charge Notices should be detailed clearly on the Garda website for the information of members of the public.
7. Where application is made to terminate a fixed ticket charge, where possible and appropriate, material to support any application made should be sought while understanding in some circumstances no such material may exist or be obtainable.

These principles were included in my statement which accompanied publication of the *O'Mahoney Report*, communicated to the Garda Commissioner for immediate implementation and provided to the Garda Inspectorate, who later incorporated them into their own report of February 2014. Pending receipt of the Garda Inspectorate's report, the Garda Commissioner swiftly moved to implement many of the key changes recommended by O'Mahoney and to strengthen the decision-making process.

I had no doubt that if not for McCabe's allegations, the dysfunctional approach to the discretionary cancellation of ticket charges would not have been identified and addressed. On the date of publication of the

O'Mahoney and GPSU reports, sensitive to McCabe's fear of his identity becoming known, I stated that there should be 'a supportive environment' in the Garda Síochána for whistle-blowers 'who have genuine concerns over apparent wrongdoing' and that they should be able to report those concerns 'without fear of adverse consequences'. I also acknowledged that 'no reasonable person could expect that a whistle-blower could or should get every minor detail right' and that what is of importance is 'the substance of a whistle-blower's concerns'.

When publishing the *O'Mahoney Report*, I could not ignore the fact that many of the more serious allegations made by McCabe against members of An Garda Síochána, already in the public domain, were not substantiated. Bureaucratic dysfunction, lack of proper oversight, procedural irregularities, inadequate record keeping and some questionable decision-making were identified. (It was not until 2017 that it publicly emerged that the same difficulties caused 15,000 road traffic summonses to be wrongly issued against motorists for failure to pay ticket charges.) However, no evidence was uncovered to suggest any corruption or criminality in the cancellation of ticket charges. McCabe's allegations of corruption, fraud and the perversion of the course of justice or the deliberate falsification or erasure of records (as opposed to a clear failure to maintain records up to date) were not upheld by the *O'Mahoney Report*. Nor were his allegations that thousands of gardaí and their family members had ticket charges wrongly cancelled. His allegations linking the cancellations of Fixed Charge Notices to any fatal road traffic accidents were also not upheld. Rejecting McCabe's allegations in relation to PULSE, the report was crystal clear, stating:

> Any changes to PULSE records made by a user will be logged in a series of 'audit' tables that are held within the database … The PULSE system does not allow records to be 'deleted', 'erased' or 'destroyed' by users once they have been saved to the database … While PULSE records can, of necessity, be updated as required for operational reasons they cannot be 'destroyed' or 'erased' and in all cases the detail of any previous version of a PULSE record is available.

Because McCabe persisted with such allegations in relation to PULSE, this issue was destined to be revisited in later reports published by other investigative bodies. In each report this conclusion is repeated.

My expression of 'concern' that some of McCabe's allegations 'were seriously inaccurate and without foundation in fact or involved an incomplete understanding of the facts' was misrepresented by Opposition TDs and wrongly presented by media commentators as displaying hostility to McCabe and garda whistle-blowers in general. Essentially, I got into trouble for telling a truth no Opposition politician or media commentator wanted to hear.

The entire garda force had been maligned by serious allegations of criminality that had not been substantiated and those bereaved by road fatalities had been led to believe that tragic deaths would not have occurred had a ticket charge not been cancelled and two penalty points imposed on specific motorists. As Minster for Justice, I believed I had a duty to set the record straight. My doing so, however, in May 2013 publicly gave birth to the personally damaging political narrative that I was in some way 'going after' McCabe. At that time I had no knowledge of the transcribed recording of the McCabe/Connolly February 2012 conversation. My expression of support for statutory reform to better protect whistle-blowers, my publication of the seven principles applicable to the discretionary cancellation of Fixed Charge Notices and my involving the Garda Inspectorate in the issue were entirely ignored.

The most serious allegations made by McCabe contended that if ticket charges imposed had been paid and not cancelled, nine road traffic deaths might have been avoided. These allegations had received significant prominence both in the print media and in the Dáil and were destined to be repeated throughout 2013, even after publication of the *O'Mahoney Report*. The allegations made and the true facts, as revealed by the O'Mahoney investigation and as published in May 2013 were as follows:

> **Allegation:** concerns a motorist who was killed in a road traffic collision and who had allegedly had a fixed charge notice cancelled 'one month earlier. She may have learnt her lesson and slowed down if she was possibly facing 4 penalty points for a second offence.'
> **Fact:** the notice was cancelled subsequent to, and as a direct consequence of, this motorist's death.

> **Allegation:** a motorist who killed a pedestrian in a hit and run collision previously had a fixed charge notice for speeding cancelled.

Fact: a duplicate notice was wrongly issued for the speeding offence and it was this duplicate notice which was cancelled. The valid fixed charge notice was not cancelled. The motorist was prosecuted and had a fine imposed by a court as well as 4 penalty points applied to his driving licence.

Allegation: a motorist lost control of his vehicle and killed a passenger, having previously had a fixed charge notice for speeding cancelled.
Fact: while the original notice was cancelled because of an error in it, a duplicate notice was issued and the motorist was prosecuted in the District Court.

Allegation: a motorist who was killed driving his car had, 6 months earlier, a fixed charge notice for driving without reasonable consideration cancelled.
Fact: what was cancelled was a duplicate notice issued in error. The motorist paid the fixed charge on the valid notice. It is also worth noting that, in the Garda investigation of the subsequent accident in which this motorist died, the motorist was not found to have been at fault.

Allegation: a person who was involved in a fatal road traffic collision, and who was arrested for killing the other driver, had 2 months earlier had a fixed charge notice for driving the wrong way up a one-way street cancelled.
Fact: a data entry error required the cancellation of the notice. A corrected notice was issued, but legal difficulties led to its cancellation. The important point here, however, is that the person concerned was a passenger in the subsequent crash, not the driver.

Allegation: a person involved in a fatal road traffic collision had 3 months earlier a fixed charge notice for speeding cancelled.
Fact: there was a very specific reason for the cancellation. The alleged speeding offence was detected by an off-duty sergeant driving his private car. The notice was terminated because of technical difficulties arising from the non-calibration of the speedometer in the sergeant's car. The motorist concerned when the O'Mahoney Report was published was awaiting trial on a charge relating to the fatality.

Allegation: a motorist who killed a pedestrian had 6 weeks earlier had a fixed charge notice for speeding cancelled.

Fact: the notice was terminated, along with other notices relating to other motorists, because of an incorrect speed limit in the area concerned, but the important point here is that the notice was issued some weeks after the fatal accident.

Allegation: a motorist who was involved in a collision where a pedestrian was killed had, 6 months later, a fixed charge notice for speeding cancelled.

Fact: in this case, a Garda investigation file was forwarded to the Director of Public Prosecutions, who directed that there should be no prosecution of the driver. The cancellation 6 months later of a notice for speeding was on the basis of a petition citing a medical emergency and clearly had no bearing on the earlier fatal collision.

Allegation: a motorist who was killed in a road traffic collision had, 10 months earlier, a fixed charge notice for speeding cancelled.

Fact: the motorist petitioned for a cancellation on the grounds that he was never at the location where the offence was detected. On reviewing the image captured by the safety camera, the Fixed Charge Processing Office validated the petition and cancelled the notice.

The *O'Mahoney Report* covered the period 1 January 2009 to 30 June 2012. The key statistics for the period were; 1,460,726 Fixed Charge Notices issued; 1,394,319 processed (95.45 per cent); 66,407 cancelled (4.55 per cent). Of the 66,407 cancellations 14,686 were cancelled for non-display of tax or insurance discs where the tax or insurance was in order or where the vehicle had changed ownership; 11,783 were cancelled because of system/detection errors and 2,554 were cancelled due to referral to the Juvenile Diversion Programme where the alleged road traffic offender was under the age of 18 years.

The balance of 37,384 cancellations (2.5 per cenr) of the total, were discretionary. Contrary to what many believed from the furore surrounding the issue, this was a nationwide rate of approximately 10,701 a year or less than two a week per garda district (garda districts can range from between one to six stations). The *O'Mahoney Report* identified 189 separate allegations made by Sergeant McCabe covering a total of 2,198 cancellations of Fixed Charge Notices. It contained a detailed analysis of 1,537 cancellations, 87 per cent of which were found to be within the correct administrative procedures, 13 per cent were not (for example, cancellations by Superintendents of notices originating outside the Superintendent's district). Due to the report referring three officers for disciplinary investigation where cancellations may not have been conducted strictly within administrative policy or procedures, the assessment of the propriety of 661 cancellations was deferred, the report stating that only some of these were to be the subject of inquiry.

At the time of publication of the *O'Mahoney Report*, discretionary cancellations were categorised as 'family bereavement' or 'medical emergency' or 'other'. I believed the 'other' category to be too broad and, as the Garda Inspectorate would later determine, it led to substantial variances in decision-making. O'Mahoney recommended the replacement of 'other' by 'humanitarian grounds' and this category was subsequently utilised but I was concerned that it was also too broad and imprecise. I emphasised the importance of 'fairness, compassion and common sense' in deciding whether to cancel a ticket charge and invited the Joint Oireachtas Justice Committee, to which I referred the O'Mahoney and GPSU reports, to consider my concern. The Justice Committee never addressed the issue, but the Garda Inspectorate did. In its report of February 2014, it recommended that legislation be enacted prescribing clear parameters for the discretionary cancellation of ticket charges. To date this recommendation has not been acted upon and the Attorney General's Guidelines on Prosecutorial Discretion continue to be applied.

In response to the O'Mahoney and GPSU reports, on 30 August 2013, Martin Callinan issued a new directive to gardaí concerning the discretionary cancellation of ticket charges and all policies and procedures associated with the management of the system were revised through an updated garda manual. As I awaited the Garda Inspectorate's report, Seamus McCarthy, the Comptroller and Auditor General (C&AG), on 30 September 2013, published a report which addressed the workings of the Fixed Charge Processing System during 2011 and 2012.

McCarthy explained that the catalyst to his report was a garda contacting his office, in July 2012, seeking a meeting and alleging 'that in many cases Fixed Charge Notices had been cancelled corruptly and illegally'. It would later emerge that Maurice McCabe had provided documentation to the C&AG on 4,000 cases. In October 2012, similar documentation provided by McCabe to Noel Brett, CEO of the Road Safety Authority had also been passed on by Brett to McCarthy. Although it was McCabe who 'prompted' McCarthy's intervention, McCarthy neither met nor spoke with McCabe prior to publication of his report. Unlike Assistant Commissioner O'Mahoney, McCarthy was not criticised for this. McCarthy's team conducted an independent analysis of ticket charges issued in 2011 and 2012 and analysed a random sample of those cancelled in six garda districts and in the Fixed Charge Processing Office in Thurles – a total of 350 cases. Contrary to some media reports, the analysis was not based on the documentation received from McCabe.

The C&AG had previously examined and reported on three occasions (2000, 2003 and 2007) on the Garda Fixed Charge Notice Processing System or its predecessor and McCabe's dossier of cases had generated concern that some previous recommendations had not been implemented. Some of these included recommendations for legislative reforms, which were the responsibility of the Department of Transport, Tourism and Sport where Leo Varadkar had been the Minister since 2011. McCarthy did not have the remit to investigate allegations of corruption or illegality made against members of An Garda Síochána, nor allegations of illegality made against members of the public, and he expressly stated that he did not do so.

The C&AG acknowledged that the gardaí were required to terminate or cancel ticket charges in certain cases where statutory exemptions were prescribed, for example, emergency response vehicles detected speeding by speed cameras. He also acknowledged that other policies allowed cancellations to be effected on a discretionary basis or in a number of specified exceptional circumstances. However, identifying 'significant operational weaknesses', he expressed concern that 'absent and inadequate records and the recorded facts of many cases gave rise to concerns that many cases have been terminated without due cause' and 'in circumstances that do not satisfy' stated policy. Replicating findings of O'Mahoney, he was concerned that senior officers were terminating tickets issued outside their districts, contrary to garda procedures. While O'Mahoney had determined that 4.55 per cent of ticket charges in total were cancelled, the C&AG covering a different time frame put the number at approximately 5 per cent. There was clearly minimal difference between their conclusions and the need to rectify operational weaknesses was undisputed.

A meeting of the Public Accounts Committee to discuss Seamus McCarthy's report, held on 23 January 2014, was attended by McCarthy and the Garda Commissioner, accompanied by senior gardaí, including Deputy Commissioner Nóirín O'Sullivan and Assistant Commissioner John O'Mahoney. By coincidence, the meeting took place exactly two years after receipt by me of McCabe's Confidential Report accusing Callinan of 'corruption'. In addition to the McCarthy report, John McGuinness, the Chairperson of the PAC, announced it had received correspondence on the issue from Maurice McCabe and retired garda John Wilson, who was assisting McCabe, and documentation from the Joint Oireachtas Justice Committee.

While the meeting was called to discuss the report of the C&AG, and Seamus McCarthy was present, it was Martin Callinan who was in the hot seat and who was extensively questioned on the Fixed Charge Notice Processing System and the discretionary cancellations. Completing his initial presentation, Callinan emphasised his commitment to ensuring the Fixed Charge Notice Processing System 'is operated in an effective and efficient manner – fairly and consistently – so as to ensure it has the confidence of the public and, most importantly, that it continues to play an important role in improving road safety by reducing poor driver behaviour'.

He acknowledged that 'the system and process have been found to be weak in a number of areas' and that there was 'no doubt' that 'record keeping has been poor' on the PULSE system, which gives 'a very limited view of the cancellations' effected. In response to questions, he clearly stated that he expected every request for cancellation of a ticket charge to be 'examined on its merits' and that he did 'not expect a member of An Garda Síochána to get involved in doing favours for their friends, family or anybody else'. He later pointed out that the *O'Mahoney Report* detailed that in 1,530 of the 1,537 terminations examined, i.e. 99.5 per cent, there was no identifiable family connection between the motorist and the garda who terminated the Fixed Charge Notice. Out of the seven cases of identifiable family members, Assistant Commissioner O'Mahoney informed the meeting that in each case the people who terminated the notices were 'not family members'.

At an early stage in the meeting, John Deasy, the Fine Gael Waterford TD, referring to the information given to Oireachtas Members and Committees by 'whistle-blowers' expressed a concern that 'in some cases it might constitute a fragment of the information around one particular case or an alleged offence'. He asserted that 'this Committee needs to be careful about how it deals with that information because it does not give the full picture' and asked the Garda Commissioner for his opinion. Callinan responded:

> that is certainly the case. If one considers the allegations that the Assistant Commissioner [O'Mahoney] has examined on behalf of all of us, it is very clear that in a substantial portion of the allegations the people who complained about corruption, malpractice, cancellations of all types had very limited access to the decision making process … they opened a screen in the PULSE system and looked at a snapshot of the actual event but they did not see the complete picture.

Where an allegation is made that a ticket has been improperly cancelled by a Superintendent, it is necessary, Callinan explained, 'to go to the District Office and examine the audit trail … to see the circumstances, to see if it has been done correctly and whether the professional judgement was proper and appropriate in the circumstances'. It was the Commissioner's view that, in the absence of such information, the PAC could not undertake a correct analysis of McCabe's allegations. However, he did acknowledge that the required information might not always be available due to poor record-keeping.

Referring to new allegations and data furnished by McCabe to the PAC which he had not seen, Callinan stated 'if I am asked in general terms whether it is appropriate for a member of An Garda Síochána to use this Committee as a platform … to make unsubstantiated allegations or provide sensitive personal data to a third party … such as this Committee – then I will have to seriously consider my position and their position'.

Saying that he had concerns about the information and data furnished to the Committee, he stated that he was taking advice as he was 'told that as we speak, I am in breach of the Data Protection Act and that it is possible that the person who supplied that information is in breach' of the Act. In his view it was 'fundamentally wrong' that a member of An Garda Síochána 'used the forum' of the PAC 'to expose material in the fashion in which it has been exposed or to make allegations that have not been substantiated'.

Emphasising the importance of An Garda Síochána's operating as a disciplined force and of he, as Commissioner, having 'control and authority over the force' he also trenchantly asserted that 'wrongdoing by any member of An Garda Síochána will not be tolerated by me or by any member of my officer corps. The Committee can take that as a given.'

For the Commissioner, there was a substantial difference between 'reporting wrongdoing and consistently putting about large volumes of material'. Referencing the 'Direction' he had issued to McCabe in 2012, Callinan continued 'in December [2012], following on from the information that the retired member of the Force [John Wilson] and the serving member, a sergeant, were working together to provide information and material for an elected representative, I took advice [from the Attorney General's office] and was advised that this is wrong.'

The fact that Callinan had acted on advice given by the Attorney General's office was, in the days that followed, ignored by his critics. Callinan asserted in a final response to Deasy that while everybody is 'entitled to be in a position to confidentially report matters of wrongdoing that come to their attention' this did not entitle individuals on a regular basis 'to make allegations that cannot be substantiated'. On being informed by the Committee's Chairman, Fianna Fáil TD John McGuinness, that the PAC intended the following week to hear evidence from McCabe, he expressed concern that he had not seen the new material furnished to the Committee and questioned the appropriateness of 'serious allegations' of a criminal and a disciplinary nature being made to the PAC by a member of An Garda Síochána and using the PAC as a 'platform to air their grievances'. It was his view that 'if any member of the Garda Síochána of any rank, anywhere, anytime, sees wrongdoing, there is an expectation and they have a statutory obligation to act on that wrongdoing'. Such action should be by 'reports through one's authorities' or by going 'through the Confidential Recipient if matters are so sensitive that one feels one cannot go any other route'. He informed the Committee that these opportunities had been offered both to Wilson and McCabe in December 2012 but that they had chosen not to use them.

Later on in the meeting Callinan disagreed with Shane Ross's assertion that if 'the whistle-blowers' did not have confidence in existing procedures their 'only option was to pursue it in the way they did', Callinan responded 'what I find extraordinary about that proposition is that both of those people engaged with the system at different stages and were selective in terms of the pieces of information they chose to bring forward without bringing forward the rest. That is what I find particularly difficult.'

Referencing the discretionary cancellation of ticket charges and '10,000 terminations a year', Ross adopted the narrative that all such terminations were wrong and accused the Garda Commissioner of 'indulging this practice'.

This clearly touched a sensitive chord with Callinan. He responded:

Of course, Deputy Ross is entitled to his view and I respect it but is it not extraordinary that it is just two individuals that are making these huge allegations of system failure and it is not dozens or hundreds of other members of An Garda Síochána that are making similar allegations ... my position is clear, anyone who makes any allegation of wrongdoing to me, I will deal with it very seriously. I am sure I speak for my officers beside me and elsewhere when I say that is the case. We will not be isolating anyone who makes a complaint of wrongdoing against another member of the Force. We have many examples within the disciplinary process where we deal with people who transgressed every year ... I will not allow anyone reporting wrongdoing to be bullied, harassed, intimidated whatever adverb or adjective he chooses to use. That will not happen on my watch ... clearly, here however, we have two people, out of a Force of over 13,000 who are making extraordinary and serious allegations. There is not a whisper anywhere else or from any other member of the Garda Síochána, however, about this corruption, malpractice and other charges levelled against their fellow officers. Frankly, on a personal level, I think it is quite disgusting. That said, I've openly admitted here to this Committee that there were difficulties within the system and that we have addressed them.

Unknown to Callinan, all future references to his response to Ross were destined to omit the last sentence and his earlier acknowledgement of garda failures.

When I first learned of the Comissioner's comments, I believed that it was likely that McCabe's repetitive allegations of 'corruption', 'criminality', 'perversion of the course of justice' and the alteration, erasure and destruction of PULSE records were to the forefront of Callinan's mind and that his reference to 'disgusting' specifically applied to such allegations and, in particular, the spurious allegation of corruption made against him two years earlier. However, I regarded his use of the word 'disgusting' as ill-considered, not only in the context of the difficult background circumstances relating to the hearing before the PAC, but also because McCabe's initial action had been the catalyst to the identification of serious deficiencies in the system.

Later in the meeting, clarifying his remarks, Callinan told Sinn Féin Deputy Mary Lou McDonald that the 'disgusting' reference related to 'the manner' in which the Ticket Charge issue had been pursued, not to the exposure of garda failures. He repeated this in a statement issued six weeks later. However, it did not prevent his comment being widely presented and viewed as his depiction and condemnation of McCabe for reporting any garda wrongdoing, failures and dysfunction.

Martin Callinan's use of the word 'disgusting' elicited no immediate response from Shane Ross TD, whose questions he was answering. But, in the days that followed, it generated enormous controversy.

The Garda Inspectorate led by Chief Inspector Robert Olsen completed in February 2014 the report I had requested on the Fixed Charge Processing System nine months earlier. I received it in early March, briefed the Cabinet on its contents on 12 March 2014 and published it that day, together with an action plan we had prepared in Justice to ensure its full implementation. The report contained comprehensive recommendations for structural, administrative and legislative reform to ensure a Fixed Charge Processing System that operated fairly, efficiently and transparently. It adopted and applied the seven principles I had prescribed in May 2013. Its recommendations covered a broad range of issues in addition to the discretionary cancellation of ticket charges by gardaí.

The Inspectorate found in its analysis of the O'Mahoney and the C&AG reports, 'that there were consistent and widespread breaches of policy by those charged with administering the Fixed Charge Notice Processing System'. With few exceptions, there was 'no meaningful evidence of consistent quality management supervision of the cancellation process' either at Garda HQ, Regional, Divisional, District or any level. In analysing cancellation practice, the Inspectorate expressed concern at the 'inconsistent nation-wide application' of the garda discretionary power to cancel ticket charges and recommended that legislation be enacted 'providing clear parameters on the use of that discretion'. Crucially, the Inspectorate recommended that the cancellation authority be centralised immediately in the Fixed Charge Processing Office in Thurles and that cancellation applications be no longer dealt with by Superintendents and

Inspectors at local district level. Resolving the dysfunction afflicting the Fixed Charge Notice System, the Inspectorate emphasised, was not solely a matter for the gardaí but required coordinated collaboration between the Department of Justice, Department of Transport, An Garda Síochána, the Road Safety Authority, the Courts Service, An Post and various appointed contractors.

I was anxious to ensure that the garda reforms needed were implemented without delay. Immediate steps were taken by Martin Callinan to start preparation of a fourth edition of the Fixed Charge Processing System Policy Procedures Manual. It became effective just five weeks after my resignation, on 16 June 2014.

Analysing seventy-six cancelled ticket charges issued for speeding to gardaí claiming to be 'on duty' while using private cars, the Inspectorate concluded that many of the cancellations granted were unjustified and lacked documentary evidence that the gardaí were 'on duty'. Robert Olson, in a radio interview, described what occurred not as 'corruption' but as 'managerial and administrative dysfunction'. The Inspectorate also identified previously highlighted long-standing deficiencies in the Road Traffic Acts relating to the enforcement of ticket charges that were the responsibility of Leo Varadkar's Department of Transport, Tourism and Sport and recommended that they be addressed in new legislation.

The recommendations for change made by the Garda Inspectorate complemented but went further than those of O'Mahoney, the GPSU and the C&AG and included twelve recommendations 'to restructure the flawed cancellation process'. In all, the report contained thirty-five recommendations for change and I secured Cabinet agreement to the establishment of a Criminal Law Working Group, as recommended by the Inspectorate to oversee their implementation. In recognition of the legislative and road safety responsibilities of Leo Varadkar, as Minister for Transport, who had already flown to the United States for St Patrick's Day events and missed the 12 March 2014 Cabinet meeting, I arranged that this group be jointly chaired by officials from both Justice and Transport and not by an official from Justice alone as proposed by the Inspectorate. It held its first meeting on 18 March 2014.

The Inspectorate reported the view of some senior garda staff that 'but for the public scrutiny the extent of the deficiencies' in the system 'would not have been detected'. Garda staff who voiced such views reflected the perspective and understanding of the general public but they were mistaken. They clearly had no knowledge of my determination to ensure McCabe's complaints were properly investigated and any deficiencies identified in the system were fully addressed. The work of O'Mahoney was well underway before the brouhaha in the Dáil and in the media about the cancellation of ticket charges. Had there been no public controversy, having read the O'Mahoney and GPSU reports, I would still have asked the Garda Inspectorate to investigate and review the operation of the Fixed Charge Notice Processing System. I had already signalled the possibility of my referring the issue to them in December 2012.

The report of the Garda Inspectorate confirmed my judgement that more needed to be done than was recommended by either O'Mahoney or the GPSU and, as it happened, the C&AG. This, of course, did not inhibit either the media or my political opponents from ignoring that it was at my initiative that the Garda Inspectorate got involved, that the difficulties and dysfunction had existed for many years preceding my appointment, that recommendations for reform repetitively made by the C&AG prior to my time in Cabinet had been ignored by my ministerial predecessors and from regarding the Inspectorate report as some sort of critique of my actions as Minister. But, of course, the ticket charge saga did not end with the Cabinet adoption on 12 March 2014 of the Garda Inspectorate report and the recommendations contained in it.

CHAPTER 21

'Real People Love the Shane and Mary Lou Show'

Melissa English, the Parliamentary Legal Advisor to the PAC warned them last week that they were crossing the line with the whistleblower stuff ... This was trumpeted by many as evidence that the PAC was out of control, out of control being regarded as a bad thing in politics, whereas ... ordinary people might regard the PAC as being out of control and beyond their remit as a good thing
– Brendan O'Connor, *Sunday Independent*, 2 February 2014

The role of the Public Accounts Committee (PAC), as detailed in its Terms of Reference, is to 'examine and report to the Dáil on accounts audited by the Comptroller and Auditor General'. The PAC can send for papers and records of relevance to these accounts and take 'oral or written evidence' of relevance to them. The report of Seamus McCarthy, the Comptroller and Auditor General of September 2013, on the Fixed Charge Notice Processing System acted as the catalyst to the committee's hearings on the issue. The committee was legally confined to considering the systems, processes and procedures employed by the Garda Síochána in the collection of money due, pursuant to the Fixed Charge Notice Processing System and, in particular, the possible loss of any money to the Exchequer. The manner in which it approached this task substantially strayed beyond its remit.

At its meeting of 23 January 2014, PAC Chairperson, Fianna Fáil's John McGuinness, for the first time in public session, informed the Garda Commissioner that additional documentation, received by the PAC from Sergeant McCabe, contained new allegations and that the PAC intended to afford McCabe a hearing. As Minister for Justice, I was not present at the meeting or aware in advance of the road the committee intended to travel. I learned from media reports that the 'additional documentation' contained allegations accusing 'over 200 senior Garda officers' of 'terminating Fixed Charge Notices inappropriately and, in most cases, corruptly'. This became a new sensational episode of the ticket charge controversy.

I knew nothing of these new allegations. McGuinness at the meeting had informed Callinan of the need for a 'comprehensive response' to these allegations 'at another time' and offered to provide copies of the documents to him. Unknown to me, correspondence had been exchanged between Callinan and McGuinness and the clerk to the PAC in the preceding two months concerning documents received by the PAC from McCabe. While Callinan did not know their content, he alleged there had been an unauthorised and unlawful disclosure of data to the PAC. The PAC denied this. Callinan objected to the PAC holding hearings on the documentation and, as the officer of An Garda Síochána legally accountable to the PAC, expressed concern about McCabe appearing before it.

'I cannot, in all fairness, have a situation where members of An Garda Síochána are coming in and making very serious allegations of a criminal nature – and a disciplinary nature – and using a platform such as this committee to air their grievances, without my having a response,' he told PAC members. He continued, 'I will not say they [McCabe and Wilson] are pursuing a particular agenda but they may very well be misguided in terms of the state of the information they feel they have.'

The PAC members were already aware that information on the PULSE system did not fully document the background circumstances to Fixed Charge Notice cancellations. It was not clear whether the 'documents' furnished by McCabe solely replicated what was on PULSE. Callinan informed the committee he would have to seek legal advice on the committee's intention to have McCabe give evidence, as proposed, for a week later. As a result, the media in the days that followed not only criticised Callinan for his use of the word 'disgusting' but also reported that the Commissioner might seek a court injunction against the PAC.

As Minister for Justice, I expected within a few weeks to receive the Garda Inspectorate report and believed Callinan had implemented substantial reform very rapidly after publication of the O'Mahoney and GPSU reports. I was surprised that new allegations of Garda corruption concerning ticket charges had been made by McCabe directly to the PAC. I was also surprised that the Committee intended that McCabe appear before it, as the PAC had no powers to properly investigate the allegations he was making or to determine whether any of the garda officers accused by him were guilty of 'corruption' or any 'illegality'. McCabe had previously complained to the Taoiseach that he had been denied fair procedures by O'Mahoney not interviewing him before finalising his report. I was now concerned that over 200 senior gardaí were going to be publicly named by him as guilty of corruption with no opportunity to protect their reputations or defend themselves.

Broadcast interviews and reported press comments of PAC members, after their meeting, convinced me that some were more interested in political grandstanding than in the substance of the issue and had given no detailed consideration to the importance of due process and fair procedures. Unknown to me then, behind the scenes during the weekend after Callinan's appearance before the PAC, Transport Minister Leo Varadkar was urging Fine Gael TD and PAC member, Eoghan Murphy, to support the proposal that McCabe appear before the committee. Murphy was one of those who doubted the wisdom of this. This unusual, and unprecedented intervention by Varadkar in the deliberative process of a committee constitutionally independent of Government, first publicly emerged in April 2018 when Murphy gave evidence before the Disclosures Tribunal. Whether Varadkar had similar conversations with other Fine Gael members of the PAC, I do not know.

I believed the PAC would be acting unlawfully and substantially outside its terms of reference if it afforded McCabe a public platform to accuse garda officers of corruption but had little doubt that some of its members would perceive such an event as a self-promoting publicity triumph. I believed it was totally wrong, enormously damaging to An Garda Síochána and would unfairly jeopardise the good name and reputation of 200 individual gardaí.

At the meeting of 23 January 2014, Shane Ross had accused Callinan and Assistant Commissioner O'Mahoney of 'indulging' a system of widespread cancellation of Penalty Points, ignoring the reforms already implemented. Speaking the next day on RTÉ's *Morning Ireland*, he had depicted Callinan's attitude to the PAC as 'most disdainful'. Ross attached no importance to Callinan's legitimate concerns about the privacy of data collected by An Garda Síochána and the use of the proper procedures to investigate allegations of wrongdoing. He displayed no concern that over 200 gardaí could be wrongly publicly pilloried as corrupt.

Unexpectedly, Niall Collins, Fianna Fáil's Justice spokesperson, criticised the approach taken by the PAC. He said, 'listening to Deputy Shane Ross this morning, I would have some serious concerns about the approach that certain members of the PAC are taking towards their interaction with the Gardaí'. Recognising the importance of the PAC's work, Collins cautioned that 'Deputies need to be careful that, in their enthusiasm to find the next villain, they do not undermine that work.'

Collins, for his troubles, was subsequently attacked by his Fianna Fáil colleague, PAC Chairperson, John McGuinness, who described Collins's reference to 'villains' as 'outrageous and absurd'. McGuinness asserted that the treatment of whistle-blowers in Ireland was 'disgusting' in response to the Commissioner's 'disgusting' remark at the PAC meeting. This was an extraordinary outburst and prejudgement by the Chairperson of the PAC in the midst of a hearing process. He then stated that the PAC 'operates above politics', and that its mission was to 'seek to find the truth'.

Over two years later, in May 2016, McGuinness would reveal in the Dáil that a meeting took place in the car park of Bewley's Hotel, on the Naas Road, unknown to both members of the PAC and to me, between him and Callinan, the day after Callinan's PAC appearance, and alleged that Callinan made 'vile' allegations about McCabe. While Callinan acknowledged they had met, he would dispute McGuinness's version of the conversation and, amidst other controversy, this issue would ultimately be addressed by the Disclosures Tribunal.

During the Tribunal's hearings in the spring of 2018, it emerged that Callinan, before arranging to meet McGuinness to attempt to persuade him against McCabe appearing before the PAC, had discussed with Brian Purcell his intention to do so. Following their meeting, he informed Purcell of the outcome. Purcell acknowledged that he did not, at any stage, discuss the meeting with me. If he had, I would have instructed Purcell to inform Callinan that a meeting between him and the chairperson of the PAC, on their own, to discuss an issue subject to public hearings before the PAC, was both unwise and inappropriate.

As Minister for Justice, I was an observer of the events relating to the PAC's engagement in the ticket charge issue and knew nothing of the allegations that would emerge in the years that followed. What I initially knew of the PAC's meeting derived from media reports. It was not until some time later, upon it being furnished to me, that I read the full transcript of the exchanges that took place at the PAC.

In the days that followed the PAC's meeting, there was much excited media commentary and speculation as to what would happen at its next meeting, whether McCabe would appear and give evidence in public or private and what action the Commissioner would take. On Saturday, 25

January 2014 Conor Lally, the *Irish Times* crime correspondent, reported that Transport Minister, Leo Varadkar, referencing the Government's commitment to transparency, believed that McCabe should be able to appear before the PAC. It was not an issue Varadkar had discussed with me and no reference was made to his personally lobbying any member of the Committee.

Labour's Minister for Communications, Pat Rabbitte, was reported as having a more nuanced perspective stating that if the committee was satisfied it had a credible witness, it was 'perfectly entitled to question him, so long as he doesn't reflect on the character of colleagues who are not there to defend themselves'. For my part I simply did not know what type of hearing the Committee would embark upon. As I believed it important to respect the Committee's constitutional independence, I refrained from making any public comment and from attempting to privately influence the approach taken by any of its members.

I had increasing concern that if we continued down this path, further damage would be done to garda morale and public confidence in An Garda Síochána. I also believed that if the PAC acted unlawfully outside its remit, it was at risk of being ultimately perceived as engaged in a witch-hunt, reminiscent of the McCarthyite era of the 1950s in the United States. All that January, I believed that the O'Mahoney and GPSU reports, the report of the C&AG together with the anticipated report from the Garda Inspectorate were a proper and proportionate response to the allegations made and the deficiencies identified and I was concerned to ensure that the work of GSOC was not overwhelmed by the ticket charge issue. However, as a consequence of McCabe newly alleging that over 200 garda officers were guilty of corruption, and in order to defuse the controversy, I decided that the public interest now required all allegations of misconduct concerning ticket charges made by McCabe be referred by me to GSOC. On Monday, 27 January 2014, I issued a statement announcing I was doing so. I expressed concern that 'some members' of the PAC 'have a tendency to prejudge issues that the committee is considering' and that 'recent comments of that minority posed the risk of bringing the work of the Committee into disrepute, undermining its role and its credibility'. On the same day, the Commissioner lifted his objection to McCabe giving evidence before the PAC and Assistant Garda Commissioner for Human Resources, Ronan Fanning offered him any supports he required.

In addition to investigating the allegations made, I also asked GSOC to investigate the manner in which they had been pursued and issues relating to the preservation of the confidentiality of garda records.

There was division within the PAC as to whether McCabe should be allowed to give evidence before it, whether if he did the Committee would be acting outside its powers and whether any evidence he might give should be heard in public, as was usual, or in private. These difficulties were resolved when McCabe expressed a preference for appearing in private and those opposed to his appearing backed off. Ultimately, on the Thursday of that week all the public got to see of McCabe was his walking up Kildare Street, through the gates of Leinster House, his garda uniform partially concealed by an anarak. McCabe gave his evidence in private and the Committee, in its report into the issue published in October 2014, stated that it did not consider the merits or otherwise of the allegations GSOC was asked to investigate. It also stated that, in the distribution of McCabe's documentation to PAC members, no personal identifying data was circulated and that the documents supplied by McCabe confirmed the findings of the C&AG. The committee also acknowledged that the records derived from PULSE 'did not have the background papers which may have supported decisions made to cancel penalty points [Fixed Charge Notices]'.

The PAC fairly found that 'the actions of the whistle-blowers have contributed to improvements in the oversight of the cancellation process'. Referencing the Commissioner's 'description' of the actions of the whistle-blowers as 'disgusting' the PAC critically commented that the Commissioner 'put a huge degree of emphasis on the need to maintain discipline within the Force'. Despite detailing 'the considerable resources taken up by the examination of the dossier by Assistant Commissioner O'Mahoney' and detailing the action taken to address the deficiencies identified, the PAC criticised 'the desire to protect the organisation' as being 'placed ahead of ensuring that the complaints from the whistleblower [McCabe] were followed up on'. While criticism of O'Mahoney for failing to address some of the questionable decisions made to cancel ticket charges would have been reasonable, the PAC's blanket criticism was not only unfair but also a total distortion of the facts. The truth is that, within days of the substantial allegations made by McCabe being furnished to the Commissioner by the Justice Department in October 2012, the O'Mahoney investigation commenced and by the time of the PAC January

2014 hearings, a substantial amount of reform had been implemented. The recommendations ultimately contained in the Garda Inspectorate's report of 2014 were a great deal more comprehensive than those ultimately published by the PAC seven months later. It was clear, however, from the Garda Inspectorate report that more change was required.

In September 2014, a month before the publication of the PAC's report on the Fixed Charge Notice Processing System, further controversy arose when McCabe made new allegations that the cancellation process was being abused. Just days before, the then 'interim' Garda Commissioner Nóirín O'Sullivan, who had taken over from Martin Callinan, had sought a report from the GPSU on the workings of the system between 1 September 2013 and 31 August 2014. She asked the GPSU to extend its work to include McCabe's allegations. This time, McCabe was not only interviewed, but nine meetings were conducted with him and he worked with the GPSU. Prior to any report being published, he was also briefed on the outcome of the investigation. The GPSU report which was ultimately published identified some minor continuing dysfunction but found that substantial improvements had been made on foot of recommendations made both by O'Mahoney and the Garda Inspectorate and, in particular, since the introduction by Martin Callinan of a new Garda Manual on 16 June 2013. As had occurred previously, some concerns raised by McCabe were validated, while others were not. New concerns raised by him, as well as being addressed by the GPSU, were also passed on by my successor, Frances Fitzgerald, to GSOC in September 2014, at Nóirín O'Sullivan's request, to be included in the investigation I had asked GSOC to undertake eight months earlier.

On publication of the GPSU report at the end of January 2015, Fitzgerald announced the appointment of Judge Matthew Deery, former President of the Circuit Court, to the new position of Independent Oversight Authority for the Fixed Charge Processing System. His remit included random inspections of Fixed Charge Notice cancellations and reporting his findings on the operation of the system to the Minister. In circumstances in which such oversight function was already exercised by the GPSU, the Garda Inspectorate, the Comptroller and Auditor General, the PAC and GSOC, it was reasonable to assume that it was hoped that the judge would pre-empt the necessity for any of these bodies to initiate any further review or investigation into the Fixed Charge Notice Processing System following GSOC concluding its then outstanding investigations.

The Independent Oversight Authority was also clearly created as a political shield to protect the Minister for Justice and the Government from any political fallout should any further dysfunction in the Fixed Charge Notice Processing System be identified by Sergeant Maurice McCabe or by anyone else in the future. It was also obviously designed to protect Frances Fitzgerald from any political blowback that might in the future result from a McCabe-related controversy.

I had been vilified in 2012 and 2013 for not initially referring McCabe's allegations about the cancellation of ticket charges to GSOC. I had finally done so on 27 January 2014 after McCabe's new allegations to the PAC, announced by its chairperson, John McGuinness TD, that over 200 senior garda officers had 'inappropriately' and 'in most cases corruptly' cancelled such notices. It took until early December 2017 for GSOC's report on the issue, completed in October 2017, to be published. The organisation had taken almost four years to produce a report following my request that it investigate all of McCabe's allegations relating to the Fixed Charge Notice Processing System and that request being supplemented in September 2014. by Frances Fitzgerald upon McCabe making new allegations. Clearly, had I simply in late 2012 requested GSOC to undertake an investigation, the reforms implemented in 2013 and 2014 would have been delayed by three to four years.

GSOC's primary role is to investigate allegations of garda misconduct. The rolling political and media frenzy that resulted from the allegations made by McCabe on the ticket charge/penalty points issue, was substantially fuelled by repetitive allegations of corruption, fraud, criminality, perversion of the course of justice by gardaí, including senior gardaí, and by allegations that records held on the garda PULSE data system had been falsified, altered, deleted, erased or destroyed. By January 2014 it had been clearly established that there was substantial administrative dysfunction in the Fixed Charge Processing System and significant action had been taken to address it. It was also publicly known that the Garda Inspectorate was revisiting the issue and about to publish its own comprehensive report. My primary objective in involving GSOC was for it to address the continuing allegations of garda corruption and criminality made by McCabe to various bodies and Dáil members, including the Department of Justice, and the new allegations made by him to the PAC that over 200 senior garda officers had 'inappropriately' and 'in most cases, corruptly' terminated ticket charges.

GSOC's report entitled *Investigation of Fixed Charge Notice Cancellations 2009–2014* finally emerged in December 2017. It was a curiously misnamed document which essentially explained why GSOC had not conducted the full investigation I had requested. It also revisited some of the linguistic inexactitude and lack of intellectual rigour exhibited by GSOC members during the so-called GSOC bugging controversy. It reported that GSOC's engagement was little more than a desktop analysis or scoping exercise involving an examination of PULSE data, a peer review of reports previously completed on the Fixed Charge Notice Processing System and the obtaining of 'statement(s) and any documentary evidence from Sergeant Maurice McCabe'. As with earlier reports published, it confirmed poor governance practices in the administration of the Fixed Notice Processing System during the period examined. It also identified some of the traffic ticket cancellations that had caused me concern and resulted in my seeking a report from the Garda Inspectorate. The report importantly confirmed that 'significant corrective' action had been taken and changes made, 'inserting rules and controls that did not previously exist'.

Some of my most prominent Dáil critics and some media commentators had denied that gardaí could lawfully exercise any discretion with regard to the imposition of ticket charges/penalty points and the initiation of prosecutions under the Road Traffic Acts. This issue had already been addressed in some of the earlier reports reviewed by GSOC, including the *O'Mahoney Report*, but what GSOC had to say on this as an independent investigative body concerned with garda misconduct was of particular interest. It stated that:

> Clearly, the use of discretion by individual Gardai is an important part of their daily work. Not all breaches of the law merit a criminal prosecution. The circumstances of a breach, the person or persons involved and the greater common good should all be taken into consideration. GSOC accepts that the public in general, would have no difficulty in accepting the use of discretion not to impose a penalty, for example, on a driver in a minor breach of the road traffic rules and regulations if they are genuinely involved in a medical emergency. However the application of such discretion must be fair and equitable, as well as transparent.

This perspective of GSOC accurately reflected the content of the seven principles detailed by me upon publication of the *O'Mahoney Report* in May 2013 and endorsed by the Garda Inspectorate in its report of February 2014. It was also consistent with the *O'Higgins Report* of 2016, discussed further on, which recognised the value of the use by gardaí 'of a transparent, intelligible system of discretion as a tool of effective policing' and acknowledged that the gardaí should not 'operate an inflexible rule of prosecuting every minor infraction'. It entirely undermined the narrative that no garda discretion was lawfully applicable to Road Traffic offences. Of course, this aspect of GSOC's report was largely ignored.

The *GSOC Report* detailed that Sergeant McCabe had attended GSOC's offices on five occasions for interviews and that GSOC had received from him 'the dossier of information from the PULSE system and other papers which had previously been passed to other agencies'. The report then continued, 'Sergeant McCabe then went into specific detail relating to a number of cancellations where he believed wrongdoing had occurred, providing details, names of Garda members involved and the situation set out in each cancellation.'

Recording that data received from An Garda Síochána 'provided some corroboration with regards to the cancellation of the Fixed Charge Notices examined' as part of its preliminary 'scoping' exercise, GSOC stated it was 'satisfied the allegations put forward by Sergeant McCabe had considerable merit'. However, GSOC did not distinguish between the different allegations made by McCabe or identify to which allegations it was attaching 'merit'. Towards the end of its report, GSOC's endorsement of McCabe's allegations appeared more qualified, stating: 'The data considered in the investigation allows GSOC to be satisfied that the allegations made by Sergeant McCabe in relation to the operation of the FCPS were merited.'

Most people reading the report would not have noticed but it appeared that GSOC somewhat opaquely confined its order of 'merit' to the allegations made 'in relation to the operation of the Fixed Charge Processing System' itself and did not endorse or substantiate the more extreme allegations made by McCabe, including those of corruption and serious criminality. Having reviewed all of the published reports preceding GSOC's 2017 publication, it reasonably and fairly expressed doubt as to whether the overhaul of the cancellation processing system would have come about 'without the intervention of Sergeant McCabe'.

GSOC's report received limited media attention and generated little political response. For those at the forefront of the political and media frenzy to which I had been subjected in 2014, it was simply seen as a further endorsement of McCabe's allegations and status as a famous whistle-blower. For most, whether any allegations made were mistaken, exaggerated, unfounded, unjustified or baseless did not matter. But the truth matters and there is considerable difference between administrative dysfunction, defective governance, inadequate record-keeping and inconsistent and poor decision-making as compared to garda corruption, fraud, criminality, the perversion of the course of justice and the deliberate falsification, alteration, erasure and destruction of garda data and records. Allegations that road fatalities resulted from such conduct also matter. On all of these, GSOC's report when carefully trawled was particularly interesting.

It referenced 'the serious nature of the allegations made, that is, corruption, perversion of the course of justice and destruction/falsification of records' and acknowledged that the pursuit of this would require an 'additional' investigative exercise and expressed concern about the costs involved in any such investigation. If there was a substantial basis for the latter allegations it would be expected such investigation would proceed and cost would not be an issue. The last allegation to be given a public airing before GSOC was asked to investigate corruption by possibly over 200 senior gardaí. In assessing this and other allegations GSOC had met on five occasions with McCabe and read all of his documentation and data. On the basis that such an investigation 'would result in considerable cost to the State' and amongst other things, there 'was a lack of supporting documentation for a large proportion of the cancellations' and 'no guarantee that the prosecution of, or disciplinary action against, any garda member could be taken' GSOC concluded that no further investigation should take place as it was 'very unlikely to provide positive outcomes'.

Translated, this meant no substantive evidence existed which could be relied upon to prove the more serious allegations that McCabe had repeatedly made and that for GSOC a 'positive outcome' required a criminal prosecution or disciplinary action. For gardaí accused of corruption and criminality, it was of major importance that GSOC's report implicitly determined that no credible and convincing evidence existed to substantiate allegations of criminal and corrupt conduct which justified any further investigation or expenditure of public funds. But this should have been explicitly stated. For my part, when Minister for Justice, I had been frequently accused of covering up garda criminality and corruption in the cancellation of traffic tickets and penalty points. Five years after the start of public controversy on that issue, when McCabe's allegations were first vigorously promoted in the Dáil by Deputies Daly, Wallace, Ming Flanagan and Joan Collins, GSOC had established that the documentation and data furnished to it by Maurice McCabe to substantiate his allegations did not merit a full criminal investigation. As for the alleged alteration, falsification, erasure and destruction of PULSE data, repeatedly alleged by McCabe, that had received considerable public prominence, GSOC had the following to say:

> For data security, all PULSE users have their own user account and password. Access to PULSE is exclusively via these security protocols, and once access is granted, each activity undertaken is logged by the system. Any change to PULSE records made by a user will be logged in a series of audit tables that are held within the database. The detail captured as part of these audit records, includes a copy of the record prior to the alteration, the details of the user who made the change, the date and the time of the change and, finally, when alterations were made. As a result, what has been changed, by whom and when it changed and what it changed to, can be definitively identified. *The PULSE system does not allow records to be deleted, erased or destroyed by users once they have been saved to the database.*
>
> (Author's emphasis)

In explaining the workings of PULSE, GSOC essentially confirmed the integrity of the *O'Mahoney Report*'s description and the information contained in Michael Flahive's December 2012 letter to McCabe after my receipt of O'Mahoney's Interim Report. However, GSOC did not expressly acknowledge it was endorsing O'Mahoney's description of PULSE nor did its own understanding of PULSE result in GSOC formally rejecting, as it should have done, McCabe's repetitive allegations of gardaí altering, deleting, erasing or destroying PULSE records. Inexplicably, in a later part of its report it revived these 'serious' allegations made by McCabe when repeating them and then concluding that no further investigation should be undertaken. As for McCabe's allegations, much publicised by Opposition TDs, media reporters and commentators, that up to nine road fatalities may not have occurred had ticket charges been paid and penalty points been imposed, GSOC had nothing to say at all.

GSOC had a public obligation to provide absolute clarity on a garda-related issue that had been the focal point of enormous public and political controversy for over five years. It totally failed to do so. Part of GSOC's remit was to examine 'the circumstances surrounding the making' of McCabe's allegations and 'the manner in which they were pursued'. This involved addressing the disclosure of confidential information held on PULSE in the national media and the right to privacy of individuals being violated. Without any reasonable explanation GSOC studiously avoided mentioning and addressing those issues. It just oddly reported that in pursuing his allegations Sergeant Maurice McCabe had 'obtained legal advice about who he was entitled to disclose information to and how to maintain the lawfulness of such disclosure'.

Referencing the 2017 *GSOC Report* has jumped our narrative forward by four years. There was still more to be played out in the ticket charge story back in the autumn of 2013 and a lot more political drama to occur in 2014. It's now time to go back there.

CHAPTER 22

A Failed Prophet and
a Ticking Time Bomb

It is only fair to acknowledge that these reports and their findings and recommendations are in response to allegations of improper cancellation of Fixed Charge Notices. However, any fair assessment must also conclude, on the evidence available, that a great many of the most serious allegations have been found to be utterly without basis, including allegations of avoidable road fatalities linked to speeding drivers being improperly let off fixed charge notices and allegations of hundreds of PULSE records being destroyed
–Alan Shatter as Minister for Justice, Dáil Éireann, 1 October 2013, Topical Issues Debate on the cancellation of ticket charges on receipt of a report into the issue by the C&AG

It was 1 October 2013, and there was yet another exchange in the Dáil Chamber on ticket charges and penalty points. It was a Topical Issues Debate originated by Sinn Féin's Padraig MacLochlainn TD and the Socialist Party Leader, Joe Higgins TD, the day after the critical report published by the C&AG. I acknowledged, as I had done previously, that the critical findings and recommendations 'are in response to allegations of improper cancellation of Fixed Charge Notices'. I also point out that 'any fair assessment must also conclude, on the evidence available, that a great many of the most serious allegations have been found to be utterly without basis, including allegations of avoidable road fatalities linked to speeding drivers being improperly let off Fixed Charge Notices and allegations of hundreds of PULSE records being destroyed'. I also referred to the fact that 'the member of the Garda Síochána who made the allegations' (Maurice McCabe's identity had not yet been publicly revealed and I continued to respect his wish for anonymity) continues to claim there has been 'widespread corruption and criminality on the part of senior members of the Force'. I informed the Dáil that the Justice Department had written 'to the member concerned, urging him to come forward with any evidence he may have to justify these allegations' and stated that he had 'not done so'. I continued: 'having engaged with members of this House and published material they [the whistle-blowers] did not cooperate with the garda investigation that took place. I do not know why that was the case.'

I believed that, following the overture contained in the Garda Commissioner's Direction and Michael Flahive's correspondence, McCabe should have clearly understood that he had an open invitation to discuss any concerns about Fixed Charge Notices and Penalty Points he wished to raise with O'Mahoney or any member of his team, and that he was not confined to discussing only those allegations originally made by him. He had insisted that his anonymity/confidentiality be preserved and I believed he should have also understood that, if his wishes were respected, O'Mahoney was not in a position to directly approach him for an interview or discussion. I was concerned that if I had ignored his request for anonymity when forwarding his allegations on to the Garda Commissioner in October 2012, either myself as Minister for Justice, or the State, would have been at risk of his initiating a court action for damages. I believed at that time had O'Mahoney directly approached McCabe, there was a risk that he and/or the Garda Commissioner could also have found themselves named as defendants in court proceedings and could have been the subject of another complaint by McCabe. Only two years earlier, Assistant Commissioner Derek Byrne had been subject to investigation after McCabe had accused him of assault and false imprisonment. Even after the DPP had determined no charges were to be brought against Byrne, McCabe had made additional allegations against Byrne in his report of 23 January 2012 furnished by the Confidential Recipient to me. I understood why O'Mahoney had not interviewed McCabe but did not understand why McCabe had not contacted O'Mahoney before his investigation had concluded.

I regarded McCabe's request that his identity not be disclosed as the complainant and his later complaint that he had not been interviewed about his allegations as incompatible and mutually exclusive. Moreover, at no stage prior to my receipt of O'Mahoney's report had McCabe or his solicitors informed me or the Department, in response to Michael Flahive's letter, that he was willing or wished to talk to Assistant Commissioner O'Mahoney or any member of his team.

McCabe continued to reject the outcome of O'Mahoney's investigation while offering no evidence to substantiate his continuing dogmatic belief in the accuracy of every allegation made by him, including his allegations of corruption, criminality and road fatalities resulting from the cancellation of ticket charges. I regarded my reference to McCabe's lack of cooperation as a reasonable description of what had occurred. Over time I had concluded that McCabe's understandable insistence on anonymity when making allegations, together with his complaints of not being interviewed about allegations for which he claimed anonymity and his insistence on the accuracy of all his allegations, including those proven to be unfounded, created a quagmire of complexity which had the capacity to detrimentally impact on anyone genuinely committed to addressing his concerns. No matter how committed one was to dealing with issues he raised, the accompanying background drama and mood music created a sense of tiptoeing on glass or sinking in quicksand. However, this was not the insight of any Opposition TD or commentator. As a result, my references to unsubstantiated allegations made by him and his 'non-cooperation' with O'Mahoney added fuel to the narrative depicting me as going after McCabe and being too close to the Garda Commissioner with whom I was supposed to be engaged in some sort of cover-up.

As far as Opposition Deputies and the news media were concerned, McCabe had, at all times, fully cooperated, acted impeccably, all his allegations were correct and I was intent on damaging his reputation. As far as I was concerned, I was simply telling the truth based on my knowledge of the background circumstances and the complexities that had arisen. Calls were made for me to apologise to McCabe and correct the Dáil record and they reached their crescendo amidst the perfect storm of garda controversies in February 2014. Despite the perception that developed, I had at no stage any personal animus towards McCabe. I was merely intent on ensuring issues raised by him were properly and reasonably addressed and that the reputations of gardaí and members of the public were not damaged by allegations that were false or exaggerated. I was also frustrated by his insistence that every allegation made by him was correct even in circumstances where the evidence overwhelmingly established he was mistaken.

In reply to Opposition criticism on 26 February 2014, in the debate in which the appointment of Sean Guerin was announced, I addressed the charge that I had misled the Dáil in October 2013, when claiming McCabe had not cooperated with the O'Mahoney investigation. I explained that 'I expected Sergeant McCabe would fully engage as a member of An Garda Síochána with Assistant Commissioner O'Mahoney's investigation team and that he would be interviewed. These are operational matters in which no Minister of Justice should interfere and, of course, any interference would be rightly subject to public criticism.' I continued stating that what was at issue was an interpretation of events. I continued:

> In what I said to the House, I relied on material which I received detailing the content of a direction given to Sergeant McCabe on a related matter, which included inviting him to participate in the O'Mahoney investigation and the fact that a letter had been sent from an official in my Department in December 2012 which, specifically, advised Sergeant McCabe that any further information which might be helpful to the investigation should be brought by him to the attention of his authorities within the Force. This letter is one of a number of letters exchanged by my Department either directly with Sergeant McCabe or with his solicitors. The situation is further complicated by the fact that, between the finalisation of the O'Mahoney report and its publication, he declined to take up an offer from Assistant Commissioner O'Mahoney to meet with a member of his investigation team. Had such a meeting taken place and some additional matters arisen of relevance to the investigation, I could have been notified of any amendments required to the report undertaken and its publication could have been delayed.

Referencing the fact that there was 'a difference of views and perceptions between An Garda Síochána and Sergeant McCabe with regard to this issue', I acknowledged that 'different Members of the House [i.e. the Dáil] may perceive these matters differently' and lamented that 'it is unfortunate that perceptions are coloured on occasion by political differences'.

Unsurprisingly, the issue did not rest there and was pursued during the debate that took place and questions afterwards. Repeated demands for me to apologise were made by Opposition TDs. By that time, Oliver Connolly's bizarre conversation recorded by McCabe was being presented as absolute proof that I was out to 'get' McCabe or to do him down.

The first two weeks in March 2014, following the Fine Gael Ard Fheis, were hectic but apart from some newspaper articles reprising the February 2014 garda controversies, my world substantially calmed down. Retired High Court Judge John Cooke and Sean Guerin SC were each embarking on their inquiries; I was confident that their reports could not create any major difficulties for me. In fact, it was my expectation that following their publication both my political opponents and various media commentators would have little choice but to back off and accept that much of the criticism and vitriol directed at me was unjustified. I also hoped that publication of the Garda Inspectorate Report on the Fixed Charge Notice Processing System and the implementation of the Inspectorate's recommendations, once adopted by Cabinet, would take the heat out of the ticket charge issue. In the background, calls for the Garda Commissioner to apologise for his 'disgusting' reference and for me to apologise for my 'non-cooperation' comment rumbled on, but it seemed the heat had temporarily gone out of the issues. What I could not foresee was that both issues would be reignited by a Fine Gael Cabinet colleague three weeks later when I was abroad on Government business and without any prior notice to me or any engagement between our special advisers.

Monday and Tuesday (3–4 March) were taken up by a meeting in Brussels of the European Union Justice and Home Affairs Ministers. I always found these meetings interesting and stimulating in addressing a broad range of justice and security issues. There could often be very differing views across the twenty-eight member states. Other events that week included meetings on aspects of the Legal Services Regulation Bill and the launch and publication of the Irish Prison Service and Probation Service annual reports. The most enjoyable event of the week was the Citizenship Ceremonies, held for the first time in Waterford City Hall, with the participation of both the Army and An Garda Síochána. I had arranged for information desks, staffed by both the Defence Forces and An Garda Síochána, to encourage some of our new Irish citizens to consider either as a career choice for themselves or their children. The warmth of the participants and the celebratory atmosphere, as always, was a great fillip. After each ceremony, over tea, cake and many photographs, I did my best to engage with as many of our new citizens as possible.

The following week was both busy and productive. Monday 10 March involved a visit to Kilkenny wearing both my Justice and Defence hats. On the Justice side, I had a detailed briefing on local crime and a variety of garda concerns at Kilkenny Garda Station and visited a Direct Provision Centre where I spoke with staff members and residents awaiting decisions on their asylum applications or outstanding court cases. The visit reinforced my determination to introduce reforming immigration and asylum legislation, substantially reduce the numbers in Direct Provision Centres, ensure that very few need reside in such centres longer than six months and, after six months, enable those still awaiting a decision on their asylum application to obtain temporary employment. On the Defence side, I had a working lunch in Stephens Barracks with members of the Defence Forces and then participated in a review of our latest contingent of troops departing on a UN mission to the Golan Heights. The mission involved overseeing the truce between Israel and Syria effective following the Yom Kippur war in 1973 and had, for many years, been largely uneventful but had now become a great deal more complicated because of the Syrian civil war and the violence being perpetrated on the Syrian side of the Golan Heights. The troop review was followed by a brief press conference at which the intense media hostility and questioning about garda matters that had characterised press engagements in the previous weeks was absent.

On that Monday, as was usual, during the drive down to Kilkenny and back to Dublin, I worked on a variety of Justice and Defence papers and took a number of phone calls from Departmental officials and others of relevance to each of my ministerial briefs. Later that week, I completed, before the Justice Committee, the Committee Stage of the mammoth and ground breaking Bill to establish a DNA database to assist the gardaí in the investigation of crime. I also attended a lunch in the Belgian Embassy for EU member state ambassadors based in Dublin to deliver an unscripted speech and take a question and answer session on EU Justice, Defence and other EU issues of interest.

Tuesday morning, 11 March, I met with officials in my Justice office to discuss legislation under preparation and worked on both Justice and Defence files. Usually Tuesday mornings were occupied by a Cabinet meeting but that week's meeting was scheduled for Wednesday afternoon. Unknown to me, that Tuesday morning a meeting of enormous importance was taking place in the Department of Justice between, amongst others, Brian Purcell and Martin Callinan. Tuesday lunchtime was spent in the Mexican Embassy discussing with the ambassador my planned St Patrick's week visit to Mexico City, starting on Saturday, 16 March

The visit to Mexico City, as planned, was a mixture of diplomacy, trade promotions, community and police meetings, engagements with the Mexican Jewish community, media interviews and participation in St Patrick's Day-related ceremonies and events. Although the programme was hectic, I was looking forward to a few days away from the hurly burly of domestic politics. Carol was accompanying me and we planned to arrive in Mexico City late Saturday evening. The official events were scheduled to take place from Sunday morning through to Wednesday evening. Before any journalist feels the need to put in an FOI request, I should explain that I paid Carol's airfare so that she could accompany me on the trip. After the official events, we had arranged to fly to Cancún for a three-day break and return to Dublin on the Sunday.

I had been embroiled in a political maelstrom since early February, the subject of continuing political and social media abuse and invective and I believed we deserved a real three-day break away from it all. As the plane took off, I was cheerfully oblivious to the ticking political time bomb that had landed in the office of Brian Purcell, just five days earlier on Monday, 10 March, when I was in Kilkenny. The handling of that bomb, both by Purcell and Michael Flahive and those working with him in the Garda Division of the Department of Justice, was to set the scene for an explosive garda-related crisis and political drama. It was destined to prematurely end Martin Callinan's career as Garda Commissioner, cause further damage to my reputation, result in a Statutory Commission of Investigation presided over by a respected retired Judge of the Supreme Court and my ultimately giving sworn evidence to that Commission contradicting evidence given by both Taoiseach Enda Kenny and Attorney General Máire Whelan. In mid-air on the way to Mexico, there was no reason to anticipate the explosion to come.

CHAPTER 23

'Distinguished not Disgusting'

Alan – saw your statement. You might bear in mind in any reference to my dept that several legislative measures in the 2010 (Road Traffic) act still have not been introduced due to delays by Gardai and court services –Text message to Alan Shatter from Leo Varadkar, Minister for Transport, Tourism and Sport, Tuesday, 11 March 2014, referencing Shatter's draft statement circulated some days earlier to Cabinet members together with a memo seeking Cabinet agreement on 12 March 2014 to publication of the Garda Inspectorate's Report on the Fixed Charge Notice Processing System

The Garda whistle-blowers ... have come in for some criticism from some quarters for releasing Garda information about private individuals. I understand this criticism but I do not agree with it. The Garda whistle-blowers only released this information after they tried and failed to have their concerns addressed through official channels and proper means. They released the information in an effort to expose bad practice and protect the public and this was done through contact with Members of the Oireachtas which is expressly provided for in the Garda Acts. Speaking on my own behalf and on behalf of the thousands of families who have had to endure the pain and loss that follows from the death of a loved one on the road, I want to thank Sergeant McCabe and Mr Wilson. They may not have got everything right but they did shine a light into a dark place and forced those who would rather turn a blind eye to face up to the truth. There have been many words used to describe their actions. But if I was to use one word, the word I would use is 'distinguished' –Leo Varadkar, Minister for Transport, Tourism and Sport, Road Safety Authority conference, March 2014

No good deed goes unpunished –Clare Boothe Lucy, dramatist, author, political activist and former United States Ambassador

Thursday, 20 March 2014. It was 4am in Mexico City and I was sound asleep in a Marriott hotel. The last official engagement of my St Patrick's week trip to Mexico had concluded at about 7.30pm on the Wednesday.

It was a radio interview recorded in the hotel lobby about the resurgence in the Irish economy, the State's improving financial circumstances and the opportunities to expand trade between Ireland and Mexico. Earlier that day I had visited the Command and Control Centre of the Mexico City police force which monitors over 8,000 security cameras across the city and stores all images for up to a week and for longer if required for a criminal investigation. My visit to one of the largest city police surveillance projects in the world would later prove to be a particular irony.

Carol and I were scheduled later that morning to fly to Cancún for a private three-day break while the rest of the party were returning to Dublin. Amongst the events scheduled for the following week was a Dáil debate on Thursday on the *Garda Inspectorate Report* into the Fixed Charge Notice Processing System. The report had been completed by the Inspectorate in February and received and read by me during the week after the Fine Gael Ard Fheis, and its recommendations endorsed by Cabinet. The report was comprehensive. It addressed a number of issues that were outside the remit of the *O'Mahoney Report* and the steps required to implement its recommendations had been initiated. The controversies relating to the issue had subsided and I believed it could no longer be fairly or credibly alleged that Maurice McCabe's allegations had been ignored or that action had not been taken by me to remedy obvious garda failures.

Mexico was six hours behind Dublin. As I soundly slept, shortly after 10am Irish time, Leo Varadkar delivered a speech in Dublin Castle opening a Road Safety Authority International Conference on Driver Distraction. He praised 'the essential work done by rank-and-file members of the Gardaí in enforcing the law on our roads' and, referencing the Fixed Charge Notice Processing System, acknowledged that 'the new procedures introduced in recent months have resulted in a step change in how the system is administered by the Gardaí and a significant fall in the number of penalty points being cancelled'. While this was an acknowledgement by him that effective action had been taken both by Martin Callinan and me to address garda failures identified by Maurice McCabe and investigated by O'Mahoney, he refrained from expressly saying this and his 'acknowledgement' was destined to be omitted from all media reports of his speech. Stating it would 'be remiss of me not to say something about the on-going controversy in relation to penalty points' (which was not that week 'on-going') he continued, asserting that the Garda Inspectorate report 'contrasted greatly with the internal investigation carried out by the Gardai'. He entirely ignored the facts that I had referred the issue to the Garda Inspectorate and the Inspectorate had addressed additional issues at my request that did not come within O'Mahoney's brief. He also glossed over the legislative failures of his Department, identified by the Inspectorate. He then referenced 'the Garda whistle-blowers' saying:

> They have come in for some criticism from some quarters for releasing Garda information about private individuals. I understand this criticism but I do not agree with it. The Garda whistle-blowers only released this information after they tried and failed to have their concerns addressed through official channels and proper means. They released the information in an effort to expose bad practice and protect the public and this was done through contact with Members of the Oireachtas, which is expressly provided for in the Garda Acts.

> Speaking on my own behalf and on behalf of the thousands of families who have had to endure the pain and loss that flows from the death of a loved one on the road, I want to thank Sergeant McCabe and Mr Wilson. They may not have got everything right but they did shine a light into a dark place and forced those who would rather turn a blind-eye to face up to the truth.

> There have been many words used to describe their actions. But if I was to use one word, the word I would use is 'distinguished'.

In Mexico, at around 7.45am, Carol and I joined Chris Quattrociocchi, my Justice Private Secretary, for breakfast and afterwards headed back to our room. Around 9.30am I brought our luggage down to the hotel lobby where Chris was waiting. He handed me his mobile phone. Independent. ie was carrying an online story entitled 'Whistleblowers: Varadkar calls on Garda Commissioner to withdraw "disgusting" remark'. The report carried extracts from Varadkar's speech delivered that morning and Chris handed me a copy, having run it off from the Department of Transport website. Reading the speech, I immediately recognised that Varadkar's description of McCabe and Wilson as 'distinguished' was designed to starkly contrast with the Garda Commissioner's use of the term 'disgusting' before the PAC and was bait for journalists to ask him some blindingly obvious questions. The speech also clearly promoted the false narrative that both Callinan and I had 'turned a blind eye' to McCabe's complaints and that they would not have been addressed but for the intervention of Wallace, Daly, Collins and Luke Ming Flanagan and McCabe contacting some of them.

The *Independent*'s report recorded that, when asked whether the Commissioner should withdraw the 'disgusting' remark, Varadkar responded, 'I think that would be appropriate. I think the Commissioner should withdraw that remark which was made on the record of the Dáil and make any other corrections that he needs to make to his testimony at the Public Accounts Committee.' Asked whether he believed Justice Minister Alan Shatter should apologise, he was reported as responding 'it's a matter for others to decide whether or not they have something to apologise about'. Similar online reports were being carried on other online news outlets. Varadkar was reported responding to one question by saying the Garda Commissioner 'is not above criticism'. He was not reported as being asked whether prior to voicing his criticism he had discussed his concerns with me. In promoting his media seducing 'blind eye' narrative, he had clearly chosen to entirely ignore the briefings and updates given both by me to him and other members of Cabinet and by Justice officials to his Department detailing the rapid response to McCabe's complaints and the mistaken nature of some of them.

I was surprised by this most public put-down of the Garda Commissioner by a Cabinet colleague and his implicit criticism of my conduct as Justice Minister in the presence of senior garda officers attending the conference. In the lifetime of the previous Dáil, even prior to Fine Gael entering Government, it was clear that Varadkar was obsessed with media self-promotion and, on an occasion when we were together and I had joked about the frequency of his appearances in the print media, he had laughingly described himself as 'a media whore'. Varadkar's ministerial St Patrick's trip to Atlanta and Savannah had been largely unreported in the Irish media. I presumed that this speech was partially media attention-seeking and his mechanism for announcing that he was back. I believed, however, that he had gone a step too far and he clearly had both the Garda Commissioner and myself in his sights. It was not the first time he had gone on a solo run without any prior contact with me or subsequent briefing and engagement as Cabinet colleagues.

Back on 11 June 2013, I learned from his being interviewed on RTÉ's *Morning Ireland* that, subsequent to publication of the *O'Mahoney Report*, he had met with one of the whistle-blowers, who I assumed to be Maurice

McCabe. He had not discussed with me his intention to meet McCabe and had not, I assumed, sought any advice from the Attorney General about the appropriateness of his doing so. He had also not briefed me on his meeting. He knew at that time, as did other members of Cabinet, of the steps being taken to implement the recommendations contained in the O'Mahoney and GPSU reports which he would acknowledge and praise in his March 2014 speech at the RSA conference. He also knew that the issue had been referred by me to the Garda Inspectorate. When asked in the radio interview about the possibility of GSOC investigating the Ticket Charge allegations, he said that the possible role of GSOC 'has to be clarified' and made no reference to the investigation underway by the Garda Inspectorate. He also made no reference to the fact that, in October 2012, then unknown to me, Noel Brett, the CEO of the Road Safety Authority, implementing a decision of the RSA, had referred McCabe's dossier of cases and allegations to GSOC. I would later discover that, at the meeting at which this was decided, it was agreed that the then Chairperson of the RSA, Gay Byrne, would brief Varadkar on events. Despite all of the media excitement and political controversy surrounding the issue, no mention had been made to me by Varadkar of the RSA referral to GSOC. I first learnt of it later that month (June 2013) when I received correspondence from Varadkar in response to my seeking comments and observations on the O'Mahoney and PSU reports. The referral was mentioned, not by Varadkar, but in an accompanying letter, which he had received from Gay Byrne as Chairperson of the RSA. By way of follow up, a constructive joint meeting with our officials and Brett took place in the Justice Department a few weeks later, in late July 2013, to ensure all necessary steps were being taken to implement essential reforms of the Fixed Charge Processing System.

I had, subsequent to publication of the *O'Mahoney Report* considered meeting with McCabe but had concerns that my doing so would undermine the statutory authority conferred on the Garda Commissioner by the Garda Síochána Act 2005 and the existing procedures for addressing garda grievances and allegations of misconduct. I had also been legally advised that such a meeting was inappropriate as McCabe had two sets of High Court proceedings against the State relating to events prior to my appointment to Government. In one of them the Minister for Justice had been named as a defendant. This advice would later be endorsed by the O'Higgins Commission.

I was dismayed by Varadkar's speech and comments. We met almost every week at meetings of Fine Gael Ministers and at Cabinet. I had briefed colleagues at those meetings of all relevant developments on the Ticket Charge/Penalty Points controversy and fully responded to any questions raised or concerns expressed. On a couple of occasions I had responded to questions asked by Varadkar. We also on occasions sat beside each other in the Dáil Chamber and both of us attended Fine Gael Parliamentary Party meetings where I had also briefed colleagues on the issue. Varadkar's office in Government Buildings was just a corridor down from mine and, on days the Dáil sat, he regularly passed by my door walking to his office. We often passed by each other in the corridor. Other Cabinet colleagues such as Frances Fitzgerald, James Reilly, Phil Hogan, Ruairi Quinn and a number of Ministers of State and TDs had no difficulty dropping into my office to discuss a variety of issues from time to time and I had no reservations doing likewise. If Varadkar had genuine concerns, no barrier prevented him from discussing them with me, dropping into my office or raising them through discussions between our special advisers or proposing that we jointly meet with the Garda Commissioner to discuss them.

On the evening of 11 March 2014, the day prior to the Cabinet adopting the Garda Inspectorate's recommendations and my publication of its report, he had texted me to ask that when speaking about the report, I 'might bear in mind in any reference to my dept [i.e. his Department of Transport, Tourism and Sport] that several legislative measures in the 2010 Act still have not been introduced due to delays by gardai and court service'.

This was not entirely accurate as some measures remained moribund because they were legislatively deficient and correcting the deficiencies was the responsibility of his Department. Clearly, however, Varadkar had no difficulty when necessary in communicating his concerns to me. There was no mention in his text of whistle-blowers, or of any concern over anything said or not said, done or not done by the Garda Commissioner or myself. He also expressed no objection to the adoption by Cabinet in his absence of the *Garda Inspectorate's Report* or to its publication.

Neither Varadkar nor any journalist reporting the Road Safety Authority event appeared to notice the contradiction between his acknowledgement of the 'step change' in how the Fixed Charge Notice Processing System was being administered as a result of the action taken by the Garda Commissioner after publication of the *O'Mahoney Report* and his assertion that a 'blind eye' had been turned to McCabe's complaints and that 'the Garda whistleblowers only released' information about private individuals 'after they tried and failed to have their concerns addressed through official channels and proper means.' He knew that the allegations received by his Departmental officials in August 2012 and forwarded to Justice in September 2012, together with those received from the Taoiseach's Department, had resulted in my communicating with the Garda Commissioner and the O'Mahoney Investigation being initiated in October 2012. He had received a personal letter dated 21 October 2012 from McCabe repeating his allegations and requesting that his anonymity be preserved which he had forwarded to me in November 2012 over two weeks later. He and his Department knew of the O'Mahoney Interim Report of November 2012, had received a copy of the correspondence sent to McCabe by Michael Flahive in December 2012 and he was present on most occasions when I had briefed Fine Gael Ministerial meetings and Cabinet meetings on the issue. He also knew that serious allegations made by McCabe attributing fatal road injuries to the cancellation of Ticket Charges were not substantiated and that both I and the Garda Commissioner had genuine concerns about the release and publication of information on the PULSE System about private individuals. He also knew that PULSE records could not be altered, erased or destroyed. He, together with other colleagues, had also, only three weeks earlier, been briefed on the difficulties I had experienced in obtaining a substantive response from McCabe's solicitors to correspondence in 2012 and throughout 2013, which I later detailed in my Dáil speech on 26 February 2014. My description of these difficulties would, two years later, be verified by the O'Higgins Commission Report. I believed that Varadkar was opportunistically reigniting a controversy, despite knowing the background to be more complex than the public could have understood or as presented by Opposition politicians and media commentators.

I had no doubt that all hell was about to break loose and that Varadkar's speech and comments would generate substantial fallout. On that Thursday morning, he knew I was abroad in Mexico on Government business. I had politically watched his back when he was abroad on publication of the *Garda Inspectorate's Report* by ensuring that the Implementation Committee for the Inspectorate's recommendations was jointly chaired by both of our Departments and had made no public reference to the statutory defects that should have been addressed long ago by his Department. My view was simply that we should get on with doing everything required to ensure no further difficulties arose in the area of Ticket Charges, Penalty Points and the recovery of traffic fines. In gratitude it seemed he had chosen to ambush me while I was in Mexico. He would not be the only Cabinet colleague to prove, in the words of the American dramatist and political activist, Clare Booth Lucy, that 'no good deed goes unpunished'.

I concluded that Carol and I had no choice but to cancel our brief holiday arranged for Cancún and immediately return home to Dublin. I had no doubt I was returning home to be embroiled in a new episode of a Varadkar-revived controversy and more media hysteria and opprobrium. As far as Carol and I were concerned, our time away together had ended before it had even begun.

CHAPTER 24

Entering a Parallel Universe

Hope springs eternal in the human breast
–Alexandar Pope, *An Essay on Man*

It is now difficult for the Garda Commissioner to withdraw the word 'disgusting' and retain his authority ... If he does not bow to a number of senior Government Ministers and withdraw use of the word "disgusting" the issue ... could turn into a full blown political controversy which Mr Kenny may find difficult to control
–*Irish Independent* editorial, 22 March 2014

Varadkar poured petrol on the flames when the Taoiseach was out of the country for St Patrick's week by calling on the former Garda Commissioner to withdraw his 'disgusting' remark about the whistleblowers. The Varadkar intervention came at a stage when the controversy had faded from the front pages but his remarks promptly put it back there with a vengeance
–Stephen Collins, *Irish Times*, 29 March 2014

It was just after 12 noon and I was sitting in my room in the Department of Justice, having reviewed the morning papers. We had landed in Dublin Airport from Mexico City earlier that Friday morning and, after about two hours' sleep, a shave and a shower, I had arrived in the Department. I was cut off from events while in mid-air and, to catch up, I got that morning's papers to read through before a meeting with Justice officials to discuss developments. Varadkar had struck media gold and was extensively quoted and praised. I knew that, from his perspective, he would regard 21 March 2014 as a particularly good day. From my perspective, I felt I had just entered some parallel universe.

'FG Ministers fall out in Penalty Points Row' claimed the lead headline on the front page of the *Irish Independent*. The story continued on page 2 with the headline 'FG Ministers barely speaking after row over Penalty Points'. It takes not only two to tango but also two to row! As Varadkar had simply delivered his speech, never discussed with me what he intended to say or the views he expressed and as we had not been in touch and I had refrained from responding, it seemed that, yet again, I had become embroiled in a fantasy narrative. It was not so much that we were 'barely speaking' it was simply that, while I was in Mexico, Varadkar had gone on a solo run without discussing his much-publicised concerns with me or the contents of the *Garda Inspectorate Report*. As I anticipated, the Garda Commissioner also featured in the headlines. 'Callinan will not withdraw comment on whistleblowers' reported the *Irish Examiner* front page. 'Now Varadkar piles pressure on embattled Garda Chief' was the Irish *Daily Mail*'s take on events. 'Tribute from Varadkar Welcomed' was *The Irish Times*' focus, reporting that both Maurice McCabe and John Wilson had welcomed Varadkar's 'tribute to them for highlighting the Penalty Points controversy'.

I knew that Varadkar and his immediate circle were dedicated to media spin and I had, until that day, found their antics more a source of amusement than irritation. In particular, because they seemed oblivious to how readily identifiable was the origin of some of the stuff that appeared in print attributed to anonymous Government sources. Journalists understandably need and thrive on such spin or off-the-record briefings. Unfortunately, all too frequently, even the experienced ones accept it at face value and fail to question or critically analyse what they are fed. In circumstances in which the spin fits neatly into an already existing popular but false narrative, the likelihood of critical assessment is somewhere close to zero. The clearly widely briefed explanations for Varadkar's speech mentioned repetitively by a variety of journalists were consistent and could not have surfaced without coming from 'a source close to the Minister'.

The much-experienced political editor of the *Irish Independent*, Fionnan Sheahan, informed the nation that morning that Varadkar 'had been dissenting from the official line on the Penalty Points affair for almost two years'. He was also wrongly depicted as having called for the involvement of GSOC in his RTÉ morning interview of June 2013. Leo's two years of dissent must have come as news to Cabinet colleagues and to their special advisers who for two years had attended weekly pre-Cabinet meetings at which this 'dissent' had never been voiced. An assertion in the same article that I had failed to acknowledge the whistle-blowers' role was at total variance with what I had previously stated on the Dáil record.

Writing in the same paper, Eamon Delany, who frequently was incisive in identifying reality in the political undergrowth, criticised my 'grating and arrogant refusal to own up' and acknowledge that both

I and the Garda Commissioner 'got it wrong' when we had 'so blithely dismissed the Penalty Points allegations'. My factually stating that some of the more serious allegations made by McCabe were both unsubstantiated and mistaken was conflated into a dismissal of all the allegations made. Of course, had all the allegations been 'blithely dismissed' no action would have been taken to address confirmed garda failures nor would the new administrative procedures Varadkar lauded have been successfully operating. But that was only a minor detail of irrelevance.

Varadkar in the eyes of the media was the conquering hero. Leo's 'roar', according to Pat Flanagan in that day's *Irish Daily Mirror*, showed 'rare moral fibre' and he was, according to the *Irish Examiner*'s Michael Clifford, 'Telling it like it is'.

Eamon Delany speculated that 'far from being a solo run' or representing a 'Cabinet division' Varadkar's intervention may well have been 'highly coordinated and considered'. Contradicting this speculation, the *Independent* in the same edition reported the Taoiseach the previous day kicking to touch, referencing the steps being taken to implement the Inspectorate and O'Mahoney reports and lamenting that 'we have been over this ground on so many occasions'.

When reading the online reports in Mexico City I knew it was inevitable that Cabinet colleagues would get calls from eager journalists seeking a response to Varadkar's comments. I was worried that someone would be tempted to say something that would pour petrol on the flames he had ignited. It was unprecedented for a Garda Commissioner to be publicly criticised by a series of Cabinet Ministers and I was concerned that yet again, the Ticket Charge issue would be elevated to a bizarre level of importance when compared to the major role played by An Garda Síochána and the important responsibilities of the Garda Commissioner in defending the security of the State and tackling serious crime. The last thing I wanted was to become embroiled in yet another week of garda-related political controversy. However, I recognised that there was a substantial likelihood I was back in that territory.

The only Cabinet Minister reported as supporting Varadkar was Joan Burton, the Minister for Social Protection, who prominently featured in the headline on the front page of that morning's *Irish Times*. 'Burton Increases Pressure on Callinan' was accompanied by a sub-headline 'Minister joins Varadkar's call on Garda Commissioner to withdraw comments'. Joan had spent over three years in Government politically nibbling at Eamon

Gilmore's heels and undermining his leadership of the Labour Party. I regarded her as totally lacking any insight into the damaging impact of her conduct on the public perception of her party and the likely damage she was causing to its future electoral prospects. She had not involved herself in Justice issues and I assumed her intervention was as much to do with constituency rivalry between her and Varadkar in Dublin West as with her obsessive need to develop a political profile at variance to that of Gilmore. *The Irish Times* reported Burton from Washington as calling on the Commissioner to withdraw his remarks saying 'I think it would be helpful if he did.' This was accompanied by a quote from an unidentified Labour spokesperson saying she 'was reflecting the generally held view within the Party'. How Joan so rapidly knew all the way from Washington the general view within the Labour Party of Varadkar's pronouncements was something of a mystery. The same spokesperson was reported as declining to say 'if the Tanaiste and Labour Leader, Eamon Gilmore, agreed with his Deputy Leader'. On my reading of it, Joan was simultaneously doing a constituency waltz with Leo while having a go at Eamon. I reckoned that the 'unidentified Labour spokesperson' did not work too far away from Burton's office!

By comparison, the *Irish Independent* reported an anonymous Fine Gael Minister as saying Varadkar had 'landed a major bucket of s**t on the Taoiseach's lap which he most certainly wouldn't have wanted' (the paper was too genteel to fully spell out the word used). It also quoted 'another senior Fine Gael figure' saying that the Transport Minister 'gets an orgasm every time he sees a microphone and a television camera'. I marvelled at the colourful language, somewhat out of character for Fine Gael, used by colleagues while I was on the flight returning from Mexico.

I thought there was some possibility if other Cabinet members refrained from commenting that the controversy might run out of steam. Clearly, Fine Gael colleagues had no wish to stir it up but I reckoned Burton's comments had created a problem, not only for Gilmore, but also for other Labour Ministers who had not necessarily closely followed the detailed complexities of the Ticket Charge issue and my dealings with Sergeant Maurice McCabe, being too busy concentrating on their own briefs.

At about 12.10 a meeting commenced in the Justice Department with my two Special Advisers, Jane Lehane and Jennifer Carroll, and two Assistant Secretaries, Michael Flahive and Ken O'Leary. Brian Purcell's mother had died the previous Saturday, the funeral had been on Thursday and Brian was on leave until at least the following Monday. If not for this sad event, he also would have been present at the meeting. I was advised that the Department only first learned of Varadkar's speech after its delivery. Before leaving Mexico, at my request, my Private Secretary had informed the Department's Press Office that I would be making no comment and to simply inform the media that the *Garda Inspectorate Report* was scheduled for Dáil debate the following Thursday. I wanted time to reflect on Varadkar's comments and to carefully consider what, if any, response or initiative to take. I regarded the concept of Cabinet collegiality to be of considerable importance not only in a constitutional sense but for the pragmatic need to ensure cooperative engagement between colleagues and Government stability. I decided that nothing was to be gained by my giving any instant response.

Having read that morning's papers, my primary concerns focussed on how to best diffuse the controversy Varadkar had reignited. I believed it would be enormously damaging to the independent statutory office and role of any Garda Commissioner, not just Martin Callinan, if he or she were to be perceived as subject to the orders and public demands of an individual or group of Cabinet Ministers. This would be a dangerous precedent that could undermine the integrity of our Justice system. I also believed it was damaging to the Government that the issue continue to fester throughout the weekend and that it was likely to evolve into an issue of confidence in Martin Callinan as Garda Commissioner and, possibly, in me as Minister for Justice.

The time reached 1pm as we considered how to best proceed. As we drank tea and ate sandwiches, we listened to RTÉ 1's *News at One* to facilitate our assessing developments.

The first radio news headline of relevance that lunchtime reported that the Garda whistle-blowers 'have been criticised by the Data Protection Commissioner [Billy Hawkes], for distributing confidential and personal data'. The next headline reported that a spokesperson for the Tánaiste, Eamon Gilmore, 'had confirmed that he shared the view of Joan Burton' and that it would be 'helpful' if the Garda Commissioner was to withdraw his 'disgusting' remark. At the end of the bulletin, RTÉ announced upcoming interviews with Billy Hawkes and my Cabinet colleague and Labour Minister for Communications, Energy and Natural Resources, Pat Rabbitte.

Hawkes's interview came first and it was of particular relevance to the revived Ticket Charge controversy. Unfortunately, it was largely ignored in the days that followed both by commentators and politicians, including Cabinet colleagues. It generated little coverage in Saturday's papers save for the *Irish Examiner,* which featured the interview on page 8. The *Examiner*'s headline neatly and accurately encapsulated the content of the interview – 'No basis for Whistleblowers to keep trawling Garda Data'. The interview took place because of an audit conducted by the Data Protection Commissioner's Office into the management of personal data on the PULSE System, details of which were published at lunchtime on that Friday. Billy Hawkes referenced the importance of ensuring that the way the gardaí handle data 'respects our rights' and, in particular, 'that it should not be disclosed outside the Force'. Asked about the activities of McCabe and Wilson, the Garda whistle-blowers, he responded 'we fully acknowledge that under the Garda Act there is a right, indeed a duty, to report corruption or malpractice, if somebody comes across it'. Once such a report had been made and there was an investigation, he believed, 'it was the duty of the Commissioner to prevent wholesale access to Garda information and, even more so, wholesale disclosure of it outside the Force, once the duty to report under the whistleblowing provisions has been met'.

Martin Callinan had been virulently criticised for his Directive of December 2012 and for restricting McCabe's use of the PULSE System. Hawkes was clearly supportive of his action. When asked whether he was 'saying you found no fault with McCabe and Wilson?', he responded 'Oh no ... we did specifically support the Commissioner's position about information being disclosed to the Public Accounts Committee' and he continued stating that, as Data Protection Commissioner, 'I had a duty to support the Commissioner when he took the position that once the whistle-blowers had discharged, if you like, their moral duty to report malpractice within An Garda then there was not a basis for them continuing to access the PULSE System, and less so for disclosing confidential information about people to third parties.'

When further pressed on the issue he responded:

Once they had stayed within the bounds of the Garda Síochána Act and the whistleblowing provisions then all was fine. It was after that there was continued access to information which was being alleged and continued disclosure of that information, that's where issues do arise in terms of the Commissioner's duty to guard personal data and to prevent it being inappropriately accessed and disclosed.

Controversy surrounding the disclosure of material on PULSE records had festered since December 2012 and Martin Callinan had been the butt of relentless criticism for restricting McCabe's access to PULSE. His action had been portrayed both by Opposition politicians and commentators as some form of retaliation for McCabe's complaints and no consideration had been given to the statutory responsibility of the Commissioner as a data controller. I considered Hawkes interview hugely helpful but did not understand why he had not prominently expressed such views previously in public. My immediate reflection on the Hawkes interview was that it should contribute to a more balanced discussion than the one revitalised by Varadkar. Of course, I should have anticipated that Billy Hawkes's comments, being at variance with the preferred media and Opposition narrative, would be given limited coverage, be entirely ignored by Opposition TDs and the commentariat, have no impact of any nature and rapidly fall out of the news cycle.

Hawkes was followed by Pat Rabbitte who, having described Martin Callinan as a 'decent and honourable man', expressed the opinion that 'it would be a great pity if we couldn't bring the controversial aspects of the saga to a conclusion' and that it would 'be helpful if the Garda Commissioner facilitated that'. When asked about the Commissioner's concerns over PULSE information passing into the public domain and his explanation for using the term 'disgusting', ignoring the concerns expressed by the Data Protection Commissioner, he deftly sidestepped the issue by responding that 'we are reigniting a controversy that has been very definitively dealt with'. Asked about my 'non-cooperation' remark made in the Dáil back on 1 October 2013 and whether I should apologise, he responded that I was 'probably badly advised' and that I had already clarified what I said. Being anxious to avoid bringing me directly into the controversy, he pointedly commented 'I have not agreed to do this interview to stoke the thing up further.' I doubted if Varadkar would have given a similar answer to that question.

By the time the *News* ended, the consensus was that I should issue no statement and that we should monitor how events evolved through the afternoon and, in particular, the impact of Billy Hawkes's interview.

I hoped that, as a result of his intervention and very explicit support for the Garda Commissioner, the pot would not be further stirred and that colleagues would keep their views for the Cabinet meeting scheduled for Tuesday, 25 March. I was, however, concerned about Labour Cabinet Ministers following Burton's lead, now her intervention had been blessed by an anonymous spokesperson for Gilmore, and believed it would be unhelpful if the issue became portrayed as being a dispute between Labour and Fine Gael members of Cabinet.

I had not been in contact with the Taoiseach, who was attending an EU Summit meeting in Brussels. Some time after 5pm there were online news reports of his intervention. Kenny was reported as stating that the Garda Commissioner deserved 'absolute respect'. He described his relationship as Taoiseach with the Garda Commissioner as 'one that has to be absolutely professional' and continued 'the Garda Commissioner, in whom I have confidence, has responsibility for the day to day running of the Gardai. He has already clarified on a number of occasions the reason for his making comments at the Public Accounts Committee and the context in which he made those comments'. There was no suggestion from anything he reportedly said that Kenny expected or demanded that the Garda Commissioner say anything further about the issue. Asked about Varadkar's remarks and those of other Cabinet members, he responded 'I certainly have a preference that if any Minister has an issue to raise, they raise it at the Cabinet or raise it where we could have discussions and deal with them, rather than have them aired in public. I'm not saying people have to be restricted in their views on anything, but there is a process by which these things should be dealt with.'

I shared and respected this view, understanding that, if all members of cabinet talked at each other through public megaphones, Government would descend into chaos and the constitutional concept of collective Cabinet responsibility would become meaningless. I decided to make no comment on or off the record on Varadkar's remarks, believing no good could come of it. I hoped Kenny's intervention would also reduce the pressure on the Garda Commissioner and result in Varadkar quietening down. I presumed there was no purpose in my attempting a reasoned discussion with Varadkar that day as I had little doubt he would be surfing on the publicity and praise lavished on him.

The Justice Press Office had been inundated throughout the afternoon with journalists seeking my response, not only to Varadkar's remarks, but also to the comments of Labour Ministers. I asked Lorraine Hall, my Press Adviser, to continue to reference the fact that the *Garda Inspectorate Report* would be debated in the Dáil the following week and, if pressed about Varadkar, to simply respond that I was 'mystified' at press reports of our falling out.

The Taoiseach's comments in Brussels were partially carried on RTÉ's *Six One* television news, together with sound bites from Joan Burton and Pat Rabbitte reflecting what they had previously said. Interestingly, in a live interview the Data Protection Commissioner went further than he had earlier on radio, stating that he had made it clear to the Commissioner that he expected him to take action to limit the access of the whistle-blowers to the Garda PULSE System. RTÉ also reported that Tánaiste Eamon Gilmore and two Cabinet Ministers had backed Leo Varadkar's call to the Garda Commissioner to withdraw his remarks.

By 6.30 pm jet lag and lack of sleep caught up with me and I went home for the night, hoping Saturday would prove a more restful day. Alexandar Pope was right when he said: 'Hope springs eternal in the human breast.'

Saturday's papers extensively reported 'the growing Cabinet crisis'. Fianna Fáil leader Micheál Martin was stirring the pot, describing the Taoiseach's Friday comments as being a 'severe rebuke of the Tanaiste, Minister Burton and Minister Varadkar'. Within days Martin would be praising Varadkar for his heroics. Consistency is not a required virtue in politics.

To add to the mix, Labour's Minister for Education, Ruairi Quinn, in defiance of the Taoiseach's wishes, was reported as having issued a statement late on Friday evening to 'join with my colleagues in encouraging the Garda Commissioner to bring an end to the controversy surrounding the Garda whistleblowers'. This resulted in the *Irish Independent* front-page headline, 'Cabinet rift deepens over Garda chief as Labour defies Kenny'. An unidentified 'Cabinet source' was quoted as saying that 'a bitter showdown was expected between Minister Varadkar and Justice Minister Alan Shatter at a Fine Gael Ministers meeting' on the coming Tuesday. In the same article, an unidentified source was also quoted as insisting Varadkar was sticking to his position. 'Minister Varadkar has raised his concerns on the Penalty Point issue both publicly and privately at Ministerial level for several months' it was reported, inaccurately. An unnamed Minister was reported as saying the party now needed to rally behind Shatter and that 'Varadkar's kicking him around the place and Shatter's in trouble. If you're on a team and one of your players is getting kicked around the place, you protect him as best you can. Callinan is not on the team – but by kicking Callinan he is kicking Shatter.' The same Minister was quoted as predicting that 'This is going to finish up badly. Varadkar could talk himself out of Cabinet.' That assessment was to prove seriously inaccurate.

Prophecy in politics is, of course, an inexact science. A Minister with leadership ambitions does not attract publicity by praising another Minister or reciting Government policy. The crucial ingredient is to be disruptive and do the exact opposite. Varadkar's 'distinguished' speech and subsequent replies to media questions elevated his status as the media's darling and made him politically untouchable. His very public praise of McCabe, criticism of Martin Callinan and perceived criticism of me would ultimately be recognised as marking the effective launch of his successful bid to become leader of the Fine Gael party.

Rifts in Cabinet were not the sole focus of that Saturday morning's papers. 'Apologise or Leave' was the stark headline directed at the Garda Commissioner by the *Irish Daily Mail*'s editorial. The *Irish Examiner*'s report was headed 'Backbench TDs cast doubt on Callinan's position'. Considering the continuing controversy and the anticipated coverage of the issue in the next day's Sunday papers and media broadcasts, I started to doubt whether my saying nothing about the issue until Tuesday's Fine Gael Ministers and Cabinet meeting was tenable. I also further considered whether I should encourage Callinan to specifically apologise for his 'disgraceful' reference when before the PAC but believed his doing so under public pressure would not end controversy. I was concerned that an apology issued by him in response to ministerial and other political pressure would have fatal consequences for Callinan's authority, standing and independence as Garda Commissioner and I had little doubt it would simply result in even shriller calls for his resignation.

CHAPTER 25

Varadkar's Source

Now it's 'coming for a head' time
–Front-page lead headline, *Sunday Independent*, 23 March 2014

Shatter has finally lost touch with reality
–Gene Kerrigan, *Sunday Independent*, 23 March 2014

Is Shatter asking Kenny; just Back Me or Sack Me
–Sam Smyth, *Irish Mail on Sunday*, 23 March 2014

The story that won't die
–Pat Leahy, *Sunday Business Post*, 23 March 2014

Political victory for Leo –*Irish Sun* editorial, 23 March 2014

It was Sunday, 23 March 2014, and Mexico seemed a long time ago. The Sunday papers, television and radio news and current affairs chat shows were dominated by what had become a full-scale Garda and political megadrama. Varadkar was depicted as the handsome hero, Luke Skywalker, and Martin Callinan and I joined at the hip as Darth Vader, with the shadow of Maurice McCabe cast across the whole stage.

After almost three weeks of relative sanity, it was Groundhog Day. The media frenzy of the dark days of February 2014 had returned. It was also the weekend of the Fianna Fáil Ard Fheis and Micheál Martin and Niall Collins tried to fan the flames of controversy but played bit parts and were no more than a sideshow.

Respecting Enda's wishes, the Justice Press Office had continued to brief all press callers that I would address the issue at Tuesday's Cabinet meeting and in Thursday's Dáil debate on the *Garda Inspectorate Report* and that 'no, Alan has not fallen out with Leo'. I expected that Varadkar would show some respect for the Taoiseach's 'preference' that the issue be kept for Cabinet. It was a great expectation.

I had not, during our three years in Government, engaged in any public row with any Cabinet colleague. Nor, through any Special Adviser or Press Officer (i.e. 'source close to the Minister') had I briefed on or off the record against a colleague. I regarded Joan's regular digs at Eamon as unfair and disingenuous and I was not going down that road with Leo. That perspective was to prove politically naive, possibly fatal.

Reading through the papers, similar stories appeared that clearly were not invented by the journalists. They could only have been the product of briefings intended to both promote Varadkar's swashbuckling image and portray me as arrogant and uncommunicative.

The respected political editor of the *Sunday Business Post*, Pat Leahy, predicting a 'Cabinet showdown over the Garda whistleblowers', wrote about Varadkar's 'growing unhappiness' for months, asserting that he had tried to press the Penalty Points controversy as 'a road safety issue' while I insisted 'it was a Garda matter'. This was fictitious nonsense as such distinction had never ever occurred to me. However, I was certain that this fantasy narrative was not invented by Leahy.

The Road Safety Authority had acknowledged that the objective of the Fixed Charge Notice Processing System was to bring about compliance with road safety measures and to reduce fatalities. As far as I was concerned, it was about ensuring that it did so and that the system was properly and fairly administered. This had been the focus of the joint Ministerial and Departmental meeting involving both myself and Varadkar held in the Justice Department in July 2013. I was so concerned about road safety that, in the spring of 2013 during a Ministerial visit to the Middle East, at my initiative a meeting was arranged, which I attended, between Noel Brett, the Chief Executive of the Road Safety Authority, Chief Superintendent Aidan Reid of the Garda Traffic Bureau and their opposite numbers in Israel. Both Israel and Ireland, in the early 2000s, had a high level of road fatalities and each in recent years had brought about a substantial and dramatic reduction. I believed both countries could further reduce road fatalities and injuries by learning from each other's initiatives. I was aware of some unique steps taken in Israel that I believed our Road Safety Authority could successfully replicate. If I had no interest or concerns about road safety this meeting would never have taken place.

The *Sunday Business Post* article unequivocally claimed that Varadkar 'had specifically asked' that the *Garda Inspectorate Report* be not taken at the 12 March Cabinet meeting because he would be abroad and that it had been discussed and disposed of in his absence. To confirm my villainous status based upon whatever briefing he had received, Leahy stated that the report 'had been with Shatter since January'. Of course, none of this was true. The report was not completed and furnished by the Garda Inspectorate to the Department until late February, was expressly dated February and given to me on 3 March. No request to postpone Cabinet discussion on it had been made by Varadkar to me. If he had made any such request before departing to the USA, I would have instantly agreed and it would have been mentioned by him in the text I received from him the day before the Cabinet meeting. Moreover, in Varadkar's absence, such a request could also have been made at the pre-Cabinet weekly meeting of Special Advisers. There would have been no reason to refuse such request. But no request was made. The only communication received by me from Varadkar of relevance to the *Garda Inspectorate Report* discussion in Cabinet was his texted request that his Department should not be blamed for the fact that some provisions in the Road Traffic Act 2010 had not yet become operative.

This fictitious version of events I knew would not have been invented by Pat Leahy and could only have derived from 'a source close to the Minister for Transport'. Sam Smyth, in the *Irish Mail on Sunday*, had clearly also been a recipient of the same briefing, referencing January as the month I had received the *Garda Inspectorate Report*. His narrative was that after receiving it, I had continued 'to attack the integrity of the whistle-blowers'. This was a reference to my explaining in the Dáil the extent of my own and my Justice officials' engagement with McCabe and his solicitors and the difficulties that arose. Smyth's article also ignored the fact that the Garda Inspectorate had reported at my request. Over two years would pass, until publication of the *O'Higgins Report*, for it to be independently determined that in my Dáil contributions of February 2014 on issues relating to An Garda Síochána, my Department and 'the whistle-/blowers', I simply told the truth.

In a front-page story headlined 'Now it's "Coming for a Head" time' the *Sunday Independent* gave the game away. Reporting that 'Mr Varadkar has been at odds with Mr Shatter for months' over the Penalty Point controversy, Jody Corcoran, John Drennan and Fionnan Sheahan informed readers that 'sources close to Mr Varadkar yesterday claimed Mr Shatter refused to engage with his Cabinet colleague on the Penalty Points issue either face to face or even by text message'. The same sources were quoted as saying that Varadkar had 'no intention' of backing down on the issue. My alleged difficulty in talking to Varadkar was said by 'the Fine Gael source' to 'be quite astonishing'. For me what was 'astonishing' was the terrible dishonesty of the briefing. Moreover, the identity of the 'source' referenced as close to Varadkar was blindingly obvious.

Reflecting on that day's news coverage and media commentary, I concluded that perhaps Gene Kerrigan's depiction of me in the same edition of the *Sunday Independent* as having 'lost touch with reality' could be accurate. As a child, I had enjoyed watching the *Twilight Zone* on television. Maybe the plane from Mexico had entered a twilight zone, and landed in some parallel universe where someone who looked like me had treated Leo the way the 'sources' were claiming?

My February 2014 experience had been of journalists creating and perpetuating a false narrative about the gardaí bugging GSOC and then fitting any emerging information into their preferred story line. Even after publication of the *Cooke Report*, I would later discover that some had difficulty acknowledging that they had simply got the story wrong. (Bizarrely, as recently as 27 December 2017 the *Irish Examiner* in a puff piece advertising its whistleblowing credentials republished, amongst others, one of its February 2014 front-page headlines which read 'Bugs and bombshells' accompanied by a tag line above it 'Garda Crises'.) But this was different. This was a Fine Gael cabinet colleague orchestrating or engaging in extensive briefing to bolster his reputation and image and deliberately damage mine. I was accustomed to this from Opposition TDs. It is an unfortunate part of political life, but I did not expect it from someone on the Fine Gael political team. It seemed clear that to justify his public stance Varadkar had, by that Sunday morning, made me his main target. He had done so knowing he would have a receptive audience based on the manner in which I had been portrayed by media commentators on the garda-related controversies throughout February. His approach could do nothing other than generate media praise and applause for himself.

Of course, on that Sunday, I was not the only media target. The Garda Commissioner also featured. *The Sunday Times*, having, a month earlier run the false GSOC bugging story, implying the gardaí were the villains, was that day moralising from its editorial pulpit. In a piece entitled 'This is a sorry state of affairs, Commissioner' the editor asserted that 'if he doesn't climb down, he should be cut loose'.

On a human level, I did not believe that Martin Callinan deserved the treatment he was receiving and phoned him that morning. He was reflecting on whether he should issue some further statement. He was appreciative of the Taoiseach's expression of confidence in him in Brussels the previous Friday, which had been widely reported. I informed him that I intended to contact the Taoiseach to discuss the desirability of my issuing some helpful media statement and providing a briefing document to Ministers and members of the Fine Gael and Labour Party parliamentary parties. During the course of our conversation, no new issue was raised by Callinan that could be a cause for concern.

I texted Enda Kenny at around 10am:

> Good morning. Think we should discuss Ticket Charge issue, where matters now stand and a possible statement I might issue today to reframe some of the discussion. Don't think it tenable or helpful that I say nothing before Cabinet meeting. Also important that we do not succumb to the mob or pour oil on troubled waters. The current level of media hysteria and misinformation (some of which is fuelled by colleagues) is damaging to the Gardai, unfair to the Commissioner and politically damaging, at least in the short term. Alan

Throughout that Sunday I declined various news broadcast media interview requests and just before 8pm emailed the Taoiseach's Private Secretary, Nick Reddy, a document I had prepared with Jane Lehane for the Taoiseach's consideration. I did not know whether he would revert to me on that Sunday evening or the next day but looking back on it now, it was far too lengthy and detailed for use as a press statement. I did at the time, however, regard it as a very useful briefing to be furnished, not only to members of both parliamentary parties, but also to Cabinet colleagues before or at Cabinet.

Enda Kenny never reverted to me on the document. Unknown to me, on that Sunday evening, Máire Whelan, the Attorney General, met Kenny in his office in Government Buildings and presented him with what would, within forty-eight hours, be universally regarded as yet another Garda scandal. She did so without making any advance contact with me. As would emerge upon publication of the *Fennelly Report*, her excuse for not contacting me was that she believed me to be 'part of the narrative' in that 'there were issues, allegations, touching on the Minister himself' and she was influenced by 'the narrative in the media that the Commissioner and the Minister were unduly close'. It is clear that by then, despite our closely working together on a variety of issues for over three years and my believing we had a genuine friendship and mutual respect, Whelan's perception had become distorted by repetitive accusations that Martin Callinan and I were 'joined at the hip' and too close. By the time she had finished her presentation to Kenny, he was fearful that when her revelations became public, either the future of the Government or his future as Taoiseach could be at risk. It is possible that by the end of Kenny's meeting with Whelan his perspective had also become contaminated by the JATH myth. Though the Garda issue raised by Whelan that Sunday evening was uniquely a Justice matter, involving An Garda Síochána. I was destined to know nothing of it until 6pm the next day, Monday. By that time, for Martin Callinan the writing was on the wall. It also seemed that for me it was just a couple of bricks below those dedicated to the Commissioner.

As Brian Purcell was on leave following his mother's death, we had not been in contact since my return from Mexico. When in Mexico, I had commiserated with him on her passing and believed it important on the Sunday evening that we talk. We had a short phone conversation briefly discussing the continuing Ticket Charge/Penalty Points controversy. Brian confirmed that he would be in the Justice Department the next day, Monday, and we agreed to again touch base on where the issue stood and review progress on a variety of other Justice matters. I also again commiserated with him on the death of his mother.

Nothing arose in our conversation to give rise to any new concerns. No mention was made by him of the issue that evening greatly exercising the Taoiseach and the Attorney General and which, unknown to me, they were discussing around the same time Brian and I spoke on the phone.

CHAPTER 26

Garda Recordings Discovered

The one thing we can all be sure about in politics is you are as well to expect the unexpected –Charles Kennedy, former leader of the Liberal Democrats and Member of the House of Commons

Unusually, my diary was blank on Monday, 24 March 2014. Carol and I had originally planned to return to Dublin early that morning. I had set the day aside to catch up with Justice files and papers that accumulated while I was in Mexico and to read Cabinet papers for Tuesday morning's Cabinet meeting. Jetlagged, distracted by the weekend's controversy and knowing that I had the day free, I waited until Monday morning at home to complete that work. I arrived in the Department at about 12 noon, dealt with some minor issues and then Jane Lehane accompanied me to the Yamamori restaurant on South Great George's Street. A table had been booked where we could have a confidential conversation. I wanted to discuss with Jane where matters now stood with the Varadkar-generated controversy and how to best resolve it.

That morning's *Irish Times* reported that Kenny and Gilmore had spoken over the weekend in an effort to calm tensions between the two coalition parties and according to 'sources', the general idea of a new independent Garda Authority was to be discussed at Cabinet on Tuesday. This had not been mentioned to me but I was not unhappy at the prospect. I was concerned about the politicisation of the gardaí and that opportunistic public demands made by Ministers amounted to political interference in an area that was the exclusive statutory preserve of the Garda Commissioner – that is the control and management of An Garda Síochána and the performance of his role as the Force's Accounting Officer. Originally, I had been opposed to the establishment of a police authority out of concern that it would prove to be just another expensive Government quango which immunised the Government and the Minister for Justice of the day from accountability to the Dáil for garda-related matters. I now perceived it as an important buffer to protect the force from being a political pawn to be played with on the political stage, regardless of consequences.

Jane and I were shown to our table in the right-hand corner at the back of the restaurant, a suitable distance from diners, to avoid being overheard. How to handle Varadkar and diffuse the controversy was the main issue to be discussed. We were also to discuss the creation of a police authority and how it would impact on the legal relationship between a Garda Commissioner and the Minister for Justice and the Minister's accountability to the Dáil for garda matters. As we sat down, I was startled to discover across the way from our table to my right, sat Varadkar, his Special Adviser, Brian Murphy, and his Press Officer, Nick Miller. Out of all the restaurants in all of Dublin!

Varadkar and I nodded acknowledgments and I think he was as surprised to find me there as I was to find him. It seemed that neither of us, at that moment, had any appetite to talk to each other. I was particularly annoyed by the nonsense briefings in the Sunday papers for which I believed he was responsible. I would like to believe that his obvious discomfort was caused by some level of embarrassment, but I doubt it. During the next hour, we each had lunch and spoke with our own Special Advisers. During the course of the lunch, Jane and I agreed that the best course of action would be for Varadkar and I to meet, together with our advisers, in advance of the Tuesday morning Fine Gael Ministerial and Cabinet meetings. Varadkar's table finished their lunch before us. I beckoned him with a friendly gesture and proposed that we would all meet that afternoon. That did not work for him so we arranged to meet around 8.45 the next morning, Tuesday. I expected that we would continue to work together in Cabinet for the remainder of the Government's term and I believed it important to mend fences. I had no wish to respond to him through a media megaphone or by unattributed briefings and act out the media narrative of two senior Fine Gael Ministers at war with each other.

Other than dealing with draft responses to Defence Parliamentary Questions and signing off on departmental letters, the rest of the afternoon was spent with Jane working on a draft of the speech to be delivered on the *Garda Inspectorate's Report*. At 6pm, Brian Purcell arrived together with Michael Flahive for a meeting to discuss the weekend controversy and the presentation I would make at Tuesday's Cabinet meeting. The discussion did not go according to plan. Shortly after an exchange of pleasantries and a brief reference to my Mexico visit, an unexpected revelation gave birth to a startling new political crisis and alleged garda scandal.

Purcell advised me that a court order for discovery had, some time ago, been made in High Court proceedings initiated by Mr Ian Bailey against the State, the Garda Commissioner and the Minister for Justice.

Madame Sophie Tuscan du Plantier, a French citizen, had been murdered in Toormore, outside Schull in West Cork in December 1996 and no one had ever been prosecuted for her murder. Ian Bailey had been a garda suspect who had consistently proclaimed his innocence. His proceedings (which he was destined to ultimately lose) sought damages for alleged garda misconduct during the course of the garda investigation into the murder. It had emerged that a number of audio taped recordings existed, made in Bandon Garda Station, of telephone conversations relevant to the Bailey court action and other conversations unconnected to the Bailey case. The tapes, I learnt, were found following a request made to the garda station to ensure that there was nothing additional to be disclosed in an Affidavit of Discovery, which was to be sworn on behalf of An Garda Síochána. I was also told that it had emerged that phone calls were being recorded in other garda stations around the country and, at that stage, the content of the recordings was unknown. It was unclear how the recordings discovered would impact on the State's or the Garda Síochána's defence in the Bailey case or the likely impact of recordings made in other garda stations on pending criminal prosecutions or on previous court convictions.

Before this conversation, I knew nothing about garda recordings and Purcell's initial briefing did not shed light on their purpose or use. As I attempted to tease out the implications of his revelations, at approximately 6.20 pm, I received a phone call from Enda Kenny. He said Attorney General Máire Whelan was with him in his office, a serious issue had arisen and he asked that I join them. Assuming his conversation with Whelan related to the recording issue, which he confirmed, I informed him that I was at that moment being briefed on it. I asked whether he wished Purcell to accompany me and he said Purcell was not required at that stage. I asked Brian to remain available and immediately went to the Taoiseach's Department where I met Kenny, together with his Secretary General, Martin Fraser, and Máire Whelan. I had no reason to anticipate that the events then unfolding would, within days, become the subject matter of a Statutory Commission of Investigation conducted by retired Supreme Court judge, Justice Niall Fennelly.

I had no detailed knowledge of the extent of the recordings or their usage, nor did I know how long the recording had been going on. I had been told that, except for 999 calls, Martin Callinan had directed that recordings cease the previous November (2013) and that a serious question mark hung over their legality. I also knew nothing about any earlier involvement in the issue of the Attorney General, Máire Whelan, officials in her office, or officials in the Department of Justice. It was my understanding that Purcell and Flahive had only first learnt of the tapes at a meeting they attended earlier that afternoon with Mr Liam O'Daly, the Director General of the Attorney General's office.

The Taoiseach's request that I join him in Government Buildings halted a myriad of questions raised by me with Purcell and Flahive. It was only after my resignation from Government and during the Fennelly Commission of Investigation proceedings, that I first learned the full backstory of what was to become the most dramatic garda-related crisis to occur during my time in Cabinet.

The Fennelly Commission of Investigation's Interim Report of 31 August 2015, unknown to me on that March evening in 2014, would later detail that Garda Headquarters up to the level of Deputy Commissioner, Nóirín O'Sullivan, knew from 18 October 2013 at a general level, if not in full detail, that 'telephone calls between members of An Garda Síochána and between a member and a civilian had been recorded in the course of the du Plantier murder investigation in Bandon Garda Station on lines' which were said to be 'not usually recorded' and that 'the tapes of these calls were in the possession of the gardaí at Bandon, that the content of the calls was potentially "unhelpful" in the defence of the Bailey case and that there were other tapes which had yet to be listened to and transcribed; and systems for recording telephone calls had been installed in divisional Garda stations generally in the 1980s and replaced in the 1990s and about 2008'.

Fennelly would conclude that by 29 October 2013 Martin Callinan 'was fully aware of the serious problem which had arisen in Bandon, at least to the extent to which it was then known' and was first alerted to the 'general recording issue on 8 November 2013'. Fennelly would also establish that, on 11 November 2013, an instruction was issued on Callinan's initiative to cease all recording of phone calls other than 999/112 emergency calls, the Commissioner believing such recordings to be 'unlawful because those speaking were unaware that they were being recorded'.

Callinan had clearly rapidly addressed the issue. He had also swiftly sought legal advice and together with Nóirín O'Sullivan and Ken Ruane, the Head of Legal Affairs in An Garda Síochána, had met with Ruth Fitzgerald, advisory counsel in the Attorney General's office, on 11 November 2013. Fennelly wrote that Callinan had informed Fitzgerald that it appeared the recording systems had been put in place in the 1970s but he did not know why. He believed he could justify recording 999 calls but not the others. Prior to meeting Fitzgerald, Callinan had not been informed, as Fennelly found, that on 18 October 2013, a Superintendent Flynn of the Garda Information and Communication Technology (ICT) section had given as a rationale for the recordings 'the gathering of evidence around calls made to Garda stations regarding bomb threats and other code words messages'. 'Code words messages' would have had authenticating code words verifying that an anonymous message came from the Provisional IRA or some other violent subversive organisation. He also did not know that Flynn stated the recording systems were in Command and Control and Divisional Garda Stations.

Essentially, Fennelly determined that three separate reports on the recordings, made by Flynn internally within An Garda Síochána during the month of October, had not been given to Callinan prior to his 11 November meeting in the Attorney General's office. As a consequence, the initial advice he received from Ruth Fitzgerald was provided on the assumption that 'there was no possible justification for the recordings'.

On 14 November 2013, following her meeting with the Garda Commissioner, Ruth Fitzgerald gave Callinan written advice that, as it was not possible to say what was the purpose of the recordings, they were unlawful under the Data Protection Acts. As the recordings could be relevant to other court proceedings, apart from Bailey, she advised they be brought together and an inventory made. Properly acting on Fitzgerald's advice, Callinan issued an instruction that all tapes of recorded phone conversation be collated and brought to Garda Headquarters. Collating the tapes took several months and Fennelly concluded that no inventory was available until late February 2014.

The Fennelly Commission reported that at the 11 November 2013 meeting Ruth Fitzgerald informed Callinan that 'the Minister for Justice should be informed' and that Liam O'Daly, the Director General of the Attorney General's office, eight days later expressed a similar view. Fitzgerald, by text and email, on 21 November 2013, asked Ken Ruane, whether the Justice Department had been informed, offering to do so. Ruane's unfortunate answer was it would be 'more appropriate' for the Commissioner to inform the Department.

Fennelly wrote that, on 22 November, Callinan told Ruane that he had contacted Brian Purcell. Fennelly concluded that 'as a matter of probability' Callinan in a phone call did report the recordings to Purcell although Purcell denied this. However, Fennelly 'was not convinced that the Commissioner conveyed to Purcell any real sense of the importance of the matter' and found that the information given was 'at a level of generality which was not sufficient to make any impact on Mr Purcell'. As a result, Fennelly determined 'the Minister [that is, me] was not informed at all'. Fennelly concluded that based on the 'significance of the information' in Callinan's possession from mid-November 2013 and his understanding of its significance, he had failed to comply with his statutory obligation to ensure that I as the Minister for Justice and Purcell as the Secretary General of the Department were kept fully informed of what he knew of the recordings.

The Garda Commissioner, Fennelly records, had in November 2013 made a judgement that a written report was required but had delayed sending one until he had greater knowledge of the recordings. In finding that Callinan could at that stage have sent 'a careful but not very detailed report based on what he then knew', Fennelly also acknowledged that Callinan was then unaware of the crucial information contained in the series of reports furnished by Superintendent Flynn to the Executive Director of the Garda Information and Communications Technology section, Mr Liam Kidd, during October 2013.

Fennelly concluded that it was 'an error of judgement of the Garda Commissioner to postpone making a written report pending the gathering of facts concerning the number of tapes at Garda stations' and that 'he could have made a partial or general report sufficient to alert the Secretary General and the Minister of the matter'. Unfortunately, Callinan did not do so. If he had, it is likely I would have learned about the recordings much earlier than 24 March 2013 and the drama that was about to unfold in the Taoiseach's office may never have occurred. I also did not know on that evening of 24 March 2014, of a detailed letter from Callinan which had been delivered to Purcell at the Justice Department exactly two weeks earlier, on 10 March 2014, giving Purcell chapter and verse about the recordings, the action taken to date and legal issues which had arisen. The letter explicitly detailed what by then was known. It should have been instantly given to me but had, it seems, 'fallen between the cracks' in the Department. Brian Purcell did not mention it when, at the Taoiseach's request, he joined our meeting later that Monday evening. The existence of this letter was destined to remain unknown to me, the Attorney General and the Taoiseach until lunchtime the next day.

I was also unaware, as Fennelly detailed, that on 10 March a meeting had taken place in Garda Headquarters at Callinan's initiative attended by him, Assistant Commissioner Nóirín O'Sullivan and Senior and Junior Counsel for the State at which the Bailey case and the recordings were discussed. Others present included Michael Flahive from the Justice Department and Ruth Fitzgerald from the Attorney General's office. Fennelly reported that Callinan had originally sought the meeting ten days earlier on 28 February but that it did not occur earlier for 'logistical reasons'. Who was responsible for the 'logistical' difficulties and what they were was not clarified.

At the 10 March meeting, Fennelly found, the Garda Commissioner had informed Flahive that he wished to brief Purcell 'personally on the implication of the recordings in the Bailey case' and on counsel's advice how to proceed. As a result, the next morning, Tuesday 11 March, Callinan met Purcell, Flahive, Fitzgerald and a solicitor from the Chief State Solicitor's Office in the Department of Justice. According to Fennelly, at that meeting not only the tapes of relevance to the Bailey case but also the general recording issue were again discussed. Incredibly, Fennelly reported that the Garda Commissioner's letter delivered that Monday was not mentioned at either meeting. I was not informed of those meetings prior to my 24 March meeting with the Taoiseach in his office, and no mention was made of them by either Flahive or Purcell during the discussion commenced in my office at 6 pm that Monday evening. Fennelly concluded that:

> Two very high-powered meetings had ... occurred, one day after the other, involving the Garda Commissioner, Mr Callinan, Deputy Commissioner O'Sullivan, Senior Counsel, Advisory Counsel from the Attorney General's office, Ms Fitzgerald and a State Solicitor ... the Assistant Secretary from the Department, Mr Flahive attended the first of these meetings and the Secretary General attended the second. The Minister with direct statutory responsibility for An Garda Síochána was not informed about the subject matter of these meetings nor was he informed about the letter of 10th March and

remained unaware of it until the letter was handed to him on the morning of March 25th 2014.

Unusually, I was in my office in the Department of Justice all that Tuesday morning, 11 March 2014, as that week's Cabinet meeting was scheduled for the Wednesday afternoon instead of Tuesday morning as was usual. It would have been very simple for Purcell and Flahive, with or without Martin Callinan, to have called into my office after their meeting, to discuss what had transpired and to hand me Callinan's letter of 10 March. I would then have known of the issue before my departure to Mexico and would have been able to address it. I have no idea why they did not do so and there is no explanation contained in any conclusions reached by the Fennelly Commission. It was certainly reasonable for Martin Callinan to assume that if I had not already been told of or given his letter of 10 March, I would be fully briefed by Purcell and Flahive shortly after his meeting with them on 11 March in the Justice Department.

CHAPTER 27

Oh what a Tangled Web

It is necessary for a prince wishing to hold his own to know how to do wrong and to make use of it or not according to necessity ... he need not make himself uneasy at incurring a reproach for those vices without which the state can only be saved with difficulty, for if everything is considered carefully, it will be found that something which looks like virtue, if followed, could be his ruin; whilst something else, which looks like vice, yet followed, brings him security and prosperity
–Nicolai Machiavelli, *The Prince*

Entering the Taoiseach's office on that Monday evening, 24 March 2014, I knew nothing of the background to our meeting that would emerge during the course of the Fennelly Commission's investigation and in 2015 be detailed in Fennelly's Interim Report. I was confronted by a very grave-looking Taoiseach and a clearly agitated Attorney General. I was told that they were discussing the Bailey court proceedings, the discovery of audio recordings of phone conversations in Bandon Garda Station of relevance to those proceedings and the general discovery of garda recordings in an unspecified number of garda stations throughout the country. I explained I had only just learnt of the recordings, that the Taoiseach's phone call had interrupted my being briefed by Purcell and Flahive and at that point I had a limited knowledge of it all. Máire Whelan launched into a briefing. She told me that on the previous Thursday she had, with her officials, been going through the quarterly list of sensitive court proceedings in which the State was involved, which was to come before Cabinet for discussion the next day, Tuesday. She advised me that when discussing the Bailey case, the recording issue had surfaced. She made no mention of having any prior knowledge of the issue. What she learned, she said, had concerned her enormously and she had subsequently read through all the relevant files and papers. It was her view that the gardaí had been involved in wholesale illegality in the recording of phone conversations in garda stations. Not only had phone calls received been recorded for many years, but so were outgoing calls made from various stations. There was a possibility that phone calls made by arrested persons to their solicitors or phone calls made by solicitors from garda stations had been recorded. Neither the content of the recordings nor what use had been made of them was known. Whelan was concerned that criminal trials may have proceeded without disclosure of crucial evidence or there may have been wrongful convictions. Privileged conversations between solicitors and their clients may have been overheard. She presented the possibility of a substantial number of convictions being overturned, convicted offenders being released from prison and pending trials being stopped in their tracks. She was also alarmed by the possibility that the gardaí would destroy the tapes and she informed us that she had ensured that would not happen. (It became clear upon publication of the *Fennelly Report* that there was no possibility of the Garda Commissioner ordering the destruction of tapes without first obtaining advice from the Attorney General's office.)

It was obvious that this was the alarming picture Whelan had painted for Enda Kenny when, as I learned, they had met to discuss the issue the previous evening. Her presentation was of wholesale criminality by An Garda Síochána and the possible meltdown of our criminal justice system with multiple applications coming before the courts by members of the legal profession to secure the release of convicted offenders. (Of course, this never happened.) I was also informed that she had obtained some advice on the issue from outside counsel prior to that evening's meeting.

Neither Kenny nor Whelan explained why neither of them had contacted me prior to the Monday evening meeting to discuss the issue. There was also nothing said that could explain Whelan's subsequent evidence to Fennelly, as detailed in his report, that she had not discussed the recordings with me earlier because 'part of the issue involved the minister himself', that I was 'part of the narrative' and there were 'issues, allegations touching and concerning the Minister himself personally'. What Whelan meant by this is unclear. Did she lead Kenny to believe at their Sunday evening meeting that I knew of and had concealed from him my knowledge of 'illegal' garda recordings? I do not know. As a result of a conversation between Michael Flahive and Liam O'Daly the previous Friday, of which she was informed by O'Daly, she wrongly believed prior to her first meeting with Kenny that I knew all about the recordings. Fennelly also wrote that she referenced as an explanation for not contacting me 'the narrative in the media' of Callinan and I as 'being unduly close'. The relevance of that statement is a total mystery as Callinan had sought advice from the Attorney General's Office in November 2013 upon learning of the tapes. Fennelly also detailed that the minutes of a meeting between Whelan and her officials on Thursday, 20 March 2014 record: 'AG queried that the Minister did not seem to have anything to do with the issue. RF [that is, Ruth Fitzgerald] said yes and noted that the issue dates back to the mid 1980s.'

Another explanation given by Whelan for her failure to discuss the recordings with me prior to the Monday evening, Fennelly wrote, was 'the tensions that existed between the Minister for Justice and Mr Varadkar'. This was a reference to the controversy subsequent to Varadkar's speech to the Road Safety Authority, delivered coincidentally on the same day Whelan stated she became concerned about the garda recordings. This explanation was totally bizarre, as the discovery of garda tapes and recordings had no connection of any nature with any issue relating to Maurice McCabe, the ticket charge/penalty points issue or Varadkar's speech.

Fennelly clearly did not regard Whelan's explanations for her conduct as plausible. First referencing that 'there were no allegations' relating to me concerning the tapes 'which created any barrier' to my 'being briefed by the Attorney General over the weekend', Fennelly, in his 2015 report, expressed puzzlement at her failure to both contact me and seek information if she believed me to be 'fully briefed' on the issue. He concluded that it would have 'been both reasonable and prudent for her to have done so'.

It is possible that having heard and read the by then popular repetitive allegation that Callinan and I were 'joined at the hip', or Oliver Connolly's depiction of us as best friends, the judgement of Kenny, as well as Whelan, became contaminated by this nonsense by the time of their Sunday evening meeting and Kenny believed I was engaged in some sort of conspiracy to cover up what Whelan referred to as 'illegal' garda recordings.

As Callinan had sought advice from Whelan's office in November 2013 there was no basis for any such belief. However, Kenny, as far as I know, on Sunday, 23 March 2014, was not told and did not know that Callinan had done so. I believe that to be the probable explanation for Kenny failing to make any contact with me between the Sunday and Monday evenings.

The Taoiseach at our meeting that Monday evening said he was 'gravely concerned'. The recordings were going to be yet another major garda scandal. An affidavit of discovery, I was told, had to be sworn in the Bailey case by the next day, Tuesday, 25 March 2014, and following that, the issue of the recordings would come out. Kenny stated that the Cabinet would have to be informed the next morning, Tuesday, at the weekly Cabinet meeting. The quarterly list of sensitive cases would be under discussion. There was also going to be a discussion about the Garda Commissioner, following on from Varadkar's public comments and calls from Labour Cabinet Ministers on the Commissioner to withdraw his 'disgusting' comment. Kenny, as Taoiseach, could not continue to express confidence in the Garda Commissioner on Tuesday if all of this could hit the fan by Wednesday.

I tried carefully to digest and analyse what I was being told. As a lawyer I knew that if an affidavit of discovery was required by the courts to be sworn by the next day, Tuesday, 25 March 2014, the material referenced in the affidavit would not normally be made available until some days later. It was my understanding, at that stage, that the issue had only emerged in the manner described by Whelan four days earlier and I queried whether an adjournment could be sought extending the time for swearing or filing the affidavit of discovery. In response, Whelan insisted that the affidavit had to be sworn by 25 March and there was no possibility of an agreed delay. Three weeks later I learned that, on that Monday, presumably unknown to Whelan, agreement had been reached to extend by two weeks the time for the affidavit to be sworn and filed in court.

Some of the concerns expressed by Whelan I had raised in the Department of Justice with Brian Purcell. Listening to Purcell and then to Whelan it was clear to me there was a huge information deficit around the recordings and I was concerned that Whelan's assessment was unduly alarmist. I was disturbed to only learn of the tapes' existence that evening and did not know why I had not been told of them earlier by Martin Callinan. At that moment I did not know whether the discovery of the tapes had been deliberately concealed from me or whether there had simply been a cock-up. I could not understand why, if Whelan had only first identified difficulties the previous Thursday which gave rise to major concerns, she had not contacted me directly upon my return from Mexico or why, following her Sunday evening meeting with the Taoiseach in Government Buildings, neither of them had discussed the issue with me. I had been available all Sunday evening and all day on Monday and had only been asked to attend the meeting in Government Buildings some twenty minutes after I understood it had started. I would later learn during the course of the Fennelly Commission's investigation, as Judge

Fennelly reported, that the 6 pm Monday meeting between Kenny and Whelan had been arranged between them the night before.

Fennelly's report also established that, contrary to the presentation Whelan made at the Monday evening meeting in the Taoiseach's office, she first learnt of the garda recordings four months earlier on 14 November 2013 when she received a memo from Ruth Fitzgerald about the issue, headed 'Nomination of Counsel – Discovery of Garda Station Recordings of Telephone Conversations'. The memo, as Fennelly detailed, informed the Attorney General as follows:

> It appears that systems were put in place in Garda stations – possibly in the 1970s – to allow for the recording of incoming and outgoing telephone calls. The reasons for the installation of the system are not known at this remove. However, in many stations the system has continued in place and recordings of telephone conversations have been made and stored. Some of the recordings are on tapes which are effectively obsolete.

Fitzgerald, in her memo, informed Whelan in November 2013 that the issue had come to light as a result of the discovery process in the Bailey case and then continued 'as regard 999 calls, these are recorded and that is both permissible and necessary. What is at issue here is calls other than 999 calls.'

A further extract from Fitzgerald's memo to Whelan (as detailed by Fennelly) states:

> As it is not possible at this remove to say what the purpose for the recording was … it would appear that the recording of telephone conversations since the introduction of the Data Protection Act is unlawful insofar as there was no purpose for the recording or the retention of the recording.

> The Garda Commissioner indicated at our meeting that he does not think there is any reason for retaining the recordings and he does not wish to do so. His concern was whether there was anything which would stop him directing the destruction of the recordings. It seems to me that this is a difficult issue upon which to advise. At one level, the recordings are illegal and illegally obtained evidence should not

be used in support of a prosecution or proceedings. Yet it may be that a party who communicated with a Garda Station may have some reason to wish to obtain the recording e.g. may claim it contains exculpatory evidence.

Fitzgerald concluded her memo by asking that Whelan nominate counsel to advise on the issue. She responded by nominating counsel but did not otherwise comment, Fennelly concluded.

Unknown to the Garda Commissioner and Ruth Fitzgerald information of relevance to the recordings was omitted from this memo. However, when the memo was furnished to Whelan, there was sufficient content in it to generate substantial concern and ring alarm bells about both the Bailey case and the general audio recordings made in garda stations. Unfortunately, in November 2013, alarm bells did not ring. Fennelly recorded that Whelan informed the Commission that 'she merely received a routine document seeking nomination of counsel,' noted it was a Data Protection matter 'and signed off on the basis that counsel would advise'. However, Fennelly detailed that less than a week later, on 20 November 2013, a Legal Management Advisory Committee (Legal MAC) meeting took place in Whelan's office which she herself attended. A brief written report of 19 November 2013 prepared by Ruth Fitzgerald on the general recording issue was considered at the meeting. It contained a 'direction' added by Liam O'Daly that the Department of Justice should be notified about the telephone recording issue. Fennelly stated that a minute of the meeting simply recorded: 'The issue of recordings of telephone conversations to and from Garda stations was noted and may be the result of the use of an automatic recording phone system in certain garda stations.' Fennelly wrote that Whelan, in her evidence, 'confirmed that she had seen that report and the recommendation of Mr O'Daly'.

I was both astonished and shocked to discover during the course of the Fennelly Commission's work the extent of Whelan's knowledge of the garda recordings prior to March 2014 as detailed in the Fitzgerald memo published by Fennelly. Had she informed me of the issue, I could have briefed both the Taoiseach and the Government and discussed the recordings with the Garda Commissioner four months earlier.

Essentially, Whelan and her officials left it to the Garda Commissioner to inform both me as Minister and the Department of Justice about the recordings. If the recordings discovered had related to the Bailey case alone, that should have been sufficient to warrant Whelan mentioning them to me, as the Minister for Justice was a named defendant in the Bailey proceedings, which were high-profile both domestically and internationally. Not only did she not do so, but at the meeting that March evening in the Taoiseach's office no mention of any nature was made by her to me of her first learning of the recordings in November 2013. Indeed, she would, some days after the creation of the Fennelly Commission of Investigation, remark to me following a Cabinet meeting that her officials had failed to brief her on the issue and she had only become aware of it on 20 March. No mention was made by her to me of the Legal MAC meeting held on 20 November 2013, her attendance at it and Liam O'Daly's advice that the Department of Justice be informed. All of this was explored in great detail in the *Fennelly Commission Report*. Fennelly acknowledged that the Attorney did not, after 20 November 2013, until 20 March 2014, see any further documentation or participate in any discussion of the recording issue and was unaware of developments in the interim period. However, I believe that she knew enough by 20 November to have understood the importance of ensuring that I was told.

Fennelly concluded that Ruth Fitzgerald expected that the Garda Síochána would inform the Department of Justice and recorded that Mr Ruane 'clearly indicated on 21st November 2013 that he would undertake to have the Commissioner inform the Department of the issue'. This did not, however, in any way preclude Whelan during one of our many phone discussions or on the various occasions that we met throughout the weeks and months that followed from mentioning the recordings to me. No legal barrier existed to prevent our having any such conversation. In circumstances in which the Minister for Justice was a named defendant in the Bailey proceedings, both the Attorney and her staff, as the legal advisers to the Government, I believe should have communicated both to me as Minister, and to officials in the Justice Department, the information received by them, any concerns it generated and should have detailed any legal action required. In the context of her knowledge of the succession of garda-related controversies in which I became embroiled in February 2014 and her attendance at Cabinet meetings in which they were discussed, her failure to discuss the recordings issue with me prior to the evening of 24 March 2014 is incomprehensible.

Fennelly recorded that it was Fitzgerald's understanding that it was both 'customary and appropriate in this specific instance' for such communication to come to me and the Department from the Garda Commissioner. On this, Fennelly recorded, Fitzgerald's view was supported by Liam O'Daly, and by Whelan who told the Commission: 'my impression was … that the Garda Síochána were very proprietorial of their relationship with the Department of Justice and … my impression certainly would be that it would be not very well received if there was any intervention directly by my office'.

Fennelly reported that the 'impression of a proprietorial relationship was disputed by Mr Callinan who told the Commission he has always assumed that the Attorney General's office would copy the Department of Justice with any advice given to An Garda Síochána'. Fennelly also reported Callinan as stating that he would have 'absolutely no difficulty' with the Attorney General's office 'informing the Department of Justice of anything that was happening between the office of the Attorney General and An Garda Síochána'. Stating that the Commission had received 'conflicting evidence from relevant witnesses as to whether a practice existed of the Attorney General's office copying advice to the Department of Justice', Fennelly concluded that it was not necessary to resolve the conflict as a consequence of Mr Ruane's commitment that the Commissioner would inform the Department of Justice of the issue.

For my part, as Minister and a member of Government, I had at all times assumed that if an important issue relevant to my Department came to the attention of the Attorney General, be it to do with litigation of relevance to the Department or legislation, that as the Attorney was the legal adviser to the Government, it would be brought to my attention and that Justice officials would be informed. During my three years in Government, there was a myriad of issues Máire Whelan and I had informally discussed and, on occasions, I had provided some assistance in addressing legal issues of difficulty that fell within my own areas of legal expertise. Unfortunately, in November 2013, Whelan did not attach the same importance to the Garda recordings issue as she did when revisiting it on 20 March 2014. It was only then that she had a 'Eureka' moment remarking to her officials, as Fennelly records, that the general recording of telephone calls in garda stations 'will be sensational'. The truth is the bizarre manner in which she dealt with the issue, her rush to judgement before taking reasonable steps to ascertain the factual background to the recordings, the premature and alarmist advice given by her to the Taoiseach and her affording me no opportunity as Minister for Justice to discover what had occurred, significantly contributed to the revelation of the recordings being a sensation.

In his report, Fennelly concluded that the information available on Garda recordings:

> and its possible implications were recognised by the Attorney General's office in November 2013 as being sufficiently important to warrant the Minister for Justice being informed of the issue. It is clear that this did not take place. The issue was not brought to the Minister's attention until March 2014. Responsibility for this must lie with either the Garda Commissioner, Mr Callinan, or the Secretary General of the Department of Justice, Mr Purcell or both.

Ultimately, Fennelly concluded that each bore responsibility for this failure but on this issue did not criticise Whelan or her officials. I believe, however, that she should have personally ensured that information on the taping issue available to her office in November 2013 was furnished to me. In fairness to Whelan and her officials it was reasonable for them to assume after the meetings of 10 and 11 March 2014 that I would have been the beneficiary of a comprehensive briefing from Purcell and Flahive but if this was Whelan's understanding, her failure to discuss the issue with me after her Thursday 20 March insight is both inexplicable and inexcusable.

In the Taoiseach's office on that Monday evening, when Whelan had completed her briefing detailing the background and her concerns, there were still substantial gaps in the information available. Other than there being three transcripts made of tapes containing content relevant to the Bailey proceedings, nothing was known about the content of any other recordings. It was also not known what use, if any, the gardaí had made of recordings or of their likely relevance to any pending or concluded criminal trials. I believed these were all issues of importance in any discussion that might take place at Cabinet the next day and substantial outstanding information was required from An Garda Síochána. I was surprised that the Taoiseach did not agree to my suggestion that we should meet with Martin Callinan. Meeting him was discussed but discounted. Kenny was worried that the Garda Commissioner being invited to Government Buildings, or to the Department of Justice, would become known and add fuel to the media frenzy that had followed Varadkar's Thursday intervention. I was not entirely convinced but the Taoiseach was adamant. Instead, Kenny stated that Purcell should be asked to join our meeting and to make contact with the Garda Commissioner to communicate to him the Taoiseach's 'grave concerns'.

The likely reaction of Cabinet members to news of the discovery of the telephone recordings was also discussed. I had little doubt that the recordings revelation would result in another political and media storm and that some members of Cabinet would demand Martin Callinan's resignation. The Taoiseach in the preceding days had regularly responded positively when he was asked by media whether he had confidence in the Commissioner. He was concerned about how he might respond if doorstepped by reporters the following morning when entering Government Buildings before the Cabinet meeting. He was also concerned that he might not be able to express confidence in the Commissioner following the conclusion of the Cabinet meeting. There was no suggestion that night that Callinan had done anything wrong or any discussion of his dismissal as Garda Commissioner but I understood that there was a possibility his position would become untenable.

Reflecting on the length of time the recordings had taken place and the action taken by the Commissioner to end them in November 2013, I had a nagging doubt as to whether the Attorney General's level of alarm was justified and had no doubt at all that the Taoiseach's perspective on the issue entirely derived from her information and advice. The Fennelly Commission would later conclude that the Taoiseach's concerns, 'arose from briefings given to the Taoiseach by the Attorney General on 23rd and 24th of March in which she informed him that An Garda Síochána had for decades been engaged in apparent widespread violation of the law the length and breadth of the country, with potentially serious implications for An Garda Síochána and the State'.

Fennelly also critically concluded that 'while briefing the Taoiseach in those terms, the Attorney believed that she had insufficient information about the matter to offer definitive advice on the real legal questions at issue'.

There were, according to Fennelly,

significant gaps in the information then in the possession of her office on matters including the origin of the recording system; the number of stations involved and the types of lines recorded; the operation, management and use of recordings by An Garda Síochána; the extent to which the recording of calls between solicitors and their clients was contemplated and/or feasible; and the extent to which members of An Garda Síochána in relevant stations were aware of what telephone lines were being recorded. In so far as it was available, any such information was likely to be in the possession of An Garda Síochána.

Fennelly criticised Whelan for not seeking the outstanding information directly from An Garda Síochána or through me as Minister for Justice in the period between 20 March and the meeting on the evening of 24 March. He made no secret of his view that Whelan should have sought 'further information before taking any stand on the matter' and that it was clear from events that occurred that 'she did not do so'.

Essentially, Fennelly concluded Whelan lacked crucial relevant information when first advising Enda Kenny on the recordings. The premature 'stand' taken by her, Fennelly found, 'injected' a 'new element of seriousness and urgency into consideration of the telephone recording issue, combined with the emergence of some recordings in the course of the investigation into the murder of Madame Toscan du Plantier' and 'contributed decisively to the subsequent very serious light in which the Garda telephone recording issue was viewed'.

The Fennelly Commission gave detailed consideration to the approach taken both by Whelan and Kenny in the period between 21 and 24 March. Judge Fennelly, in his report, stated that:

It is difficult to avoid the conclusion that a decision was made not to include the Minister for Justice in discussions of the matter on Sunday, 23rd March, and for most of Monday, 24th March. The Taoiseach maintained that he was entitled not to do so, but the information he was receiving from the Attorney General could not have been more alarming and it does raise the question as to whether it was the most appropriate decision. It is impossible to know what would have happened if the Minister had been taken into the confidence of the Taoiseach and the Attorney General. Mr Shatter has said that he would himself have contacted the Commissioner. It is true that the Commissioner was not contacted, either by the Taoiseach or the Attorney General, following the meeting on Sunday evening, the

23rd March 2014. It is very likely that, if the Minister had been kept informed of the issue, it would have made a significant difference to the events as they unfolded.

Unfortunately, Fennelly did not investigate or explore what conversations, if any, about the issue took place prior to the Monday evening meeting in the Taoiseach's office between Kenny and his special advisers, Mark Kennelly and Andrew McDowell. That remains unknown.

In the Taoiseach's Department that Monday evening, 24 March 2014, events continued to unfold. At about 9pm, Brian Purcell joined us. There was some further discussion about the discovery of the Garda tapes and Kenny informed Purcell that he wanted him to meet Callinan that evening to explain his grave concerns about the matter. In Purcell's presence, reference was made to the next day's Cabinet meeting and to the difficulty Kenny might have after that meeting in expressing confidence in the Commissioner. At no stage was Purcell asked to seek any 'views' or 'information' of any nature from Callinan, as Kenny would later claim, nor was any express statement made that Callinan should consider his position. However, I had no doubt that a message conveyed to Callinan stating the Taoiseach's 'grave concerns' and that following the Cabinet meeting the Taoiseach may be unable to express confidence in him implicitly carried with it the message that he should also consider his position. I believed that this was intended by Kenny and, as the meeting evolved, I suspected it was his intention to get to this point from the very start of the meeting. It all made sense in the context of his resistance to Callinan being asked to meet with us that evening and his preference that Purcell, and not I, would meet with him. If Kenny wished Callinan to fall on his sword, he likely had concerns that if I met Callinan he would not do so. From the Taoiseach's perspective, it was obvious that if the Commissioner swiftly resigned or retired, the difficulties surrounding the following day's Cabinet meeting would be resolved. Kenny would also be immunised from political criticism and attack resulting from his earlier expressions of confidence in Callinan.

Brian Purcell clearly understood the nature and likely consequence of the message he was to deliver. He became agitated, stood up and, unusually in the presence of the Taoiseach, paced up and down, constantly repeating the words 'this is wrong', 'this is wrong' and 'this is all wrong'. I doubt that the Secretary General of any Government Department has ever so behaved in the presence of a Taoiseach. I regarded Purcell's reaction as creating an opportunity for me to meet Callinan to attempt to ascertain the full story. As Kenny was insistent that Purcell meet with him, I offered to accompany Purcell on what had by then been agreed to be a visit by him to the Commissioner's home. It is my recollection that Kenny directed that Purcell should go alone and that Purcell also turned down my offer to go with him. The Fennelly Commission would later conclude that it was simply Purcell who turned down my offer.

The time approached 10pm and the meeting ended. Purcell was to first phone Callinan and then drive to his house and he did so. I was convinced there was more to the story and conflicted about whether I should phone Callinan before Purcell's arrival at his home. I had always respected Kenny's authority as Taoiseach and his role as head of Government. I was concerned that a phone call by me at that moment to Callinan would be seen to be not only disloyal but to be disrespectful. I was also concerned that my making such a call could result in a charge that I was in some way complicit in concealing the discovery of the recordings and attempting to fabricate some story with the Commissioner. In addition, I was annoyed that I had not been informed by Callinan of the recordings issue prior to that evening and wrongly suspected that he might have concealed the issue from me because of the multiplicity of garda-related controversies and media labelled 'scandals' of the preceding weeks.

If I had phoned Callinan, it is likely I would have learned that, exactly two weeks earlier on 10 March 2014, a detailed letter explaining the Garda taping issue, signed by him, for my attention, had been delivered to Purcell's office. While Purcell had protested in the Taoiseach's office that what he was being asked to do was wrong, he had neither brought the Garda Commissioner's letter along with him nor mentioned its existence nor his meeting thirteen days earlier with Martin Callinan in the Department of Justice at which they had discussed the recordings issue. The letter would not surface until towards the end of the next day's Cabinet meeting, over three hours after Martin Callinan had announced his premature retirement. It was only upon receipt of the letter that I learnt the Garda Commissioner had first furnished information to and sought advice from the Attorney General's office on the recordings the previous November. When I read the letter, I wrongly assumed the issue had been dealt with by Máire Whelan's officials without her knowledge. The extent of the information furnished to her of the recordings in November 2013 did not fully emerge until the hearings of the Fennelly Commission of Investigation. It only became public knowledge upon publication of the *Fennelly Interim Report* in September 2015. And by then few noticed or really cared.

CHAPTER 28

The Garda Commissioner Retires

The immediate and direct cause of his [Martin Callinan's] decision to retire was the visit from Mr Purcell and the message conveyed from the Taoiseach during that visit
–Interim Report of the Fennelly Commission, September 2015

As I was leaving the Taoiseach's office that Monday evening, the Taoiseach told me that he had met Leo Varadkar that morning and discussed with him his speech of the previous Thursday and his criticism of the Garda Commissioner. Varadkar had not mentioned this meeting to me in the Yamamori restaurant. Saying that Leo was a 'troubled young man' due to a family member dying in a crash, Kenny asked that I meet Leo the next day before the Cabinet meeting. Kenny gave no details of the Varadkar family's bereavement. It was only upon my reading Philip Ryan and Niall O'Connor's book *Leo* published in September 2018, that I first learned that, almost nine years earlier, in June 2005, in Carlow, in a 'freak road traffic accident' Varadkar's 82-year-old maternal grandfather had been killed when a loose horse on the road panicked and jumped on the bonnet of the car in which he was travelling.

I informed Kenny that Leo and I had already arranged to meet in Government Buildings and that I had fine-tuned the briefing document on the Ticket Charge/Penalty Points issue emailed to him on the Sunday for distribution at Cabinet on the Tuesday morning. We had not discussed that issue or any other garda-related controversies that evening. However, I had little doubt that they were in the background. The Cooke inquiry into the allegation that the gardaí had GSOC under surveillance and the Guerin inquiry into allegations of garda corruption and misconduct made by Sergeant Maurice McCabe had only been underway for a short few weeks, Cabinet Members were publicly calling on the Garda Commissioner to withdraw his 'disgusting' remark and now the Taoiseach had been presented, in the most alarmist fashion by Máire Whelan, with what was inevitably going to be referred to by the media as another 'garda scandal'.

I knew Varadkar had a great capacity to rock the boat and had no concept of collegiality. It was my experience that if he believed there was an issue to be addressed which would generate a headline and attract praise, rather than discussing it privately with a Ministerial colleague to assist in its resolution, he was guaranteed to talk at you through a public media megaphone – or you would find out through an unidentified source quoted in a newspaper, most often the *Sunday Independent*, which would credit him as having a particular view. This made him a favourite of the print media. I had no way of knowing the influence, if any, of Varadkar's meeting with Kenny that Monday morning and how it figured in Kenny's assessment of how to best address the garda telephone recordings issue. I was conscious that he was entirely reliant on Whelan's advice that there had been a 'wholesale violation of the law by An Garda Síochána' and that he must have had concerns about Varadkar's likely response to this information coming up at Tuesday's Cabinet meeting. Having repeatedly publicly expressed confidence in Martin Callinan, any implications for his continued leadership of Fine Gael, his position as Taoiseach and for the stability of the Government, I knew, had to have figured in Kenny's approach. I believed it was likely that these considerations substantially influenced his behaviour and the dynamic of our meeting in his office.

Checking my mobile phone as I was being driven home, I found a text from Varadkar confirming our Tuesday morning meeting suggesting 'we bring advisors' but stating also 'one on one is fine with me too'. I responded: 'That's grand. See you in the morning' and informed him my advisers would be there. From the outside looking in we appeared to be the best of buddies. I made no reference to the night of drama in Government Buildings.

At home, I reflected on what had occurred and my concerns grew as did my regret that I had not insisted, as Minister for Justice, that Martin Callinan be invited to discuss the issue with us that night in Government Buildings. Just after midnight I sent a text to Brian Purcell. It read: 'This is horrendous. Phone me when u can at any time. A.'

About thirty minutes later, Purcell telephoned. He had left the Commissioner's home and, shortly after, Callinan had phoned him proposing to announce that he would retire, his retirement to take effect in three months time. Brian had informed Martin Fraser who would contact the Taoiseach. Purcell sounded very distressed and described his visit to Callinan's home as the worst meeting of his life. He made no mention of Callinan's letter of 10 March. It was agreed that we would talk again in the early morning and he would make contact in the meantime if there were any developments.

I went to bed feeling exhausted and emotionally drained. I slept until 3am, then went downstairs, made a cup of tea and read through that day's Cabinet papers and then the morning papers online. While the Garda recordings issue did not feature, the controversy triggered by Varadkar the previous Thursday continued to dominate the headlines.

'Warring FG Ministers ordered to cool Penalty Points row' was the headline on the front page of the *Irish Independent* followed by 'Labour won't push for Garda Chief Callinan to quit post' on the inside. The *Irish Daily Mirror*'s headline reported 'Whistleblower row splits the Cabinet' while in contrast, the *Irish Times* story was headlined 'Gilmore denies Cabinet tension over Callinan'. It was all about Ticket Charges/Penalty Points, Sergeant Maurice McCabe and Varadkar's intervention over the Garda Commissioner's 'disgusting' reference.

Irish Times columnist Fintan O'Toole's article was headlined 'Disgust means Callinan must go' while the *Irish Independent* editorial read 'Callinan in tough position ahead of Cabinet meeting'. All of the stories and articles maintained the theme that Callinan was the villain of the piece and Varadkar the hero with whom I was involved in a row. This despite the fact that five days had passed and I had not uttered a single word in public in response to his intervention the previous Thursday. Clearly, nothing was yet known of the garda recording issue or of the dramatic meeting the night before in the Taoiseach's Department or of Brian Purcell's late-night visit to the Commissioner's home. RTÉ Radio 1's *Morning Ireland* reported on the continuing ticket charge controversy and broadcast an interview with Clare Daly calling on the Commissioner to resign. Shortly after that, Brian Purcell got in touch to tell me that the Taoiseach was insisting on the Commissioner's immediate retirement and would not agree to it being delayed. Martin Callinan was being informed.

I arrived in Government Buildings in good time for my 8.45am meeting with Varadkar. Purcell was already in my office as we had arranged. No major developments had occurred since our phone discussion and it was expected there would be a meeting in the Taoiseach's office later. Together with my two Special Advisers Jane Lehane and Jennifer Carroll I met Varadkar who arrived with his Special Adviser, Brian Murphy and his Press Officer, Nick Miller. Having briefly exchanged pleasantries we commenced discussing the Ticket Charge and Penalty Points issue, the allegations made by Sergeant Maurice McCabe and the Garda Commissioner's remarks before the Public Accounts Committee. As far as I know, Varadkar knew nothing of the drama being played out in the background and I did not believe it appropriate that I discuss it with him until the position of Martin Callinan was fully clarified. The truth was my head was not in the discussion. Although annoyed by Varadkar's intervention when I was away in Mexico and the damaging briefings against me that I believed he had orchestrated, I tried to avoid any recrimination of any nature whatsoever but simply factually explained what I understood to be the context of the Commissioner's 'disgusting' comment and the reality that while Maurice McCabe had certainly acted as the catalyst to substantial changes being implemented to the Fixed Charge Notice Processing System, he had also made very serious damaging allegations which were not substantiated.

I have little memory of what else was said at the meeting other than Varadkar was brooding and largely silent and, when it was over, I thought it one of the oddest meetings in which I had ever participated. At one point, I was called out to be updated on where matters stood with Martin Callinan. After we finished, I met with the Taoiseach, Martin Fraser and Brian Purcell in the Taoiseach's office. Callinan had agreed to instantly retire and I was advised that he would shortly issue a statement.

Callinan had presided over the Garda Síochána at an enormously difficult time. Due to the State's dire financial circumstances there had been a dramatic reduction in funding for An Garda Síochána. Badly needed investment in garda technology and software had been postponed, 139 garda stations had been closed, recruitment to the gardaí had stopped in 2009 and the numbers within the force had been significantly reduced. Nonetheless, Callinan had played a crucial role in protecting the security of the State and in the fight against crime and subversion. Despite all the controversies surrounding the workings of the Fixed Charge Notice Processing System, there had also on his watch undoubtedly been a dramatic reduction in road fatalities and he had rapidly reformed that system after publication of the O'Mahoney and GPSU reports. What he had said at the Public Accounts Committee had repeatedly been selectively edited and quoted and his critics did not know that a groundless accusation that he was corrupt made against him by McCabe in January 2012 would, two years after his retirement, be said by the O'Higgins Commission to be 'unfounded' and 'unsupported' by any evidence.

Regardless of the back story into the garda recording issue, of which I had no visibility that morning, I believed that Callinan had been consistently unfairly pilloried by the media and Opposition TDs, had been targeted for politically opportunistic reasons by some of my Cabinet colleagues and, in the end, wrongly hounded out of office. While Fennelly ultimately concluded that Callinan should have reported to me earlier on the garda recordings, looking back on it all now it is clear that he responded correctly to the discovery of the recordings and sought and relied upon the advice of the Attorney General's office in dealing with them. There was no question of tapes or recordings being destroyed in the absence of advice from that office. Nor, as Fennelly would ultimately conclude in his final Report of March 2017, was there any evidence of information recorded being misused by An Garda Síochána. Callinan also ultimately fulfilled his statutory obligation to inform me of the discovery of the recordings and the action taken by him in his letter of 10 March 2014. He was entitled to assume that his specific request in his letter to Brian Purcell that it be furnished to me would be swiftly complied with.

I did not know that further allegations and controversy would surface in the years that followed concerning Callinan's conduct around the time of the PAC hearings on the ticket charge issue and his interaction with the head of the Garda Press Office and would be addressed in 2018 by the Disclosures Tribunal.

I also did not anticipate the dispute which Judge Fennelly narrated occurred before his Commission of Investigation over the exact mission given by Enda Kenny to Brian Purcell on the night he visited Callinan in his home. This centred around whether Purcell was asked to inform the Commissioner that the Taoiseach may be unable to express confidence in him after the Tuesday Cabinet meeting. To my surprise, as Fennelly records, in their evidence both Kenny and Máire Whelan denied that this was part of Purcell's mission and that it had been discussed at the meeting in the Taoiseach's office. A meeting between Kenny and Eamon Gilmore unexpectedly facilitated Fennelly unravelling the truth.

Shortly after 9am on Tuesday, 25 March 2014, Kenny met Gilmore who, for the first time, was briefed by Kenny on the events of the preceding twenty-four hours. The *Fennelly Report* records that Kenny informed Gilmore of 'very alarming' information he had received from Máire Whelan in relation to the Bailey case and the general recording issue. Fennelly continued that:

The Taoiseach, according to Mr Gilmore, went on to say that, if he were asked in the House [i.e. the Dáil] if he had confidence in the Garda Commissioner, he would not be able to say that he had. He added that, if he said that he had confidence in the Garda Commissioner on the Tuesday and information relating to these tapes emerged on the Wednesday he would then be in a very difficult position.

Gilmore's evidence was regarded by Fennelly as 'significant corroboration for the proposition that the Taoiseach did express doubts about whether he could continue to express confidence in the Commissioner' at the Monday evening meeting that took place in his office. Fennelly recalled that Kenny spoke to Gilmore 'very much in the same terms as are attributed to him by his Secretary General, Martin Fraser, Mr Shatter and Mr Purcell' and concluded that: 'there is no reason to doubt the evidence of Mr Fraser, Mr Shatter and Mr Purcell that it was said the Taoiseach might not be able to continue to express confidence in the Commissioner. The Commission finds their evidence to be plausible and credible.'

In so concluding, Fennelly essentially rejected evidence given under oath by Enda Kenny and Máire Whelan as being both implausible and lacking credibility. In most Western European democracies in such circumstances it would have been universally regarded as untenable that the Prime Minister and the Attorney General remain in office. But not so in Ireland. It was politically expedient for members of both the Fine Gael and the Labour Parties to look the other way and ignore Fennelly's rejection of sworn evidence given by Kenny and Whelan, the former being the leader of Fine Gael and the latter being a member of the Labour Party. This was also facilitated by Fennelly accepting Kenny's word that he did not intend to put pressure on Callinan to retire as a consequence of Purcell's unprecedented late-night visit to his home while concluding that

> when all the circumstances are viewed objectively, the mission on which Mr Purcell was being sent was liable to be interpreted as suggesting to the Commissioner that he should consider his position ... the message delivered by Mr Purcell, in all the attendant circumstances, in explicit contemplation of the risk that at the next day's cabinet meeting the Taoiseach might possibly be not able to express confidence in him, carried with it the obvious implication that the Commissioner's own position was in question.

Essentially, it was a conclusion that Kenny either lacked the intelligence or insight to foresee the blindingly 'obvious' or did not understand the natural consequence or outcome of the 'mission' on which he sent Purcell. In other circumstances that would have been insulting but confronted by the allegation that he had unlawfully forced the Commissioner to resign Kenny celebrated Fennelly's conclusion, the media being widely briefed by Government sources that he had been vindicated by Fennelly. Interestingly, Fennelly reported that Kenny's own Secretary General, Martin Fraser 'was not surprised that a decision by the Commissioner to retire was the ultimate outcome'. Fennelly's report also recorded my evidence that I 'was firmly of the view that the Commissioner was expected by the Taoiseach to consider his position'. My view has not changed.

In September 2015, after some huffing and puffing in the immediate aftermath of publication of the *Fennelly Report* and some political slapstick in the Dáil Chamber after the summer recess, Opposition politicians and media commentators, who had wrongly accused me of not telling the truth about my knowledge of garda recordings and Callinan's 10 March 2014 letter, rapidly moved on to other business. Perhaps they were discombobulated by Fennelly's findings discrediting false allegations made which had resulted in my being publicly pilloried in the immediate aftermath of Martin Callinan retiring. To have politically and repetitively honed in on Fennelly's rejection of parts of Kenny's and Whelan's sworn evidence would have required an eventual public acknowledgement that I had been wrongly excoriated, that I had stood up to both Kenny and Whelan before the Fennelly Commission and that I had told the truth. For both Opposition politicians and media commentators that was, it seems, a step too far and risked debunking the preferred narrative casting me, when it came to each of the garda-related controversies, in the leading role as the deviant cabinet villain.

****

In again reporting on Varadkar's revival of the ticket charge controversy and my Dail reference to the whistle-blowers' lack of cooperation with the O'Mahoney investigation, the morning papers on Tuesday 25 March 2014 quoted Eamon Gilmore as saying that 'I think it would be helpful if the remarks were withdrawn'. I had addressed that issue only four weeks earlier in the Dáil and Gilmore had not asked that I say anything more about it. I anticipated that in the discussions taking place that morning between Kenny and Gilmore the issue of my 'apologising' to McCabe to lower the political temperature and call off the media hounds would arise.

The creation of a policing authority had been Labour Party policy for some time but it had not been agreed as part of the Programme for Government. It was clearly now back on the political agenda. A balanced approach to addressing critical issues relating to the gardaí, I believed, had been totally abandoned in the thirty-first Dáil. Where there was credible evidence of significant garda failures or illegal conduct, I believed it was entirely right that such issues be addressed in the Dáil. However, I was concerned that unverified allegations were being politically weaponised and that it had become acceptable that the Garda Commissioner be regularly politically targeted and attacked and his authority undermined without his being heard. I also had growing doubts about the workings of the Garda Division within the Department of Justice. The emergence out of the ether of the recordings issue, without my having any prior knowledge or forewarning convinced me that the departmental structures were dysfunctional, in particular those of the Garda Division. Following the Taoiseach's meeting with Gilmore, I readily agreed to a proposal to Cabinet for a policing authority, on condition that the required legislation maintained appropriate democratic accountability to the Houses of the Oireachtas for An Garda Síochána.

Unsurprisingly, the Garda recordings and Callinan's retirement dominated that morning's Cabinet meeting. A statement published after the meeting revealed that the Government had considered 'a new and very serious issue relating to An Garda Síochána' the implications of which 'are potentially of such gravity' that a decision had been made to establish a statutory Commission of Investigation. It continued:

> In the context of ongoing legal proceedings in a particular case, the Government has learnt that a system was in place in a large number of Garda stations whereby incoming and outgoing telephone calls were taped or recorded. The Government was informed of this new information at its meeting today. As the matter is before the courts, it is not appropriate to make any further comment on the specific case.

The statement explained that it had been discovered that such recording systems were 'in place for many years', had been discontinued in November

2013 and expressed the Governments 'extreme concern' that 'it is not yet clear why this practice was in operation'.

Of course, neither I nor any of my Cabinet colleagues were at the time aware of the fact that the information was not 'new'. It had, in partial form, first become known to the Attorney General in November 2013. Unusually, Máire Whelan was not present at the Cabinet meeting as she had to attend a funeral outside Dublin following a family bereavement.

The statement disclosed that the Government had sought 'a full, detailed report on all aspects of this matter from An Garda Síochána and the Department of Justice and Equality' to enable an informed decision to be made on the legal and other consequences of the recordings with the assistance of the Attorney General. In addition, the statement formally thanked Martin Callinan for his 'long and dedicated service to the State' as Garda Commissioner; announced the appointment of Nóirín O'Sullivan as interim Garda Commissioner and that there would be an 'open competition' for a permanent appointment to the position. Reiterating its commitment to Garda oversight and accountability, the statement announced 'the establishment of an independent Garda authority' appropriate to Ireland's needs and 'which will maintain appropriate democratic accountability to the Oireachtas'.

At one point the Cabinet meeting adjourned to facilitate the statement's preparation so that it would be formally approved by Cabinet members. At approximately 12.35pm, a buzzer rang in the Cabinet room to indicate a document for a Cabinet Minister had been delivered to the outer office. Shortly after that, Martin Fraser left the room and on his return placed a large brown envelope in front of me. I did not immediately open it as the statement was under discussion. Then Pat Rabbitte and I briefly left the room and agreed some amendments to the statement, which were approved by colleagues. Around 1pm I opened the envelope and was shocked at what I found. It contained a letter dated 10 March 2014 signed by Garda Commissioner Martin Callinan, addressed to Brian Purcell. The letter explicitly requested, in its first sentence, that it be brought 'to the Minister's attention'. This was the first time I had seen or had knowledge of it. The letter ran to three pages and was headed 'Recording of telephone conversations made and retained in Garda stations. Data Protection Acts – retention of data.' It detailed the background to the recordings, their relevance to the Bailey case, what was known at that stage and the action taken by the Commissioner. It also expressly referenced that the Commissioner had 'consulted with the Attorney General's office on this issue on 11 November 2013 and also established a Working Group who will be in a position to report to me [the Commissioner] once they have further liaised with the Attorney General's office in respect of all recordings which have been collated to date'. The letter also stated that 'it is the case I expect that consultation with the office of the Data Protection Commissioner will be necessary which I will consider following further advices from the Attorney General'.

I did not immediately fully digest the fact that the Attorney General's office had been aware of the issue since the previous November as my focus was on Purcell's failure to give me the letter earlier or to mention it at all on the Monday evening. I was completely gobsmacked. The meeting ended and I gave the letter to Enda Kenny, informing him that I knew nothing of it until it had arrived into the Cabinet meeting. I asked that he give a copy of it to both the Tánaiste and the Attorney General and told him that I would ask Brian Purcell why it had only just surfaced.

When I returned to my office, Brian Purcell was waiting. I demanded an explanation for why I had only received a copy of the Commissioner's letter after his retirement and over two weeks after it had been received in the Department. Purcell's response was 'It shouldn't have happened, the Department let you down, Minister'. I reminded him that this was the second occasion within four weeks that it had emerged that I had not been given an important letter received from the Garda Commissioner. Purcell went into a long explanation about the number of departmental officials within the Garda Division of the Department, the pressures under which they worked, perhaps he should have allocated additional staff to that section, something about new structures to ensure a similar difficulty does not arise. In exasperation, I asked how was I to know what other important correspondence or documentation was sitting in the division of which I knew nothing. Purcell's response could best be described as a shrug of his shoulders. I then informed him of the Cabinet's decision to appoint a Commission of Investigation and to hold a Dáil debate the next day on Callinan's retirement and the recording revelations. Having read Callinan's retirement statement and issued a response acknowledging his very distinguished service and enormous contribution in fighting crime, the Dáil bells ringing signalled it was time for me to go down to the Chamber as Minister for Defence for Defence Question Time. At 7pm I phoned Callinan to personally wish him well. He was courteous but sounded stressed and shell-shocked.

Rushing out of my office, I was met by an anxious Vincent Lowe, my Defence Private Secretary, holding the Defence questions file. As I waited for Question Time to begin, it occurred to me that while those in the Dáil Chamber knew by then of the Garda Commissioner's retirement, I was the only one present who knew of the drama of the preceding twenty-four hours or of the revelations to come.

The Chamber was an oasis of calm. I used the few moments before the Ceann Comhairle's entrance to temporarily park that day's tumultuous events and to focus solely on my Defence brief. As is usual, questions with 'priority' status by the spokespeople for the various Opposition political parties and political groupings came first. The third priority question of the day was from Mick Wallace, who had been hunting for the Garda Commissioner's head for over two years. In it, Wallace asked that the Defence Forces review their admissibility criteria for new recruits in relation to the 'visibility of tattoos'. He was particularly concerned about a rule that prohibited 'tattooing above the collar of the shirt' as it rendered an otherwise suitable applicant with a neck tattoo ineligible to join up. Wallace believed the rule to be unfair. Responding, I pointed out that the policy of our Defence Forces is 'not in any way unique' and that a number of armies including the British, Australian and US armies have a similar rule. Wallace explained that an applicant about whom he expressed concern had passed his physical fitness test on the first occasion but did not make the final list for recruitment. On his second physical his tattoo had been deemed too high although Wallace alleged 'with his head tilted forward where the tattoo was' it was 'not visible'. Wallace had received a letter from the disappointed applicant and I assured him I would inquire into what occurred. He courteously thanked me. Privately I regarded the rule as archaic and worth revisiting. As this was Defence question time, no mention of any nature was made of Martin Callinan's departure. The letter that caused me the greater concern that afternoon was the one from Callinan to Purcell and the consequences of its languishing in the Department of Justice for over two weeks.

CHAPTER 29

Shedding Crocodile Tears

He is a man who gave a lifelong commitment to An Garda Síochána and gave distinguished service. That should be acknowledged in this House
–Micheál Martin, leader of Fianna Fáil, speaking in the Dáil on the retirement of Martin Callinan, Leaders' Questions, 25 March 2014

I would like to put on the record my appreciation of the 41 years of service given by the Commissioner, Martin Callinan ... It must have been a very difficult decision for the Commissioner to announce his retirement
–An Taoiseach Enda Kenny, speaking in the Dáil on the retirement of Martin Callinan, Leaders' Questions, 25 March 2014

After Defence questions, tributes were paid to my Fine Gael colleague Nicky McFadden, a good, decent and brave Deputy, afflicted by Motor Neuron disease, who died far too young. The Dáil then adjourned for fifteen minutes. It reassembled at 3.45pm for Leaders' Questions. Having intended to return to the Chamber, I discovered that arrangements for the next day were changing and that not only was there to be a debate on the Commissioner's retirement and the garda recordings but that the debate originally scheduled for Thursday on the *Garda Inspectorate Report* had been brought forward.

I received a message that the Taoiseach was anxious that I revisit and bring to an end the controversy over whether Maurice McCabe did or did not cooperate with the O'Mahoney investigation. Kenny, I was told, regarded it as important that there be no more Cabinet instability or division and that McCabe's non-engagement with O'Mahoney and my reference to it no longer remain a focal point for upset and disagreement.

As far as I was concerned, I had fairly and reasonably addressed the issue in the Dáil on 26 February. Nonetheless, I fully understood that the comments attributed to the Tánaiste, Eamon Gilmore, meant that, if I did not put the issue to bed, the future cohesion and stability of the Government was at risk as was my membership of Government.

I appreciated that Kenny had been supportive throughout the course of the garda controversies during February of 2014 and recognised the inevitability of political mayhem resulting from the recording revelations. Within a short period of time there had been too many garda-related controversies. I had been accused of lying and incompetence just a month earlier in relation to the issues which resulted in the creation of the Cooke and Guerin inquiries and that train was again coming down the tracks at breakneck speed.

In the introduction to its report, the Garda Inspectorate had acknowledged all of the assistance provided to it by many gardaí. There was no reference to any garda member failing to cooperate and I assumed that McCabe had engaged with the Inspectorate. I also knew by then, from his evidence to the PAC, that Superintendent John O'Mahoney was aware or at least suspected by the time he submitted his report to me, that McCabe was the source of the allegations he was investigating. Due to the seriousness of the allegations and the public controversy surrounding them, I believed he should have enquired whether McCabe would meet with him or one of his investigators before completing his report. It would have been a simple matter for him, through the Commissioner, to ask the Department to expressly ask the complainant to meet with him or a member of his team. However, no such step had been taken, which I personally regarded as a common-sense initiative that I would have taken in O'Mahoney's position. However, he had not. I decided that at the start of my speech on the *Garda Inspectorate Report*, I would address the issue of McCabe's 'lack of cooperation' with O'Mahoney and put it to bed.

As I finalised my Dáil speech, the garda recordings and Martin Callinan's unexpected retirement took centre stage during Leaders' Questions. An hour or so earlier, while I was in the Dáil answering Defence questions, unknown to me, Enda Kenny had met Micheál Martin and Gerry Adams to brief them on the Garda Commissioner's retirement and the discovery of the garda recordings. At the commencement of Leaders' Questions, Martin expressed his 'regret' that Callinan had 'resigned' from his post. He continued:

He is a man who gave a lifelong commitment to An Garda Síochána and gave distinguished service. That should be acknowledged in this House. It is a very sad reflection on how the Government has handled this entire series of crises in the administration of justice that things have come to this pass. Commissioner Callinan played a role in bringing a number of significant criminals to account.

In shedding his crocodile tears, Martin failed to mention the role Fianna Fáil had played in demonising both Martin Callinan and An Garda Síochána and its promotion of the Gardai bugged GSOC narrative. He had a cut off me for my treatment of whistle-blowers, referenced all of the various garda controversies of the month of February and the garda recordings issue. The Taoiseach, responding, also expressed his 'appreciation' for the forty-one years of service given by Callinan. He disingenuously acknowledged that 'it must have been a very difficult decision for the Commissioner to announce his retirement' making no reference of any nature to his own role in Brian Purcell's late-night visit to the Commissioner's home.

The Garda Commissioner gone, Martin had his sights firmly trained on me. Politically embracing 'the very forthright and frank … assessment of the situation' of the whistle-blowers, by his new best friend, Leo Varadkar, he described my position as 'untenable'.

Off the subject of Callinan's retirement, Kenny gamely defended me stating that 'the Minister, Deputy Shatter has proven to be probably the most reforming Minister for Justice in the past 50 years and so many issues of societal consequence that have been left lying around have been, are and will be dealt with by him as Minister for Justice and Equality'. Gerry Adams avoided the hypocrisy and went straight for the jugular. It was his view that 'while the Commissioner has undoubtedly done the State some service, his decision to resign was the right one because his position had become untenable'. Varadkar was also Gerry's new best pal and he wanted to know would the Taoiseach require me 'to go?'

The Taoiseach said 'No' and as he had done with Martin, addressed decisions made at that morning's meeting by the Government to put in place a new police authority. In response, Adams demanded that the Taoiseach 'do the decisive thing and ask the Minister, Deputy Shatter, to resign'. Kenny fought back accusing Adams of only wanting 'another head on a plate', referred to the Garda recording issue and the establishment of an independent police authority and repeated what he had previously informed Martin and Adams at their earlier meeting.

Following the Dáil exchanges on the monitor in my office, I was surprised that nothing was said by Kenny about the Garda Commissioner's letter of 10 March and Purcell's visit to the Commissioner's home and concluded that he must not have mentioned either to Martin or Adams.

The Taoiseach explained that 'as Leader of the Government' he thought it important to bring information about the garda recordings to the attention of the Members of the House 'having checked the validity and veracity of the issues all day yesterday and all night last night'. At that time, I had no idea what, if anything, Kenny had done on the Monday to 'check the validity and veracity' of the information received by him from Máire Whelan. His depiction to Adams of his action the previous day turned out to be untrue. The *Fennelly Report*, in its conclusions, determined that if the Taoiseach during the course of that Monday had been truly seeking information required to check the 'validity and veracity of the issues' either he or the Attorney General at his behest, would have been in contact with the Garda Commissioner and myself as Minister for Justice. Fennelly also went on to conclude that, had he been in contact with me, events might have turned out differently. Following publication of the *Fennelly Report* the fact that Kenny had misled the Dáil on this was ignored.

Some time after 6pm, I received from the Garda Division within the Department of Justice a draft of my Dáil speech for the following morning on Martin Callinan's retirement and the garda recording issue. For the first time I learnt that Departmental officials were made aware of the recordings of relevance to the Bailey court proceedings as result of papers received by the Department on 28 February. I was less than impressed. Meeting Brian Purcell that evening I expressed my annoyance and dissatisfaction at the continuing revelations and asked how could I still be sure I knew the full story.

I was not happy with either the formulation or content of the speech and, together with Jane Lehane, I worked on it until late in the evening. I was anxious to ensure that its content was totally factually accurate and that I did not unknowingly lay a new political landmine. Before the evening was over, RTÉ's Paul Reynolds was reporting Brian Purcell's late-night visit to the Garda Commissioner's home and that Martin Callinan had written to Brian Purcell a fortnight prior to his retirement about the garda recordings. It would emerge during the hearings of the Disclosures Tribunal in 2018 that Superintendent David Taylor, head of the Garda Press Office, furnished a copy of the letter to Reynolds, at Callinan's request, after his retirement was announced.

Callinan's letter had referred to his engagement with the Attorney General's office and this was also detailed in the draft speech. It was particularly important to fully explain the chronology of what occurred. I wanted no issue to later arise over the accuracy of my speech. I knew that my account of events and my lack of knowledge of the garda recordings would be challenged in the Dáil and I had no wish to generate any additional controversy.

I left the Dail at about 10pm and a copy of the draft speech was sent to both the Taoiseach's and the Attorney General's office for feedback. I was certain that it would require further work after I had slept on it and that some amendments or additions might be suggested to me. I also wanted to review the Wednesday morning papers before finalising it. I reckoned that Tuesday, 25 March 2014 would long remain in my memory as the most stressful day so far during my time as a Cabinet Minister and that Wednesday would not be much better.

CHAPTER 30

Tapegate, Twin Egos, Leo Lionised and God's Earth

Every issue turns into a calamity and a crisis ... the Minister's statements are not credible and it is time for him to leave the Ministry of Justice
–Niall Collins TD, Fianna Fáil Spokesperson on Justice, speaking on the Garda recordings issue in the Dáil, 26 March 2014

Why his whole explanation is incredible is that nobody on God's earth can believe that a letter of this importance arrived from an officer of the State of significant importance on a matter of apparently considerable urgency and the Minister was not told –Shane Ross TD, speaking on the Garda recordings issue in the Dáil, 26 March 2014

The fact is that the letter of 10 March 2014 was not given in any form to the Minister at any time from its delivery on 10 March 2014 up to the 25 March 2014 ... Mr Shatter has said that he was not involved in any way in the matter of the garda telephone recording, which appears to be correct. Nobody has suggested he was. He was not even aware of it –Conclusions contained in the Interim Report of the Fennelly Commission, September 2015

It was 5.10am on Wednesday, 26 March. Having fallen at midnight into an exhausted deep sleep for about two and a half hours, I woke and spent the rest of the night tossing and turning, the events of Tuesday spinning around in my head. I was now sitting at the kitchen table with a cup of tea and reviewing the morning's papers on my iPad. Predictably, this latest controversy had been dubbed 'Tapegate'. There was wall-to-wall coverage of the Commissioner's retirement, the Taoiseach's Dáil exchanges of the previous day, the Government's statement and the revelation of the garda recordings. There was much speculation about the content of the recordings and their implications for the criminal justice system. Commentators and journalists adopted the usual default position, questioning whether I knew of the garda recordings earlier than disclosed as a result of the Garda Commissioner's letter of 10 March 2014 'revealed' by Paul Reynolds on the previous evening's RTÉ television *News*.

Taking a different approach, *The Irish Times'* leading political correspondent and columnist, Stephen Collins, reported that 'the last straw' for Mr Kenny was discovering the Garda Commissioner, Martin Callinan, knew of the recording of calls at garda stations the previous November. This report obviously derived from some briefing given to Collins by a Government source. What Collins could not have known, but the *Fennelly Report* would reveal seventeen months later, was that Máire Whelan also knew of the recordings in November 2013 and did not inform either the Taoiseach or me about them until March 2014. He also could not have anticipated that *Fennelly's Final Report* of March 2017, while confirming the gardaí had for many years systematically recorded non-999 or non-emergency telephone calls from members of the public in initially eighteen and then later twenty-one Divisional Garda Stations outside the Dublin Metropolitan District without lawful authority, would find no evidence of improper Garda access to or use made of the recordings. Fennelly would also ultimately establish that the gardaí operated a telephone recording system which 'had been beset from its beginnings by misunderstanding, poor communication, imperfect information and a sequence of errors rather than any conspiracy'. It was essentially a system operated without any specific guidelines, only known to the Telecommunications section of An Garda Síochána and about which 'there was almost total ignorance at the highest levels of the force' within the Department of Justice and other State agencies. My predecessor Ministers for Justice were also found to have no knowledge of the recording system. While Fennelly would confirm that the systems installed and operated at garda stations to record non-999 calls were not authorised by law, breached the constitutional right to privacy and had resulted in the gardai having 'unlawfully' in their possession 'a very large volume of recorded material', he would not validate 'the alarming picture' of the issue first painted by Máire Whelan which generated the Taoiseach's serious concerns. Neither that nor Whelan's knowledge of the recordings in November 2013 would be regarded by Enda Kenny as the 'last straw'.

There can be little doubt that Kenny's more benign view of Whelan derived from the fact, as readily discernible from Fennelly's interim report, that in various respects her evidence to the Fennelly Commission was supportive of evidence given by Kenny, not all of which was accepted by Fennelly as an accurate portrayal of events. It is also clear that parts of Whelan's evidence were rejected by Fennelly and he was critical of her attempt to contradict and withdraw sworn evidence that she had previously given. Neither this nor Fennelly's accurate description of the advice given by her on the fateful evenings of 23 and 24 March 2014 as 'alarmist', in circumstances in which she lacked crucial information to form any definitive judgement, in any way inhibited Enda Kenny from reappointing Whelan to the office of Attorney General following the February 2016 General Election and his forming a minority Government. It also did not inhibit him at his last Cabinet meeting in June 2017, a day before being replaced as Taoiseach by Leo Varadkar, from arranging to obtain the Cabinet's agreement to Whelan's appointment as a judge of the Court of Appeal. Perhaps, it incentivised his promoting her judicial appointment as a mechanism to attempt to immunise her from future criticism for the manner in which she dealt with the recordings issue and for her bizarre and inconsistent conduct and evidence as narrated by Fennelly. It also provided a mechanism to try and ensure that should she at any future time be subject to criticism, any critic could be accused of failing to respect the judiciary and as attacking judicial independence, a concept never intended to immunise from questioning and criticising the pre-judicial conduct of a serving judge.

In that Wednesday's *Irish Times*, under the headline 'Twin Egos once Joined at the Hip Threaten Coalition', Miriam Lord applied her acerbic wit to Martin Callinan's departure and the recording revelations. In her eyes the 'affair blew up into such a mess' because:

> An alliance of twin egos conspired to tough out the crisis. Callinan and Shatter – the former obstinate and authoritarian and the latter, obstinate and arrogant, refusing to accept that they, in their lofty domains, or in the institutions of the State they represent, could ever be anything but above reproach. Between them, they would see off those irritating whistleblowers and parliamentary nuisances daring to question them.

In her worldview 'the shiny phone-tapping bauble' was a contrived distraction from the whistle-blower row preceding it. Even for satire this theory was bordering on bonkers. It was, however, consistent with most of the media's obsessive and enthusiastic demonisation of me and promotion of ever more imaginative conspiracy theories.

Lord recorded that 'the intervention of Minister for Transport, Leo Varadkar (who was being congratulated by the likes of Roisin Shorthall and Peter Mathews in the Chamber yesterday) escalated the situation'. 'The Cabinet', she wrote, 'doesn't seem to care that the Minister for Justice has become a long-term tenant in the Last Chance Saloon. Because if they avert their gaze for long enough, even Shatter will have to emerge eventually through the swinging doors. Won't he? In the meantime, all they have to do is create enough distractions and diversions to keep the media occupied.'

Lise Hand's colour piece in the *Irish Independent* was amusingly entitled 'A story moving so fast it should have been given Penalty Points of its own!' Both she and Lord in their columns that morning poured scorn on the Taoiseach's assertion in the Dáil that Martin Callinan had 'retired' and not been pushed to resign. This particular insight I regarded as a fair and accurate analysis of events.

I amended my draft speech for the Dáil to ensure any questions raised in the morning newspaper coverage were comprehensively answered. Political opponents and some commentators were already asserting that I must have known of the recordings in garda stations a great deal earlier and certainly by June 2013 when GSOC published a report which had mentioned the recording of phone calls in Waterford Garda Station. The allegation was that I had received the GSOC report, knew of the widespread recording of telephone calls in Garda stations and, predictably, that I was not telling the truth.

I knew nothing of the *GSOC Report* until this allegation surfaced. There had been no mention of it to me by any Justice official nor had it been referenced by any Opposition TD, as far as I was aware. Contacting Brian Purcell at 7am, I requested that the position in relation to the *GSOC Report* be clarified. Within a short time he informed me that GSOC had published the report in summarised form as a press release on its website in June 2013. The report related to the recording of two phone calls made to the control room of Waterford Garda Station by two gardaí charged with assault. The content of their conversations had been ruled inadmissible in their criminal trial and that of two other gardaí before Waterford Circuit Court, as they did not know their conversations were being recorded. GSOC had prosecuted the case and, in its report, stated that the Garda Commissioner 'may wish' to re-evaluate the practice of recording such calls and the consents required if it is to be permissible to use such recordings in evidence. I concluded that had GSOC considered that there was a major difficulty with garda telephone recordings in garda stations across the country, it would have reported its concerns directly to me, been more definitive about the action the Commissioner should take and, if necessary, could have initiated its own independent public interest investigation having completed its work on the Waterford case. GSOC had not done so and its online report had attracted no major attention of any nature whatsoever. In the context of the general recording issue, as first revealed to me on the Monday evening, the Waterford case was simply a red herring pickled for political ammunition. *Fennelly's Final Report* of March 2017 later concluded that, while GSOC could have examined the 'the practices, policies and procedures of An Garda Síochána' in relation to the internal recording of telephone calls following its report on the Waterford case, there was 'no reason why they should have done so'.

I was scheduled to be in the Dáil Chamber to deliver my speech at 10.50am. Following my arrival, some useful small amendments were made to the speech suggested by the Taoiseach's Department. I do not know whether they were suggested by one of Enda Kenny's Special Advisers or by Kenny himself.

Máire Whelan also made contact to express concern about the reference to the Garda Commissioner's engagement with her office in November 2013. Until receipt of the Commissioner's letter, I had assumed that the first she knew of the recording issue was in the days immediately preceding her Sunday meeting with the Taoiseach. She was concerned my reference in the draft speech attributed to her a greater degree of knowledge in November 2013 than she then had. As a result, the final text of the speech read that, in November, the Attorney General, 'in the context of the civil proceedings previously mentioned' i.e. the Bailey proceedings, 'was made aware of the existence of tapes and the possible existence of other tapes' and continued 'I am advised that she had no knowledge at that time of the circumstances surrounding the making of the tapes, the legal background to their being made, the content of such tapes or the number of such tapes.' I had no wish of any nature to cause any difficulties for Whelan and teased out over the phone with her the wording ultimately used. It was the first time we had an uncomfortable conversation. I got the clear impression that she would have preferred if I had made no reference to Martin Callinan's November engagement with her office. I thought this odd as it was expressly mentioned in Callinan's 10 March letter. I had a growing unease about the events of the weekend and was determined to ensure that I would omit no information that could result later in a valid allegation that I had been less than truthful.

During our conversation, Whelan did not mention the meeting that took place in her offices on 20 November 2013 to discuss the Garda recordings, as detailed by the Fennelly Commission, or the detailed memo she had earlier received from Ruth Fitzgerald. The first I learnt of that meeting and the view expressed at it, as reported by Fennelly, that the Justice Department should be informed of the recordings was during the Fennelly inquiry process. It was also the first time I learnt, as Fennelly details, that in November 2013 the Attorney knew of the actual, not the 'possible', existence of tapes in addition to those relevant to the Bailey case and the recording of telephone conversations in Garda stations other than Bandon.

Just prior to 10.50am, I sat down in the Dáil Chamber beside Simon Coveney, Minister for Agriculture and Fisheries. He was just finishing Question Time. Mick Wallace was asking about fishing boats and there was one more question before Question Time ended. I reckoned it would not be Wallace's only fishing expedition of the day.

As I stood up to speak, the Dáil Chamber began to fill up. I paid tribute to Martin Callinan, referred to the Government's post-Cabinet statement and stated what I knew of the Garda recordings and the chronology of events. I also detailed the contents of the Garda Commissioner's letter of 10 March, and when I first received it. I explained that 'we are dealing here with a system of recording phone calls into and out of garda stations over a period of up to thirty years' and 'as with other matters under investigation, there are issues which far pre-date my tenure as Minister for Justice'.

Pointing out that the recording issue 'existed throughout the lifetime of the previous Government', I told Deputies that 'the recording system was upgraded during the [previous] Government's term of office in 2008', the implication being that if funds were allocated at that time, the existence of the recordings should have been known to my predecessors in Government. *The Fennelly Report* of 2017 would later conclude that no previous Minister knew of the recording system.

By early 2013, I believed that there was a need for a root-and-branch reform of An Garda Síochána. I understood, in order to achieve that, buy-in was required from the Garda representative bodies from the start in order to encourage their engagement and, ultimately, their co-operation in implementing recommended reform. Under the Haddington Road process, which dealt with public service pay and related issues, it was agreed that an independent comprehensive review would be undertaken of An Garda Síochána. It took considerable time to get the Garda Representative Association (GRA) and the Association of Garda Sergeants and Inspectors (AGSI) to agree the person or body to be appointed to undertake the review. The Garda Inspectorate was the obvious choice, as it could build on work it had already done. I also believed it would be valuable to get a comprehensive account from the Inspectorate of garda progress in implementing recommendations previously made. Initially, the garda bodies resisted the Inspectorate taking on this role and it was not until February 2014 that agreement was finally secured. As result of the agreement, I was able to inform the Dáil that day that the Inspectorate had 'very recently commenced the work required'. I over-optimistically expected that the work would be completed before the end of 2014 but the Inspectorate's very detailed and valuable report was not completed and published until November 2015. By then, I was long gone from the Justice Department. Many of the reports' recommendations still remained to be implemented when it was superceded in September 2018 by the *Report of the Commission on the Future of Policing in Ireland*.

When I concluded my speech, Opposition Deputies immediately went on the attack, revisiting all of the Garda controversies of February 2014 and regurgitating the many false charges then made. As the focus was politics and not facts, Leo Varadkar and the Labour Ministers who had been prominent in the news headlines and stories of the previous days, found themselves unexpectedly verbally embraced, lionised and praised by Opposition Deputies. Unwittingly, they were cementing the foundations for Varadkar's campaign for leadership of Fine Gael. According to Fianna Fáil's Niall Collins, they were the only Members of Cabinet 'living up to their responsibilities'. Alleging that 'the Government knew about this [the Garda recording] for a long time', Collins questioned why the recording issue emerged on the day of the Commissioner's 'resignation' and 'dropped into the political mix'. Clearly adopting Miriam Lord's 'shiny phone tapping bauble' theory, he asserted that 'The Minister and the Taoiseach are getting caught up in their own web of spin and beginning to meet themselves on the way back.'

In the midst of hyperbole and accusation, Collins hit one nail on the head. 'Is it not the case,' he asked, that the Attorney General 'should have informed the Minister or the Government of these matters?'

Sinn Féin's Padraig MacLochlainn took up a similar theme to ask 'are we ... to believe the Minister was only told' about Commissioner's letter after his retirement? He was sure I would 'understand why many citizens would be very sceptical about all of this'. Listening to both Collins and MacLochlainn, I could readily understand that most people would be astonished that a letter of such importance as the one sent by Martin Callinan had languished within the Justice Department for over two weeks and not been given to me. I was not merely astonished – I was outraged. Yet again the instant assumption was that I was lying. According to MacLochlainn this, like each of the other 'scandals', 'demonstrated an unhealthy close relationship' between me and the former Garda Commissioner.

After a break of about four weeks, we were back in JATH territory yet again. What I could not fathom was how my lack of knowledge of the Garda recordings or Martin Callinan's premature departure from Garda Headquarters in the Phoenix Park could be credibly depicted as demonstrating our alleged 'unhealthy close relationship' or that we were joined at the hip. MacLochlainn called on me 'like my friend Martin Callinan to resign'.

Mick Wallace, fresh from his fishing adventures, accused me of 'misrepresentation of the facts and the law'. According to Wallace, I was trying to save face and was engaged in 'frantic finger pointing at anyone who might act as a fall guy' to save my political career. Wallace, as an incessant and compulsive finger pointer, saw no irony in his charge. He continued claiming that I had 'dispensed' with the Garda Commissioner and the Confidential Recipient, that I had 'overstayed' my welcome and was 'no longer fit for office'. Wallace's political partner, Clare Daly TD, believed it was 'not credible' that I did not know about the recordings and accused me of contaminating 'the process beyond [my] sell by date'.

In an act of constituency collegiality, Shane Ross TD could not resist temptation. 'I do not think there is a sinner outside the House who believes a word of the scenario painted by the Government today. It defies credibility,' he roared. According to Ross 'nobody on God's earth' would believe I was not told of the Commissioner's letter of 10 March 2014 before the Commissioner's departure. It was all fire and brimstone with a theological bent!

The debate followed a predictable path. When replying, I knew I was engaged in a dialogue of the deaf and was simply re-enforcing the truth of what I first told the Dáil for the benefit of both the media and the public. Again stating that I first learnt of the 10 March letter at the previous day's Cabinet meeting, I continued: 'If it had been furnished to me earlier, why would I not have read it? Why would I not have shared it with colleagues? What possible advantage is there in my so dealing with matters … Who in their right mind would want another issue of difficulty or controversy relating to the Garda Síochána?' To which Independent TD Thomas Pringle, going all Shakespearean, responded, 'That is the question!'.Two minutes later the Dáil sitting was suspended, the curtain came down and that morning's theatrics ended.

Seventeen months later, the Fennelly Commission would publish its report and unequivocally establish that I had told the truth, confirming that I 'was not involved in any way' in the garda recording issue, knew nothing of it until the evening of 24 March and was not informed of the Commissioner's letter until it was delivered into the Cabinet meeting some four hours after his retirement. But by then it had become apparent that the truth really mattered to very few beyond me – my family and my close friends. It was of no major interest to the media commentariat or to Opposition Deputies by whom I had been pilloried.

Later that day, the whole issue was revisited in the Dáil Chamber on Leaders' Questions while I watched from my office. Micheál Martin got straight to the point, asking the Taoiseach 'to explain why the Attorney General did not go to the Minister for Justice and Equality in the four-month period during which she would have been aware of both the specifics of the [Bailey] case and its importance'. He also wanted to know why she did not inform the Taoiseach earlier than the previous Sunday evening. The Taoiseach responded, stating that 'the Attorney General's constitutional position is to give legal advice to the government. She is bound to have all the facts at her disposal before she makes a judgement'.

Of course, alerting a Government Minister and the Taoiseach to a major issue of concern that comes across her desk did not require that the Attorney must first 'have all the facts' or that any definitive judgement need be made by her. This was nonsense. *The Fennelly Report* unequivocally established that the Attorney, when first informing Kenny of the issue in March 2014, was clearly making judgements without having 'all the facts at her disposal'. Entangled in a new set of false allegations that I had lied, and preparing to deliver my speech on the *Garda Inspectorate's Report*, I barely digested Enda Kenny's evasive response to Micheál Martin.

Asked about media reports of Brian Purcell's late Monday night visit to Martin Callinan's home, Kenny responded that in the context of the 'nature of the information' furnished to him, he believed 'that the Commissioner should be made aware of its gravity and how I felt about it and the implications'. The second part of this response contradicted the Fennelly Commission's report of Kenny's evidence to it. Fennelly accepted that Kenny wished Purcell to inform Callinan of his grave concerns. However, Fennelly also stated that Kenny said, in his evidence, that the other purpose of Purcell's mission was to obtain the former Garda Commissioner's 'views'. *The Fennelly Report* quoted Kenny's above Dáil response to Martin and, rejecting Kenny's evidence, Fennelly concluded that Purcell was not asked to seek either views nor information from Martin Callinan during his late-night visit to his home.

Fennelly determined that included within Purcell's mission was a message to be conveyed to Martin Callinan that the Taoiseach may be unable the next day to express confidence in him after the Cabinet meeting. Presumably, these were 'the implications' that Kenny had in mind but which he refrained from explaining to the Dáil.

There is only one conclusion that can be drawn. Either Enda Kenny as Taoiseach misled the Dáil on 26 March 2014 or he misled the Fennelly Commission in his evidence. It was Brian Purcell's job that night, not to seek the views of the Garda Commissioner, but to inform him of the possible 'implications' arising from the discovery of the Garda recordings, that is, that the following day the Taoiseach might not be able to express confidence in him as Commissioner.

Enda Kenny, when meeting Micheál Martin and Gerry Adams the previous day, had not only concealed the existence of the letter of 10 March but also had not mentioned Purcell's late-night visit to the Commissioner's home. They only learnt of the visit overnight from media reports. Martin accused Kenny of 'essentially sacking Callinan'. Kenny bristled in response and 'deplored' what he called Martin's accusation that he was a liar and that he had used 'some perception of authority to remove people from office'.

He then entirely ignored Martin's comment that it seemed 'somewhat dysfunctional' that a conversation would not have occurred between the Minister for Justice and the Attorney General, similar to the one between the Taoiseach and the Attorney on the Sunday. Despite Martin's best efforts, Kenny avoided explaining why Máire Whelan had not talked to me about the recording issue before the Monday evening meeting in his office.

Unlike Martin, Gerry Adams had no hard questions to ask about the Commissioner's departure. As far as he was concerned it was Commissioner gone, Shatter next. Criticising me over all of the preceding Garda controversies and for not informing the Taoiseach of the discovery of garda recordings, he asked Kenny to do 'the right thing and ask the Minister, Deputy Shatter, to go'. In response, the Taoiseach again accused Adams of 'focussing on a head'.

Unknown to us all, I was destined for decapitation within six weeks!

****

The next major event on that day's Dáil agenda was the debate on the Garda Inspectorate investigation into the ticket charge/penalty points issue. I began by acknowledging that my saying the previous October 'that the whistle-blowers did not cooperate with the Garda investigation that took place in respect of their allegations' relating to the Ticket Charge/ Penalty Points issue 'has been the source of upset and distress to the whistle-blowers'. Stating I had reconsidered the matter in detail, I noted that on a previous occasion I had informed the Dáil that I 'expected that Sergeant McCabe would be interviewed during the course of the O'Mahoney investigation' and continued:

> I note that he fully engaged with the Garda Inspectorate in the work undertaken by it to prepare the report which is the subject matter of today's debate. I want to say very clearly that, having re-examined the facts and further considered the matter, I believe more should have been done during the course of the O'Mahoney investigation to obtain information from and ascertain the views and experiences of the whistle-blowers. Further and better efforts could and should have been made to secure productive engagement with them in the investigation of their claims. I therefore wish to correct the record of

the House that the whistle-blowers 'did not cooperate with the Garda investigations that took place'.

I acknowledged the statement was incorrect and explained that it was never my intention to mislead the House. I then apologised to both McCabe and Wilson.

I made no reference in the statement to the difficulties created for O'Mahoney by McCabe's insistence, in his correspondence, that his identity remain confidential nor did I reference McCabe not contacting O'Mahoney in response to the Garda Commissioner's and Michael Flahive's December 2012 communications.

I continued, stating:

It was never my intention to cause any upset. If any upset was caused, I hope that my correcting the record of the Dáil today will put this matter to rest. In doing so, I again acknowledge, as I have done many times previously that the reports published and findings and recommendations that have been made with regard to the Fixed Charge Notice System and Penalty Points are a response to the allegations made by Sergeant McCabe and supported by former Garda Wilson.

I then reprised the history of the issue and before I was again politically pilloried, I reminded Fianna Fáil's Justice Spokesperson, Niall Collins that, at the time of publication of the O'Mahoney and GPSU Reports, he had publicly stated that he 'had no issue with those reports' and that he had welcomed 'the finding that there was no corruption'.

The debate, thereafter, took a predictable course and much praise was again lavished on Varadkar by Opposition TDs for my being 'dragged kicking and screaming into the Chamber' to apologise to the Garda whistle-blowers. In the debate, Deputies did not confine their contributions to the Garda Inspectorate Report, Ticket Charges and Penalty Points but yet again ranged far and wide repeating many of the charges previously made that would later be found to be false in judicial inquiries and investigations. Varadkar delivered a straightforward and reasonable speech, entirely ignoring the controversy he had generated and fuelled and ignoring Opposition Deputies' plaudits. In it, he specifically referenced and praised the substantial reforms of the Fixed Charge

Processing System that had been implemented. He did not mention the departed Garda Commissioner. For Varadkar, Martin Callinan's fate was beneficial collateral damage inflicted to elevate his public stature as Enda Kenny's likely successor and there was no need to say anymore. Being praised by Opposition TDs was the icing on the cake. It did not matter that their praise was little other than cynical political mischief-making.

During the question and answer session that followed, the role of the Attorney General and the Taoiseach in dealing with the Garda recordings was explored by some Deputies. Based on my knowledge at that time, I vigorously defended them both against criticism, describing them as working 'extraordinarily hard and long hours'. I detailed what I knew of their meeting on the Sunday evening and asserted that 'there is absolutely no reason for the Attorney General to be the subject of criticism'. Had I known the full details of her November 2013 briefings and meeting with her officials on the recordings issue and if I had possessed some prophetic vision of her evidence to the Fennelly Commission as detailed in its report, I would not have been as enthusiastic in defending Máire Whelan against criticism. Had I anticipated the Taoiseach's evidence to Fennelly and what I learned subsequent to publication of the *Guerin Report*, I would not have been extolling his virtues. For me it was a more innocent time.

CHAPTER 31

Fake News Irish-Style and Alternative Facts

The Commission has seen no evidence to suggest that any Minister for Justice was informed or put on notice, in any way, of the fact of Garda telephone recording. The lack of knowledge of successive Ministers for Justice is the simple consequence of the fact that senior ranks of An Garda Síochána were almost totally unaware of such recording systems as existed, as well as the lack of such knowledge in the Department
–Final Report of the Fennelly Commission, April 2017

In the days that followed media reports were consumed by the latest garda-related drama. What was termed 'the garda tapes scandal', having dominated Wednesday's Dáil business, took over the Thursday morning papers. Conspiracy theorists were convinced that the tapes were revealed only to distract from the Taoiseach pushing Martin Callinan overboard and to resolve Cabinet difficulties caused by Varadkar. The truth, of course, was that Máire Whelan's alarmist and dilatory revelation of garda recordings, compounded by Brian Purcell's extraordinary failure to inform me and the Taoiseach of the Commissioner's letter, resulted in the Commissioner being pressurised to 'retire'.

The truth of my narrative of events was, predictably, challenged and judged implausible. *The Irish Times* reported that the Tánaiste and Labour Leader, Eamon Gilmore, had reassured anxious Labour TDs that I had told the truth. On the Tuesday evening following the Garda Commissioner's resignation, at Gilmore's request, he and I discussed Callinan's 10 March letter. Gilmore had observed an envelope being handed to me in Cabinet and was entirely satisfied that my account of events was true.

The Irish Times, as did other newspapers, reported speculation that Whelan's role 'had been highlighted' to 'help protect the position of Mr Shatter since Labour would not push for his resignation if Fine Gael could demand the same of the Attorney General'. Whelan's knowledge of events had been referenced in my Dáil speech for no reason other than to ensure that the chronology I gave the Dáil was accurate and without ulterior motive. I had unknowingly minimised the nature of the information on the garda recordings given to her in November 2013. The Minister for Public Expenditure and Reform, Brendan Howlin, had told RTÉ's *Six One News* the previous evening that I 'absolutely' had his 'full confidence, that of the Labour Party and, indeed, every member of the Government' and this was reported as also were calls by Opposition TDs that I resign or be fired.

The *Irish Independent* reported that 'embattled Garda Commissioner stepped down after a blunt warning by a senior civil servant that he was unlikely to survive a looming Cabinet meeting'. Unnamed Ministers were reported as 'privately' admitting that his resignation (not 'retirement') prior to Tuesday's Cabinet meeting had been 'politically desirable' and one unidentified Minister as apparently rejoicing that in the context of the whistle-blower controversy 'there was a head delivered'. Reading that, I wondered who had anonymously welcomed Martin Callinan's departure and the delivery of his head.

Callinan's departure, the *Independent* explained, had 'alleviated the crisis, healed the rift between the two Government parties, avoided a stand-off at Cabinet and eased the pressure on Justice Minister Alan Shatter to resign'. In the following days, there was much speculation about the impact of the garda recordings on the criminal justice system. There were concerns that trials would be abandoned, convictions set aside and hundreds of convicted offenders released from prison – essentially the Armageddon scenario painted by Máire Whelan to the Taoiseach on Sunday evening 24 March, and repeated the next evening in the Taoiseach's office to both of us. As I write this, almost five years later, Armageddon and the meltdown of our criminal justice system is still awaited.

Both Miriam Lord and Lise Hand penned their satirical depictions of Wednesday's Dáil proceedings. The Dáil, Lord wrote, 'had witnessed the conscious uncoupling of the Minister for Justice from his pride'. My apology to McCabe and Wilson was 'nothing more than a procedural formula of words uttered to get himself, and more importantly, a severely rattled government out of the mess he helped create for them'. For Miriam, my malevolence was clearly established and there were no complexities involved in McCabe's engagement with me and the Garda Commissioner. 'By seeking to disregard their claims while unable to neutralise their persistent presence, Minister Shatter and the former Garda Commissioner set in train a chain of events which have grown to a full blown government crisis,' she wrote. For Miriam, there was only one side to this story. Reflecting on her column, I wondered whether she had given any thought to how the extensive and effective reforms had come about, that even Varadkar had acknowledged in his Dáil speech the previous day, if I had disregarded their claims. Unfortunately, perception trumps facts for those unwilling to question and challenge a preferred narrative within the media bubble. In this pre-Trump era fake news Irish style was in the ascendancy.

Lise Hand, with prophetic intuition wrote that 'no Minister – not even one protected by the unstinting loyalty of a Taoiseach whose role in this drama is to play Laertes to Alan's Hamlet – can survive indefinitely an endless wave of controversies and the resulting blizzard of negative publicity'. Personally, I thought that for most of February and now again in March a blizzard would have provided some light relief. On the scale of things, this was more a tornado and truth a casualty blown away by its destructive vortex of violently rotating winds. Alternative facts ruled the post truth world I politically inhabited.

Hand concluded by asserting that I 'may have survived the day but many ghosts in this tangled tale haven't been put to rest and any one of them could yet rise again to strike the fatal blow to the Minister'.

Reading both columns over breakfast that morning, I did not anticipate that Sean Guerin's report would cause the tale to become further entangled. I am not sure whether Miriam Lord would today regard this failing as a symptom of my pride or my ego. Looking back on it all now, I regard my own lack of prophetic vision as resulting from a mixture of political naivety and optimistic belief that truth would win out and that false accusations levied against me on the issues subject to non-statutory inquiries by both Cooke and Guerin would be given no credibility once their reports were published.

While Cooke's 'truth' had the capacity to set me free as Feargal Purcell the Government Press Secretary had predicted, it unfortunately came far too late. By the time of publication of the *Cooke Report* my goose had been truly cooked. By then I was already a political corpse as a consequence of Sean Guerin's flawed inquiry and his unexpected critical commentary on my conduct as Minister for Justice.

CHAPTER 32

The Arrogant and Perfidious Jew

The Minister's name has become a watchword for hubris, arrogance, intellectual superiority and the inability to admit even the slightest mistake –Speech by Fianna Fáil's Willie O'Dea TD during a Dáil Confidence Motion, 1 April 2014

In the following days, broadcast and print media continued to focus on the discovery of the garda recordings and the departure of the former Garda Commissioner. The discovery of almost 2,500 garda tape recordings and an unspecified number of digital recordings of uncertain legality was a big story but the related political controversy got most attention.

There was continuing speculation that the Government had overplayed the 'crisis' over the recordings to distract attention from what one journalist described as 'the deep rifts' between the coalition partners over my handling of the whistle-blowers controversy and from the retirement of Martin Callinan. Unidentified legal sources were also reported to be sceptical of the concerns, originating from Máire Whelan, that pending criminal prosecutions and trials could be at risk and a large number of convictions overturned as a consequence of the discovery of the recordings. In time they would be proved right.

Behind the scenes, the Attorney General's office was working on the terms of reference for what became the Fennelly Commission of Investigation. Following the Cabinet meeting of 1 April, the appointment of Judge Niall Fennelly as chair of the Commission was announced. A week later, on 8 April, the Commission's detailed terms of reference were published. It was originally envisaged that the Commission would focus exclusively on the recordings issue. But at the Cabinet meeting on Tuesday, 8 April, it was agreed that the Commission would also investigate 'the furnishing' to me of Martin Callinan's letter of 10 March 2014 and 'the sequence of events leading up to the retirement' of the former Garda Commissioner. This was done in response to proposals received from the Joint Oireachtas Justice Committee and to address allegations that neither the Taoiseach nor I had told the full truth in our account of events and, in particular, with regard to Martin Callinan's departure. Comments in media reports from unidentified Government and Fine Gael party sources added credibility to these claims. For example, Pat

Leahy and Michael Brennan, in the *Sunday Business Post* reported that 'Callinan was told to go and that's it. There's no getting away from that, a senior party source said.' It sounded like the unnamed 'senior party source' was proclaiming some sort of personal victory. Who? Your guess is as good as mine.

While clearly critical both of me and the Taoiseach, Tom McGurk in his weekly column in the same paper had some interesting insights that transcended the week of garda-related controversy. He wrote 'First of all, whether he deserves it or not – and as a reforming Minister for Justice few could deny that he has been hugely energetic and hardworking – Alan Shatter has become the big political target, a kind of political pariah dominating the 24 hours news cycle.' Acknowledging the dynamic of present-day media reporting, he continued:

> However regrettable it may be, modern media works on the simplest of blood-letting principles, seek out the public enemies and take them out. It's the twenty-first-century version of the lynch mob and the hue and cry. People like complex stories told in simple terms and they want their heroes and villains sketched out in the broadest strokes. Hence, it is my belief, that once you are the starring villain in one of these grim pantomimes, then there's no way back. You might limp on for a time but they'll get you eventually.

McGurk's major criticism of the Taoiseach was Kenny's failure to yet sack me or, as McGurk framed it, to cut me adrift. He viewed my remaining in Government, mired in continuing controversy, with the European and local elections approaching, as damaging to the prospects of both Fine Gael and Labour and seriously damaging to the Taoiseach's political future. Still confident that the truth would triumph, I gave little weight to McGurk's words. As things turned out, he was right on the button, as were his colleagues, Michael Brennan and Pat Leahy. Deploying a banking metaphor, in the same paper they wrote that 'The political capital in Shatter's account is at an all time low and, if there is another withdrawal, expect Kenny to close him down, rather than offer him another last minute over-draft.'

In the middle of it all Monday, 31 March 2014, provided an enjoyable diversion from continuing controversy. I spent the day in the Convention

Centre in Dublin, together with retired High Court Judge Bryan McMahon, officiating at four citizenship ceremonies. The Garda Band was on stage and before each ceremony they had the auditorium rocking and swaying to the sound of jazz. Members of the Defence Forces proudly carried the tricolour on stage at the start of each ceremony and I got a lump in my throat every time. Despite having presided over dozens of citizenship ceremonies since their invention and inauguration in June 2011, they continued to have an emotional impact on me. There is something truly special about them. The atmosphere is both celebratory and electric. By 5pm that day over 4,000 new Irish citizens had joyously recited the oath of loyalty to the State and wildly applauded their becoming new Irish citizens. The day was a welcome refuge from the awfulness of the preceding days. In my final remarks on stage at what would, unknown to me, be my last citizenship ceremony, in a reflective moment, I told those present that citizenship ceremonies were the highlight and most enjoyable part of my job as Justice Minister. Leaving the stage I wondered what led me to say that and whether I would be back for more citizenship ceremonies three months later.

On April Fool's Day, Tuesday 1 April, and the preceding weekend, Fianna Fáil were promoting a motion of no confidence tabled in me for debate in the Dáil. In response, as is traditional, a counter motion of confidence was tabled on behalf of the Government. Seventeen months later I would discover that, on the same day, a civil servant in the Taoiseach's Department telephoned Sean Guerin to find out whether he would complete his preliminary inquiry in the 'timeframe' designated in his Terms of Reference. The designated 'timeframe' Guerin and the civil servant clearly had in mind was eight weeks and no longer. Documentation obtained through a Freedom of Information request, strenuously resisted by the Taoiseach's Department, recorded Guerin's 'firm intention and desire' to do so.

Some would perceive the phone call to Guerin as putting inappropriate pressure on an individual appointed to conduct an independent inquiry. Others would regard it as an innocent and appropriate enquiry by the Department ultimately responsible for publishing Guerin's report. As Guerin had only commenced his work a month earlier, it was at the very least a strange coincidence that the phone call was made on the very day Fianna Fáil's no confidence motion in me was on the Dáil agenda. There can be little doubt that the civil servant's phone call was made in response to instructions given. Who gave those instructions is a matter for conjecture.

Before the confidence motion was debated, Opposition leaders returned at Leaders' Questions to the events of the previous week. Micheál Martin regarded it as 'inconceivable that the Minister would have been briefed by Departmental officials at 6pm on the Monday (24 March 2014) about the telephone recording system and would not have been told … that a letter had been received two weeks earlier from the Garda Commissioner detailing in a reasonable comprehensive manner the background to this issue'. For Martin it was 'even more incredible' that the Secretary General who received it was 'the very man' sent by the Taoiseach to the former Commissioner's home. In response, Kenny confirmed that I had neither been furnished that Monday evening with the Commissioner's letter nor knew of its existence or content. Clearly, Martin was not convinced by this response.

The confidence debate started at 7.30pm. The allegations that I had been untruthful in detailing my knowledge of the garda recordings and the Commissioner's letter as well as untruthful and incompetent in the manner in which I had dealt with issues under examination by both Cooke and Guerin and in addressing McCabe's Ticket Charge/Penalty Points complaints were the central themes of contributions from the Opposition. Most political observers and commentators regard such debates as political slapstick warranting limited attention, unless there is a real prospect of a Minister resigning or being sacked or a Government falling. The Opposition had no expectation of winning the Dáil vote that evening as the Government had a safe majority. However, they knew that another week consumed by a Shatter-related controversy was damaging to the Government, continued to undermine my public credibility and increased pressure on the Taoiseach to throw me to the wolves.

Opposition contributions to the debate were predictable and nothing dramatically new emerged. The contribution which stood out for me was that of Fianna Fáil's Limerick TD Willie O'Dea, which was simply abusive and deeply personal.

The 'arrogant Jew' is a centuries old anti-Semitic depiction of Jewish people who stand up for themselves, have the courage of their convictions and who are neither servile nor compliant. Accusations of my being 'arrogant' were commonplace by the date of the confidence motion and surfaced several times during the debate. I assumed that most, if not all, of those who resorted to it had no understanding of the backdrop to the narrative used by them, were not consciously anti-Semitic and would be outraged if accused of anti-Semitism. Whenever I truthfully addressed false allegations, attempted to correct inaccurate narratives or simply defended myself against political attack, the 'arrogance' accusation surfaced either in the Dáil or in the print media. Some reporters and media commentators were particularly addicted to it. It may be a risky thing to write but, without fear of contradiction, I do not believe there is a single public servant with whom I directly worked during my time in the Department of Justice or the Department of Defence who regarded me as arrogant. In fact, compared to stories that circulated about the conduct of Ministers past and some of more recent vintage towards civil servants working in a variety of Government departments, I was perhaps, more understanding and less critical than was wise when mistakes occurred.

While his Fianna Fáil colleagues on that night did not enter this territory, Willie O'Dea plunged in head first: 'The problem is that the Minister, Deputy Shatter, does not deal with people on an equal basis. He sees everybody at a distance from the towering heights of his own regard.' Willie sounded as if he was reading an extract from one of Miriam Lord's more recent colour pieces in *The Irish Times* or a Dearbhail McDonald commentary in the *Irish Independent*. It is extraordinary how on occasion politicians and political commentators meet at the political crossroads and cross pollinate each other's perspective and influence public opinion. But Willie did not stop there. He continued in full flight, 'the Minister's name has become a watchword for hubris, arrogance, intellectual superiority and the inability to admit even the slightest mistake'.

Until that evening's debate, I had refrained from responding to such charges but when Willie sat down with a look of self-satisfaction at his way with words, I decided to do so in as dignified and considered a way as I could.

I responded:

Like everyone else in this House, I do not get everything right. It is extraordinary how people think that an individual can never make a mistake or that he or she can never be forgiven for making that mistake. I do not have a monopoly of wisdom and neither does anyone else. I have stated as much on many occasions in this House.

We all get some things wrong sometimes. If we do not address issues which require to be dealt with and if we simply remain paralysed when confronted with difficulties, however, then nothing would ever change. The status quo would continue to obtain to the detriment of people in this State.

No one else that evening or on the Wednesday evening walked through the door opened by O'Dea. To my surprise, the next day, on Leaders' Questions, Gerry Adams commented that while he had 'no confidence in the Minister, Deputy Shatter, it was nauseating to listen to the former Fianna Fáil Minister, Deputy Willie O'Dea, pontificating last night in a highly vindictive, personalised and inappropriate way about the Minister'. It was the first, and as far as I can recollect, the only time that Gerry Adams, albeit somewhat grudgingly, came to my defence.

The confidence debate finished shortly after 9pm on Wednesday, with the Fine Gael and Labour parties joining together to vote confidence in me. The next day, Thursday, the Dáil moved on to other issues.

The events of the previous week and my being continuously derided that week both in the Dáil, the print media and on current affairs programmes resulted in the predictable abuse and anti-Semitic tropes on social media. More seriously, it resulted in the delivery of a suspicious envelope to our home and, a short time after I had sounded the alarm, a visit by the gardaí and the army bomb disposal team. The envelope contained images of German Nazi soldiers at a rally, a series of Nazi swastika flags and of a group of emaciated Jewish inmates of a concentration camp. The envelope also contained white powder, samples of which were taken both by the gardaí and the army disposal team for analysis. Ultimately, the white powder was identified as ashes, presumably symbolising the remains of cremated Jewish concentration camp victims.

Within a week, a second incident occurred and An Post at the local Ballyboden Sorting Office called the gardaí after powder was spotted coming out of an envelope addressed to my home. That package also contained anti-Semitic material. Around the same time and in the weeks immediately preceding the posting of the package, a stream of anti-Semitic emails were received in the Department of Justice which, amongst other things, accused me of being 'a perfidious Jew' and a 'Yiddish whore'. The gardaí successfully identified the origin of the emails and, in November

2015, following a guilty plea, the person responsible was sentenced to one hundred hours of community service.

To survive in frontline politics, you need a thick skin and a capacity to stay emotionally detached from criticism voiced where it is unjustified and false charges made by political opponents and media commentators. It is inevitably part of the territory. Unfortunately, we live in an age in which many people have little respect for the jobs that politicians do and little thought is given to the personal impact of abuse and the stress it causes to politicians and their families. Of course, politicians are their own worst enemies in the manner in which they treat each other.

I greatly enjoyed the work involved in being Minister for Justice, Equality and Defence, up to the end of 2013. But, except for a brief period during March 2014 it had been a pretty lousy and torrid year. To do the job, it is important that your home is a safe haven where you can relax. It is bad enough that your spouse and family have to cope with the exigencies of a family member in public life. It is a step too far when threats intrude into your home. Despite maintaining an outwardly sanguine appearance, I was shaken by the envelope delivered to our home and was concerned it could undermine Carol's sense of security despite our 24/7 garda presence. I was, however, determined not to be undermined or driven out of office either by my critics or those who hate.

Coincidentally, the following Tuesday, 8 April 2014, my 'Irish Human Rights and Equality Commission Bill 2014' came before the Dáil. It was a Bill I regarded as enormously important, bringing together the Irish Human Rights Commission and the Equality Authority into one body with a wider overall remit. Vested interests attached to each body had created difficulties in progressing the legislation and my objective was misrepresented as being to curtail rather than enhance human rights and equality protection. A great deal of work, both on the domestic and international political scene, was needed to correct that perception. However, by the time I was moving the Bill in the Dáil, Departmental officials had been informed by their European Commission counterparts that the Bill would prove to be an important template to be copied in other European Union states.

During Ireland's EU Presidency in 2013, when chairing meetings of Justice Ministers, I had raised the need for more effective action to be taken at European level to counteract hate crime, racism, anti-Semitism, xenophobia and homophobia and I made reference to this in my speech that day in the Dáil. I expressed concern about growing anti-Semitism across Europe and regarded progressing the Bill through the Dáil that week as particularly appropriate in the context of what I had experienced in the days and weeks preceding the debate. Unfortunately, in the years that have followed the scourge of anti-Semitism has further spread throughout many European countries, resulting in Jewish people being targeted, murdered and maimed by those who hate. The new norm is the necessity in too many European countries for the permanent presence of police or private security guards outside Jewish institutions, such as synagogues and schools.

Good Friday was 18 April 2014 and the Easter weekend finally arrived. In the two weeks leading into Easter, my world calmed down. The garda controversies no longer featured in Leaders' Questions and the Dáil motion to establish the Fennelly Commission and detailing its terms of reference was approved.

In the background, the Cooke and Guerin inquiries were ongoing and Judge Fennelly's Commission of Investigation was getting underway. When moving the Dáil motion on the Fennelly Commission, which of course included provision for a comprehensive investigation into the garda recordings issue, Enda Kenny told the Dail that his 'sole interest' was 'to establish the truth'. He had made a similar statement in the Dáil when Sean Guerin was appointed to undertake his non-statutory inquiry. It was not only in the public interest but also in my own interest that the truth be fully established about the issues that had been the focus of so much frenzied controversy and false accusation going back to the start of the year. What I did not anticipate was that the Taoiseach would construct his own version of the truth and that his interest in the 'full truth' was partial. This would only slowly become apparent to me in the months following my resignation from Cabinet.

After attending the annual Easter Sunday commemorations outside the GPO in O'Connell Street in which the Defence Forces played a central role, Carol and I took a badly needed week's break. The first major event I attended after the break was the launch of Fine Gael's European election campaign in the Royal College of Physicians on Monday 28 April. There was a great buzz at the launch and happily no mention of garda controversies. On that Monday evening the first meeting of a newly formed Cabinet Justice Committee took place to consider in detail the creation of the new proposed Police Authority.

The weekly Cabinet meeting was held on Wednesday, 30 April when the Dáil reconvened after the Easter break. Justice Questions were the first item on the Dáil agenda that day and only one Priority Question tabled by Fianna Fáil's Niall Collins related to the garda controversies. It seemed that, at least temporarily, there was some recognition that they had been politically flogged to death. Opposition parties and TDs had clearly decided to await publication of the pending reports and were now focusing on other issues.

Responding to the question from Niall Collins, I informed him that I expected that the Cooke and Guerin Reports would be 'received shortly', while emphasising that 'their finalisation is exclusively for Mr Justice Cooke and Mr Guerin'. I did not wish there to be any new or credible accusation made of my interfering in any way with either Guerin or Cooke and neither I, nor any civil servant on my behalf, made any enquiries to find out how rapidly their work was progressing. They were each required to present their reports within eight weeks of their appointment 'or as soon as may be thereafter' and this phrase gave each of them as much flexibility as they required to take any additional time necessary to complete their task. As Judge Cooke's job seemed less onerous than Sean Guerin's, as it involved a good deal less documentation and engagement with fewer people, I expected the *Cooke Report* would be received and published first.

On 1 May I completed, in the Dáil, the report and final stages of the Criminal Justice (Forensic Evidence and DNA Database System) Bill informally known as the DNA Database Bill. It had yet to complete its stages in the Seanad but its passage through the Dáil was a giant step forward and the fulfilment for me of a major personal reforming objective. It was one of the lengthiest Bills I had processed since entering Government and was a pet project. For many years, I had been critical of the fact that we did not have a DNA Database for garda use in crime detection. The Bill was 217 pages long, had just under 170 sections and was, I believe, the most important piece of legislation on criminal law enacted in the Thirty-First Dáil.

The week ended with my attending a reception for the Mexican Dublin Business Conference in the Mansion House, where I met some of the business people I had first met in Mexico City six weeks earlier. The food was good and the event enjoyable.

My visit to Mexico in March had been the prelude to major domestic political turmoil and garda-related controversy. As I was heading home that Friday evening, I did not know that the reception I had just attended would be my second last official engagement as a member of Cabinet. While the relationship between Ireland and Mexico is mutually advantageous and positive, each time in 2014 when I officially engaged with Mexico there was unexpected personal political damage and drama. Of course, Mexico is not to blame.

CHAPTER 33

The *Guerin Report* is Born

Need to give you the Report from Guerin this morning. It's very Problematical –Text message to Alan Shatter from An Taoiseach Enda Kenny, Wednesday, 7 May 2014

Early Tuesday morning, 6 May, as usual, I started work on papers at home. I was concerned about a Defence issue and anxious to have it dealt with as soon as possible by Cabinet.

Within a few weeks of the Government being formed in 2011, I had secured Cabinet approval for the construction and purchase of two new Naval vessels at a total cost of approximately €100 million that the outgoing Fianna Fáil-led Government had planned to purchase. The purchases were crucial because two of our Naval ships had already passed their 'use by' date and were due to be decommissioned. The first of the new vessels was undergoing sea trials and scheduled to be formally commissioned and launched on 17 May 2014, an event I was looking forward to attending. There was a third ship that would soon have to be replaced and we had an option to contract for the construction and purchase of a third vessel at 2011 recession pricing. I needed Cabinet approval to sign the contracts. It was hugely advantageous financially to the State that we did so and time was running out. A memo had been submitted to the Cabinet Secretariat and I was hopeful that the issue would be dealt with at that Tuesday morning's Cabinet meeting, or if that were not possible, at the next one. So just after 7.35am, I texted Enda Kenny: 'Can I have a brief word with u about our option to purchase a third ship for navy before Cabinet as it is something we need to deal with this month.'

I also said it 'would be advantageous to make a decision before the launch of the new ship', which I had named, with Cabinet approval, the *Samuel Beckett*. This would be the second last text by me to Kenny as Minister for Justice, Equality and Defence. As it turned out purchase of the third new naval vessel was not on that Tuesday's Cabinet agenda and was not agreed until a week later, by which time I was no longer a member of Cabinet. Ultimately, the contract for the third ship was signed by Kenny as acting Minister for Defence and today our Naval service has three fine recently commissioned vessels, the *Samuel Beckett*, the *James Joyce* and the *William Butler Yeats*. Without these vessels our Navy would have lacked the capacity to save the lives, in recent years, of many thousands of refugees being trafficked across the Mediterranean. While I selected the names Beckett and Joyce, the name Yeats was selected by Simon Coveney, following the Defence brief being transferred to him. Despite the contribution of Yeats to Irish literature, when Minister for Defence I had deliberately excluded Yeats from my list of possible names because of his anti-Semitism. I had Maeve Binchy in mind for the third ship.

On Wednesday 7 May 2014, I received a text from Enda Kenny at 6.52am. It read 'Need to give you the report from Guerin this morning. It's very problematic. Have health committee at 8. Call over at 7.45. E.' Engrossed in work, having forgotten to take my phone off silent, I failed to notice the text till close to 8am when I headed back upstairs to shave and shower. I arranged to meet the Taoiseach after his Health meeting in Government Buildings. When I arrived in his office at approximately 9.15am he handed me the *Guerin Report*, informed me its contents were very serious and the future of the Government depended on how I responded to it. I was stunned, as I did not expect Guerin could properly complete his inquiry so quickly nor did I expect any report he wrote would contain any criticism of my actions as Minister for Justice. I assumed that if any issues arose for which I was responsible during the course of his inquiry which generated concern, or about which Guerin required information from me, he would either interview me or write directly to me. I did not anticipate a report would be completed with conclusions critical of my actions without any direct engagement of any nature with me.

I understood both from the Taoiseach's expression and our conversation that the report was critical and that he expected my resignation. I believe that Andrew McDowell, the Taoiseach's economic adviser, was sitting in the Taoiseach's room during our brief meeting but I am not entirely certain of the accuracy of this recollection. I was totally focussed on what Kenny said to me and totally taken aback. I muttered something in response about having learnt of another letter that had not been furnished to me by Justice officials (upon reading the Guerin Report I was to discover reference to more than one letter) and the meeting ended. The resignation word was not used by Kenny, but the message was clear.

I was scheduled that morning to attend the Church of the Sacred Heart in Dublin for the Arbour Hill commemoration of those who lost their lives in 1916 and, as Minister for Defence, to greet the guests as they arrived for the 10am service. Among the expected guests were the Taoiseach and the Attorney General. I informed the Taoiseach I would read the report upon my return.

I returned to my office, informed Jane Lehane of my exchange with Kenny and asked that she start reading the report in my absence. There was a sense of unreality in what was happening. I was driven to Arbour Hill, went into acting mode and assumed an appropriate ministerial demeanour. The event, which was attended, amongst others, by Government Ministers, a large number of TDs and Senators, members of the judiciary and relatives of those who died in 1916 was surreal. I was there but not there. As I conversed with some of those arriving for prayers and with others upon completion of the religious service and ceremonials, it felt as if I was watching the event, not participating in it. It was difficult to believe that this could be my last official engagement as a Government Minister. There remained a whole agenda of legislative reform and change to be implemented, which I had mapped for completion over the remaining two years in Government. Substantial work had also been completed on a Defence White Paper that I hoped within a few months to bring before Cabinet and then publish. I loved my involvement in both Justice and Defence and had never envisaged it would prematurely end.

The many false allegations I had been subjected to in connection with garda-related controversies in the first quarter of 2014 had made life difficult and, on occasion, very unpleasant but I believed things had settled down. I also expected that the Cooke and Guerin reports would set the record straight and raise no questions about my ministerial conduct and competence. Ironically, I was confident that when viewing the correspondence sent to McCabe's solicitors, Guerin would be in no doubt that I had taken McCabe's allegations seriously and would understand the difficulties I had encountered in making progress because of McCabe's erratic engagement. I had actually been looking forward to the publication of both reports.

I arrived back in Government Buildings from Arbour Hill just before 12 noon and Jane, who was clearly upset, briefed me on what she had read so far. I was scheduled to take Defence question time in the Dáil chamber at 2.30pm and first had to check through some of the answers to questions prepared by Defence officials. Bizarrely, ensuring I was happy with the responses prepared was my first priority. I was clearly in denial.

I then glanced over the Guerin Report and knew there was no possibility that I could fully read and digest the 300-page report before 2.30pm. I understood it had only been received by the Taoiseach the previous evening and wondered how he could have fully read it before 7am that morning. I wondered whether it had been read overnight by one of his special advisers and simply summarised for him or extracts contained in it had been identified for him to read. I still do not know the answer to that. A message was left with Kenny's private secretary that I wished us to meet again. I also unsuccessfully attempted to make phone contact with Máire Whelan. It was a very basic legal principle that an individual could not be criticised in an inquiry without being given a fair hearing and I could not understand how a Senior Counsel appointed by the Government to conduct an inquiry could have violated this basic principle – but I never got to discuss that issue with Whelan.

I chose to read three out of the twenty chapters of the Report that appeared from its index to be most relevant to my engagement as Minister and that Jane had already read. It was clear that I was severely criticised and that Guerin had no understanding of my true approach to the complaints made by McCabe or of the difficulties that had arisen. Amongst other things, he concluded that there was cause for concern 'as to whether all appropriate steps were taken by the Minister for Justice and Equality to investigate and address the specified complaints' of McCabe and also that I had failed to 'heed' his voice 'despite ... having an independent supervisory and investigative function with specific statutory powers'. The conclusion that I had 'failed to heed' McCabe's voice coincided with a similar charge made by Micheál Martin in the Dáil in February 2014 two days after he had met with McCabe. The report merely recited but contained no legal analysis of the flawed provisions in the Garda Síochána Act and the relevant Whistleblowers Regulations. I was also astonished to discover that despite his remit, which required Guerin to read all documents of relevance to his inquiry, he had chosen to complete his report without reading what he recorded GSOC referring to as its 'voluminous' documentation of relevance to the issues he was addressing.

Guerin attributed his failure to read GSOC documentation to the time constraints imposed for the completion of his report. I regarded this explanation as nonsensical. His terms of reference, like those of Judge Cooke, gave him leeway to take as much time as he required to properly complete his report and, if in doubt, there was no obstacle preventing him from informing the Taoiseach that he needed extra time. More often than not, those conducting either statutory or non-statutory inquiries at the request of Government or a Government Minister require more time than originally envisaged. Moreover, whenever extra time is requested and an explanation provided, it is never denied. As a lawyer and a politician, I did not know of any person or tribunal conducting any previous inquiry at the request of Government making a deliberate decision to not read documentation known to be relevant to the outcome of their inquiry.

I knew GSOC had an important role with regard to protected disclosures made through the Confidential Recipient. It also had investigated the circumstances surrounding the despicable murder of Sylvia Roche-Kelly, as a result of a complaint to GSOC made by her bereaved husband. I could not understand Guerin completing his report without reviewing GSOC's own internal documents and files and, if required, meeting with GSOC, as I would later discover Judge Cooke did during his inquiry into GSOC's mistaken suspicions of being bugged.

Guerin's report detailed that he had met Maurice McCabe on four occasions involving nineteen hours of discussion. No transcript or extract from any transcript of their discussion had been provided to me to enable me to respond to anything that might have been said about how I addressed McCabe's allegations. To this day I am unaware of the content of any transcript that exists.

It was clear that Guerin had a broad remit to meet or communicate with anyone he decided could assist him in his task. I could not fathom how he could seriously question or criticise the appropriateness of my response as Minister for Justice to McCabe's complaints and accuse me of failing 'to heed' his voice without giving me any opportunity to explain my actions.

It was about 2pm and, following a phone call from Kenny's private secretary, I again met him in his office. I complained that Guerin had criticised me without giving me any opportunity to respond, mentioned his failure to read GSOCs papers, challenged his critical conclusions and asked that I be allowed twenty-four hours to complete reading the report and to reflect on its content. I also informed him that the report referenced additional correspondence of importance received by Justice Department officials that was never furnished to me. (The correspondence of relevance predated Martin Callinan's letter of 10 March 2014 that had recently generated much controversy.) Kenny's response was that, if he were asked later that afternoon in the Dáil chamber whether he had confidence in me, he would be unable to give a positive answer. I immediately recognised the similarity of this to the message conveyed by Brian Purcell to Martin Callinan on the Taoiseach's behalf just six weeks earlier. I knew my ministerial career was over.

Kenny was scheduled to be in the Dáil chamber at 4.30pm. I informed him that in the circumstances he would have my resignation letter by 4pm, after Defence question time had concluded. The meeting had lasted for no more than five or six minutes.

I returned to my office, dictated in part my letter of resignation and then went down to the Dáil chamber for Defence question time. I calmly responded to questions and no one in the chamber could have guessed the drama going on in the background. Appropriately for the day that was in it, one of the Priority Questions was concerned with whistle-blowers in the Defence Forces. The very final question answered by me as Minister for Defence concerned the total length of service allowed in the Defence Forces to privates and corporals, asking that I revise the twenty-one-year rule limit to allow those who wished to do so to continue in service. In responding, no hint of any nature was given by me to the fact that my term of service as Minister for Justice and Defence was destined to finish within ten to fifteen minutes of that day's question time ending.

Looking back on it now, I think I was on automatic pilot and in a state of shock and disbelief. Exiting the chamber at 3.50pm, I returned to my office and completed my letter of resignation. It was delivered to Enda Kenny's office about 4.10pm.

Once Kenny informed me that he would be unable to express confidence in me I knew my position was untenable. Had I tried to hold out there would have been an unedifying controversy. I also understood it was the Taoiseach's prerogative to sack any Minister he chose and, if he did not sack me, I reckoned upon publication of the *Guerin Report*, not only the Opposition but also the Labour members of Government and some of my Fine Gael colleagues would be calling for my head. I was determined to depart with dignity. After weeks of unrelenting criticism and pressure, Guerin's unexpected conclusions, together with Kenny's immediate withdrawal of support and refusal to respond to my concerns about Guerin's report, left me with no choice. I knew that to attempt to counteract the inevitable deluge of criticism and condemnation would be the political equivalent of swimming against a flood tide. It can be done for a while but if you cannot reach dry land and the tide never turns, drowning is inevitable.

To me, involvement in political life was public service and involved no personal gain, as my salary as Minister for Justice and Defence fell substantially below my earning potential as a partner and advocate in Gallagher Shatter, a reasonably well known and successful solicitors' firm. My objective was to address issues that had for too long been ignored by Government and simply to make people's lives better. I also enjoyed the international dimension of my political engagements in Justice and Defence, in particular with regard to the EU and the Middle East on which I have considerable expertise. I was concerned that another high-octane political controversy fuelled by a media lynch mob would seriously damage Fine Gael, would be horrendous for my family and that it could dramatically impact on my health. A capillary had not burst in either of my eyes for about six weeks. While I had been medically assured that such an event was not a cause for major concern, I was convinced that this was a physical reaction to the emotional stress which I suppressed and concealed from the public.

My letter of resignation stated that I was resigning to avoid any controversy arising upon publication of the *Guerin Report* distracting from 'the important work of government' or creating difficulties for the Fine Gael or Labour parties heading into the European and local government elections. In it I criticised Guerin's failure to interview me prior to reaching conclusions about my ministerial conduct, detailed my concerns over his failure to read GSOC's documents and lavished praise on the Taoiseach and the Attorney General, Máire Whelan. While I believed that Kenny should have allowed me more time to read the report, I wrongly believed that he knew nothing of Guerin's approach to his task until he had received his report. I recognised that my staying in office following its publication would place him in an impossible position. I was grateful and privileged to have been a Minister for three years in two great Departments and appreciative of the support of the Taoiseach and Attorney General throughout that time. The letter was written by me in good faith. I absolutely believed at the time that Kenny would follow up the concerns I expressed to him on the afternoon of 7 May in his office and which were repeated in my resignation letter. It was only after my resignation I would discover that he had no interest in doing so and that my beliefs were seriously mistaken. I felt totally betrayed. My letter read:

OIFIG AN AIRE DLÍ AGUS CIRT AGUS COMHIONANNAIS
OFFICE OF THE MINISTER FOR JUSTICE AND EQUALITY

An Taoiseach Enda Kenny TD
Department of An Taoiseach

7th May 2014

Dear Enda

Thank you for furnishing to me this morning a copy of the report received from Sean
Guerin SC on a "Review of the actions taken by An Garda Siochana pertaining to
certain allegations made by Sergeant Maurice McCabe". As you know, the Report
runs to over 300 pages and I have neither had the time to fully read or fully consider
the contents of the Report. I have, however, fully read Chapters 1, 19 and 20 of the
Report and a copy of the letter accompanying it of the 6th May 2014 by Sean Guerin
SC.

I note that Mr Guerin states that "it is beyond the scope" of the Review "to make any
determination of the complaints Sergeant McCabe has made". However, having
regard to all of the controversy surrounding allegations made by Sergeant Maurice
McCabe and the seriousness of the various issues raised by him, I agree with Sean
Guerin's conclusion (his having examined the Garda files and accessed information
not furnished to me) that it is appropriate that these matters be the subject of a
statutory inquiry.

I would, however, be less than honest if I did not also record my concerns and
reservations with regard to his Report and, in particular, certain conclusions reached
by him. I was surprised to learn that he received no documentation from the Garda
Siochana Ombudsman Commission (GSOC) and, as he states in his letter, that "the
process of drafting the final report was well underway" when he learnt of
"difficulties" being expressed by GSOC with regard to the furnishing of
documentation to him. Complaints made to GSOC and GSOC's dealings with those
complaints and the statutory role of GSOC were all, amongst other matters, of
relevance to the consideration given by me to issues raised by Sergeant McCabe.
Under the Terms of Reference furnished to Mr Guerin, he was requested to conclude
his review within 8 weeks of 27 Feb 2014 "or as soon as may be thereafter". In his
letter, he notes that GSOC was willing to release what is described as its
"voluminous" documentation subject to certain safeguards which he stated to be "not
unreasonable". I would have expected that, prior to finalising his report, he would
have agreed reasonable safeguards with GSOC and obtained and considered
documentation held by it with regard to the matters under review prior to formulating
his conclusions. Moreover, I note that, under the Terms of Reference, Mr Guerin was
authorised to "interview Sergeant Maurice McCabe and any other such person as may
be considered necessary and capable of providing relevant and material assistance".

At no time did he ask to interview me and I would have expected, if it was his intention to reach a conclusion or form an opinion with regard to my approach or the extent of my concern with regard to the issues raised by Sergeant McCabe, that he would have done so.

I am anxious that any controversy that may arise on publication of the Report does not distract from the important work of Government or create any difficulties for the Fine Gael or Labour Parties in the period leading into the European and Local Government elections. It is my judgement that the only way in which such controversy can be avoided is by my offering you my resignation from Cabinet.

It has been a particular privilege to serve as both Minister for Justice and Equality and also Minister for Defence. I want to thank you for affording me the opportunity to be of public service in these positions and I hope that the reforms and change implemented over the past three years will endure and prove to be of lasting benefit to all who reside in our State.

I believe you are an extraordinary Taoiseach doing an extraordinary job during what has been a very difficult time for our country and I want to thank you for all the assistance and support you have given to me. I also want to record my thanks to the Tanaiste and all my Cabinet colleagues in both parties and to the Fine Gael and Labour Parliamentary Parties. In a cynical age, when politicians are given little public credit for anything they do, I want to especially acknowledge the dedicated commitment of members of both parties, Ministers and non-Ministers, to the welfare of our country. I know on occasion there are issues that give rise to disagreement but what has been extraordinary over the past three years has been the constructive engagement which ultimately has facilitated resolution of the most difficult of issues.

In addition, I want to thank the Attorney General for her assistance and wise counsel on a variety of issues. I am sure that, in the context of the legislative programme, I have put her and her officials from time to time under substantial pressure in my enthusiasm to progress badly needed and long awaited legislative change. Without their help, the progress made would have been impossible. I also want to thank all of the outstanding officials in both of my Departments for the work they do.

Finally, I hope I will be forgiven if I especially thank the many members of the Fine Gael Parliamentary Party, the wider Fine Gael membership and the general public who have been supportive over the past three years through some difficult times and who also have enthusiastically supported and embraced the legislative and other changes which you gave me the opportunity to bring about. I wish the Government well for the remainder of its term in office.

Sincerely

Alan Shatter TD
Minister for Justice, Equality and Defence

When the terms of reference were being finalised for Guerin's Inquiry, Kenny had proposed he be required to complete his task within six weeks. I believed that impossible and ultimately eight weeks 'or as soon as may be thereafter' was agreed on the understanding this would afford Guerin any additional time he considered necessary to properly do his job. In the Dáil, Kenny had emphasised the purpose of the inquiry was to 'find out the truth'. In retrospect, for Enda Kenny I believe the primary purpose of the exercise was to end all political controversy on garda-related issues under examination at least a full three weeks before the upcoming local and European elections. For him, time was more important than truth.

It was not until September 2015, in response to a Freedom of Information (FOI) request that I first learnt that emails sent by Guerin to GSOC's solicitors, Arthur Cox & Co, while conducting his inquiry were also copied by him to the Taoiseach's Department. In one of those emails dated 25 April 2014, two weeks before completion of his report, Guerin informed the Taoiseach's Department that he intended to complete his report without reading 'voluminous' GSOC documentation of relevance. Through an FOI request to GSOC, I also discovered that GSOC's solicitors urged Guerin to read GSOC's documentation before completing his report. The Guerin email of 25 April was emailed to Martin Fraser and there is no reason to doubt that he gave a copy of it or communicated its contents to Kenny. The email expressly signalled that Guerin intended to complete his report and not read documentation directly relevant to his inquiry in defiance of his terms of reference. Put simply, in advance of furnishing his report, Guerin was warning that his inquiry was flawed.

Had I, as a Cabinet minister, received such a communication from a lawyer conducting an inquiry under the aegis of my Department, I would have specifically insisted that all documents of relevance be read and reviewed and all necessary enquiries undertaken before conclusions were reached and a report delivered. I would also not have expected to receive copies of correspondence sent by the person conducting an independent inquiry to a Government agency subject to that inquiry. I was astonished to discover that such emails had been copied to the Taoiseach's Department. So, I discovered, were GSOC's solicitors, Arthur Cox & Co. In a response to Guerin, they noted that his email of 25 April 2014 stated it had been copied to the Taoiseach's Department. They confirmed their understanding from his Terms of Reference 'that your inquiry is an independent inquiry' and stated that they were 'unclear' what was the 'role in the inquiry' of the

Department of the Taoiseach. The correspondence released by GSOC in response to my FOI request included no explanation given by Guerin in response.

Had Enda Kenny informed me, as Minister for Justice, that Guerin had notified him of his intention to not read 'voluminous' GSOC documents of relevance, the alarm bells would have rung. I would have advised him that under the Government's Terms of Reference, Guerin was required to read all relevant documents and had no discretion to simply discard or ignore some. However, instead of informing me of this communication, Kenny concealed from me any prior knowledge of Guerin's intended flawed approach. Initially, his Department refused to release the relevant emails to me on foot of my FOI request in 2015. I appealed their decision and they again refused. I further appealed to the Information Commissioner and it is my understanding that he made it known to the Taoiseach's Department that, if they did not voluntarily release the emails, he would order their release.

If Kenny believed it appropriate that he receive from Guerin copies of emails sent by him to GSOC, Kenny's motive in concealing his knowledge of them from me is unclear. It is also unclear why, when furnishing his report to Kenny on 6 May 2014, in an accompanying letter, Guerin again stated he had not read the GSOC material as if this was the first time Kenny was being informed. As he explicitly referenced this in his report, the reason for mentioning it specifically in his letter is a mystery.

CHAPTER 34

A Uniquely Irish Political Coup

*The duty of the law is to be fair to all and not to limit its protection to
those who are seen to represent popular causes*
–From posthumous statement of Sean O'Leary, former judge of the
Circuit and High Court, Irish Times, 3 January 2007, subsequent to
his death aged 65 on 22 December 2016

We are slaves of the law so that we may be able to be free
–Marcus Tullius Cicero

Jane Lehane handed my resignation letter to Chris Quattrociocchi
without explaining its content and requested that he deliver it to the
Taoiseach's Private Secretary, Nick Reddy. Jennifer Carroll, Lorraine Hall,
Brian Purcell and Ken O'Leary (an Assistant Secretary in the Justice
Department) arrived in my office for a meeting as Jane returned. They
had no inkling of the day's happenings and were completely stunned.
At 4.30pm, Enda Kenny informed the Dáil of my resignation. At that
moment, Chris and Vincent Lowe first learned that I was no longer their
Minister. My failure to explain events to my Private Secretaries gives an
insight into how traumatised and distracted I was at the time.

We silently watched the proceedings in the Dáil Chamber on my office
monitor like participants at a wake. I did not digest what the Taoiseach said
as he announced my resignation nor did I read the Dáil record afterwards.
I only first did so online almost two years later when I was writing this
book. I was surprised to discover that he attributed my resignation to my
accepting responsibility for the 'inadequacy of my response' to Sergeant
Maurice McCabe's allegations as depicted in the *Guerin Report*. I had
not done so and this was not true. A few days after publication of the
O'Higgins Report, as a result of a letter sent to him, in the Dáil Debate on
the report, Kenny corrected the Dáil record, acknowledging that I 'did not
in fact accept responsibility for criticism made' by Guerin. Of course, at
the time of making his original statement on 7 May 2014, the reason given
by him for my departure from Government conveniently fitted into the
prevailing favoured narrative.

Kenny had, on 7 May 2014, bizarrely and repetitively stated that Guerin had not spoken to me before reaching his conclusions. No TD on the Government or Opposition benches, other than me, has any time since questioned how an individual appointed by Government to undertake a non-statutory inquiry could severely criticise and condemn the conduct of a Cabinet Minister without speaking to him or directly engaging with him. This silence was not broken following the publication of the *O'Higgins Report* which irrefutably established his criticism to be wrong. My forced departure from Government remains a uniquely Irish political coup that no Oireachtas member has had the courage or decency to fully or truthfully address.

On that afternoon and evening of 7 May 2014, both Jane and I behaved very strangely. Reflecting on it now, I have no doubt that we were both traumatised. I cannot otherwise explain why I failed to inform either Chris or Vincent of my resignation before they learnt of it from the Taoiseach's Dáil announcement. I think neither I nor Jane were capable that afternoon of verbalising to either of them that I was resigning.

It was only at lunchtime that day that I had made phone contact with Carol, informed her of what was happening and that I believed, following my early morning engagement with the Taoiseach, I had no choice but to resign. Carol questioned my judgement and urged me to delay doing so. After my second meeting with Kenny I believed my continued membership of Cabinet politically untenable. I next phoned her as Jane was handing Chris my resignation letter but I have no recollection of our conversation.

Between 5pm and 6pm, robot-like Jane and I, with the help of those present, gathered up all my personal possessions in our office in Government Buildings. Sometime shortly after 6pm we were driven by Sean Cahill, one of my garda protection officers, to the Department of Justice at 94 St Stephen's Green so that I could say my goodbyes and clear my office. Both Sean and my other garda protection officer, Norman King, in the three years of our working together had become great friends. Sean was so upset he was unable to speak as he drove around the Green.

A couple of hours was spent in the Department gathering up all personal items and papers and thanking some of the officials who had worked closely with me for all their support and help. Brian Purcell's office was across the corridor from mine. My recollection is that we had some conversation and that over the next couple of hours, he wandered in and out of my room on a couple of occasions looking both upset and deeply uncomfortable. Again, I have no recollection of what we said. There was an overwhelming sense of gloom and people speaking quietly to each other as they would at a funeral. It reached 8pm and I was concerned that Carol was both upset and home alone. There was nothing left for me to do in the Department. Sean drove me home. Neither of us said much. I do not believe it fully sank in that I would never again, as a Government Minister, attend Cabinet meetings, help draft and steer new legislation through the Dáil, participate in Citizenship Ceremonies, engage with the fantastic members of our Defence Forces or attend a Justice or Defence EU Ministerial meeting. I felt responsible and guilty that, as a consequence of my resignation, Jane, Jennifer, Lorraine and some others had automatically that evening lost their jobs. Each had worked under pressure, put in long hours, done a great job and I believed deserved to be better treated.

On that drive home it all felt unreal, as if I was in a nightmare. When I arrived, Carol emerged, tears streaming down her face. That was the moment I accepted this was reality. I believed my political reputation was enormously damaged, possibly irreparably, and my reputation as a lawyer destroyed as a result of the *Guerin Report*.

I have no memory of the rest of that evening or night. Carol tells me I slept for about two hours, then got up and made tea. The next day is also a blur. I recall Carol, Jane and I spending a great deal of time together going back through the previous day's events, driving from my home to Jane's house to escape from reporters and photographers gleefully gathered outside our front gate and reading various commiserating texts and emails from a variety of people. I was surprised at how many officials/public servants working at various levels within the Departments of Justice and Defence and related agencies as well as some members of the Defence Forces took time to communicate with me and to express regret at my departure. One of the odder texts I received was from Oliver Connolly, who clearly lacked any personal insight or understanding of the damage done by his bizarre conversation with Maurice McCabe. Connolly expressed himself as 'very saddened' by my departure and that 'perhaps we can meet up at some time for a drink when the dust settles'. As far as I was concerned there was no question of my ever doing so and the only subsequent occasion on which our paths crossed was the day he gave evidence before the O'Higgins Commission.

On Friday, 9 May, Sean drove me to the Department of Defence's headquarters in Newbridge for the last time. I wanted to thank the officials there for all their work and support while I was their Minister and clear out some personal papers and memorabilia from my office. I also spoke with the Department's extremely competent Secretary General, Maurice Quinn, and very able Chief of Staff, Conor O'Boyle, and informed them that, at my brief second meeting with the Taoiseach prior to Defence Question Time on the afternoon of my resignation, I had reminded him of the importance of the contracts being signed for the purchase of the third new Naval vessel and expressed my optimism that it would be secured for the Navy's benefit.

Before leaving the Department of Defence that morning, I received word that the Rehab Group had lost High Court judicial review proceedings they had taken against me as Minister for Justice and against the State. They had challenged a decision I made in December 2012 to phase out a scheme, set up in 1997, to compensate a number of charities which claimed to be losing out to the new National Lottery. Under the scheme, annual payments were made by the State to designated charitable bodies in proportion to the gross funds they raised selling their own lottery products. Rehab was annually the largest recipient of money under the scheme. In 2012 Rehab had received €3.924 million out of €6 million and the figures were similar in 2011. It had received over €80 million since the scheme's inception.

Shortly following my appointment to Cabinet, responsibility for the scheme had been transferred from the Department of Finance to Justice. I had personally examined the papers received from Finance, became very concerned about the scheme and asked that it be audited. I concluded from the information I received that the scheme was being abused. Rehab and other designated charities were making minimal profit from their own lottery products and some were making no profit at all. It was clear that their lotteries had essentially become a means of leveraging State funds. People buying lottery products from the designated charities believed that their money was being used to provide charitable services. In reality, most of it was being used to administer the lotteries, pay salaries and commissions to lottery sellers and for prizes. The real value to Rehab and the other designated charities of the lottery products they sold was the money they received from the State to match their gross turnover. I concluded that the charitable bodies had long ceased to operate their own fundraising schemes for profit and were simply using them as a means to leverage public funding.

It was Rehab's contention that the State should, in perpetuity, continue to pay them millions of euro annually under the scheme. I disagreed. I believed it was not a justifiable use of taxpayers' money and that it should be ended in the public interest. In order to put me and the Government under pressure, Rehab initiated a second High Court action claiming over one billion euro damages against the State for losses allegedly resulting from the establishment of the National Lottery.

There had been substantial concern within Justice in the lead-in to the court hearing over the consequences should Rehab be successful. Rehab had also lobbied the Taoiseach and Cabinet colleagues to persuade me to back off, the most prominent lobbyist being Frank Flannery who had long associations with Fine Gael. I had directly engaged with the Justice officials dealing with the proceedings and kept an eagle eye on the court papers exchanged. I believed the Rehab lottery products sold were generating completely inadequate profits for charitable purposes. It was unfair both to those purchasing Rehab lottery tickets and to taxpayers and I insisted we stood firm. I thought it was a particular irony that, two days after my resignation, the High Court had dismissed Rehab's proceedings and, in so doing, diminished the likelihood of the group succeeding in their enormous damages claim against the State.

In the weeks that followed, the Rehab Board resigned, announced that it was not appealing the High Court decision and withdrew their claim for damages. Rehab also stopped running the lotteries used to leverage funds from the State scheme.

That Saturday morning's newspapers gave some coverage to the High Court's Rehab judgement but it generated minimal media interest. No mention of it was to be found in the Sunday papers. The fact that the State had been saved many millions of euro at a time of financial difficulty was not regarded as of any great relevance to readers.

Predictably, that weekend's papers had wall-to-wall coverage of the *Guerin Report*, my resignation and acclaimed Sergeant Maurice McCabe in heroic terms. There was no exploration of how a Cabinet Minister could have been criticised and condemned without being given any opportunity to explain his actions. Not a single media commentator attached any credibility to the concerns I had expressed in my resignation letter about Guerin's flawed inquiry process or questioned why McCabe was the only person he interviewed. There was simply universal agreement that I was guilty as charged and deserved my fate.

CHAPTER 35

Guerin v O'Higgins:
The Truth Two Years Too Late

I am of the opinion that there is cause for concern as to the adequacy of the investigation of the complaints made by Sergeant Maurice McCabe to the Minister for Justice and Equality and a sufficient basis for concern as to whether all appropriate steps were taken by the Minister for Justice and Equality to investigate and address the specified complaints
–Guerin Report, May 2014

No complex organization can expect to succeed in its task if it cannot find the means of heeding the voice of a member whose immediate supervisors hold him in the high regard in which Sergeant McCabe was held. Ultimately, An Garda Síochána does not seem to have been able to do that. Nor does the Minister for Justice and Equality, despite his having an independent supervisory and investigative function with specific statutory powers –Guerin Report

There were pertinent and cumulatively most compelling considerations which amply justified the Minister in acting as he did …The Minister promptly consulted the Secretary General … he was manifestly right to seek the views of the then Commissioner. It was an obvious prudent and sensible thing to do. Indeed, he would be open to justified criticism had he acted otherwise … Sergeant McCabe does not now question (that) decision of the Minister … The exchanges between the department, the minister and the Commissioner during the handling of Sergeant McCabe's complaint were at all times professional and appropriate … (The Minister) displayed personal and active concern … The enquiry made by the department as to confidentiality (of documentation and correspondence received from Sergeant McCabe's solicitors) was perfectly reasonable in the context of all the previous correspondence between Sergeant McCabe and the department … Neither the department nor the minister can be faulted for failing to take further action on a request for an inquiry under section 42 of the Garda Síochána Act 2005, as amended, in circumstances in

which Sergeant McCabe continued to assert a claim of confidentiality
over relevant correspondence and enclosures
–O'Higgins Commission Report, May 2016

Sean Guerin's Report entitled *Review of the action taken by An Garda Síochána pertaining to certain allegations made by Sergeant Maurice McCabe* was published two days after my resignation, on 9 May 2014. In his introduction Guerin asserted that what he termed his 'review' was 'conducted in accordance with the terms of reference agreed by the government on the advice of the Attorney General'. This assertion, unfortunately, was not entirely accurate. Guerin's terms of reference prescribed that he 'interview Sergeant Maurice McCabe and any other such person' considered 'necessary and capable of providing relevant and material assistance' to his review in respect of allegations made by McCabe 'of grave deficiencies in the investigation and prosecution of crimes in the county of Cavan'. They also required him 'to receive and consider any relevant documentation that may be provided by Sergeant McCabe or such other person'. Additionally, he was obliged to 'examine all documentation and data held by An Garda Síochána, the Department of Justice and Equality and any other entity or public body' deemed relevant to McCabe's allegations. The requirement that he 'receive and consider any relevant documentation' that could be provided and that he 'examine all documentation and data' was, under his terms of reference, an absolute duty. Guerin was not entitled, when conducting his 'review', to simply not read, consider or examine relevant documentation or data that he knew existed or to arbitrarily decide not to interview readily identifiable people who were 'capable of providing relevant and material assistance'.

Guerin was also obliged 'to communicate with An Garda Síochána and any other relevant entity or public body in relation to any relevant documentation and information and to examine what steps, if any', were 'taken by them to investigate and resolve' McCabe's allegations. His remit to 'communicate' was designed to not only facilitate Guerin make written requests for 'relevant documentation' but to also enable him to seek any 'information' necessary for the purpose of his fully and properly completing his task. It enabled him to seek clarification in writing on any issue or to simply interview a relevant person who could shed light on an issue.

Central to Guerin's task was an obligation to consider whether there was 'sufficient basis for concern as to whether all appropriate steps were taken by An Garda Síochána or any other relevant entity or public body to investigate and address' McCabe's complaints. This obliged him to identify whether there was sufficient basis for such 'concerns' as to require in the public interest that they be addressed by a formal statutory inquiry or commission of investigation. His task did not envisage or require that he pass judgement on anyone.

Immediately following his appointment, Guerin wrote to me, as Minister for Justice, requesting that I nominate a Justice official with whom he could directly communicate to obtain any documentation he required. An official was duly nominated and I instructed that there be full cooperation with Guerin and that he be provided with all documentation of relevance concerning our engagement with McCabe. I assumed that he would seek and obtain from An Garda Síochána, GSOC and the DPP all relevant documentation held by them. I believed that the Department's documentation would clearly illustrate that, as Minister, I had at all times promptly and appropriately dealt with McCabe's allegations and that any difficulties that had arisen derived from McCabe's request for anonymity, his assertion of confidentiality over documentation provided to me and his solicitors' failure to reply to correspondence. I also believed if Guerin had any concerns arising out of his documentary review, or required additional information before completing his task, he would either 'communicate directly with me' and seek my response or interview me. As Guerin was undertaking an 'independent' role and as I could not anticipate what, if anything, might be of 'concern' to him, I believed it was for him to determine what, if any, information or clarifications he required from me rather than for me to unilaterally communicate with him. The fact that the Department of Justice was the 'lead Department' for the Cooke Inquiry had already resulted in some alleging that the outcome of that inquiry would be in some way improperly influenced by me. I had no wish for a similar allegation to be made as a consequence of my directly contacting Sean Guerin rather than responding to questions raised by him. I believed it to be of crucial importance that his independence be unimpeachable.

I did not understand Guerin's terms of reference as mandating him to criticise any individual and I believed that he would afford me an opportunity to address any concerns of relevance that might arise from his documentary review. For decades the legal principle 'audi alteram partem' (hear the other side) has been one of the most cherished and sacrosanct principles of our law, prescribing that no person shall be condemned without first having been heard. It had been automatically applied by judges and lawyers undertaking both statutory and non-statutory inquiries. I had no reason to believe that Guerin would stray outside his terms of reference, that he would ignore the relevance of this principle to the task he was undertaking and at no stage was I concerned that he would criticise me. I was mistaken. His condemnation of me came as a complete bombshell.

Guerin concluded that I had not 'heeded' the voice of Maurice McCabe and that there was a sufficient basis for concern as to whether all appropriate steps were taken by me as Minister for Justice to investigate and address McCabe's 'specified complaints'. I could not fathom how an experienced lawyer could complete a report containing conclusions about my conduct as a Government Minister without directly engaging with me in any way whatsoever. I learnt from Guerin's report that he had conducted four interviews with McCabe, totalling nineteen hours. He had also criticised the Garda Authorities in trenchant terms for 'a fundamental procedural flaw in the Investigation' of one of McCabe's complaints, the alleged flaw being a failure to afford McCabe 'an opportunity to comment' on a senior officer's account of a meeting that took place with McCabe. It was right that Guerin took whatever time he believed necessary to interview the Sergeant, but it was a total mystery why he had not given me the benefit of even a one-hour engagement or provided me with a transcript of McCabe's interviews and sought my response to any allegation made about my Ministerial conduct.

The report not only disclosed that his interviews with McCabe were the only major substantive interviews undertaken by him but that, contrary to his Terms of Reference, he had not, as he was required to do, examined and considered all relevant documentation and data. In his report, as well as in his accompanying letter to Enda Kenny, he astonishingly admitted that he had completed his work without his first reading what GSOC described as 'voluminous' documents of relevance to his inquiry.

Judge John Cooke was conducting his non-statutory inquiry into the 'Gardai Bugged GSOC' allegations simultaneously with Guerin undertaking his inquiry. Documentation released in response to an

FOI request established there was some delay in GSOC compiling the documentation required by Guerin because the Cooke inquiry had started one week earlier. In order to protect the confidentiality of their documentation, GSOC proposed to give Guerin full access subject to conditions or safeguards which Judge Cooke had no difficulty in accepting. What Guerin described in his letter to the Taoiseach of 6 May 2014 as 'not unreasonable' safeguards were referred to in his report as 'obstacles' to his accessing GSOC documents. Because of what he described as the 'tight timescale' imposed on him, contrary to the advices of GSOC's solicitors, he completed his report without reading GSOC's documentation. As a consequence, his report did not fully address the action, if any, taken by GSOC when they were informed by successive Garda Commissioners of complaints made by Maurice McCabe through successive Confidential Recipients or of the outcome of internal Garda investigations into those complaints. Having not directly engaged with me or fully engaged with GSOC, Guerin's report also failed to fully consider the relevance of GSOC's role to the response sent by me to McCabe's January 2012 complaints. Neither did he have any insight into the flawed nature of the Confidential Recipient provisions for the conduct of a Ministerial investigation or for the conduct of an inquiry under Section 42 of the Garda Síochána Act, 2005.

Despite the 'tight timescale' under which Guerin operated and the Taoiseach's apparent urgency to establish the truth of McCabe's complaints and allegations, it was over eight months before the Government brought before the Dáil, in January 2015, a motion to establish the Commission of Investigation recommended by Sean Guerin. The Commission of Investigation's terms of reference were practically identical to those proposed by Guerin in his report and included no additional substantive issue of concern. As a result, the Commission of Investigation, conducted by retired European Court and High Court Judge Kevin O'Higgins, was not tasked with conducting a comprehensive investigation into the adequacy of the approach taken by GSOC when informed of complaints received through a Confidential Recipient and the outcome of investigations, if any, conducted into those complaints. This issue, having not been properly addressed by Guerin, was then largely omitted from the O'Higgins Commission's terms of reference. Nothing was done to ascertain whether there was any basis for concern as to whether GSOC had negligently failed to initiate any public interest inquiry following receipt of McCabe's complaints emanating from the Confidential Recipient where an inquiry was warranted. This was despite Guerin in his report speculating that GSOC also may not have 'heeded' McCabe's voice. The O'Higgins Commission, did, however, address the approach taken by GSOC to complaints it directly received alleging Garda misconduct, which overlapped with complaints made by McCabe relating to the same incidents.

Over two years after publication of the *Guerin Report*, the O'Higgins Commission Report was published on 11 May 2016. During his sworn statutory investigation Judge Kevin O'Higgins fully engaged with all the parties who were given the opportunity to present oral evidence, to be legally represented and to cross-examine witnesses.

The work of the O'Higgins Commission was meticulous, evidence was given on oath, fair procedures were fully complied with and everyone affected by the Commission's Investigation was given a fair hearing and an opportunity to respond to the parts of its draft report affecting them. The Commission undertook its investigation in private modules that examined specific issues which arose under its terms of reference. It did not seek or consider the content of any transcripts made of Guerin's meetings with McCabe.

The portion of the O'Higgins hearings that I attended concerned my response as Minister for Justice and that of the Department of Justice to the complaints made by Maurice McCabe in his report of 23 January 2012 received from the Confidential Recipient, Oliver Connolly, and in related correspondence. The same module also addressed the garda response to McCabe's complaints concerning the specific garda investigations he had identified as flawed.

Addressing my Ministerial role and actions, the O'Higgins Commission report contained conclusions that completely contradicted those reached by Guerin. It also rejected all allegations it addressed made by Maurice McCabe about my conduct as Minister for Justice. In doing so, the Commission irrevocably established the untruth of widely believed accusations made in the Dáil by Micheál Martin, Niall Collins, Mick Wallace, Clare Daly, McCabe's many other Dáil advocates and by numerous media commentators.

In his letter to me through the Confidential Recipient in May 2012, McCabe had complained about my seeking observations from the Garda Commissioner on the allegations made by him, alleging that I had asked the Garda Commissioner to investigate himself. This allegation had also surfaced in the Dáil chamber. In his report, Guerin stated that:

> he [Sergeant McCabe] complained that the Minister had acted in an inappropriate way and that it was wrong of him to request a report from the person Sergeant McCabe had complained about. Sergeant McCabe said it defied logic and was not fair or in keeping with natural justice and fair procedures … while it would, of course, be entirely reasonable to expect that, where a complaint is made, opportunity will be given to the person the subject of the complaint to respond to it, it is a different matter altogether to be entirely satisfied by that response … the process of determining Sergeant McCabe's complaints went no further than the Minister receiving and acting upon the advice of the person who was the subject of the complaint [that is, Martin Callinan, the Garda Commissioner].

The *O'Higgins Report* substantially differed from Guerin, stating that:

> the Minister promptly consulted the Secretary General of the Department and asked him to obtain the observations of the Commissioner as a matter of urgency. He also spoke to the Assistant Secretary of the Department, Mr Michael Flahive. Before deciding on what course of action to adopt, the Minister was manifestly entitled to seek the views of the Commissioner. Any suggestion to the contrary is rejected. It was an obvious, prudent and sensible thing to do. Indeed, he would be open to justified criticism had he acted otherwise.

McCabe believed that as Minister for Justice, I should have personally investigated the allegations made by him. Guerin concluded that my not instigating such investigation, gave rise to 'a sufficient basis for concern as to whether all appropriate steps' had been taken by me. Addressing this issue, the *O'Higgins Report* stated:

> the fact that there had been an extensive investigation of the matter by an Assistant Commissioner and an experienced Superintendent, that their findings had been reviewed by a Deputy Commissioner, that the report had been sent to the DPP [Director of Public Prosecutions] for consideration, were all matters which had taken place before the

Commissioner was asked for his comments [by the Minister]. It is clear that from the matters mentioned in the preceding paragraphs, that in seeking the views of the Commissioner, the Minister was not asking him to investigate himself or to adjudicate on a complaint made against him. Sergeant McCabe in a report made through the Confidential Recipient in May 2012, rhetorically asked '[h]ow can any member of An Garda Síochána make a complaint against a senior Garda officer or the Commissioner when the result is asking that particular officer in question to investigate himself?' The Minister simply requested a report from the Commissioner on the matters raised.

O'Higgins recorded that in his evidence to the Commission, McCabe 'did not take issue with that course of action'. The report continued: 'it was appropriate for the Minister to rely on the Commissioner's report ... Sergeant McCabe does not now question the decision of the Minister to consult the Commissioner and to rely on the information supplied by him in coming to his determination'.

Essentially, when before the Commission, giving evidence on oath, McCabe took a different stance on this issue to the stance previously taken not only by him but also by members of the Dáil with whom he had been in contact. It was starkly different to the criticism voiced by Fianna Fáil leader Micheál Martin in the immediate aftermath of his meeting with McCabe in February 2014. The Commission concluded that my initial response to McCabe's letter of complaint received through the Confidential Recipient in January 2012, which had been the subject of so much public criticism and ridicule, was entirely appropriate.

Guerin's report depicted both the Department of Justice and myself as simply referring issues of complaint to An Garda Síochána and my accepting without question and being satisfied by the resulting Garda response. He also criticised the absence of any Departmental memo briefing me on the statutory powers relevant to my considering the complaints and allegations made by McCabe. The *O'Higgins Commission Report* provided an entirely different understanding of events, which I could have easily explained to Guerin had he taken the trouble to ask me. The truth was that I did not require a memo from Justice officials to understand the statutory powers available to me, and the Justice officials criticised for not furnishing me with a memo knew this.

The *O'Higgins Report* records that 'the former Minister, Mr Shatter, was, as he told the Commission "intimately aware of the legislation in this area, of the contents of the particular statutory instrument made under the Garda Síochána Act that set up the Confidential Recipient and of the other related legislation that we have had a lot of discussion on."'

O'Higgins also concluded that it was apparent from the evidence of Mr Michael Flahive, Assistant Secretary of the Department of Justice and Equality, that the Department was 'fully aware of the legal situation regarding confidential reports and how they should be dealt with'. Later on, O'Higgins concluded: 'on receipt of the reports transmitted to the Department by the Confidential Recipient they were taken seriously and addressed promptly. The evidence of the Assistant Secretary of the Department, Mr Flahive, establishes that the gravity of matters was immediately appreciated. The statutory provisions applicable to the complaint were fully understood.'

Had Sean Guerin asked either myself, Brian Purcell or Michael Flahive, this could have been explained to him. Instead, he criticised Departmental officials for not providing me with a memo I did not need and arbitrarily assumed that the absence of a memo justified concern that I had failed to either understand or properly fulfil my ministerial duties. Bizarrely, I was damned by Guerin because of my legal knowledge and expertise.

Guerin also criticised the absence of any information detailing the consideration I gave to the Garda Commissioner's response to McCabe's complaints before replying to Oliver Connolly, the Confidential Recipient. This is also comprehensively addressed by the O'Higgins Commission. It records:

> The former Minister told the Commission that it was not on the basis of one single factor but on the 'conglomeration of the background information' furnished to him that he came to the conclusion 'at that point in time there was no basis for me taking further action'.
>
> Those factors were as follows:
>
> - A wide-ranging investigation had been undertaken by Assistant Commissioner Byrne and Chief Superintendent McGinn.
> - Their investigation had been reviewed by Deputy Commissioner Rice.

- Eleven of the twelve matters had been referred to the Garda Síochána Ombudsman Commission under the regulations. The former Minister told the Commission that GSOC had statutory powers which enabled it if it thought 'there was something untoward in the manner in which these matters were being dealt with or something that should have alerted them ab initio once they learnt of them, to engage in an investigation independent of the Gardai.'
- That the papers had been considered by the DPP who had not recommended any prosecutions.
- 'The implausibility of the allegation that the Garda Commissioner had effectively put someone onto the promotion list in circumstances where there was an independent interview system and examination system' as the former Minister put it.

An additional factor in (the) former Minister's response was that he was aware that the complaints of Mr Lorcan Roche-Kelly were the subject of an investigation by GSOC.

All of this could have been explained to Guerin had he informed me of his concerns or reservations about the appropriateness of my actions. No explanation should have been required concerning the relevance of GSOC's investigation into allegations of garda misconduct preceding the dreadful murder of Sylvia Roche-Kelly. Guerin ascertained from garda papers, as the *O'Higgins Report* confirmed, that GSOC's independent investigation into Lorcan Roche-Kelly's complaint had concluded in August 2012, almost a year and a half before the tragedy was first mentioned in the Dáil by Micheál Martin as if that investigation had not occurred. The O'Higgins Commission accepted that: 'These were pertinent and cumulatively most compelling considerations which amply justified the Minister in acting as he did.'

Contrary to Guerin's view, O'Higgins concluded that: 'The exchanges between the Department, the Minister and the Commissioner during the handling of Sergeant McCabe's complaint were at all times professional and appropriate.'

Referencing Department of Justice correspondence, seen by Guerin, sent to McCabe's solicitors between October 2012 and May 2013 to which no substantive reply had been received, the Commission described the correspondence as 'perfectly reasonable in the context of all the previous correspondence between Sergeant McCabe and the Department' and reached a conclusion that escaped Guerin. Having referred to the initial letter sent, O'Higgins continued 'a number of reminders were sent to Sergeant McCabe's solicitors and the former Minister had personal input into at least three of them. This displayed personal and active concern on his part.' O'Higgins observed that: 'despite numerous requests, it had not been communicated to the Minister whether he had permission to refer the confidential material onwards for advice' and 'neither the Department nor the Minister can be faulted for failing to take further action on a request for an inquiry under Section 42 of the Garda Síochána Act 2005, as amended, in circumstances where Sergeant McCabe continued to assert a claim of confidentiality over relevant correspondence and enclosures'.

Following publication of the *O'Higgins Report*, it was indisputable that the critical opinions and conclusions of Sean Guerin about my conduct as Minister for Justice were entirely refuted and Maurice McCabe's criticism of my conduct proved entirely wrong. On the day I received Guerin's report I believed that, had Guerin openly engaged with me and afforded me the luxury of even a quarter of the time he gave to interview McCabe, there would have been no basis for his expressing concern about the appropriateness of my actions nor would I have had to resign from my Ministerial position. There would also have been no reason for him to recommend my actions be the subject of investigation by a Commission of Investigation nor for my life being turned upside down.

By reigniting the inevitable media and Opposition frenzy of criticism and condemnation and validating it, the *Guerin Report* did enormous damage to my reputation both as a politician and a lawyer. Validation given by Enda Kenny, other members of Cabinet and TDs to the report both inside and outside the Dáil in the immediate aftermath of my resignation and its publication by Government added to the damage. To this day my reputation and credibility has not been fully restored despite my vindication by O'Higgins.

As a direct consequence of the *Guerin Report* and Enda Kenny's response to it, I had no choice but to resign as Minister for Justice, Equality and Defence. A substantial portion of my time in the years that followed was taken up with the Fennelly Commission and the O'Higgins Commission, court proceedings against Guerin and, after publication of the *O'Higgins Report*, in attempting to firefight articles, publications and online content that largely ignored my vindication by O'Higgins and reproduced Guerin's damning criticism and extracts from the McCabe/ Connolly transcript. Both Guerin's criticisms and Connolly's fantasised nonsense continued to appear in print and online, including in narratives published by mainstream media, through into 2018 without reference to O'Higgins's undisputed conclusions which Maurice McCabe fully accepted.

A great deal happened in the weeks and months following publication of the *Guerin Report*. My further engagements with Enda Kenny in relation to Guerin, Kenny's evidence to the Fennelly Commission of Investigation as detailed in its Report and other matters resulted in my having unexpected disappointing new insights into the character and actions of a Fine Gael leader I had both liked and admired. The conduct and evidence of the Attorney General, Máire Whelan, as detailed in the *Fennelly Report* was also for me a devastating eye opener.

I found myself, for over four years, conducting a war on all fronts to establish the truth with regard to what had happened, to attempt to restore a remnant of my good name and reputation, to ensure no person in the future could be condemned in a report published, following a preliminary or any form of non-statutory inquiry without a fair hearing and to achieve some semblance of justice. I was largely shunned by Fine Gael Cabinet and Parliamentary Party colleagues, some of whom I had prior to my resignation, mistakenly regarded as genuine friends and many of whom I had carefully ensured received any assistance or information they required from me personally or from either the Department of Justice or Defence during my time as a Minister in Cabinet. A particular disappointment was Frances Fitzgerald. I had regularly provided any help she sought with her brief and in implementing, as Minister for Children, a Fine Gael programme of reforms I had originated when in Opposition and ensured were included in the 2011 Programme for Government.

The main focus of those former Cabinet colleagues who briefly engaged with me following my resignation was to advise me to keep my head down, cause no waves and take no action to challenge Guerin or upset Kenny. Whether they did so out of any genuine concern for my political or personal welfare or as emissaries for Kenny, I cannot be sure. None of them had considered that what happened to me could happen to them, at any time in the future, if they were denounced in the Dáil and by a frenzied media mob, or condemned in a report published following a non-statutory inquiry, without due process and a fair hearing. Ironically, in November 2017, the Dáil denunciations and frenzied media mob was destined to re-emerge on an issue relating to Maurice McCabe, the Garda Síochána and the O'Higgins Commission. Frances Fitzgerald, who had entirely ignored what I had to say about Guerin, was wrongly and unfairly targeted and after two weeks of political controversy forced to resign from Government.

CHAPTER 36

A Rush to Judgement, Legal Guff and Reformers Beware!

You can't defend yourself against this court; you have to acknowledge your guilt. Acknowledge your guilt at the first opportunity. Only then are you given the possibility of escape, only then –Franz Kafka, *The Trial*, in which Josef K is on trial without having done anything wrong as a result of unknown information derived from an anonymous informant, and struggles to defend himself against secret charges

My accusation is that it is a fundamentally flawed preliminary inquiry and report and an unprecedented rush to judgement ... I stand by the rule of law, the personal rights protected by our Constitution and the European Convention on Human Rights, the core principles of constitutional and natural justice and the core values of this State and the European Union whose objectives include ensuring justice is not arbitrary and that no body or individual can trample on such rights, including the right of all to receive a fair hearing where allegations are made against them –Alan Shatter referencing the *Guerin Report*, Dáil Debates, 19 June 2014

Why Shatter's Hold Me Back, Let Me At Him Legal Guff Rings So Hollow On Guerin Report –Headline of article by Remy Farrell SC, *Irish Independent*, 23 June 2014

Shatter Deserved Better Than To Be A Warning To Reformers –Headline of article by Labour Party TD, Michael McNamara BL, *Irish Independent*, 27 June 2014

I stayed away from the Dáil debate on the *Guerin Report* which took place on 15 May 2014. I knew there was no point in my participating in it. I had not been believed in February 2014 when telling the truth about my dealings with Maurice McCabe's complaints and allegations and Guerin's critical conclusions had provided my political opponents and Government colleagues with the political ammunition to excoriate me.

I was still very stressed and severely shaken. Not even a masochist would have volunteered for the roasting I knew was inevitable had I appeared in the Dáil chamber that Thursday afternoon. I also had no wish to listen to the praise that I knew would be lavished on Sean Guerin.

After the debate I contacted Enda Kenny to reiterate my concern about Guerin's failure to directly engage with me, to read GSOC documentation and inaccuracies in his report. I eventually met Kenny in his office on 12 June 2014. He took notes, promised to follow up my concerns and to revert to me. He never did. On 19 June 2014, I decided to use the opportunity of the Dáil debate on the *Cooke Report* to publicly highlight the *Guerin Report*'s deficiencies. Frances Fitzgerald, whom I still regarded as a friend, was present for the debate. I wrongly believed she would take my concerns seriously.

Addressing the *Guerin Report* I stated that

It was right that Mr Guerin met with Sergeant McCabe for as long as he deemed necessary. It is a mystery to me, however, as to how he believed he was properly fulfilling his remit and his obligation to observe fair procedures to reach accurate conclusions and make recommendations by meeting for nineteen hours with Sergeant McCabe but meeting with no one else whose good name, reputation and credibility could or would be affected by his report … I believe that fair procedures and the principles of natural and constitutional justice required that Mr Guerin should have interviewed me or at the very least, communicated his concerns and questions to me in writing and afforded me the opportunity to address them and also to address his draft conclusions which he had to know would render my continuing in office, as Minister for Justice and Equality, untenable.

I continued:

I believe all of us should be entitled to know that we cannot by way of any form of inquiry or review or other means, be secretly put on trial: have charges levied against us of which we have no knowledge: be prosecuted without being informed of the evidence and be convicted without being given the opportunity to speak or defend ourselves. I believe that the unprecedented approach to this review or examination or preliminary inquiry which was undertaken and conducted must never be repeated. I believe no one in the future requested to undertake such a task should be enabled to take unto himself or herself the role of investigator, prosecutor, judge, jury and executioner and to ignore entirely fair procedures prescribed by our courts and which are specifically prescribed for the undertaking of a statutory inquiry pursuant to the Commission of Investigation Act 2004.

I was both angry and distraught when delivering that speech. To hide my emotion, I just kept my head down and because of the limited time available to me, quickly read through my pre-prepared script. Stating that the principles of fair procedures and natural justice were crucial to the rule of law and ignoring them put 'in peril a value system crucial to the well being of all our citizens and of all who reside in the State' I asserted that 'to ignore them is to endorse the creation of kangaroo courts'.

My speech was entirely ignored not only by subsequent speakers but also by Frances Fitzgerald, as Minister for Justice, in her response to the debate. While it was reported in the next day's newspapers, it generated no real interest amongst the band of reporters who had written copious critical articles and commentary pieces on the various alleged Justice and Garda 'scandals'.

Remy Farrell SC, a Law Library colleague of Sean Guerin who, like Guerin, has a substantial criminal law practice, in a shameless derogatory article in the *Irish Independent* four days later likened me to a 'hapless crank' and a 'disgruntled litigant bedecked in a sandwich board disclaiming various grievances' standing outside a courthouse engaged in 'public ravings'. Anticipating that I would 'skulk into obscurity' and accusing me, as he had done in a previous article, of 'characteristic bluster', he asserted that my 'complaints don't withstand the most superficial scrutiny'. His bilious attack, lacking any filter and jettisoning all legal learning, derisively dismissed my 'musings about the various constitutional imperatives and the primacy of the rule of law' and sarcastically denigrated my claim that Guerin's inquiry was fundamentally flawed and that I should have been given an opportunity to address Guerin's concerns. He also inaccurately asserted that 'the Guerin Report never made any findings against Alan Shatter'. It was a nasty, vitriolic and unhinged personal attack that outdid anything previously published on the McCabe-related controversies. It was not the first time Farrell had targeted me in a critical article but it was by far his most abusive. I was astonished by the amount of pure bile displayed by a member of the Law Library.

I had lost the will to engage and did not have the energy to offer any response. By then Farrell's dismissive narrative suited both my Fine Gael colleagues and all members of the Opposition who, like Farrell, wished me to simply disappear into obscurity. But Farrell's unpleasant diatribe was a step too far for the courageous Labour Party TD and barrister Michael McNamara. His was the only voice to respond.

In a replying article published four days later in the *Irish Independent* criticising Farrell, McNamara noted that:

> Reforms proposed by Alan Shatter to the provision of legal services in Ireland made him very unpopular with many on the Bar Council. As Michael Noonan pointed out this week, the motto of King's Inns is Nolumus Mutari (We Shall Not Be Changed). Shatter's Legal Services Bill which since his departure has been delayed, not only proposes profound changes for the Bar, but if enacted will result in a drop of income for many in the legal profession. Hence his unpopularity. His lack of deference to his 'learned friends' attracted a level of resentment unparalleled since Roger Casement was denied legal representation by the Bar of Ireland. His resignation was greeted with glee in the Law Library with some of Ireland's finest legal minds punching the air in frenzied scenes of jubilation. Nevertheless, like every Irish citizen he remained and remains entitled to fair procedures.

Referring to Farrell's views as 'disturbing', McNamara asserted that 'One of the most basic tenets of the Rule of Law is that anyone be made aware of the accusations made against him or her and be given an opportunity to respond.' He concluded that my fate 'will serve as an example to any overly zealous reforming post shuffle ministers'.

Michael McNamara whose legal scholarship and analysis in time would be proved correct was the only sitting TD in the Thirty-First Dáil to publicly support me and express any doubts of any nature about Sean Guerin's conduct of his inquiry and his criticism of my ministerial conduct. I will always be grateful to him for his support at an enormously difficult time. Unfortunately, like me, he lost his Dáil seat in the February 2016 election. McNamara's insight into the attitude of many senior barristers to my attempting to end restrictive practices within the legal profession was right on the money but did not reflect the views of many junior counsel who were privately supportive of the reforms I had been piloting.

The same week McNamara's article appeared for the first time, I obtained a copy of a surprising letter received by Enda Kenny in September 2011, the very month the Legal Services Regulation Bill had been published. The author was Frank Callanan SC, a much-respected Senior Counsel whom Kenny had appointed as Chairperson of the Fine Gael Board of Trustees in 2012. A short time after I became minister, at Máire Whelan's suggestion, I had appointed him to conduct an informal inquiry into a long-ignored issue of concern relevant to the Department of Defence and his report, in September 2011, was incisive and brilliantly written. About a week after my resignation, Frank Callanan had visited me in my home to discuss a data protection dispute which had arisen involving Mick Wallace TD, and on which Callanan was advising me. He expressed condolences on my ministerial demise. My immediate reaction was gratitude for his kindness but towards the end of his visit the conversation became weird. Still stunned and distressed by events, I asked him did he understand how Guerin could have condemned me unheard. He initially ignored the question. Presuming he had not heard, I repeated it. There was a strange awkward silence as he gazed out the window into the distance. Time momentarily seemed to stand still, then avoiding commenting on Guerin's report he simply announced 'Oh, I share offices with Seán Guerin but we rarely see each other. He specialises in criminal law while I work in the civil law area.' With that he lapsed again into silence. Upon my again asking how Guerin could have criticised me without affording me any opportunity to respond, he ignored the question, announced he had to leave and rapidly departed.

Callanan's letter was dated 16 September 2011 and addressed to 'An Taoiseach, Enda Kenny'. Referring to the Legal Services Bill 'as proposed by the Minister for Justice', much of its content reflected criticism of the Bill voiced in the weeks and months that followed by members of the Bar Council, some of which was useful in the context of fine tuning and improving the Bill. However, part of the letter was unexpectedly personal. While saying that he 'had the highest regard for Alan Shatter as a Minister, parliamentarian and jurist', Frank Callanan wrongly asserted I had 'never made any secret of [my] view that members of the Bar need to be taken down a few pegs, and the more pegs the better'. Directly addressing Kenny further on in his letter, Callanan continued 'I am concerned, not only as a barrister, but as a supporter of Fine Gael and a huge admirer of yours. This Bill is very un-Fine Gael. It is not in your style as Taoiseach. It should not be adopted by the rational, pragmatically reforming government you lead.'

I had never expressed the view that 'members of the Bar' should be 'taken down a peg' to anyone. I had never met or spoken with Callanan before asking him to take on the Defence issue, and had met with him a number of times to discuss the Wallace data protection dispute. He had never attempted to discuss the Legal Services Regulation Bill with me or mentioned his letter to Enda Kenny. For me it was all profoundly unsettling. Reflecting on it now, I have no doubt that his critical perspective as detailed in his letter to Kenny was mild compared to that of many of his senior counsel colleagues. It is also likely that his odd reaction to my mention of Guerin's report resulted from discomfort in being asked about the conduct of a Law Library colleague and friend with whom he shared offices.

Subsequent to my discovering Callanan's September 2011 letter to Kenny I discharged him as my counsel in the Data Protection Act dispute and appointed another barrister. My explanation was that there was 'a conflict of interest'. The only time our paths again crossed was when I was giving evidence before the O'Higgins Commission and Frank Callanan was present, acting as counsel for Justice officials.

Four weeks after publication of the Guerin Report, an 'Independent Review Group' was established by Frances Fitzgerald to examine the workings of the Justice Department and required to furnish its report by 11 July 2014. What became known as the *Toland Report* was published on 28 July 2014 and its publication resulted in the resignation of Brian Purcell as Secretary General of the Department. While praising the 'strengths' of the Department, the report indentified a range of weaknesses and issues and prescribed wide-ranging reform of departmental structures and practices. In doing so, it criticised poor management routines and practices, including 'poor political antennae for issues with serious potential impact'. Referencing 'recent events' it concluded that 'on a number of occasions there were serious leadership and management failures, particularly in the Garda Division within the Department and senior management of the Department regarding how briefings between the Minister and senior management were handled'. The 'culture' of the Department was described as 'closed and unnecessarily secretive', the need for secrecy not being restricted to only areas of 'particular sensitivity'. While most of the media regarded the euphemistically referenced 'recent events' as relating solely to issues addressed by the *Guerin Report*, they also included the failure of Brian Purcell and the Michael Flahive-led Garda Division to furnish me with important letters from Garda Commissioner Martin Callanan upon their receipt and briefings on the Garda recording issue. Revelations of issues then unknown to me would later, during the Fennelly Commission and Disclosures Tribunal hearings, validate Toland's assessment.

I expected that within two to three weeks of publication of the *Guerin Report*, the Statutory Commission of Investigation recommended by Guerin would be established. After all, it had taken no more than three weeks to agree Terms of Reference and establish the Fennelly Commission and Guerin had published draft terms for the Commission he recommended. As May stretched into July it became clear that Kenny and my former Cabinet colleagues were in no hurry and the long Dáil summer vacation period was approaching. The impact of Guerin's report on my life was of no concern to Kenny or, I slowly understood, to any of my Fine Gael colleagues and there had been no new major garda-related public controversy since my departure from Cabinet. I realised the last thing Kenny wanted was to remind people of the controversy that had occurred by proposing and debating the possibly troublesome Dáil motion needed to create the Commission. He was also put under no pressure by Opposition TDs on the issue as they had achieved their objective – I was no longer a member of Cabinet.

In the immediate aftermath of publication of Guerin's report, I had considered and obtained advice and then rejected the notion of taking judicial review proceedings in the courts. I did not want my life taken over by potentially lengthy litigation. I had for many years been in age denial and had never really acknowledged that I was in my early sixties. Somewhere in my head I had stopped at 39! For the first time in my life age became an issue. Court proceedings, including a possible appeals process, I conservatively and wrongly estimated could take between two to three years. I would by then be 65 or 66. I wanted to look to the future and not dwell on the past. As a lawyer, I had met too many people with an obsessive sense of injustice as a result of something bad that had happened in their past and who could not move on and enjoy life. Life is a short and transient experience and I did not want to become one of those people.

By the second week in July my perspective changed. I was angered by the destruction of my political career and reputation and distressed at being totally abandoned by former 'friends' in the Fine Gael parliamentary party. I was also fed up with being continuously targeted by online abuse, being verbally abused in the street and, on more than one occasion, spat upon. I also felt betrayed by Kenny's failure to ask Guerin to address issues raised by me relating to the conduct of his inquiry and his deceitful pretence that he would do so. Unable to defend myself against continuing demonisation, I decided to take on Guerin in the courts. I issued High Court proceedings seeking a declaration that Guerin's conduct of his inquiry violated natural and constitutional justice and my rights to due process and a fair hearing.

With no sign of a Commission of Investigation on the horizon my alternative was to 'skulk into obscurity'. I was not in any circumstances going to do that and fulfil the fantasies of Sean Guerin's Bar Library colleague, Remy Farrell and those who thought like him.

CHAPTER 37

Complaints Upheld, Exaggerated, Unfounded and Withdrawn

Some of the complaints have been upheld in this report, especially in respect of the quality of the investigations examined by this Commission. Other complaints made by him (Sergeant Maurice McCabe) have proven to be overstated or exaggerated. Some were unfounded and some have been withdrawn –O'Higgins Report, May 2016

The *O'Higgins Report* was not all about me. Its terms of reference required that the Commission investigate and report on garda investigations conducted into a number of incidents of varied seriousness raised by McCabe, his allegations 'of corruption and malpractice' in relation to garda PULSE computer records which he claimed were seized from him by Assistant Garda Commissioner Derek Byrne and the general conduct of policing at Bailieboro Garda District in 2007–8.

All of the Garda Investigations McCabe complained about occurred in 2007–8, three to four years before I became Justice Minister. An internal Garda investigation by Assistant Commissioner Byrne and Chief Superintendent Terry McGinn into his complaints had also been completed in 2010. Some serious garda failures were identified. The conduct and outcome of that investigation had been reviewed by Deputy Garda Commissioner Nacie Rice and some disciplinary action had been taken against members of the garda force. Details of the investigation had also been furnished to the DPP who declined to initiate any prosecutions.

There can be no doubt that McCabe had rightly complained about the quality of garda investigations and garda dysfunction and his complaints had been taken seriously by the garda authorities. However, McCabe had difficulty in accepting that all of his complaints were not upheld and that some senior members of the force were not criticised and disciplined. As would later emerge, during the course of the Byrne/McGinn investigation McCabe had been badly treated and ridiculed by some of his garda colleagues and subjected to false allegations. Unfortunately, McCabe's understandable distress at false allegations being made against him did not inhibit his making exaggerated or unfounded allegations or allegations for which there was not a scintilla of evidence against others.

McCabe's Confidential Report that I received on 23 January 2012 through Oliver Connolly, had some content blacked out by Connolly to preserve McCabe's anonymity, citing McCabe's fear of 'revenge and harassment against me and my family'. It detailed his concerns about various incidents and investigations. All but one of these had previously been investigated by Byrne and McGinn. Acknowledging that they had been investigated by Assistant Commissioner Byrne, the report complained that 'no adverse findings' had been made against a Superintendent Michael Clancy who had been the 'Superintendent in charge of Bailieboro Garda District from July 20017 until March 2008'. The report I received did not reveal that its author had previously made complaints to a Confidential Recipient, had revealed his identity as the complainant to the garda authorities, his complaints had resulted in the Byrne/McGinn investigation being undertaken, that the DPP had previously declined to prosecute Byrne following the complainant alleging that Byrne had assaulted and falsely imprisoned him in the Hillgrove Hotel or that GSOC were investigating the circumstances which resulted in the murder of Sylvia Roche-Kelly.

Referencing what he reported as Byrne's 'decision' that 'complaints against Superintendent Clancy were not substantiated in any way' and critical of 'no adverse findings' having been made against Clancy, McCabe's report continued, 'Alarmingly, Commissioner Callinan and Deputy Commissioner Rice agreed with Byrne.'

He then alleged that 'it may be the case that Derek Byrne hid evidence, material and certain findings from his superiors because he was the Commissioner in charge of the region at the time of the wrongdoing and received a bonus'.

The Confidential Report continued: 'I find it hard to understand that the Commissioner of An Garda Síochána has rewarded Superintendent Clancy and placed him on a promotion list for the rank of Chief Superintendent. One of the incidents alone is enough to question Superintendent Clancy's suitability for his present rank, let alone promotion.'

It alleged that the Garda Commissioner had

made a serious error of judgment by placing Superintendent Clancy on a promotion list. The evidence is clear and it is corruption as defined by An Garda Síochána's Charter on Confidential Reporting. Gardai engaged in falsifying records, erasing official records, erasing reported incidents, destroying official records, covering up serious investigations and gross dereliction of duty on a massive scale and it appears that the Commissioner was or is aware of it all. It also questions the whole PULSE system when gardaí can erase, alter, destroy, etc. etc. any record or information without any accountability or sanction.

McCabe also complained that senior garda management found 'no fault whatsoever' with either Superintendent Clancy, or Superintendent Cunningham who took over from Clancy. Bizarrely, having named Callinan directly in his report and unequivocally asserted that 'the evidence is clear' and that Callinan was guilty of 'corruption', towards the end he appeared to partially retract the allegation stating 'Callinan may not have been given all evidence in my complaints and he may have been misled by the investigation team. The evidence is shocking.'

In addition to investigating how An Garda Síochána had dealt with the specific incidents highlighted by McCabe and deciding whether I had dealt properly with his complaint to me, the O'Higgins Commission also addressed whether Callinan was 'corrupt' as McCabe alleged, how the Garda Síochána had responded to McCabe's complaints and the allegations made by him against other senior officers and members of the force.

If no allegation of corruption had been made by McCabe against the Garda Commissioner, McCabe's report containing his other complaints and allegations would have been handed by Oliver Connolly directly to Martin Callinan who would have been obliged to pass it on to GSOC. In addition to any internal Garda response to McCabe's complaints, GSOC would have been obliged to decide whether it should commence its own independent investigation.

The O'Higgins Commission confirmed many but not all of the findings of the Byrne/McGinn investigation which had, by 2010, validated many of McCabe's complaints about garda investigative failures and the absence of professionalism, competence and standards to which the public is entitled. The Commission was also critical of aspects of the Byrne/McGinn process and findings, in particular for 'failing to address certain specific complaints of Sergeant McCabe', 'and for dealing with them in vague and general terms'. However, the Commission categorically rejected all allegations made by McCabe to me against Garda Commissioner Martin Callinan and other serious allegations made by him against Byrne, McGinn and Cunningham, including McCabe's allegation that Callinan was corrupt, that Byrne had covered up 'serious corruption' and his speculation that he did so because he had received 'a bonus'. All of the more extreme allegations made by him against Superintendent Clancy concerning garda failures and dysfunction in the investigation of the specific incidents he detailed were also rejected. The Commission also rejected his allegation that Callinan had unlawfully placed Clancy on a promotions list, an allegation that had immediately raised doubts in my mind about the validity of parts of McCabe's 23 January 2012 report.

There can be no doubt that the *O'Higgins Report* confirmed that McCabe had highlighted legitimate concerns about procedures and practices in Bailieboro Garda Station and operational and investigative failures where the public and victims of crime had not been well served. In a number of instances those failures were because young probationary or inexperienced gardaí failed to properly perform their duties, together with a total lack of adequate supervision and oversight. Some flaws in the Byrne/McGinn investigation were also identified that escaped the review of it conducted by Deputy Commissioner Nacie Rice. However, the *O'Higgins Report* also established that a number of McCabe's complaints were not valid, and neither was some of his criticism of the Byrne/McGinn investigation. In fact, during the course of the O'Higgins Commission sworn hearings McCabe withdrew some of his allegations.

McCabe's conduct and his understandable stress, caused by instances of his being badly and wrongly treated resulted in his Dáil advocates and many journalists and commentators assuming that every allegation he made was true. An incapacity or unwillingness to critically assess the allegations he made was the catalyst to both my being vilified and the demonisation of anyone else who challenged any part of McCabe's narrative. It also fostered a belief that the only function of the O'Higgins Commission was to validate his claims. Those parts of the *O'Higgins Report* critical of McCabe, rejecting very serious allegations made by him and detailing those he withdrew, or which were determined to be 'unfounded', to lack even 'a scintilla of evidence' or to have 'no basis', were largely ignored by most media commentators and both Government and Opposition politicians in Leinster House. Within the media bubble, Paul Reynolds, RTÉ's Crime Correspondant was a standout exception objectively reporting the totality of O'Higgins's findings. By doing so, he unknowingly laid the foundations for the integrity of his reporting, being subject to public scrutiny and put under a legal microscope by the Disclosures Tribunal.

Those who were understandably outraged by bad treatment and false allegations to which McCabe was subjected suspended all critical faculties when it came to unsubstantiated allegations made by McCabe against others. The plight of garda colleagues whom he had wrongly accused of corruption, malpractice, pervsion of the course of justice, or not properly fulfilling their duties and who had lived under the stress and shadow of these allegations for years was barely, if at all, acknowledged. No consideration was given to the impact on Martin Callinan and other garda officers of being wrongly accused of corruption by a member of An Garda Síochána.

There can be no doubt that Maurice McCabe shone a spotlight on garda failures that should not have occurred. However, in doing so, he also did enormous damage to those he wrongly accused. This is something the O'Higgins Commission did not fully address. Its partial avoidance of that issue facilitated it being ignored by both the political and media establishment and laid the foundation for subsequent controversy and political crisis.

Ultimately, it resulted in the strategy of Garda Commissioner Nóirín O'Sullivan and counsel representing An Garda Síochána before the O'Higgins Commission being, in early 2018, one of the issues subject to public hearings held by the Disclosures Tribunal.

The *O'Higgins Report* described McCabe as 'a dedicated and committed member of An Garda Síochána', as never being 'less than truthful in his evidence' as 'a man of integrity' and acknowledged that he 'acted out of genuine and legitimate concerns'. The Commission stated that he had 'shown courage and performed a genuine public service at considerable personal cost' and that it accepted his 'bone fides'. It also quoted Assistant Commissioner Derek Byrne, against whom McCabe had made extremely serious allegations of misconduct, as describing McCabe as being 'regarded as a highly efficient sergeant' and endorsed this description. However, some of this is strangely inconsistent with the largely ignored and forgotten conclusions of the Commission which sit uncomfortably with its fulsome praise and its benign reference to it not upholding some of McCabe's complaints and the Commission's brief but restrained depiction of their impact on those subject to them.

While the report stated that McCabe had never been 'less than truthful in his evidence', the Commission did not examine how he portrayed the events it investigated to Sean Guerin or to Dáil members in the years preceding the Commission's hearings or how they came to be portrayed by most of the media. In conducting its investigation, the Commission never sought the transcript of Sean Guerin's nineteen hours of interviews with McCabe. Although the *Guerin Report* was the starting block for its investigation, it did not regard doing so as relevant to its remit.

The O'Higgins Commission stated that McCabe was 'prone to exaggeration at times'. However, it seemed to excuse his propensity to exaggerate in its next sentence when noting that 'In common with many other witnesses, his recollection of some events is diminished with the passage of time.'

But, having done so, the report continued: 'Some of the complaints have been upheld in this Report. Other complaints made by him have proved to be overstated or exaggerated. Some were unfounded and some have been withdrawn.' Some of those withdrawn included some complaints made about my conduct as Minister for Justice which had contaminated political and media discourse for over two years prior to publication of the *O'Higgins Report*. The same can be said for some withdrawn, exaggerated and unfounded complaints made against various senior garda officers.

An unfounded complaint or allegation is defined by the Merriam/Webster online dictionary as one 'having no basis in reason or fact' or 'an accusation that is baseless, foundationless, invalid, groundless, unreasonable, unsubstantiated, unsupported or unwarranted'. The O'Higgins Commission did not dwell on the meaning of the term 'unfounded' but did to a degree expand on its use of that term.

Referencing what it understood to be McCabe's January 2012 allegation of 'corruption' levelled at Martin Callinan, the *O'Higgins Report* stated:

> It was submitted on behalf of Sergeant McCabe that he had not intended to make allegations of criminal conduct against the Commissioner, but rather of an abuse of power only. The allegation was understood by the Commissioner to be one of criminal conduct.

The hurtful allegation was based on the belief, unsupported by any evidence, that the Commissioner had put Superintendent Clancy on a promotion list.

The report continues:

> It must be stated clearly and unambiguously that there is not a scintilla of evidence to support an allegation of any type of corruption against the former Commissioner. In the context of any such grave allegations the former Commissioner is entitled to have his reputation vindicated. In the matters under consideration any aspersions cast on the integrity of the former Commissioner were unfounded and deeply hurtful.

Referencing Clancy's promotion, the report explained, as I knew within a short time of receiving McCabe's Confidential Report of January 2012, that Clancy had been 'through the normal selection process set out in the Garda Síochána (Promotion) Regulations 2006. This involved a competitive process, held by a promotion board ... No criticism has been made of that process. There is no evidence to suggest that the process was not carried out appropriately, or in accordance with the requirements of the regulations'.

The *O'Higgins Report* concluded Clancy was entitled to be named on the promotion list and to be promoted. Had the Garda Commissioner tried to prevent this, the report stated 'he might well have been subject, not only to criticism, but to possible legal action by Superintendent Clancy' as 'the Commissioner had no reasonable grounds' to suspect Clancy was 'guilty of any conduct that would render' him 'unsuitable for promotion'. O'Higgins dismissed as totally baseless the complaints made by McCabe which caused his Confidential Report to be furnished to me as Minister for Justice, and which resulted in my being wrongly criticised by Sean Guerin and being compelled to resign from Government.

The remit of the O'Higgins Commission did not include ascertaining how many members of the Dáil had been furnished with McCabe's report of 23 January 2012 alleging corruption and impropriety by Martin Callinan and Clancy's unsuitability for promotion. Nor was it tasked with determining how much the report contributed to the media frenzy after it was selectively quoted by Micheál Martin on the plinth and subsequently in the Dáil chamber. While the Commission described McCabe's 'unfounded' allegations against Callinan as 'hurtful', it did not address their impact on him in any greater detail.

While the O'Higgins Commission concluded that McCabe's 'hurtful' allegation that Martin Callinan was corrupt was 'in part, a device to ensure that the complaint came before the Minister for Justice', it also concluded that he did 'hold genuine concerns that there was some impropriety in the promotion of Chief Superintendent Clancy' and declined to regard his 'unfounded' allegation as an 'abuse of process'. It is notable that the Commission determined that McCabe's 'concerns' were based on a 'belief' for which, as the Commission decided, there was not 'a scintilla of evidence'. A consequence of the O'Higgins Commission's approach is that any Garda could perceive that using a confidential disclosure mechanism or the Garda Síochána Act to give information to a member of the Houses of the Oireachtas, ensures impunity from any consequences resulting from making 'unfounded' or 'exaggerated' allegations or allegations lacking a 'scintilla of evidence'. While the conclusions of a statutory investigation or inquiry cannot be used as a precedent in law, there is good reason for concern about the implication of this particular conclusion.

The unfounded allegation of 'corruption' made in 2012 by McCabe against Callinan is minimised by McCabe's biographer, *Irish Examiner* journalist Michael Clifford, in his account of these events in his book *A Force for Justice*, published in September 2017. He attributes and excuses the allegation to McCabe's 'desperation' to have his complaints addressed by an outside agency and simply describes the accusation of corruption as 'unfair' and as 'what some might term reckless'. He carefully avoids quoting the O'Higgins Commission's conclusion that the allegation was 'hurtful' and made 'without a scintilla of evidence'.

Other conclusions of O'Higgins critical of McCabe's 'unfounded' and 'exaggerated' complaints were also largely ignored by members of the Oireachtas and most journalists. The report rejected 'complaints of corruption' made by McCabe against Assistant Commissioner Byrne, Chief Superintendent Rooney and Superintendent Clancy and, where any allegation may be implied, against Superintendent Cunningham. It concluded that, in each case 'the Commission has found those hurtful complaints unfounded' and acknowledged that 'those against whom such complaints were made had to live for many years under the strain of those allegations'. Noting that the Commission examined in detail 'a large number of complaints made against Clancy', the report also asserted that 'he is exonerated of any wrongdoing and is the subject of only occasional and mild criticism'. Amongst those 'hurtful' and 'unfounded' complaints firmly rejected by O'Higgins was one in McCabe's January 2012 report to me that wrongly alleged 'that Sylvia Roche Kelly would be alive today but for the sheer incompetence and gross dereliction of duty of Superintendent Clancy'. No such finding was made against Clancy by either the O'Higgins Commission or GSOC. In relation to Assistant Commissioner Derek Byrne, whom McCabe had accused of assault and false imprisonment, the report also recorded that in his evidence to the Commission 'Sergeant McCabe withdrew all allegations of impropriety of any type' against him. It was not within its remit to address for how long such allegations had been in circulation or their impact on Byrne's reputation or wellbeing.

The only remaining complaint made by McCabe against Byrne the O'Higgins Commission had to address was the quality of the Byrne/McGinn investigation. It praised Byrne for giving evidence to the Commission in 'a forthright, honest and helpful manner' and described him as 'a man of integrity and a highly competent member of An Garda Síochána committed to the good of the force'. This starkly contrasted with McCabe's damning depiction of Byrne in his report to me of January 2012 when, amongst other things, he alleged Byrne had given 'findings' to Commissioner Callinan 'which cover up serious corruption'. Moreover, the Commission determined that in her dealings with McCabe, Chief Superintendent McGinn 'showed experience, kindness and sensitivity'.

The O'Higgins Commission acknowledged that the Byrne/McGinn investigation had upheld eleven of McCabe's complaints while criticising it for failing to address 'certain specific complaints' made by McCabe 'and/or for dealing with them in vague and general terms'. Stating that 'any criticism' it made of Byrne/McGinn 'must be taken in context' the Commission asserted that, 'It would be quite wrong and unfair to suggest that Sergeant McCabe's complaints were not taken seriously or that they were brushed aside.'

It recorded that the garda investigation into McCabe's complaints involved more than twenty interviews with McCabe and his furnishing eleven statements. Referencing complaints not properly addressed, the Commission concluded that it considered that 'there was a corporate closing of ranks' which was not done 'consciously or deliberately' stating 'there was no question of bad faith'. Describing McCabe's complaints as 'extensive', 'some specific and some generalised', 'some very difficult and extremely sensitive', O'Higgins acknowledged that McCabe 'was not always the easiest person to deal with'. O'Higgins concluded that the Byrne/McGinn investigation took his complaints seriously, that their investigation 'involved a great deal of hard work … took nearly two years to complete', that 'the completed file consisted of eight modules comprising a report and appendices' and that 'very considerable resources were put into the investigation'.

McCabe alleged in relation to PULSE that 'Gardaí engaged in falsifying records, erasing reported incidents, destroying official records [and] covering up serious investigations'. O'Higgins concluded, as McCabe alleged, that gardaí had failed to fully record information on PULSE and to keep it up to date. O'Higgins also questioned the integrity of additional information placed on PULSE by individual gardaí after Deputy Commissioner Rice requested that incomplete PULSE records be updated after he received clearly deficient records from McCabe. However, O'Higgins rejected McCabe's allegation that 'many of the PULSE incidents were corruptly updated or updated to cover up wrongdoing', concluding that Rice's decision, made in good faith, to return the records to the Cavan/Monaghan Garda division for completion was not corrupt, nor was updating the incidents of itself corrupt. O'Higgins did not uphold McCabe's allegation that PULSE records had been erased or destroyed. GSOC, in its 2017 report on the ticket charge issue, confirmed that PULSE did not permit the erasure or destruction of records.

While criticising aspects of the Byrne/McGinn investigation, O'Higgins's narrative confirmed that Guerin's conclusion that the garda organisation had not heeded the voice of McCabe was not an accurate picture of an investigation conducted into complex allegations and events. It also confirmed the widely inaccurate nature of much of the Dáil Opposition and media narrative during the frenzy of February 2014. However, in a world in which truth is of casual relevance, controversies are simplistically portrayed and in which people are attached to politically opportunistic narratives, there was no chance that any member of the Opposition would voluntarily, in the Dáil Debate following publication of the *O'Higgins Report*, correct the Dáil record and withdraw false charges trenchantly made in 2014.

CHAPTER 38

Betrayal, Conscience, Excoriation and Vindication

I am pleased to acknowledge that the O'Higgins Report has found clearly that the former Minister acted properly at all times in relation to the handling of allegations made by Maurice McCabe ... I would like to emphasis, as I did at the time of his resignation, that Alan Shatter was an exceptionally hard working, radical and reforming minister who has left a positive legacy across the wide range of areas for which he had ministerial responsibility –An Taoiseach Enda Kenny opening the Dáil Debate on the *O'Higgins Report*, 25 May 2016

My predecessor was excoriated across the floor of this House about matters which some considerable time later he was found to have dealt with properly. Whatever passion members of this House may have in pursuing what they believe to be great wrongs, we would all do well to reflect that righting the wrongs done to some by doing wrongs to others is not what justice is about
–Tánaiste and Minister for Justice and Equality Frances Fitzgerald responding to the Dáil Debate on the *O'Higgins Report*, 26 May 2016

I lost my Dáil seat in the general election of 26 February 2016. My election campaign in what was the new Dáil constituency of Dublin/Rathdown was an uphill battle. The *Guerin Report* copper-fastened in the public consciousness my alleged failure to 'heed' Sergeant Maurice McCabe's concerns. My difficulties were exacerbated by a local controversy. Stepaside garda station was one of 139 garda stations closed by the Garda Commissioner three years earlier. It was part of a process to consolidate the network of garda stations across the State and make An Garda Síochána more efficient and cost effective at a time of shrinking resources and fewer gardaí. The Stepaside station closed by 8pm each evening and was structurally unfit for purpose. Despite €3.5 million invested in modernising and doubling the size of Dundrum Garda Station three miles away and a need for gardaí to spend more time out in the community instead of behind desks, many in the local community were demanding that the station be re-opened. As the Minister for Justice when the station closed, I was perceived by some as the enemy and responsible, following its closure, for every crime committed in Stepaside. The fact that this was a garda operational decision was entirely ignored, as was the reality that when 138 other stations were closing across the country it would have been entirely unethical for me to intervene and exclude Stepaside.

What I did not know, when Stepaside station closed, was that the Commission on the Future of Policing in Ireland in its report published in September 2018, would place substantial importance on the 'operational independence of the Garda Commissioner' and assert that the Commissioner 'should determine the operational structure of An Garda Síochána' and 'manage the police estate'. In doing so, it would also state that the Minister for Justice should not compromise such independence and the Commissioner should determine the number of garda stations required, stating that 'police stations do not in themselves enhance police visibility or engagement in the community'.

The Stepaside issue only affected one part of the constituency and both I and my campaign team felt that my personal campaign, in difficult circumstances, was going reasonably well and my prospects of re-election were good. Then, with eleven days to go, I received a draft of Chapter 13 of the *O'Higgins Report*. It covered the parts of the inquiry I had been involved in and included the draft conclusions from that chapter and a request for any final submission I might wish to make. I believed that the hearings had gone well but I was both relieved and delighted to learn that I was fully exonerated. I could tell no one, as the draft was confidential. The draft I received would also have been provided to all the officials connected to the Department of Justice subject to the Commission's Investigation and to the lawyers representing them. I do not know whether Frances Fitzgerald, then Justice Minister, was given a copy of the draft or briefed on its content by Justice officials or whether the Taoiseach, Enda Kenny, learnt of the conclusions in the draft chapter before polling day. I felt not only legally bound but also honour bound by the confidentiality of the O'Higgins process. As a result, during the last ten days of the election campaign, when challenged or criticised over McCabe-related controversies, I could not mention O'Higgin's conclusions or that I had been vindicated.

Exactly one week after my receipt of O'Higgins's draft Chapter 13 and just four days before polling day, I was informed that Brian Hayes

MEP, Fine Gael's Director of Elections, on instructions from Fine Gael's election committee, was arranging for a leaflet to be dropped in strategic locations in the constituency. The leaflet was in the form of a letter, signed by the Taoiseach and Brian Hayes, asking Fine Gael voters to give their first preference vote to my Fine Gael running mate, first time Dáil candidate and member of Dún Laoghaire/Rathdown County Council, Josepha Madigan, and their second preference to me, in order to secure two Dáil seats for Fine Gael. I knew that this decision would be heavily influenced by Fine Gael's General Secretary, Tom Curran, and Head of Research and Development, Terry Murphy, and, in my case I believed not made without Enda Kenny's knowledge. In the lead-in to the election Kenny had promised me any support I needed during the campaign. I had asked for none from him but had discussed with him the difficulties caused to my re-election campaign by the *Guerin Report* and the garda-related controversies.

By the last weekend of the campaign Fine Gael was in trouble. A nightmare opening press conference, a confused presentation of Fine Gael's election programme, poor media performances by Kenny, public disillusionment with established politicians and increased support for independent candidates, together with a resurgence in Fianna Fáil support and greater support for the Green Party and Sinn Féin was a deadly political cocktail. Fine Gael's support was eroding nationally. I knew there was no chance of winning a second seat in Dublin Rathdown.

Between 1981 and 2011 I had represented Dublin South, a five-seat constituency. Dublin South had been renamed, redrawn and reduced to a three-seat constituency, Dublin Rathdown. Fifty per cent of my traditional vote was now lost to our neighbouring constituency. This was the other complication in my getting re-elected and well understood by Kenny and those in Fine Gael headquarters. In every preceding election I had always supported strategic action to maximise Fine Gael's Dáil seats and, where necessary, to encourage Fine Gael supporters to vote tactically. I had done so to my cost in 2002 and lost my Dáil seat. In 2016, for the first time in thirty-five years, I said no, protesting that if the proposed leaflets were dropped Fine Gael would still only win one seat and I would be the loser. I had started the campaign with a genuine hope that we could win two seats but knew by the Monday evening before polling day, when I was informed of the leaflet drop, that two seats were impossible. I also knew that the message in the leaflet clearly wrongly implied that my seat was safe.

Despite my protests, the leaflet drop went ahead in the twenty-four hours prior to polling day. From the voting tally in the areas where the leaflets were delivered, it was clear they were effective and substantially contributed to my losing the election.

My constituency was not the only one in which Fine Gael voters were asked to strategically vote. In some constituencies the tactic was successful, in others not. There is also nothing unusual about over-anxious and paranoid candidates opposing such tactics. So, from the outside looking in, there was nothing unusual about the leaflets distributed in Dublin/Rathdown. But given the circumstances in Dublin/ Rathdown, and, in particular, the personal battle I was fighting, there was only one rational conclusion. There was a determination to ensure if there was only one Fine Gael seat to be won, I would not win it. Why else, with Fine Gael's vote shrinking, in a five-seat constituency redrawn and reduced to three, would a leaflet giving the impression my seat was safe, signed by the Taoiseach as party leader, be selectively delivered into strong Fine Gael areas, urging voters, for the benefit of the party, to vote Madigan No 1, knowing its content would rapidly become known across the entire constituency? Was this Kenny's revenge for my contradicting his evidence before the Fennelly Commission? Or for my rocking the boat by challenging Guerin in the courts? Did Kenny know of my vindication by O'Higgins and want me out of the Dáil before the *O'Higgins Report* was published for fear I would prove troublesome? It is not possible to definitively answer these questions but the conduct of Kenny and others after the election gives some interesting insights on which others can make their own judgement.

Had the leaflet drop been a strategic mistake, I would have expected after the election to hear from Enda Kenny or Tom Curran or someone in Fine Gael headquarters to apologise for ignoring my protests. I had been a Fine Gael TD for over thirty years and a Cabinet Minister for three years, with an unprecedented area of responsibility. I had drafted major sections of Fine Gael's 2011 General Election reform programme and been part of the team that had negotiated the 2011 Fine Gael/Labour Programme for Government. Apart from the legislative programme I had implemented and progressed, I had also led two successful referendums – one a controversial referendum on judicial pay at a time of major financial crisis, the other to establish a Court of Appeal. Prior to becoming a member of Cabinet, I had published more parliamentary Bills from the Opposition benches and had more enacted into law than any other Opposition Dáil Deputy in the history of the State. I was also the only member of the small Irish Jewish community to have ever stood as a Fine Gael election candidate, to become a member of the parliamentary party and become a Fine Gael Cabinet Minister. I had, as Minister for Justice, been wrongly vilified (by then the Cooke and Fennelly reports had been published for some time so the truth of events had begun to emerge) and I had been subject to anti-Semitic abuse and threats. If a mistake had been made in good faith one would expect that I would have been contacted by someone in a leadership position in Fine Gael. But I was not.

Even if insincere, for no reason other than the optics, some post election communication from Kenny or Curran or Murphy would have been expected, I believe, by most people. Could it be that conscience made cowards of them all or simply that once I was out of the Dáil maintaining any pretence was perceived as an unnecessary encumbrance?

About ten days after the general election, Brian Hayes visited me at home to apologise for allowing the leaflet drop to take place against my wishes but this was a personal apology of little value as he was frank enough to admit his wife, Genevieve, insisted he do it. From my perspective, Brian was only fronting the campaign, as National Director of Elections, and I had no doubt he was obediently acting on the orders of others when it came to the leaflet drop. But for me, acting under orders was not a good enough excuse for allowing it to proceed and giving it legitimacy. If positions were reversed I would never have done it to him. For many years Carol and I had regarded Brian and Genevieve as friends. We had socialised together occasionally. Brian, Carol and I had golfed together and, during the election campaign, I had taken a little time out to assist Colm Brophy, a Fine Gael colleague and friend of Brian's, with his election campaign.

I had foolishly trusted Kenny and party officials to behave honourably during the election campaign. I understood I was at risk of losing my seat and ultimately it was for the electorate to determine my fate. What I did not expect was that the Taoiseach, as leader of the party, and those who worked closely with him would cynically manipulate Fine Gael voters into redirecting crucial first preference votes and undermine the integrity of the election process. I felt totally betrayed and Brian's role in it all was particularly upsetting.

Three months after the general election, on 25 May 2016, Enda Kenny opened the Dáil debate on the *O'Higgins Report*. Having briefly and selectively referenced the background to the establishment of the O'Higgins Commission he stated that he was 'very pleased to acknowledge that the *O'Higgins Report* has found clearly that the former Minister acted properly at all times in relation to the handling of allegations made by Maurice McCabe'.

Referring to a letter I had sent him following publication of the *O'Higgins Report*, he continued:

> I would also like to take the opportunity to correct the Dáil record of the 7th May 2014. I am happy to state on the record that the former Minister, in resigning, did not in fact accept responsibility for criticism made in the Guerin Report of the adequacy of the Department and the Minister for Justice and Equality in responding to allegations made by Sergeant McCabe. The former Minister set out his reasons clearly in his letter of resignation.

A little further on came Kenny's public virtual embrace which, viewed by an uninformed observer, could have been perceived as resembling the level of warmth and support displayed by him after his Ard Fheis speech in March 2014 when, at his instigation, we raised our arms in unison to the acclaim of the Fine Gael faithful.

Referring to my period in Government, he continued:

> I would like to emphasise, as I did at the time of his resignation, that Alan Shatter was an exceptionally hard working, radical and reforming Minister who has left a positive legacy across the wide range of areas for which he had ministerial responsibility. As Taoiseach I again thank him for his service, both as a Minister and a Dáil Deputy over many years.

In different circumstances Kenny's words of apparent warmth and praise and the correction of his inaccurate explanation to the Dáil of the reason for my resignation from cabinet in 2014 would have been welcome. However, my immediate reaction upon reading what he had said was an overwhelming feeling of nausea and a splitting headache. The insincerity and hypocrisy was mind-blowing, coming from a man who had denied me any reasonable time to fully read and digest the *Guerin Report*, entirely ignored my criticism of the manner in which Guerin had conducted his inquiry, pretended to have no advance knowledge of any of its flaws, ensured that, following my resignation from Cabinet, I could play no meaningful role of any nature in the Fine Gael party, undermined my general election campaign and had last talked to me at a Dublin/Rathdown General Election event held two weeks before polling day. Moreover, even in the midst of his very public praise, Kenny exhibited a casual self-serving relationship with the truth. He spoke of my having resigned from Government 'following publication of the Guerin Report' conveniently side stepping any reference to his pressurising me into resigning two days before the report was published. He could have acknowledged that Guerin's condemnation of me was clearly mistaken but he did not do so. He used my 'ongoing litigation in the courts' with Guerin to avoid that acknowledgement. He also avoided addressing serious issues concerning the conduct generally of non-statutory inquiries that I had raised in my letter to him shortly after publication of the *O'Higgins Report*.

For Kenny to explicitly recognise Guerin's flaws and mistakes, his own role in my resignation and to apologise for the way I had been treated was a step too far. So also was any reference to the way in which I had been vilified and demonised both inside and outside the Dáil chamber. Kenny rightly acknowledged the role of Maurice McCabe in the revelation of garda failures and dysfunction. But he also carefully avoided any reference to 'unfounded' or 'exaggerated' allegations or to those allegations withdrawn by the Sergeant during the O'Higgins Commission hearings or to the damage done by them being politically weaponised and my being targeted by Opposition TDs in the Dáil chamber and their 'hurtful' or 'damaging' impact on the people against whom they were made.

As Tánaiste and Minister for Justice, Frances Fitzgerald tentatively entered some of that territory in her initial speech. Emphasising the importance of the Garda Síochána taking seriously allegations of wrongdoing made by its own members and primarily focused on the treatment of Maurice McCabe, she remarked: 'We never again want to see the situation in which Maurice McCabe found himself, nor do we want to see people for long periods having to live under the shadow of unfounded allegations.' In doing so, she was careful to avoid identifying those who 'for long periods' lived under the shadow of unfounded allegations and anyone directly responsible for making them.

Later on in her speech, she spoke of the *Guerin Report* as a prelude to the creation of the O'Higgins Commission and of that report's 'acceptance' by Government, but there was no mention at that stage of my vindication, the flawed approach taken by Guerin, his mistaken conclusions and to the now proved accuracy of my June 2014 Dáil critique of the *Guerin Report* which she had sat through and ignored. Despite the explicit findings of O'Higgins, she also said nothing about the dangers of assuming all allegations made by 'whistle-blowers' are true and of people being condemned without a fair hearing. The fear of a political and media backlash resulting from any criticism voiced of anything said or done by Maurice McCabe ensured her silence. As was the case in 2014, it clearly never occurred to her that she might one day become personally entangled in a McCabe-related garda controversy and be wrongly accused of behaving badly.

The Opposition speeches that followed were predictable. Like those of Kenny and Fitzgerald, they addressed the findings and conclusions of O'Higgins, Garda reform, the treatment of whistle-blowers and the background to the *O'Higgins Report*. Little recognition was given to the conclusion of O'Higgins that the Byrne/McGinn investigation, although flawed, had taken McCabe's 2007/2008 allegations seriously and had substantiated many of them. Nor did a single Opposition TD engage in any serious discussion or analysis of the damage done to individuals by allegations made by McCabe which he withdrew or which were exaggerated or rejected by O'Higgins as 'unfounded'. For some, doing so would have involved an unprecedented public act of self-criticism having been the principal promoters of 'unfounded' and 'exaggerated' allegations both inside and outside the Dáil. There was also no prospect of any acknowledgement by any Opposition TD that I had been vindicated by O'Higgins, wrongly criticised in the Dáil and maligned by Guerin when so many had validated and celebrated Guerin's conclusion that I had not 'heeded' McCabe's voice. There was no question of any Opposition TD withdrawing false charges from the Dáil record or offering any apology. Despite presentations to the contrary, for most of my former Dáil critics it was all a political game and the twisting of truth and the promotion of alternative facts was all part of it.

Micheál Martin excelled himself. There was no possibility of him acknowledging that accusations made by him against me on the Leinster House plinth in February 2014 and then repeated by him and other Fianna

Fáil members in the Dáil chamber were mistaken. It was a simpler matter to just reframe history. He focused on his providing to the Taoiseach the 'papers and dossier' he had received from Maurice McCabe and denied that he had engaged in 'a partisan political attack or an agenda-driven stunt'. It was a curious denial to make in a debate where no prior speaker had made any such accusation. While asking that the debate not 'descend into petty point scoring', a coded request that he be not criticised, Martin washed his hands of any responsibility for my vilification and political demise and gave Guerin a free pass. In doing so, however, he did touch on one truth.

> The Guerin Report did not cause the resignation of the former Minister. The Taoiseach made clear to the then Minister what had to happen when he presented him with the Guerin Report. The former Minister has focussed too much on saying that Guerin caused his resignation. That is not what happened. Even before we discussed the Guerin Report in this House, the Minister had resigned saying he was doing so for political reasons because of the forthcoming local elections.

Martin's reference to Kenny's conduct was perceptive and his correction of Kenny's timeline for my resignation accurate but the contention that the *Guerin Report* had not 'caused' my resignation and essentially had nothing to do with my departure from Government was mere sophistry and a totally disingenuous false narrative. Martin then resorted to intellectual gymnastics, giving fulsome praise to McCabe while also welcoming the exoneration of Martin Callinan, stating: 'The findings of the Commission underline the staunch reliability of Sergeant McCabe and exonerate the former Commissioner, Martin Callinan, which is important and which I welcome.'

How to reconcile 'staunch reliability' with a rejected allegation of corruption made by McCabe against Callinan in 2012 for which there was 'not a scintilla of evidence' was not something he felt the need to explain. For Micheál Martin his speech was also not an appropriate moment to publicly address 'unfounded' and rejected allegations of corruption and criminality made against other members of the garda force, false allegations he had promoted nor his accusations that I had 'undermined the administration of justice' and ignored McCabe's concerns. He was not prepared to accept any responsibility for promoting any allegation which was exaggerated, unfounded or simply mistaken. Predictably, neither Martin nor any other member of the Dáil saw fit to address the difficulties and complications that directly arose from McCabe's expressed wish to remain anonymous and his solicitors failure to respond to crucial letters from the Justice Department. The fact that these issues were addressed in the *O'Higgins Report* did not matter. It was all a bridge too far. McCabe's celebrity and the fear of political, public or media backlash ensured it was all strictly off limits for politicians opportunistically surfing on the slipstream of McCabe's verified complaints and his media and public acclaim.

The Dáil debate on the *O'Higgins Report* concluded on 26 May 2016. It was Frances Fitzgerald's responsibility to respond to the debate. She entered political territory related to McCabe's allegations and complaints she had until then studiously avoided. Saying that during the debate a 'number of Deputies raised the treatment of whistle-blowers and the specific cases of other Garda members who have made allegations', she continued:

> Any dispassionate reading of the O'Higgins Report and an objective assessment of the events of the past couple of years demonstrate two things: the dangers of rushing to judgement and the need to have fair, independent and objective procedures in place for dealing with allegations of wrongdoing within An Garda Síochána. We should all face up to the fact that my predecessor was excoriated across the floor of this House about matters which some considerable time later he was found to have dealt with properly. Whatever passion members of this House might have in pursuing what they believe to be great wrongs, we would all do well to reflect that righting the wrongs done to some by doing wrong to others is not what justice is about.

It was an interesting insight clearly intended to remonstrate only with Opposition TDs and presumably stimulated by their selective and politically partisan references to the *O'Higgins Report*. However, her comment was also relevant to the way Sean Guerin had conducted his inquiry and reached his conclusions. For two years she had ignored my Dáil criticism of Guerin's rush to judgement, his flawed approach to his inquiry and the consequent damage done to my reputation, but Fitzgerald did not explicitly go there. She was also careful to avoid any direct critical reference to Maurice McCabe's 'unfounded' or 'exaggerated' allegations or to allegations withdrawn by him when before the O'Higgins Commission or rejected by the Commission. Her defence of me in the Dáil chamber, her insights about the importance of 'fair' procedures and the 'dangers of rushing to judgement' while welcome were, for me, over two years too late.

Exactly a month later, the court proceedings I had taken against Guerin were scheduled to be heard by the Court of Appeal and I had no choice but to continue my court battle for which I had received no support of any nature from a single member of the Fine Gael parliamentary party. Frances Fitzgerald's belated recognition of the importance of 'fair, independent and objective procedures' remained central to that battle and as far as the Taoiseach, Tánaiste and the Government were concerned the chosen position was to look the other way. Despite my vindication by O'Higgins there were no private messages of encouragement or support from any former Cabinet or Fine Gael colleague. As far as they were all concerned, I was bucking the system and creating unnecessary controversy when I should long ago have compliantly accepted my fate and disappeared from public view.

CHAPTER 39

Watergate Irish-Style

Who does Alan Shatter think he is? The Columbo of Dáil Éireann it seems – skulking around thinking he has the lowdown on his political rivals –Email of a John Murphy, published on 20 May 2013 by the *Irish Daily Mail*, portraying with humour the prevailing media narrative around a controversy involving Alan Shatter and Mick Wallace TD relating to a minor road traffic incident

I want to make it perfectly clear that I had not sought out this information in regard to Deputy Wallace nor did the Minister request that I seek it out. The Minister at no time sought from me information of any kind on Deputy Wallace –Letter of 21 October 2013 from Garda Commissioner Martin Callinan, responding to a questionnaire received from the Standards in Public Office Commission (SIPO)

The information regarding the incidents concerned was provided to you by the Garda Commissioner in accordance with section 41 of the Garda Síochána Act and was not therefore improperly obtained –From SIPO letter, 14 January 2014, to Alan Shatter following SIPO concluding its preliminary inquiry rejecting complaints made against Alan Shatter by Mick Wallace TD

A bizarre offshoot of the ticket charge controversy with surreal consequences originated with an offbeat public intervention by Roscommon-South Leitrim TD, Luke Ming Flanagan, in the Dáil on 12 March 2014. Flanagan, together with TDs Mick Wallace, Clare Daly and Joan Collins had been critical of gardaí cancelling traffic tickets. They were the four who organised the press conference initially arranged for Buswells Hotel, in December 2012, to disclose a dossier of alleged incidents and names derived from the confidential garda PULSE system. On 9 March 2013, before I had received the *O'Mahoney Report*, a story appeared in the *Sunday Independent* claiming that Flanagan had traffic tickets and penalty points terminated on two occasions in 2011 for using a mobile phone while driving. The incidents described were identical to one of the alleged examples of wrongdoing 'exposed' and on display in the Buswells December 2012 press conference. A media furore ensued.

Ming was accused by some commentators and politicians of hypocrisy. He resisted calls to resign.

On 12 March 2013, in the Dáil, Flanagan attempted to explain his benefiting from circumstances he had stridently condemned. Having confirmed that he had 'received a fixed penalty notice in the post' as a result of using his mobile phone when driving in June 2011, he continued:

> A few days later I bumped into a Garda Sergeant who informed me he was aware I had received a notice. He asked me what had happened and I told him the story. [Flanagan claimed he had been on route to a Dáil meeting.] He told me I was covered under the rule on travelling to the Dáil. I informed him that there was no point but he insisted I write to the station and explain. I did so and no points were added to my licence. I will supply the name of the Garda in question to the Minister for Justice and Equality, Alan Shatter, in order that he can use it in his internal review of the penalty points issue. I had planned to name him in the Dail but I was informed … that I would be stopped and that would be the end of my speech … I did not ask the Garda Sergeant in question to get involved, but he insisted that he should.

Later in his speech, Flanagan confirmed that, in December 2011, he had again been stopped for using his phone, this time when driving to a meeting in Roscommon County Council offices. He claimed that when at the meeting, he 'casually' mentioned being stopped and that, after the meeting, he received a phone call from 'a senior council official' who informed him that 'he had sorted out his penalty point issue for him'. Flanagan stated he neither received penalty points nor a fine and, from his Dáil account of what occurred, it appeared that no Fixed Charge Notice was ever issued. He claimed that he had intended to reveal all of this upon publication of the *O'Mahoney Report*. Blaming the gardaí for what the next day he referred to in an interview as his own 'corrupt' action, he had a credibility difficulty when attempting to explain the letter he sent to An Garda Síochána specifically asking that the June traffic ticket be cancelled.

Flanagan's Dáil speech was swiftly followed by a statement from the Roscommon County Manager, Frank Dawson, asserting that he 'assumed' he was the county official Flanagan referred to in the Dáil as he had mentioned the second mobile phone incident to him. Dawson 'utterly' rejected 'his allegations that I "sorted out his penalty points issue" for him'. He stated he was forwarding his account to the Garda Commissioner.

To ascertain the truth, I requested the Garda Commissioner to have Flanagan's account of events investigated and to inform me of the outcome. We had now entered a farcical world in which Flanagan was publicly criticising the gardaí for complying with his written request that they exercise their discretion and cancel a traffic ticket he had received.

Flanagan informed the Dáil that he had contacted the fines office in County Roscommon to ascertain how he could have 'the punishment that should have been imposed on me in the first place – my fine and my penalty points – restored'. This incongruous action announced by Flanagan, taken almost two years after the June 2011 incident, was treated seriously by Clare Daly who was speaking after him, and who admiringly described his speech as 'a hard act to follow'. I marvelled at Flanagan's brass neck and the uncritical response of Clare Daly. Daly's admiration was not shared by Joan Collins who criticised Flanagan's conduct in the days that followed, when it became a focus for media and public ridicule. I never discovered whether Flanagan was successful in reviving the missing fines and penalty points.

Later that month, I received a letter from Flanagan naming individuals he claimed were involved in the cancellation of his penalty points stating he believed 'the truth about the situation must be established'. However, Flanagan declined to engage with the gardaí appointed to investigate his claims and ascertain the truth. In early May 2013, I asked to be informed where the investigation stood so I could issue a public statement on Flanagan's claims on the day the *O'Mahoney's Report* was published. I wished to avoid any suggestion that he had been ignored. In the end, all I could do was express disappointment at his unwillingness to engage with the garda investigation he had sought. He had clearly lost interest in establishing the truth.

If nothing further had occurred, the Ming Flanagan episode would have been a ridiculous but largely forgotten and irrelevant comic example of political hypocrisy. However, it laid the foundation for some real trouble which, on reflection, I should have avoided. But, unfortunately, I have a particular difficulty with people lecturing and denigrating others from a counterfeit moral pulpit.

Under section 41 of the Garda Síochána Act, the Garda Commissioner has a duty to keep the Minister for Justice fully informed of significant developments that could adversely affect public confidence in the gardaí, garda matters relevant to the accountability of Government to the Houses of the Oireachtas and any other matter the Commissioner believes should be brought to the Minister's attention. In the aftermath of the brouhaha around Ming Flanagan's revelations, public self-flagellation and naming of names in his letter to me, during a conversation with Martin Callinan on the exercise of garda discretion and ticket charges, he mentioned an incident involving Mick Wallace. He had learnt, during the course of the O'Mahoney investigation that, in May 2012, a garda in a patrol car had spotted Wallace using his mobile phone while stationary at a traffic light-controlled road junction in Dublin. The garda had applied his discretion by issuing a warning. No traffic ticket was issued and no penalty points imposed. It was my judgement that, as Wallace's car was stationary at a red traffic light, it was an entirely reasonable and proper exercise of Garda discretion. However, Callinan was concerned to ensure that, should Wallace choose to disclose the incident and replicate Ming Flanagan's conduct, I would have prior knowledge of what occurred. I had never sought any information of any nature from the Commissioner about Wallace or any other member of the Oireachtas. If not for Flanagan's antics I do not believe Callinan would have felt obliged to inform me of the Wallace incident.

The day after publication of the *O'Mahoney Report*, I appeared together with Wallace on RTÉ's flagship current affairs television programme, *Prime Time*, for a joint interview with Pat Kenny. Kenny, doing his job and being deliberately provocative, correctly stated that the report found fault with the gardaí but 'no corruption, no criminality'. He asked Wallace: 'Do you accept you went off a bit half cocked on this?' Wallace replied 'No, I do not' and then denied that there was any legislation in place 'to actually justify this use of discretion' and asserted that its use was 'not lawful'.

In response to Kenny's questions to me I detailed the findings of the *O'Mahoney Report*: garda failings identified: 'wild and exaggerated claims' established as untrue and the fact that, five hours before publication of the *O'Mahoney Report*, before he could have read it, Wallace had labelled it 'a whitewash' on Pat Kenny's earlier radio show on RTÉ. I then spoke about some circumstances in which gardaí had lawfully and correctly exercised their discretion 'as Deputy Wallace knows'. Believing there was a legitimate public interest in defending lawful garda conduct, I continued:

> Even without issuing tickets the gardai exercise discretion. Deputy Wallace himself was stopped with a mobile, on a mobile phone last May by members of An Garda Síochána and he was advised by the gardaí who stopped him that a Fixed Ticket Charge could issue and he could be given penalty points. But the garda apparently as I am advised ... used his discretion and warned him and told him not to do it again.

Wallace's immediate reaction was denial of any incident, saying: 'I'll tell you what first of all that's news to me.'

Pat Kenny: 'You don't recall that incident?'

Mick Wallace: 'I don't know.'

Shortly after, Kenny asked whether he was 'not concerned that the Minister should know about your private business dealing with the Gardai?'

Wallace responded, 'I'm not remotely worried about what the Minister knows.'

When Kenny then asked Wallace whether motorists should always end up in court, Wallace replied: 'No listen. If the motorist is stopped with a Garda using his discretion there and then is perfectly reasonable [sic]. But once it goes up on the system then they should go through the courts system. Now listen ...'

Pat Kenny: 'So if you enjoyed the on-the-beat discretion of the Gardai, which you don't remember, so be it, but once it goes into the system you have to go all the way.'

Wallace responded, 'that's the law', I contradicted him and the interview briefly returned to issues arising out of the *O'Mahoney Report*. But Pat had the bit between his teeth.

Pat Kenny: 'The Minister has thrown in a grenade though about you benefiting from discretion with the Gardai ...'

Mick Wallace: 'Well listen that's news to me Pat right, but listen ...'

Pat Kenny: 'You don't remember that?'

Mick Wallace: 'I don't know.'

And with that, Wallace rapidly moved on to another issue. We returned to discuss the *O'Mahoney Report* and Wallace, who continued to criticise it and make allegations irrefutably proved bogus, ultimately admitted he had not finished reading the report. It was not clear to me what part, if any, of the report he had read.

I did not regard our *Prime Time* interview as a major political event. I believed Wallace had not emerged particularly well out of it but that our exchanges would produce minimal feedback. My main objective that night was to tell the truth about the workings and the failings of the Fixed Charge Processing System, acknowledge that some garda decisions made to cancel traffic tickets should not have been made and to correct false allegations of corruption and that road fatalities had resulted from traffic tickets being unlawfully cancelled. I also believed it was important that the general public should know that I had asked the Garda Inspectorate to conduct a further investigation. I was surprised that Mick Wallace had not fully read the *O'Mahoney Report* before the programme and at his denial of any knowledge of his mobile phone incident, which was similar but not identical to Ming Flanagan's. I anticipated his *Prime Time* appearance might result in his having to respond to a few media questions the next day but that was about it.

The next morning Wallace appeared happy with the broadcast. He tweeted 'Last night's Prime Time well worth a watch #FixedChargeNotices'. By the weekend he was no longer 'not remotely concerned about what the Minister knows' but reported to be asking the Data Protection Commissioner and the Standards in Public Office Commission to investigate my comments. By the Monday, Wallace had remembered the incident and Tuesday's papers reported that he admitted an encounter with a garda after being spotted at traffic lights in Dublin while using his mobile phone. The *Irish Examiner* reported that when asked on an RTÉ interview did the gardaí exercise discretion, he replied: 'Yes they did.'

Ming Flanagan had been accused by media commentators of hypocrisy over his road traffic incidents and relying on garda discretion to avoid ticket charges and penalty points. No such charge was levelled by media commentators or Opposition TDs at Wallace. I was now accused of using my 'powerful position' to target and spy on Opposition TDs and, like Richard Nixon, to develop an enemies list. The charge was that I had wrongly sought and used confidential Garda information to attack a political opponent. The hyperbole got the Labour Party angsty and Joan Burton was quoted as expecting 'a frank and full reply' from me to clarify how I learnt of the Wallace traffic incident. A minor event was being portrayed as a major Government crisis and scandal and Wallace as an innocent victim of unlawful wrongdoing.

The Taoiseach tried to bring some sense of proportion to the furore. Kenny was reported by the *Irish Independent* from Boston as stating:

> It was brought to his [Mr Wallace's] attention that discretion has applied in the past in regard to fixed penalty points before fixed notices were issued. And that's relevant information to the general public. The point here is the deputy in question was adamant that no discretion should be used by Gardai, when he himself was the recipient of discretion, before a fixed penalty point notice was actually issued. That information is relevant to the background to this discussion.

Fine Gael Ministers rowed in asserting that I had acted in the public interest. Minister for Public Works, Brian Hayes, did not hold back. The same paper reported him asserting that 'We're not going to be lectured, quite frankly, by people who don't pay their tax and have a huge tax liability to the Irish State.'

The most serious allegation made was that I had unlawfully violated Wallace's right to privacy under the Data Protection Act, on the assumption that I had wrongly sought and disclosed confidential data improperly obtained from An Garda Síochána. Of course, I had not done so, but it would take until 2017 for that to be irrefutably established.

In the midst of the frenzy that developed, in the days following the programme, media reporters and commentators ignored the fact that the four TDs – Wallace, Ming Flanagan, Joan Collins and Clare Daly had, approximately six months earlier, revealed confidential information originating from the PULSE system. Under the cover of Dáil privilege, some had named individuals as if guilty of wrongdoing, giving them no opportunity to defend themselves. Of course, the names revealed in the Dáil had generated considerable news coverage and, because journalists were quoting Deputies speaking in the Dáil chamber, they were protected from any possible action. The double standards involved became starkly apparent when Wallace opted into the false narrative that I had violated his Data Protection rights. He complained to both the Standards in Public Office Commission (SIPO) and the Data Protection Commissioner about my conduct. Somewhere along the line, his morning-after tweet expressing his satisfaction with the *Prime Time* programme, inconsistent with his new-found unhappiness, was deleted from his Twitter account.

On Monday, 20 May 2013, following up the weekend controversy, RTÉ television's *Six One* evening news interviewed Billy Hawkes, the Data Protection Commissioner. He revealed that Wallace had, that afternoon, lodged a complaint with him that he would investigate. He then added to the political excitement by identifying the 'key issue', as being that 'the personal data of Deputy Wallace … was disclosed by Minister Shatter' and by stating that 'it is for Minister Shatter to justify the basis and the justification for disclosing data that came into his possession as Minister for Justice'. This was a totally inappropriate comment by Hawkes, partially publicly pre-judging an issue on which he had to adjudicate. It was the equivalent of a High Court judge taking to the airwaves to partially adjudicate on a case prior to hearing the evidence and the submissions of disputing litigants. As his perspective fitted neatly into the prevailing media narrative it generated no critical comment. It simply added fuel to the story.

I was taken aback by the unexpected media onslaught and surprised by the extent to which Wallace was immune to criticism. I was also surprised by Hawkes's public intervention. Having initially defended my comment on *Prime Time*, I concluded that the issue was an unnecessary distraction. I also believed that all reasonable perspective had been lost. I was being depicted as the Irish equivalent of Richard Nixon, spying on political opponents. The controversy led to Dáil time being allocated on Tuesday evening, 21 May 2013, to discuss the issue and I decided, in so far as I could, to end the controversy. I told the Dáil that I regretted that my comments on *Prime Time* had 'inadvertently resulted in concerns being expressed that I am prepared to use confidential Garda information to damage a political opponent'. I continued:

> Nothing could be further from the truth, but I am happy to offer reassurances to deputies on this point. I give a solemn assurance to the House that I am not in the business of receiving, seeking or maintaining confidential sensitive information from An Garda Síochána on members of this House, Seanad, anyone in political life nor are Gardai in the business of providing it.

I then explained how I knew of the Wallace incident, asserting that 'there is nothing sinister about it' and that 'my discretion in maintaining confidences and not revealing information inappropriately is well known to many who have been writing and commenting on this controversy'. This was a reminder to journalists that I had never sought any political benefit or advantage by leaking confidential information or anonymously briefing reporters about any issue during my time in Cabinet. I explained I had mentioned the Wallace incident on *Prime Time* as:

> I believed in the performance of my duties as Minister for Justice and Equality it was necessary for me to ensure continuing public confidence in the [garda] force and it was wrong for Deputy Wallace to pillory others for the proper exercise of a lawful discretion. It was my judgment that it was both necessary and in the public interest that I point out he had been a beneficiary of that discretionary exercise. I believed there was an extraordinary inconsistency between what the Deputy had to say and what had occurred in his case. I made the point not to make a political charge against him, nor for any personal benefit, but to defend the integrity of the gardaí.

Stating that Wallace, like tens of thousands of others, had been a beneficiary of Garda discretion properly exercised and that I had made no allegation of any wrongdoing, I then acknowledged that no one has a monopoly of wisdom and continued, 'If Deputy Wallace believes I did him a personal wrong by mentioning it, I have no problem saying I am sorry.'

My apology, unsurprisingly, did not elicit any positive response. After all, the controversy as hyped in the Dáil had more to do with political opportunism and point scoring and less to do with principle. In response Fianna Fáil's Niall Collins called for my resignation, a call he made with some regularity, and Wallace confirmed he had written to both the Data Protection Commissioner and SIPO. From then on, the universal media perspective remained that I had despicably violated Wallace's rights under the Data Protection Act and that accusation reappeared from time to time in the months that followed as part of the Opposition's ongoing critical political narrative.

Within a few days, letters were received in the Department of Justice from both the Data Protection Commissioner and SIPO detailing Wallace's complaints. Surprisingly, notification was also received of a complaint to SIPO made by Ming Flanagan that his rights had been violated by my issuing a statement detailing his failure to engage with the gardaí in the investigation he had sought in order to establish 'the truth of the situation'.

The main complaints of both Wallace and Flanagan to SIPO were that I had failed to properly perform my duties as a Minister, had breached SIPO's code of conduct, failed to respect confidences wrongly disclosed to me and that these were matters of significant public importance. Each complained, in almost identical language, that I had subjected him to a 'politically motivated personal attack' which was 'a serious abuse of the Minister's power and privileges'. The number of politically motivated personal attacks to which I had been subjected by Wallace and Flanagan was of no relevance to this narrative. Responding to the allegations, I detailed to SIPO the relevant facts and background circumstances, the persistent demands of Wallace and Flanagan for transparency in the Fixed Charge Notice Processing System, Flanagan's allegation of wrongdoing by third parties both in the Dáil and in correspondence to me, Wallace's denial that gardaí could lawfully exercise a discretionary power to terminate ticket charges, the importance of maintaining public confidence in the gardaí and the public interest in transparency. Stating that I was not influenced by any personal considerations, I told SIPO that I had acted at all times impartially and in good faith in the proper exercise of my Ministerial functions.

The Garda Commissioner, in October 2013, in response to SIPO's detailed questions, stated that the information provided by him to me was fully consistent with his statutory obligations and that I had 'at no time sought information from him about Deputy Wallace'. In relation to Luke Ming Flanagan, he stated that he had informed the Secretary General of the Department of Justice of the position relating to the investigation being undertaken 'in the context of an update sought by the Minister into the examination of assertions made in Dáil Éireann by Deputy Flanagan' and that doing so 'was significant with regard to public confidence in An Garda Síochána and relevant to the Minister's accountability to the Houses of the Oireachtas'.

In January 2014 I was notified by SIPO that both Wallace's and Flanagan's complaints had been rejected. Having concluded its preliminary inquiry SIPO determined that I had properly received the information from the Garda Commissioner who had been under a statutory duty to provide it to me and that I had not done 'a specified act' of 'significant public importance' requiring the conduct of any further investigation.

Unfortunately, the proper, fair and careful approach of SIPO was not replicated by the Data Protection Commissioner, Billy Hawkes.

Wallace's allegation to the Data Protection Commissioner was similar to that made to SIPO. He specifically alleged that I had abused my ministerial 'power and privilege' by disclosing 'improperly obtained personal data'. A letter I received on 25 May 2013, signed by Tony Delaney, the Assistant Data Commissioner, informed me that the Commissioner was satisfied 'the personal data of Deputy Wallace was processed' by me and that he was going to conduct 'an investigation to determine whether that data processing was carried out' in compliance with section 2 of the Data Protection Act. This section details circumstances in which 'data' can be properly processed or disclosed. This replicated Hawkes's disturbing RTÉ interview prejudging as true the allegation that I had 'processed' Wallace's 'personal data', without first considering the full facts. At that stage neither Delaney nor Hawkes had any knowledge of the records, if any, maintained by An Garda Síochána, the Department of Justice, or by me, as Minister, of the Wallace incident and neither were in a position to determine whether what the Act refers to as 'personal data' existed or whether such data had in fact been 'processed'.

This matters because the specific purpose of the Data Protection legislation is to protect the confidentiality of manual and electronic data and to specify the circumstances in which it can be properly accessed and disclosed. It has no role in regulating verbal communications between individuals that do not disclose confidential information maintained electronically or in manual records. Nor does it confer a role on the Data Protection Commissioner to prevent the Garda Commissioner fulfilling his statutory obligations, where it is in the public interest, to disclose information to the Justice Minister. It is Dáil Éireann to whom the Minister for Justice is properly accountable in relation to such matters. If the Data Protection Commissioner could exercise this role, there would be no information received from a Garda Commissioner which a Minister for Justice could publicly disclose without being at risk of investigation. The Data Protection legislation would morph into a political weapon for a Minister's political opponents to opportunistically invoke. It would also be extremely dangerous if the Data Protection Acts could be used to limit legitimate public debate on important issues of public interest. This would have serious implications for press freedom and freedom of expression. This, of course, was not a difficulty that occurred to those critically commenting on the continuing controversy and stoking the media frenzy.

The letter from Tony Delaney, the Assistant Data Commissioner, was received after I had explained in the Dáil the background to my *Prime Time* interview and apologised for upsetting Mick Wallace. There is a procedure for the voluntary amicable resolution of a complaint under the Data Protection Act and I proposed that this be tried, without prejudice to my position should any investigation proceed. The Data Protection Commissioner explored this possibility and for some months I heard nothing more. When SIPO rejected his complaint, Wallace turned down the offer and insisted the investigation go ahead. He seemed to be intent on pursuing the issue as much as possible.

Responding to the Data Commissioner, I informed him that the information about Wallace was not in my possession nor in the Department's possession in any documentary form and there was no record maintained of it. It merely derived from a verbal communication of the Garda Commissioner that I remembered. It was not data as understood by the Act. It also later emerged that prior to furnishing me with his draft decision on 17 April 2014 for my 'observations', the Data Commissioner had not seen or examined what record, if any, of the Wallace incident was maintained by the gardaí.

In his draft decision Billy Hawkes ruled that I was a 'joint controller' of Wallace's data with the Garda Commissioner and had violated Wallace's Data Protection rights. I continued to contend in my response to him, on 2 May 2014, that the information did not and could not constitute data for which I was responsible, nor could I be a 'controller' of data not in my or the Department's possession. Despite this, on delivering his final decision four days later, on 6 May 2014, the Data Commissioner concluded that I was a 'Data Controller for the purposes' of the Data Protection Act of the 'personal data' of Deputy Wallace and had contravened its provisions and, as a consequence, Wallace's rights to privacy.

I was astonished by the decision. It would emerge over two months later that the only garda record that existed of the incident was contained in an internal Garda email, referencing Wallace being cautioned, first shown to Hawkes on the day of his final decision. I did not know of the existence of the email and Hawkes had not sought my views on it. It became absolutely clear that the Data Commissioner also knew nothing of the email when framing his draft decision nor had he taken any reasonable time to reflect on its relevance to Wallace's complaint. He had simply rushed to judgement.

Most of my exchanges on Wallace's complaint took place with the Data Commissioner between February and May 2014. This coincided with all the Garda-related controversies resulting in the creation of the Cooke and Guerin non-statutory inquiries and the Fennelly Commission. It also coincided with me being under a deluge of criticism as a result of a multitude of false charges and fake news stories. In normal circumstances where genuine concern exists that a complaint has been prejudged, the person adjudicating is asked to stand aside. Having already been convicted by the media of violating Wallace's rights and being under sustained political attack on a variety of fronts, I concluded that asking Billy Hawkes to stand aside would provoke another political 'scandal' and allegations that I was interfering in an independent adjudication process. I believed that anything I might say would inevitably be either entirely ignored or denigrated as a 'political stroke'. The toxic political environment in which I was working and its double standards were starkly illustrated by the unprecedented disclosure in the *Sunday Independent* on 4 May 2014 of Billy Hawkes's confidential draft decision.

The draft decision had been confidentially furnished by the Data Commissioner only to Wallace and to me for our 'observations' and to no one else. I presume Wallace, like me, properly shared it with his advisers. Under the front-page headline 'Last Straw as Shatter Breaks the Law', Niamh Horan and John Drennan dramatically reported that 'a shocking finding that Justice Minister Alan Shatter broke data protection laws could spell the end of his cabinet career' and predicted that 'the damaging finding ... will certainly compound existing tensions within the coalition'. Reporting that both the Cooke and Guerin Reports 'could spell further trouble for Mr Shatter', the story quoted an unidentified 'senior' Fine Gael source as stating that 'Enda is very loyal, too loyal for his or our own good. He feels Shatter has been hounded by the media and vested interest groups who want his head.' An anonymous Fine Gael Minister was also quoted saying 'Shatter has ruined us' asserting that my 'performance' has been 'devastating' for Fine Gael's core vote. Labour ministers were also reported to be unhappy, one anonymously quoted saying that 'Shatter is on the brink, his line of political credit is very thin.'

The *Sunday Independent* concluded its story quoting 'a source close to Mr Wallace', in celebration mode, stating 'This is a massive coup for Mick, who has long argued that the public cannot have a Minister for Justice, who abused his position by using his power to find private information on an individual to smear their reputation for political point scoring.' There was no space in the story to include the fact that SIPO had, less than four months earlier in a published decision, rejected the allegation that I had abused my position to 'find' anything and concluded that the particular information had been properly provided to me by the Garda Commissioner in accordance with his statutory obligations.

I did not expect the Data Commissioner's final decision to issue, as it did, on 6 May 2014, within four days of his being furnished with my detailed submissions challenging his draft conclusions. Hugely concerned about the political fall out, that evening I met with Attorney General, Máire Whelan, in her office in Government Buildings, together with my counsel, Frank Callanan SC, who had been advising on the dispute, my special advisers, and the Attorney's and Justice officials. A decision was made to appeal to the Circuit Court and we assumed that Billy Hawkes's decision would not withstand judicial scrutiny.

Unknown to me, by the time I was heading home from Whelan's office that evening, the Report of Sean Guerin, with whom Frank Callanan shared offices, had already been delivered to the Taoiseach's Department. Less than twenty-four hours later I would cease to be a member of Cabinet and the decision of the Data Protection Commissioner would be referred to in my political obituaries by both political opponents and commentators as an additional reason to welcome my departure from Government.

The following morning, 7 May 2014, as I was heading into Government Buildings for my initial discussion with Enda Kenny about the *Guerin Report*, the Data Commissioner's decision was being widely reported, together with an accusation by Mick Wallace that I had abused my office and his demand that I resign. Commentators made no critical analysis of the report's content and gave no consideration to the long-term consequences of the Data Commissioner's interpretation of the law and his own powers. I do not know the impact on Enda Kenny and those around him of the *Sunday Independent*'s revelation of Hawkes's draft decision and that morning's news reports, as he considered Guerin's critical conclusions. One thing is certain, they could not have been helpful.

****

When condemned by both an inquiry and an investigation conducted by two different independent individuals into two separate issues, you are unlikely to be taken seriously when you cry foul, complain of a lack of fair procedures and mistakes in findings or conclusions with regard to either the facts or the law or both. It gets worse when the conclusions correspond with a popular narrative. The perception is that you are in denial, unwilling to acknowledge your failings and to take your deserved medicine. That is where I found myself in May 2014. The headline over Miriam Lord's satirical and acerbic colour piece in *The Irish Times*, on 8 May 2014, referencing my resignation letter, summed up the prevailing perspective, 'Minister for Self Defence stayed true to form to the end'.

I regarded the decision of Hawkes as entirely wrong, damaging to my reputation, totally disruptive of the statutory relationship between a Garda Commissioner and a Minister for Justice and contrary to the public interest. I did not anticipate that my successor in Justice, Frances Fitzgerald, would be anything other than supportive of the court action Whelan, as Attorney General, had recommended. But I was wrong. Enda Kenny's imperative was to distance the Government as far as possible from the issue. Some days later I was taken aback to read a newspaper report that Fitzgerald, as Minister for Justice, would not be party to the Circuit Court appeal. Totally traumatised by events, the legal complications that could result from her decision did not instantly occur to me.

CHAPTER 40

The Rule of Law

It must be considered absolutely fundamental that before a person is severely criticised in a significant public undertaking by an eminent person in a report to the government in regard to a matter of urgent public importance that he or she would be afforded some notice of the criticisms and opportunity to comment on them: audi alteram partem
–Judgement of Mr Justice Sean Ryan, President of the Court of Appeal, in court proceedings Alan Shatter (Appellant) v Sean Guerin (Respondent), 10 November 2016

I am of the view that the respondent [Billy Hawkes] made 'a serious and significant error or series of errors'... in applying the definitions in the (Data Protection) Acts to the appellant in the circumstances that gave rise to the complaint
–High Court judgement of Mr Justice Charles Meenan in Alan Shatter (Appellant) v Data Protection Commissioner (Respondent) & Michael Wallace (Notice Party & Complainant), 9 November 2017

The rule of law matters. It is what ensures individual rights are not violated, constitutional norms are respected, mob rule does not prevail and result in individuals' lives being wrongly blighted or reputations wrongly destroyed or their being arbitrarily condemned or jailed without fair procedures or a fair hearing. It requires that laws enacted are uniformly properly interpreted, applied and administered and, where disputes arise, they are resolved by courts composed of competent and independent judges who impartially and fairly carry out their duties. The rule of law is at the very heart of the Irish constitution and central to the proper functioning of our parliamentary democracy. It is a concept to which I am passionately committed and which I advocated as a crucial principle for greater European Union activism during Ireland's Presidency of the EU in 2013 at a time when it was, as it still is today, under threat in some EU member states. In 2015 I lost confidence in the Irish Courts' commitment to the rule of law.

In the Circuit Court appeal issued against the Data Protection Commissioner, Paul Anthony McDermott BL, who represented the Commissioner, contended that I had no entitlement to bring the appeal as

I had ceased to be Minister for Justice. This was because, he told the court, the Data Protection Commissioner's decision related to the Minister for Justice only, not to me personally. Had Frances Fitzgerald as Minister for Justice filed an appeal this issue could not have arisen. As the Data Protection Commissioner's decision detrimentally impacted on my good name and reputation not only as a Government Minister but also as a TD, lawyer and a citizen and as the good name and reputation of Irish citizens is constitutionally protected, I did not believe the Court would take this objection to my appeal seriously. I also believed that the court would conclude that the way in which the Data Protection Commissioner decided Wallace's complaint and his application of the relevant legislation was fundamentally flawed.

On 21 January 2015, Circuit Court Judge Jacqueline Linnane unceremoniously dismissed my appeal, holding the objection to my 'standing' to take the court action to be 'well founded'. She also determined that, should she be wrong on that issue, the decision of the Data Protection Commissioner was not 'vitiated by any serious or significant error or series of errors' and that even if I could properly bring the appeal, having ceased to be Minister for Justice, she would dismiss it. She had no interest in the impressive and compelling legal submissions made on my behalf by my Senior Counsel, Eileen Barrington, ably assisted by Emily Gibson BL.

In the High Court proceedings taken against Sean Guerin, Paul Gallagher SC together with Paul Anthony McDermott BL represented Guerin. They also argued that, as I had ceased to be Minister for Justice before initiating the proceedings and was 'a private citizen', I could not seek 'judicial review' of the Guerin Report. Included amongst other contentions on behalf of Guerin was that his report was not 'justiciable' and did 'not give rise to a requirement for fair procedures and natural justice'. In so far as the court may conclude fair procedures were required, it was also contended any such requirement had been satisfied.

On 20 May 2015 High Court Judge Seamus Noonan, having excoriated me in some preliminary commentary, dismissed my proceedings. He held Guerin's report to be not justiciable and determined that I was not in a position to properly challenge it. He took, however, a somewhat different approach to deciding I lacked standing to challenge the *Guerin Report* to that taken by Circuit Court Judge Jacqueline Linnane in my appeal against the Data Protection Commissioner.

Judge Noonan referred to the fact that 'the Government decided to accept the Report, to publish it to the general public, to accept the recommendations contained in the Report and to establish a Commission of Investigation. These were all decisions for which the applicant bears responsibility as a member of the Government that made them'.

Further on he continued that, if I 'were still a member of the Government and sought to bring these proceedings it is difficult to escape the conclusion that he [I] would, in effect, be seeking to judicially review' myself. He concluded that I could not 'improve' my 'position by resigning and then bringing proceedings as a private citizen'.

According to Judge Noonan my court action had not passed the first hurdle and I was not entitled to bring it, whether or not I was still Minister for Justice, as I had been a member of the Government that had accepted the *Guerin Report*, agreed to implement its recommendations and had, following its receipt, agreed to its publication. The difficulty with this analysis was its factual inaccuracy. I had, of course, resigned from Government prior to the Cabinet meeting held to discuss the report and any decisions made by Cabinet following its receipt. This was clear from the documentation before the court and the submissions made to it by my eloquent Senior Counsel, Paul Sreenan, who represented me together with Patrick O'Reilly SC and Cathal Murphy BL.

For good measure Judge Noonan also determined that, even if the report were justiciable, I had been 'accorded fair procedures entirely commensurate with the nature of the review being undertaken' by Guerin. He concluded that I knew Guerin's terms of reference and was 'perfectly free' to furnish any additional information I anticipated he might require to carry out his role. There was, in the judge's view, no obligation on Guerin to interview me, ask me any questions or afford me an opportunity to comment on a draft of his report. It was Noonan's view that the circumstances were such that I 'must have known that the documents on their own would give rise to conclusions reasonably obvious to any intelligent reader'. Of course, my difficulty was that Guerin had not reached the conclusions that I believed were 'reasonably obvious'. Noonan's version of fair procedures required a person subject to an inquiry to prophetically anticipate the reasoning and likely conclusions of the person conducting it and provide whatever additional information they anticipated might influence the outcome of the inquiry. This was an unprecedented diminution of an individual's right to a fair hearing and a surprisingly novel application of the constitutional protection of a citizen's good name and reputation. The 'intelligent reader' dig was also surprising coming from a judge of the High Court.

As a practising solicitor who had acted as an advocate in both the Circuit and High Court for over thirty years, I knew that cases that initially appear straightforward can become unexpectedly complicated. I was also keenly aware that the outcome of any court case cannot be predicted with absolute certainty. The rejection of both court applications, the judgements delivered in both courts that I could not challenge the flawed procedures that had denied me a fair hearing and mistaken conclusions which had destroyed my reputation as a Minister, TD and a lawyer and the failure of both judges to properly address legal issues came as a complete shock. These issues were of huge importance, not only to me, but also to public administration, the manner in which government does its business and to the general public. I was also astounded by the curt manner of both judges, neither attaching any credence to a single submission made on my behalf by the very competent, experienced and articulate barristers representing me.

In both cases appeals were lodged, in the Data Protection case in the High Court and in the Guerin case in the Court of Appeal. However, my confidence was severely undermined and I started to doubt whether in either case the law, as I understood it, would be applied. I perceived the approaches of both judges who dismissed my actions in the earlier hearings as arbitrary, extraordinarily subjective, lacking in logic and contrary to long established legal principles.

I decided that I should prioritise the Guerin appeal. A major obstacle in both cases was the decision that I had no entitlement to take either case despite my reputation being damaged by both Guerin's and Hawkes's conclusions. This was a vital issue that required resolution by the Court of Appeal in the Guerin case before it was revisited by the High Court in the Data Protection case.

The Court of Appeal hearing was scheduled for June 2016. Approximately six weeks beforehand, on 11 May 2016, the *O'Higgins Report* was published. Its conclusions entirely contradicted Guerin's criticism of me and established his concerns about and condemnation of my ministerial conduct to be unjustified. I momentarily hoped this would result in Sean Guerin acknowledging that he was mistaken and that a contested appeal hearing would be unnecessary. After all, the truth had now been established and Enda Kenny as Taoiseach in the Dail on 25 May acknowledged that the Report found that I 'had acted properly at all times in relation to the handling of allegations made by Maurice McCabe'. Accepting he had got anything wrong or made any mistake was not something clearly that featured on Guerin's horizon. A fully and highly contested appeal hearing took place before three Appeal Court judges, the President of the Court, Judge Sean Ryan, and Judges Mary Finlay Geoghegan and Mary Irvine. Much to my relief, on 10 November 2016, the Court disagreed with the High Court decision and granted the appeal. The decision of the three Appeal Court judges was unanimous. The Court's main judgement was delivered by its President, Judge Sean Ryan. His initial conclusion was that 'It is clear that the Taoiseach's withdrawal of confidence and Mr Shatter's response by resigning happened because they considered that the statements in the report contained serious criticisms of the latter in the performance of his responsibilities as Minister for Justice and Equality.'

Judge Ryan ruled that Guerin's opinions and conclusions were 'deleterious' of my good name and were 'severe criticisms' and that he had made findings of fact or reached conclusions 'that reflect serious criticism of the Minister in the conduct of his office'. He continued: 'The statements reflect on Mr Shatter's good name because they impair his reputation generally as a competent Minister who is discharging his responsible position efficiently with integrity. They also indicate or suggest that he is not interested in ascertaining the truth about grave allegations of misconduct by Gardai.'

The damage, he held, did not only apply to me solely in my role as a Minister or as some 'disembodied formal functionary' but also to me personally as I 'had been found to be neglecting [my] duty'. The nature of the task Guerin was asked to undertake was not, according to Ryan, 'a justification for abandoning every element of fair procedures'.

Further on he continued:

Mr Guerin was mistaken in thinking that he was under no obligation to ensure the appropriate level of concern for Mr Shatter's position as Minister for Justice and Equality in light of what he was proposing to submit to the government as his conclusions ... It must be considered absolutely fundamental that before a person is severely criticised in a significant public undertaking by an eminent person in a report to the government in regard to a matter of urgent public importance that he or she would be afforded at least some notice of the criticisms and opportunity to comment on them: audi alteram partem.

Contrary to the view of Judge Noonan in the High Court, Judge Ryan had no doubt that I was entitled to initiate the judicial review proceedings. The fact that I had been a Minister in the Government that commissioned the Report, he held, did not deprive me of my right to my good name and reputation or abrogate any of my rights to fair procedures. He 'did not think such a position makes legal or constitutional sense' and did 'not also believe it accords with logic'. For Judge Ryan the right to a fair hearing for someone at risk of adverse findings was central to the concept of natural justice and Sean Guerin was 'obliged to observe the rules of natural justice'. He made no comment on Judge Noonan's mistaken narrative that I was still a member of Government at the time when the Cabinet discussed and made decisions on Guerin's Report.

Both Judges Finlay Geoghegan and Mary Irvine agreed with Judge Ryan that my appeal be granted. In her judgement, Judge Finlay Geoghegan stated that the court was required to consider the appeal on the basis of what was known in May 2014 and that the conclusions contained in the *O'Higgins Report*, which was not published until May 2016, were not relevant to the outcome of the appeal. She had no doubt about my standing to bring the court proceedings as the 'criticism in respect of acts done or not done by the Minister while the appellant was the holder of the office can only be objectively viewed as criticism of him personally with the potential to damage his good name and reputation'.

In confirming my right to fair procedures and 'entitlement to be heard' before Guerin criticised my actions as Minister for Justice in his report, she stated she

cannot agree that it was a matter for him [that is, the Minister for Justice] to make contact with the respondent [Sean Guerin] and provide information that he would wish to be taken into account. The obligation to ensure that fair procedures were afforded to an individual whose good name was at risk in the process was on the respondent. The appellant only had a right to be heard because the respondent proposed including statements critical of him in the Report. If no statements critical of the appellant were to be included the respondent would not have been obliged to give him an opportunity to be heard.

The outcome was of importance not only to me but also ensured that no one in the future could be similarly condemned in a report published after a preliminary or informal inquiry without being afforded a fair hearing. Within days of the decision of the Court of Appeal, the *Guerin Report* was removed from the Government's website but its content remains otherwise widely available and readily accessible and as it was laid before the Dáil, it remains on the record of the Houses of the Oireachtas and available unamended in the Leinster House library.

The Appeal Court had to further consider the action required as a consequence of my successful appeal. In March 2017, in further judgements delivered, the State's obligation to vindicate the good name of every citizen and protect it from attack, including mine, was referenced by the Court's President, Judge Ryan, who suggested that the State should arrange to redact offending content from the *Guerin Report* explaining such action as due to the court's judgement. This was merely a suggestion. The court essentially determined that any further action required to protect my reputation as a result of the court's decision was an issue to be resolved between me and the Government or, as expressed by Judge Finlay Geoghegan 'and any other person under whose control the Report continues to be published or public record maintained'. The court also made an order for costs against Sean Guerin.

Following the Court of Appeal's November 2016 decision one current Fine Gael Cabinet member, currently Tánaiste and Minister for Foreign Affairs and Trade, Simon Coveney, texted me. 'Well done today', the text read, 'a difficult legal process for you that should not have been necessary, your approach has been fully vindicated. I just wanted to say well done on a personal level.' We had sat beside each other for more than three years at Cabinet meetings. It was the first time he had communicated with me since my resignation from Cabinet in May 2014. Unfortunately, no such public comment was volunteered by him or by any former or current Cabinet member. A short time later Coveney was reported in the *Irish Examiner* as denying I was owed any apology by Enda Kenny for the manner in which I had been treated. It was an interesting and depressing insight into the prevailing ethos of today's Fine Gael.

In March 2017 those around me believed the saga was finally over and that, following my vindication by O'Higgins and the unanimous decision of the Appellate Court judges, there was little likelihood of Guerin appealing to the Supreme Court. I had my doubts and, unfortunately, I was right. An application by him to the Supreme Court for leave to appeal was granted in July 2017 and my court proceedings were destined to be placed in limbo and re-fought before the Supreme Court on 3 May 2018. Guerin remained intent on defending the indefensible and contending that I had no entitlement to challenge his flawed inquiry in the courts and his discredited criticism and condemnation of my conduct as Minister for Justice. In the meantime, the Court of Appeal's decision facilitated bringing my proceedings appealing against the Data Protection Commissioner's ruling to a sane conclusion.

On 11 May 2016, the day the *O'Higgins Report* was published, a man arrived at my home. When I opened our front door, I was handed a High Court Plenary Summons. The named Plaintiff was 'Michael Wallace' and, together with 'The Minister for Justice and Equality, Ireland and the Attorney General', I was a named defendant. The timing was exquisite. I thought it particularly ironic that on the very day the public learnt that the O'Higgins Commission had determined as spurious a plethora of false allegations, touted by Mick Wallace together with Opposition leaders and other TDs, which had destroyed my political career and public credibility, I should be served with court proceedings initiated by Wallace seeking damages. It was less than three months since I had lost my Dáil seat in the 2016 general election. The serving of the court writ left me in no doubt that the imbroglio I was involved in was not going away any time soon.

As a result of Judge Linnane's dismissal of my Circuit Court appeal against the Data Protection Commissioner's decision, Wallace was claiming aggravated or exemplary damages for breach of the Data Protection Acts and violation of his right to privacy. Checking the court summons, I discovered it had been issued almost a year earlier, on 15 May 2015, and that Wallace's Senior Counsel was Remy Farrell, the barrister who had viciously attacked and ridiculed me in an article published in the *Irish Independent* shortly after my Dáil speech criticising the *Guerin Report*.

If Judge Linnane's decision went unchallenged neither the State nor I had any defence to Wallace's claim for damages and the only outstanding issue would be 'how much'?

As Frances Fitzgerald, in her capacity as Minister for Justice, had not appealed Billy Hawkes's original decision, Wallace's claim could only completely fail if my appeal to the High Court was successful. I was considering not pursuing the Data Protection case any further. The Court of Appeal hearing in the Guerin case was only six weeks away. I believed the outcome of that appeal uncertain because of my Guerin High Court experience and the result of Data Protection Circuit Court Appeal. I had had enough of the courts, wanted to get on with my life and did not want to be imprisoned in a time warp and engaged in further litigation. But now Wallace had left me with no choice. Whether I processed the data appeal or not, the Data Protection issue was going to end up in the High Court.

My appeal to the High Court was the last line of defence to Wallace's claim and it was far too late for Frances Fitzgerald to reverse the decision made by her shortly after her appointment to Justice to not get involved. The Department was now involved whether she liked it or not. Like me, the State was at risk of having to pay financial damages to Wallace.

The High Court appeal in the Data Protection case was in hearing for four days commencing on 20 July 2017 before Judge Charles Meenan. It commenced just over three months after the finalisation of the Guerin proceedings in the Court of Appeal. Again, it was contended that I could not properly bring the appeal as the original decision made related to the Minister for Justice and I was no longer the Minister. However, Judge Meenan in his judgement delivered on 9 November 2017 rejected this contention, citing the judgements delivered by the Court of Appeal almost exactly a year earlier in the Guerin case and concluded I was entitled to challenge a decision that impacted on my good name and reputation. He then proceeded to conclude that Billy Hawkes had wrongly predetermined 'an important issue' in Wallace's complaint by concluding that the information furnished to me was 'data' which I had 'processed'. However, as I had 'acquiesced' in his determining the complaint and did not ask the Data Protection Commissioner to recuse himself, he ruled I could not rely on that issue in the appeal. This did not greatly matter as he entirely disagreed with Circuit Court Judge Linnane's perspective that the decision of the Data Protection Commissioner was not vitiated by any serious or significant error or series of errors.

Referring to the fact that in both his draft and final decision Hawkes had referenced the 'data' involved in Wallace's complaint as a 'written note', he stated that all Hawkes knew on the date of his decision was that the written note was in fact an email internal to the gardaí dated 11 January

2013 having 'been shown' it for the first time on the day of his final decision. He did not know who was the sender or recipient of the email and had neither obtained a copy of it nor furnished a copy to me. Hawkes not doing so, Judge Meenan ruled, violated 'fair procedures' as I had been 'deprived of an opportunity to make any observations or submissions concerning this central piece of evidence in the complaint'. He determined the procedures followed by the Data Protection Commissioner to be fundamentally flawed and that Hawkes's 'significant error' required the court to reverse the Circuit Court's decision.

But that was not all. Judge Meenan then proceeded to agree with submissions originally made to the Data Protection Commissioner in 2014 and repeated by my Senior Counsel, Eileen Barrington, in the Circuit Court hearing. The written note or email, he determined, comprised neither automated nor manual data as defined by the Data Protection legislation. The information contained in it was recorded neither on the Garda PULSE system nor in any filing system, so there was no evidential basis for Hawkes's conclusion that the email was 'data'. Neither, contrary to Hawkes's view, could I be regarded as a 'data controller' as it was 'difficult to see' how I 'could control the contents' of an email 'internal to An Garda Síochána'.

Having rejected the conclusion that I was a 'data controller', Judge Meenan noted that the Data Protection legislation provided that having found a person in breach of its provisions, such person may be required 'to block, rectify, erase or destroy any of the data concerned'.

How I could 'block, rectify, erase or destroy' information I remembered or, as was submitted to both Hawkes and the Circuit Court, 'information in my mind' was a major mystery. Was a lobotomy required or should I simply be ordered to shoot myself? Judge Meenan simply addressed this conundrum by stating: 'It is difficult to see how the appellant could comply with such request.'

The High Court essentially ruled that the Data Protection Commissioner had made a series of serious and significant errors and that Circuit Court Judge Linnane had 'erred in law' in holding that I lacked the standing 'to bring and maintain the appeal', in her finding that the Data Protection Commissioner followed fair procedures and in her application of the Data Protection Acts to Mick Wallace's complaint. My appeal was successful and an order for costs was made against the Data Protection Commissioner. Surprisingly, although a notice party to the appeal, neither Wallace nor his lawyers appeared to participate in it.

The result of both the Guerin and Hawkes appeal cases was an enormous relief. For those who in the future might have to address false allegations made against them, they shone a spotlight on how inquiries should be properly conducted and the importance of fair procedures. The Data Protection Act ruling ensures that in the future greater care will be taken in addressing complaints and that our data protection laws will be more carefully applied. It should also ensure no artificial barriers are erected which inhibit open communication between a Garda Commissioner, the Minister for Justice and various garda oversight bodies and that no artificial impediments exist to the communication or reporting of information that is in the public interest. It should also ensure that no Data Protection Commissioner in an interview again pre-judges a complaint that requires adjudication. The Guerin Appeal Court judgements, I knew, if upheld by the Supreme Court, should ensure that no one in the future will be unfairly and wrongly condemned by any individual or body conducting a preliminary or informal inquiry and fair procedures will be used in the conduct of such inquiry. It was my hope that the outcome of both cases would result in a lesson being learnt not only by politicians and journalists but also by those appointed to undertake important public duties about the danger of rushing to judgement and the injustice that can result. The likelihood of this hope being truly fulfilled as the seasons moved on from the summer of 2017 into the autumn and then the winter and the birth of a new year was for me entirely dependent on the outcome of Guerin's Supreme Court appeal.

The outcome of both appeals restored my faith in our courts' adherence to the rule of law and my belief that if you fight hard enough and persist truth can trump falsity. But I also recognised that, even with an unshakable belief in the value of truth and both the determination and resources to overcome obstacles and false narratives, there is no certainty the truth will ultimately prevail.

It would be untruthful to pretend that my joy at the Data case ending successfully and the Court of Appeal reversing the decision of Judge Noonan was not somewhat tainted by too many 'might have beens'. Had Guerin properly undertaken his inquiry and not rushed to judgement, I might not have been criticised by him, or become entangled in an investigation by the O'Higgins Commission and might have remained a member of Cabinet. Had Billy Hawkes not prejudged the complaint he received and properly applied Data Protection law, Mick Wallace's complaint would have been rejected, the allegation I had improperly used confidential garda information might have been discredited and Hawkes's ruling might not have negatively affected the perspective of Enda Kenny, Cabinet colleagues and others. Having been vindicated in 2014 by Judge Cooke, had I not been condemned by Hawkes and Guerin, Opposition politicians and the media might have backed off and let me get on with implementing my reform agenda, including some major reforms that remain outstanding to this day. Had I not lost both court cases in 2015, my reputation might have been at least partially restored and I might have retained my Dáil seat despite Enda Kenny's malign intervention in the electoral process. Had issues been addressed as they should have been, the champagne corks I am told were popped by some members of the Law Library on 7 May 2014 to celebrate my departure from Government would have remained in their bottles.

Of course, all of this is 'might have beenism', as in the febrile atmosphere of the time there is no guarantee that different and right outcomes would have substantially changed or prevented continuing false narratives about my villainy, arrogance and incompetence. While the *Irish Examiner* unexpectedly acknowledged in an editorial of 11 November 2016 that I 'was hounded from office because of public opinion driven by strident commentary – some from this newspaper' and that I had been vindicated, had things been addressed differently there is no certainty that the stridency of the critical media commentary would have in any way diminished or that the truth would have prevailed. I have learnt this as, through into 2018, whenever garda or Maurice McCabe-related controversy again arose, some involved in Irish media remained prone to revive, recycle and republish allegations established as false by the O'Higgins Commission and they continued to be regularly referred to on social media.

Curiously, publication of the *O'Higgins Report* did not result in any articles questioning how it came about that Guerin's conclusions about my ministerial conduct were so erroneous. It was also noticeable that few media outlets gave any major coverage to Judge Meenan's damning judicial exposure of the fundamentally flawed decision-making of Billy Hawkes as Data Commissioner. Despite his prejudging Wallace's complaint, utterly failing to properly apply the legislation he was appointed to administer and inflicting serious reputational damage on a member of Cabinet, few members of the public to this day know the extent to which he got it wrong. For example, Independent Newspapers, which trumpeted its original coverage, publishing Hawkes's confidential draft decision as a dramatic *Sunday Independent* front-page political scandal story, relegated Judge Meenan's High Court's decision to a five-sentence report on page ten of the *Irish Independent*. Unlike the *Irish Examiner* it did not engage in any public soul-searching. Not a single newspaper ran any detailed analysis or commentary piece on the High Court's decision. Nor was a single article published by the mainstream papers criticising Billy Hawkes's prejudgement of Wallace's complaint or demanding that he publicly explain his total failure to properly interpret and apply the Data Protection Act. The fact that his term as Data Commissioner had ended and he had retired in August 2014, shortly after my resignation from Government, did not render him unaccountable for his adjudication. It was also not an issue RTÉ's *Prime Time* felt the need to revisit despite the programme's central role at the very start of the story. Critical analysis of what had occurred and how Wallace's complaint was addressed by the Data Commissioner may have resulted in too many uncomfortable conclusions, contradicting a narrative that all of the media, both print and broadcast, had favoured, heavily invested in and revisited with some repetitive regularity in the too recent past.

Unfortunately, it seems that this saga is not yet completely over. Just two weeks before the Supreme Court was scheduled to deliver its judgement in Guerin's appeal and almost fifteen months after Judge Meenan in the High Court determined that his privacy rights under the Data Protection Act had not been violated, Mick Wallace unexpectedly revived the High Court action first initiated by him in 2015 against me personally and the Minister for Justice. His solicitors, in correspondence, stated he was no longer pursuing his claim for damages based on his right to privacy under the Data Protection Act being breached and served a Notice for Trial to process, as his lawyers described it, a claim for compensation for breaches of 'the right to privacy and a breach of confidence'. As I write this, it feels like *Groundhog Day*. Will it never end?

CHAPTER 41

Outside Looking In

When once you were in the grip of the Party, what you felt or did not feel, what you did or refrained from doing, made literally no difference. Whatever happened you vanished and neither you nor your actions were ever heard of again –George Orwell, *1984*

There is a general constitutional obligation to protect the good names and reputations of persons who may be the subject of untested allegations … People are entitled to fair procedures, justice and the proper way of doing things –Tánaiste and Minister for Justice and Equality Frances Fitzgerald rejecting Sinn Féin Deputy Leader Mary Lou McDonald's demand that Garda Commissioner Nóirín O'Sullivan 'step aside' pending allegations against her being investigated by Judge Peter Charleton, 9 February 2017

From the date of my resignation as a member of Cabinet in May 2014, I felt semi-detached from many of my Fine Gael colleagues in the parliamentary party. As I was fighting battles on a series of fronts they were understandably getting on with their lives and as time passed becoming focused on their personal prospects in the next general election and their own election campaigns. As a member of the party I continued to attend some parliamentary party meetings and Fine Gael and local meetings in my own constituency. In September 2015 I started my own personal campaigning, leaflet drops and door knocking. I had little enthusiasm for it before publication of the *Fennelly Report* that month and following its publication I remained weighed down and distracted by the O'Higgins Commisssion, the ongoing court proceedings, the constant media recycling of my alleged villainy and incompetence, and repetition of Guerin's criticism. In the immediate aftermath of my resignation none of my former colleagues in Cabinet, no member of the Oireachtas or any media commentator was prepared to consider that either McCabe in his allegations or Guerin in his report could have got anything wrong. A whole body of work was being undertaken with the *Guerin Report* as its foundation stone on the assumption that the totality of his opinions and conclusions could be relied upon.

I doubted any value was attached to anything I said at parliamentary party meetings and I was deeply frustrated by the slowdown in my reform agenda. I watched as some important legislation I had drafted and fought for was dropped, including legislation addressing the issue of surrogacy and providing legal rules and a mechanism to determine the legal parentage of a surrogate child. Legislation to establish separate and independent family courts, to radically reform and modernise our gambling laws, to require the mandatory disclosure of medical error and to comprehensively reform our emigration laws was abandoned and enactment of the Legal Services Regulation Bill was delayed and some of its provisions diluted. However, over time it became clear that although delayed, Justice officials were continuing to work on many legislative measures I had initiated and that Frances Fitzgerald and later, her successor at Justice, Charlie Flanagan, were adhering to a substantial part of my reform agenda. The enactment of the Children and Family Law Reform Act in 2015, albeit omitting the issue of surrogacy, was an important follow-up to the Children's Rights referendum and a crucial but late prelude to the Marriage Equality referendum. Its passage through both Houses of the Oireachtas made the many early morning hours and the holiday time I had spent in preparing a very detailed first draft of the Bill and the time spent discussing it with Justice officials and officials in the Attorney General's office worthwhile. The reforms contained in it were centrally focused on protecting the best interests of children during family breakdown, clarifying parental rights and obligations and recognising the true diversity of Irish family life.

In the autumn of 2013, I had secured the Cabinet's agreement to my proposal that the Marriage Equality referendum recommended by the Constitutional Convention be held in the first half of 2015. Support for the proposal from Labour Cabinet Ministers was not in doubt as, prior to the Cabinet meeting, Eamon Gilmore had asserted Labour's determination that the referendum take place. I was uncertain of the stance of some Fine Gael Cabinet colleagues, including the Taoiseach and Leo Varadkar, but the proposal received general support. I was determined that the proposed constitutional reform would succeed. Sidelined by Fine Gael central, in April and May 2015 I threw myself into campaigning for a majority 'Yes' vote in my constituency and enjoyed the company of an enthusiastic and optimistic band of mostly gay canvassers with whom I knocked on doors, together with Jane Lehane, who was then working as my parliamentary assistant in Leinster House. The campaign was a great distraction from the Commissions of Investigation and court cases as was the victory celebration on the day of the count. There was a joyous, somewhat chaotic and irreverent celebration of the referendum's successful outcome in The George pub on Dublin's South Great George's Street. TV3 was there to broadcast a referendum count show hosted by an elated and normally irascible Vincent Browne. It will always remain with me as a beautiful memory of the day. It was difficult to fight back the tears of joy as my Fine Gael colleague Jerry Buttimer and I were jointly interviewed, knowing the 'Yes' side had won. Thank you Vincent and TV3.

Those interviewed on Vincent's programme that afternoon included Oireachtas members who fought for constitutional change at a time when it was politically hazardous to do so. Some sections of the political media obsessed on Leo Varadkar who had come out as gay in January 2015 when the pioneering, openly gay Leinster House political hero was Independent Senator David Norris followed by then Senator Katherine Zappone and her then partner and sadly deceased spouse Ann Gilligan, Fine Gael's Jerry Buttimer and Labour Party TDs Dominic Hannigan and John Lyons. A week after the referendum Carol and I had a great and memorable party in our home for all of those with whom Jane and I had canvassed. Carol had been unable to canvass because of a knee problem, which was only later resolved by a partial knee replacement.

When in Leinster House, other than turning up in the Dáil chamber to vote, I had a minimal role. My position was similar to that of many backbenchers and I remained, to a degree, on the inside looking out. When I lost my Dáil seat in February 2016 I became a non-person as far as the movers and shakers in Fine Gael were concerned. There was no offer of a Taoiseach's appointment to the Seanad as made to some other former colleagues who had lost Dáil seats and no opportunity or invitation to positively use my expertise to the Party's or the country's benefit. Despite my chairing meetings of both EU Justice and Defence Ministers during Ireland's Presidency of the EU in 2013, attending EU Council of Ministers meetings for over three years, during the Presidency initiating a number of important new EU initiatives in both the Justice and Defence areas and just prior to my resignation being asked to chair regular meetings of the European People's Party Justice Ministers, no invitations arrived to attend any of the Government's consultative meetings on Brexit. For personal psychotherapy before the complexities of the Brexit issue were fully generally understood, I wrote an article on the subject published by *The Irish Times* and a year later a prescient letter that the paper published correctly predicting approaching difficulties. Neither generated any interest and, politically impotent, I fulminated at home. I recognised that my personal credibility as even a political commentator had been totally destroyed by Guerin's conclusions and the widespread perception that I had not only ignored Maurice McCabe's concerns but had also been intent on doing him down and covering up garda wrongdoing. As my battles continued, I was firmly on the outside looking in.

As I awaited the Court of Appeal's judgement in the Guerin case, new Maurice McCabe-related controversies arose and two others were revived. The *Irish Examiner*'s Michael Clifford reported on 4 October 2016 that 'two senior Gardai' had made allegations under the Protected Disclosures legislation that senior garda management had engaged in a concerted campaign to destroy the character of a garda whistle-blower. Clifford, in a commentary piece published in the paper the same day, assumed all the allegations to be true, calling them 'revelations'. He asserted that the 'two Protected Disclosures alleging the maltreatment of a whistleblower suggests that little has changed'. The disclosures had been given to then Tánaiste and Minister for Justice Frances Fitzgerald the previous day and although supposed to be confidential became an instant focus for contentious Dáil exchanges and media controversy.

It rapidly became known that the disclosures were made by Superintendent David Taylor who, while I was Minister for Justice, was head of the Garda Press Office, and Sergeant Maurice McCabe. The whistle-blower alleged to be the victim of the alleged campaign was McCabe. It was also reported that those accused were former Garda Commissioner, Martin Callinan and the then Commissioner, Nóirín O'Sullivan. Taylor had 'confessed' to McCabe that he had engaged in the campaign and he alleged he had done so as Press Officer under the direction of Callinan with the knowledge of O'Sullivan. Clifford had met both Taylor and McCabe. In his biography of McCabe published in September 2017, Clifford synopsised what allegedly occurred. According to Clifford, Taylor told McCabe that the alleged campaign included the sending of 'hundreds, if not thousands, of text messages to media and Garda personnel casting McCabe in a bad light'.

The day of Clifford's first article revealing the alleged campaign, Fianna Fáil leader Micheál Martin demanded in the Dáil a 'dramatic response from the government' in relation to the 'character assassination' of whistle-blowers who he claimed had been 'strategically undermined and under attack'. In response, Taoiseach Enda Kenny voiced the concern necessary to appease the media and to meet the political demands of the moment stating his 'determination' to deal 'properly' with the protected disclosures. Careful examination of the credibility of the allegations made and investigation into the background was not required before Micheál Martin alleged 'a very high level of wrongdoing' and another media frenzy erupted, with Clifford playing a prominent role.

Within days, on 7 October 2016, the Government announced that a review would be conducted into the allegations, by retired High Court Judge Iarfhlaith O'Neill. In a statement, Frances Fitzgerald stated the importance of the claims of those making the disclosures 'being properly addressed'. She did not detail the nature of the claims but they had been referred to by Clifford in articles and broadcast interviews and then repeated by other journalists and media commentators. As a result, O'Sullivan, as Garda Commissioner, was repetitively pilloried both inside and outside the Dáil. By 7 December 2016 O'Neill had completed his review and furnished his report to Fitzgerald. He meticulously followed fair procedures, sought and obtained responses to allegations made and stated that he could reach no conclusions through the informal review he had conducted because of 'conflicting accounts from key witnesses'. Both Callinan and O'Sullivan had denied the allegations made by Taylor and McCabe. O'Neill recommended that a further Commission of Investigation be established.

Nothing inappropriate had ever been said to me about McCabe by Callinan, O'Sullivan or by Taylor who I had met on occasions when Callinan and I were jointly engaged in media briefings or events which generated media interest. Watching events from the outside, the differences between the approach of O'Neill compared to Guerin were stark. O'Neill, like Guerin, was given a specific number of weeks to conduct his much less complex review. He sought extra time and Fitzgerald agreed. He gave all concerned the opportunity to respond to allegations made against them. His report contained no adverse conclusions damaging to any party. It simply recommended that a sworn Commission of Investigation was required to resolve conflicting accounts of events. The approach to the allegations by Taoiseach Enda Kenny, Fitzgerald and other Government Ministers was also markedly different to what I had personally experienced.

On 5 October 2016, the day after the allegations were first raised in the Dáil by Micheál Martin, Deputies Clare Daly and Mick Wallace, who it would later emerge had also met Taylor and maintained ongoing contact with McCabe, led the charge in calling for the resignation of Nóirín O'Sullivan. Sinn Féin's Deputy leader, Mary Lou McDonald, called for her to 'stand aside'. Enda Kenny in response to McDonald expressed his confidence in both O'Sullivan and in Fitzgerald, who was also subject to criticism.

Some Opposition Dáil deputies were back in kangeroo court mode and in search of a head. In response to escalating controversy, O'Sullivan issued a statement that she 'was not privy to nor approved of' any action targeting a garda officer. Fitzgerald resisted pressure to instantly condemn O'Sullivan. On 6 October 2016, rightly stating that the Protected Disclosures legislation prevented her from commenting on the allegations made to her, Fitzgerald told the Dáil:

> It is vitally important that the claims people make in such disclosures are properly addressed. However, this must be done in a way that is fair, proper, just and within the rule of law. It would be a cruel irony if a system that was introduced to deal with wrongdoing were to lead us in turn to do wrong to people. Everyone is entitled to his or her good name unless it can be fairly and objectively shown that he or she had been involved in wrongdoing.

A little later she stated:

> I do not believe it is right for anyone to rush to judgement about these matters. It offends all the principles of fairness for conclusions to be drawn on the basis of claims against persons which have not been properly tested or where those who have had claims made against them have not had a chance to tell their side of the story.

Fitzgerald detailing her totally correct principled approach to the protected disclosures received by her, having ignored my criticism of the *Guerin Report*, as I awaited the Court of Appeal decision in the Guerin case was, for me, a particular irony and source of irritation.

Pending completion by Judge Iarfhlaith O'Neill of his review, the Taoiseach and Fitzgerald were repetitively asked whether O'Sullivan retained their confidence. Their consistent and correct response and that of other Cabinet Ministers, including Leo Varadkar, likely derived from an official briefing note, was to refer to the importance of fair procedures and a fair hearing. After the Court of Appeal's decision in my proceedings against Guerin, the phraseology used by them echoed the phraseology contained in the judgement of the Court's President, Judge Sean Ryan. Following receipt of O'Neill's report, Fitzgerald announced that, because of the allegations contained in it and 'the fact that third parties are mentioned', she was seeking the Attorney General's advice 'as to what material might properly be put into the public domain, having regard to the rights of all concerned'. Two months later, in February 2017, when announcing the terms of reference for establishing a commission of investigation, the Government also announced that the *O'Neill Report* would not be published 'because of the nature of the allegations contained in it'. A statement issued stated simply that the *O'Neill Report* had recorded that allegations of serious wrongdoing had been made against Callinan and O'Sullivan which they 'wholly denied' and that an 'inquiry should be established immediately to ascertain the truth or falsity of these allegations'.

Quite correctly no criticism was voiced, uncertainties expressed, pejorative comment made by O'Neill about anyone, nor published by Government. The Government's approach was clearly heavily influenced by the Court of Appeal's judgement in my case against Guerin. On the day the Dáil was scheduled to debate the terms of reference for the Commission of Investigation, which Frances Fitzgerald announced would be chaired by Supreme Court Judge, Peter Charleton, Sinn Fein's Mary Lou McDonald once again asked Fitzgerald whether she retained confidence in Garda Commissioner Nóirín O'Sullivan and whether she would ask the Commissioner to 'stand aside for the duration of the Commission's Investigation'. This was consistent with the Shinners' approach to shoot first and ask questions later. Fitzgerald gave her short shrift, responding that she did not believe there was any reason for anyone to stand aside and rightly asserted 'that people are entitled to fair procedures, justice and the proper way of doing things'. Later that day in the Dáil, Fianna Fáil's spokesperson on Justice and Equality, Jim O'Callaghan, essentially agreed with Fitzgerald on the importance of fair procedures and, upon allegations being made, individuals being entitled to defend themselves. This was very different to my personal experience in 2014 of the perspective and actions of both Fine Gael's Kenny and Fitzgerald and the leadership of Fianna Fáil. Of course, O'Callaghan was first elected to the Dáil in February 2016 and was not a TD when I was a Cabinet member. However, a year later O'Callaghan would adopt a different approach towards Fitzgerald when another McCabe-related controversy blew up.

At the same time as the Government correctly declined to publish the *O'Neill Report*, Kenny was ignoring my solicitors' requests that the un-amended *Guerin Report* as placed in the Oireachtas library be withdrawn and a statement made in the Dáil chamber correcting the Dáil record in so far as it contained commentary replicating or validating criticism of my conduct as a member of Cabinet directly derived from Guerin's discredited conclusions. While the report was removed from the Government's website, Kenny had no difficulty with the falsities contained in it remaining available to read and regularly regurgitated online and by the media. He felt no obligation to expressly acknowledge, on the Dáil record, that Guerin's questioning of my Ministerial competence and his criticisms were mistaken, to apologise for their consequences and for entirely ignoring the concerns I had expressed about the report. He was, of course, under no political or media pressure from anyone to do so.

The day after the Government announced its intention to establish a further Commission of Investigation, on 8 February 2017, another McCabe-related controversy arose. Labour leader, Brendan Howlin, claimed in the Dáil that he had been told by an unnamed journalist that the journalist 'had direct knowledge of calls made by the Garda Commissioner to journalists during 2013 and 2014' during which 'the Commissioner made very serious allegations of sexual crimes having been committed by Sergeant Maurice McCabe'.

The Garda Commissioner Howlin referred to was Nóirín O'Sullivan, who speedily denied the allegation. Although Howlin acknowledged that he did not know whether the charges made against O'Sullivan were 'true or not' he commented that 'if it was a fact that the Garda Commissioner was in direct contact with the media making allegations against one of her own officers … it would be quite extraordinary'. Broadcast and online media went into overdrive reporting Howlin's explosive Dáil intervention and O'Sullivan was again called upon to either stand aside or resign. Sixteen months later, by June 2018, it would be clearly established that Howlin had entirely relied on what he claimed he was told by Alison O'Reilly, an *Irish Mail on Sunday* reporter, for the allegation; that she had no 'direct' knowledge of any such calls; that her information was based on alleged conversations with a colleague and friend, the *Mail on Sunday*'s crime correspondent, Debbie McCann, who denied any phone conversations of any nature had taken place between her and Nóirín O'Sullivan during the relevant period; that no such calls could be identified from a trawl of Nóirín O'Sullivan's phone records; that a dispute existed between McCann and O'Reilly as to the content of conversations in which they engaged; that O'Reilly had said nothing to Howlin of any such alleged calls being made by O'Sullivan to any other journalists and that Howlin did nothing to independently verify what he claimed he was told.

The day after the Howlin-generated drama, Michael Clifford of the *Irish Examiner* and Katie Hannon on RTÉ's *Prime Time* reported that in August 2013 a false allegation of serious child sexual abuse made against McCabe was contained in a HSE Counselling Agency Report furnished to its Children and Family Services Department. On 1 January 2014, the department and its staff transferred to TUSLA, the Child and Family Agency. The report was forwarded by TUSLA in May 2014 to An Garda Síochána. The information in the report was said to be a 'clerical error'. The 'error' was only discovered in mid-May 2014, a couple of weeks after the report was furnished to the gardaí. It was claimed that neither the allegation nor the 'error' was then disclosed to McCabe, although it was known to 'senior' Garda officers. The serious sexual abuse alleged against McCabe, which included an allegation of digital rape, had never occurred. Despite recognition of the error, in reliance on the original report, a TUSLA social worker had sent a letter at the end of December 2015 to McCabe informing him the allegation was being investigated. It was only upon receipt of the letter on 5 January 2016 that he first learnt of it. McCabe denied the allegation, informing TUSLA of an incident that occurred in 2006. In that year an accusation had been made by the young teenage daughter of a garda colleague that, eight years earlier, she had been a victim of sexually inappropriate behaviour by McCabe. The allegation had been investigated, no crime of any kind had been disclosed, the file was furnished to the DPP who directed there was no basis in fact or in law for any prosecution and the matter was closed. In the summer of 2013 the girl, who became known as Ms D, had sought counselling. The counsellor who composed a report on their meeting, using an earlier unrelated report as a template, had retained in her report information relating to an entirely different case containing allegations unconnected to either Ms D or McCabe. When seeking counselling, Ms D had clearly stated she did not want her complaint re-opened. It was not until June 2016 that McCabe was told a mistake had been made. By the time the story publicly emerged in February 2017 McCabe had been in contact with and privately met the Children's Minister Katherine Zappone to complain about the conduct of TUSLA who subsequently acknowledged in a letter to Zappone that TUSLA 'did not meet the high standards set for the service and intended to apologise to Mr McCabe'. Both the HSE and TUSLA apologised to McCabe who initially was reported as rejecting their apologies.

Whether the 'error' resulted from negligence or incompetence or was a deliberate attempt to smear McCabe and was the result of a conspiracy between employees of TUSLA and members of An Garda Síochána became a major issue, as did the origin of the story. Without any facts to substantiate the allegation, the conspiracy theory was the one predictably favoured and advocated by most commentators and Opposition TDs. The 'protected disclosures' of Taylor and McCabe complicated the background. So did an allegation first made in May 2016, after publication of the *O'Higgins Report*, by Fianna Fáil Deputy and former chairman of the Public Accounts Committee, John McGuinness, that former Garda Commissioner Martin Callinan had made 'vile' allegations to him about McCabe when they met, at Callinan's ill-advised request, in January 2014, in the car park of the Bewley's Hotel, Newlands Cross, in Dublin. An added factor was the revival of an allegation that McCabe had been badly treated and pilloried by counsel representing Garda Commissioner, Nóirín O'Sullivan, before the O'Higgins Commission. This allegation was based on the leaked content of selective extracts from transcripts of the Commission's confidential hearings that had been furnished by an anonymous source to McCabe's biographer and journalist Michael Clifford and first published by the *Irish Examiner* on 13 May 2016, just two days after publication of the *O'Higgins Report*. The extracts published had fuelled a public perception that McCabe had been wronged during the Commission's hearings and, because selective, did not accurately fully reflect events before the O'Higgins Commission.

Following it all from the outside looking in, as yet another predictable political and media tumult and frenzy erupted, I presumed a foul up by both the HSE and TUSLA and no conspiracy. Reference to the 'clerical error' and later to an 'administrative error' alleging serious child sexual abuse deriving from 'a report template' which was 'cut and pasted' into another report solidified my view. However, past events foretold that there cannot be a McCabe-related controversy involving allegations of corruption or conspiracy without an accompanying political crisis. It arrived on cue.

CHAPTER 42

Enda Kenny Resigns

I might say mea culpa as I did say and I am guilty here of not giving accurate information, I understood from thinking myself that I had, that she had asked me about meeting Sergeant McCabe in the first place. It actually was her office that consulted with my officials who told me –An Taoiseach Enda Kenny admitting, somewhat incoherently, in the Dáil that he spoke inaccurately in a radio interview when fabricating a conversation that never took place with Minister for Children Katherine Zappone

Over the weekend following the TUSLA revelations it was reported that, at the Cabinet meeting the previous Tuesday in which the creation of the Charleton Commission of Investigation was discussed, the Minister for Children, Katherine Zappone had not informed Cabinet members that she had met Lorraine and Maurice McCabe on 25 January 2017 and of her knowledge of the TUSLA debacle. While it was understood that both Taoiseach Enda Kenny and Justice Minister Frances Fitzgerald had been informed of her intention to meet the McCabes, it was also believed that she had not briefed them on her discussion with them. The conduct of Zappone, why she withheld information from her Cabinet colleagues and who said what to whom and when, was put under a media and political microscope. For some it became of greater importance than the fact that the HSE and TUSLA had seriously screwed up.

Both Kenny and Fitzgerald stated they knew nothing of the TUSLA issue until the *Prime Time* revelations, two days after the Cabinet agreed to the setting up of the Charleton Commission of Investigation. On RTÉ Radio's *This Week* Sunday news programme Kenny acknowledged that Zappone had informed him she intended to meet the McCabes and claimed that upon her doing so he told her 'If you do have a meeting make sure you have a thorough note of it.' Within twenty-four hours it became clear that Zappone had merely notified the Taoiseach's office of the intended meeting and no conversation about it had occurred between them before it took place. Under media pressure on the Monday, following a Zappone press briefing, Kenny then acknowledged he was mistaken in referring to a conversation that never happened. He also accepted, as stated by Zappone, that prior to the Cabinet meeting Zappone had mentioned to him her meeting with McCabe and had informed him that false allegations of sexual abuse made against McCabe had been received by TUSLA without revealing the full details of what had occurred. The exact details were withheld, it was said, to preserve confidentiality and initially there was some confusion as to whether TUSLA had even been mentioned. A central issue was whether the extraordinary conduct of HSE and TUSLA employees fell within the proposed Charleton Commission of Investigation's terms of reference. Zappone stated she had been assured by Kenny that it did, even though Kenny did not know what TUSLA had done.

Under questioning in the Dáil on the Tuesday, 14 February 2017, Kenny acknowledged he was guilty of not giving accurate information when referring to his fictitious conversation with Zappone prior to her meeting the McCabes, acknowledged that the conversation he had referred to on RTÉ's *This Week* had not taken place and expressed a 'mea culpa'. As a result, the Dáil exchanges that day addressed not only the HSE and TUSLA foul up or, as some insisted, TUSLA's conspiracy with the gardaí to blacken McCabe's name, but also communications between Kenny and Zappone and how the Government had dealt with the issue.

To add to the complexity of it all, on the evening of Monday, 13 February 2017, Maurice McCabe and his wife Lorraine issued a four-page statement entitled *Truth Today – Justice To Follow*. In it they demanded a public inquiry and rejected the Government's proposal to establish a further Commission of Investigation. They did not want, they said, 'another Commission of Inquiry' [sic] conducting 'a secret investigation behind closed doors' and producing a report into which they would have 'no input as of right'. In so far as this assertion implied that Maurice McCabe had been deprived of his right to make input into the deliberations of the O'Higgins Commission it was an extraordinary misrepresentation of how the Commission had conducted its business. McCabe had given evidence to the Commission and been represented throughout the Commission's hearings by his legal team lead by Michael McDowell SC. His legal team had cross-examined witnesses and made extensive submissions. A draft of the *O'Higgins Commission Report* had been furnished to him to submit amendments to it and the draft report had been amended as a result of his lawyer's intervention.

The McCabes' statement also claimed that throughout the proceedings before that Commission, Maurice at the hands of the legal team representing the current Commissioner was cast in the role of culprit or defendant, and as a person making those complaints in bad faith and without cause. The McCabes stated that when challenged the 'legal team' confirmed they were acting on the Commissioner's – that is Nóirín O'Sullivan's, 'personal instruction' and accused O'Sullivan of claiming 'in public to be supportive of us while seeking in private to discredit Maurice McCabe before the O'Higgins Commission'. This selective depiction of the O'Higgins Commission's proceedings painted a limited and distorted picture of the hearings that took place before it. The statement also wrongly asserted that during the O'Higgins Commission's hearings lawyers representing Garda Commissioner Nóirín O'Sullivan, had 'repeatedly' attempted to introduce in the proceedings the 'entirely false allegation made of sexual abuse in 2006 against Maurice ... for the purpose of discrediting his motives and testimony'.

The McCabes' statement was perceived in both political and media circles as adding to the perception of McCabe being wrongly treated and traduced during the O'Higgins Commission's proceedings as originally fuelled by the leaking by an unnamed source to Michael Clifford in May 2016 of the selective extracts from the O'Higgins hearings transcript. It resulted in Fianna Fáil leader Micheál Martin that night visiting McCabe and his family in their home and informing the Dáil the next day that he had 'no doubt' that 'there was an attempt and a campaign to undermine the integrity of Maurice McCabe because he was proving to be a major thorn in the side of senior people within An Garda Síochána or on foot of the fact that he was raising issues that have been subsequently vindicated by a Commission of Investigation'. Martin asserted, without qualification, that the 'lethal aspect of all of this is the fact that the [TUSLA] Report ... was used to fundamentally undermine the integrity of Maurice McCabe'.

Referring to the O'Higgins Commission and repeating McCabe's call for a Tribunal of Inquiry, Martin criticised the Commission, asserting that it 'was conducted in an unacceptable manner' and described the McCabes' experience before it as 'shocking, with the kitchen sink and all thrown at them by senior counsel representing the Garda Commissioner' – that is, Nóirín O'Sullivan.

Fianna Fáil promptly withdrew its support for the minority coalition Government's proposed Commission of Investigation and demanded the establishment of a Tribunal of Inquiry that would hold public hearings. As the Government formed after the 2016 general election was entirely dependent on Fianna Fáil's support to remain in office and did not want to be involved in any conflict with the McCabes, Enda Kenny rapidly agreed. The Cabinet and the entire Dáil and Seanad supported the establishment of the Tribunal sought. Prior to its creation no member of Government or Opposition TD gave any consideration to the full transcript of the O'Higgins hearings first being inspected to ascertain whether McCabe's complaints about his treatment before the Commission stood up. It was apparently enough that he asserted that his 'comments' could 'easily be verified' by inspecting it.

What was to be the Charleton Commission of Investigation became the Disclosures Tribunal of Inquiry chaired by Supreme Court Judge Peter Charleton. Its name derived from the fact that the major issues it had to address originated with the protected disclosures made by Superintendent David Taylor and Sergeant Maurice McCabe in the early autumn of 2017. On the day of its creation by orders of both Houses of the Oireachtas, Michael McDowell, who had been elected to the Seanad in 2016 and who as a Senior Counsel had for a number of years represented and advised McCabe, in two Seanad contributions joined the chorus of those demanding that Garda Commissioner Nóirín O'Sullivan step aside 'temporarily' until the Tribunal reported. In calling on her to step aside, he acknowledged that 'due to professional duties of confidentiality and professional rules on privacy' he had been unable to publicly comment on 'the demonisation of Sergeant McCabe and his family' and excused his intervention as fulfilling his constitutional and statutory duties as a member of the Oireachtas on the proposal to establish the Tribunal. Having regard to his professional engagement with McCabe and the likelihood he would both represent him before the Tribunal and cross-examine Nóirín O'Sullivan before it, as ultimately occurred, I regarded McDowell's Seanad intervention as totally inappropriate. While alleging the 'demonisation' of McCabe he was contributing to the 'demonisation' of O'Sullivan.

By the beginning of 2017, if not sooner, the delicacy of engaging with allegations made and issues raised by Maurice McCabe and the fear of critical media commentary and public opprobrium had resulted in the stage being reached whereby McCabe was, on garda-related issues he raised or those connected to him, determining the response and actions of the Government, all Opposition parties and all Oireachtas members. No one was prepared, where possible, to check the accuracy of any statement he issued or resist any demand he made for fear of adverse personal political consequences. The financial consequences to the State of a Tribunal of Inquiry instead of a less costly Commission of Investigation or the impact of unsubstantiated allegations made on the lives of others and on the capacity of senior Garda officers to fulfil their myriad of duties had long ceased to matter. No lessons of any nature had been learned from the fact that the O'Higgins Commission had concluded that some of McCabe's complaints were exaggerated, others unfounded or made without a scintilla of evidence and had recorded that some of long duration were simply withdrawn during the Commission's hearings.

The controversy and accompanying media and political frenzy, which included an unsuccessful Dáil motion tabled by Sinn Féin of 'no confidence' in the Government, generated fears amongst Fine Gael TDs of an accidental early general election. Fine Gael's 2016 general election campaign had been a political disaster and Kenny's leadership of it abysmal. It had for some time been understood that Kenny would step down well in advance of the next election and Fine Gael TDs had no wish for him to lead them into another election campaign. Kenny's invented conversation with Zappone as recounted by him on RTÉ's *This Week* was for some the last straw. Anonymous Fine Gael TDs were reported as predicting his leadership was coming to an end and political pundits predicted he would resign within weeks. On 17 May 2017 he announced he was resigning as leader of Fine Gael at midnight. He remained Taoiseach until 14 June 2017 when he was replaced by Leo Varadkar, who twelve days earlier had been elected leader of the Fine Gael party.

Watching it all from the outside looking in I thought it both extraordinary and ironic that Kenny was forced to fall on his sword primarily as a result of an unnecessary invented parable of an imagined McCabe-related conversation with the Minister for Children. I could not fathom why he had invented the conversation as there was no political necessity or benefit in his doing so. As far as I was concerned it was not the first time that he was 'guilty of not giving accurate information'. It was just that this time, on a detail of no or minimal consequence, it had caught up with him. In the overall circumstances, whether Kenny had or had not advised Zappone to take notes at her meeting with the McCabes was a thing of monumental irrelevance blown out of all proportion. But it was not the only irrelevant issue related to the McCabe political and media narrative, destined to be blown out of all proportion before the end of 2017.

CHAPTER 43

The Resignations of Nóirín O'Sullivan and Frances Fitzgerald

When allegations are made against an individual and the individual in question denies those allegations, that individual has a constitutional right to his good name. We do not hear much about that right but it is a right that has meaning. It is not an anachronistic right. That means an individual who denies allegations is entitled to defend himself against those allegations –Deputy Jim O'Callaghan, Fianna Fáil's spokesperson on Justice and Equality, stating that he was not calling for Garda Commissioner O'Sullivan to step aside or resign, 9 February 2017

Following the Disclosures Tribunal commencing its work, the final report of the Fennelly Commission was published on 6 April 2017 and a series of new garda-related controversies occurred. The garda issues included the revelation that gardaí had between 2011 and 2016 falsely reported over 1.9 million bogus alcohol breathalyser tests and, unconnected to the breathalyser revelation, had also secured approximately 14,700 Road Traffic convictions against motorists wrongly summoned to court. The latter were the result of gross administrative dysfunction, which exceeded the level of dysfunction involved in the ticket charge/penalty points controversy, with greater consequences. On this issue, however, no one alleged corruption, widespread criminality or perversion of the course of justice. Ultimately, procedures had to be put in place to have convictions wrongly obtained set aside. The bogus breathalyser tests reported were the result of dishonesty, gross dereliction of duty, irresponsibility and inadequate oversight and supervision. Revelation of both of these matters was rapidly followed by the uncovering of serious financial irregularities in the Garda Training College in Templemore and major new questions arising about the accuracy of garda data and crime statistics. This all resulted in further pressure on Garda Commissioner, Nóirín O'Sullivan, predictions that her position was becoming untenable and generated more political controversy.

When Leo Varadkar's Cabinet was appointed, Frances Fitzgerald moved out of the Department of Justice and Equality and became Tánaiste and Minister for Business, Enterprise and Innovation. It seemed at that point that she had politically survived her time in Justice. She was replaced in Justice by Charlie Flanagan, who had been Minister for Foreign Affairs. Máire Whelan's nomination to the Court of Appeal was agreed by Cabinet at Kenny's final Cabinet meeting the previous day and generated some brief controversy. Six days later Whelan was pictured at the ceremony in Áras an Uachtaráin in which she swore the judicial oath sitting beside President Michael D Higgins and new Taoiseach Leo Varadkar. She took up her position as a member of the Court of Appeal and the political world and the media rapidly moved on to other business. It is highly unlikely that in any other European democracy an individual would be appointed to a senior judicial position so soon after the conclusion of a Commission of Investigation detailing the conduct and poor judgement attributed to Whelan by the *Fennelly Report*.

As the Disclosures Tribunal continued its work, various investigations were initiated and Oireachtas hearings took place relating to the spring 2017 revelations of new garda failures, dysfunction and incompetence accompanied by more calls for Nóirín O'Sullivan to step aside or resign as Garda Commissioner. On 10 September 2017, she announced her early retirement stating that the 'unending cycle' of investigations and inquiries were taking up the 'vast majority of [her] time' and impeding her implementing 'deep cultural and structural reform' of the garda organisation, rectifying past failures and meeting 'obvious policing and security challenges'. Then in November 2017, a Sergeant McCabe-related political controversy reignited with a new twist, accompanied by the inevitable political and media frenzy and Government crises.

McCabe alleged in February 2017 that he had been wrongly treated by Garda Commissioner Nóirín O'Sullivan and her legal team during the O'Higgins Commission hearings. It was further alleged by Micheál Martin that Frances Fitzgerald, when Justice Minister, knew of and passively acquiesced in what Martin referenced as the 'adversarial strategy' of the Garda Commissioner before the O'Higgins Commission. McCabe had claimed in his February 2017 statement that 'the entirely false allegation of sexual abuse' made against him in 2006 'was repeatedly the subject of attempts at introduction in the [O'Higgins] proceedings for the purpose of discrediting his motives and testimony'. This resurfaced and Micheál Martin alleged that Fitzgerald by failing to intervene had given An Garda Síochána 'free rein' and 'allowed' them to 'undermine' McCabe's credibility by relying on an allegation made against him rejected by the DPP. He accused her of 'a fundamental failure to protect a man' who 'was wronged on several occasions by this State'. Nóirín O'Sullivan having resigned, Frances Fitzgerald was the primary target and yet again the fear loomed of the Government falling and an unexpected general election.

What advance knowledge Fitzgerald and Justice officials had of O'Sullivan's alleged strategy before the O'Higgins Commission and the action, if any, taken by her became the dominant political story for over two weeks and occupied substantial Dáil time. It was repeatedly alleged that McCabe's character and integrity had been wrongly and maliciously attacked by the Garda Commissioner's legal representatives before the O'Higgins Commission and that there was a conspiracy to smear him and destroy his reputation. Dáil questions tabled by Labour TD, Alan Kelly, lit the fuse that created the controversy which trespassed on territory to be examined by Judge Charleton's Disclosures Tribunal. Labour leader Brendan Howlin alleged there had been a legal strategy to 'go after' McCabe and asked when this was known by Fitzgerald and her successor at Justice, Charlie Flanagan. The 'go after' McCabe allegation replicated the false accusation to which I had been previously subjected.

Taoiseach Leo Varadkar asserted that Fitzgerald had informed him that she 'had no hand, act or part in' nor any prior knowledge of the alleged strategy of the former Garda Commissioner's legal team and that she first found out about it 'around the time' it was first in the public domain, that is, after publication by the Government of the *O'Higgins Report* in May 2016. Flanagan also knew nothing of it having only been appointed Minister for Justice the previous June, over a year after publication of the *O'Higgins Report*. Officials in the Department of Justice, Varadkar stated, first learned of the strategy after McCabe's cross-examination before the O'Higgins Commission concluded. The phraseology used by him, denying any earlier knowledge of the strategy within the Department, implied for some that he accepted that a strategy intent on damaging McCabe in fact had been deployed before the Commission. A week later Varadkar had to correct the information first given by him.

He informed the Dáil that the previous evening he had been given a copy of an email exchanged between two Justice officials describing a conversation one of them had with an official in the Attorney General's office concerning a dispute that had occurred before the O'Higgins Commission. He also acknowledged that the email had been received before McCabe was cross-examined but after the O'Higgins Commission had in 2015 commenced its hearings. Fitzgerald had forgotten the email, which had been sent to her for information only. (It later emerged that the Justice official who circulated the email was Michael Flahive, who was one of the officials who neither mentioned nor furnished to me in 2014 Martin Callinan's letter about Garda recordings prior to Callinan's resignation.) The email stated that counsel for the Garda Commissioner had raised before the O'Higgins Commission an allegation of a 'serious criminal complaint' against Sergeant McCabe on which the DPP had directed 'no prosecution' and that McCabe's counsel had objected.

The serious criminal complaint referenced was that made by Ms D in 2006. The email speculated that the issue had been raised as 'potentially relevant' to McCabe's motivation in complaining of garda misconduct and failures. Fitzgerald, who had met McCabe and his wife in October 2014, was accused of giving an impression of being supportive of McCabe and whistle-blowers generally while being aware earlier than she had claimed of the Garda Commissioner's alleged criticised strategy to attack McCabe's character and integrity, of failing to intervene and of doing nothing to stop it. Despite both Varadkar and Fitzgerald rightly asserting that the gardai were separately legally represented before the O'Higgins Commission, its proceedings were private and that Fitzgerald could not lawfully interfere in the hearings of the Commission nor influence another's legal strategy, Opposition Dáil Deputies insisted that Fitzgerald should have intervened.

Mary Lou McDonald alleged that An Garda Síochána and the Department of Justice had participated in a conspiracy to 'malign a good man' and 'smear him as a sex abuser in order to shut him up'. Micheál Martin alleged with regard to the O'Higgins Commission that 'an appalling set of actions were afoot to undermine the man's credibility and character'. An extra layer of confusion was added following Martin and the next day, Varadkar, each having had separate phone discussions with McCabe, reporting that McCabe had challenged the accuracy of the email. Varadkar informed the Dáil that McCabe had 'denied' that criminal allegations concerning sex abuse were 'raised at all at the O'Higgins Commission'. Assuming Varadkar accurately reported his conversation with McCabe to the Dáil, this was distinctly odd as it contradicted McCabe's own allegation of repeated attempts to raise the issue contained in his February 2017 public statement. At that stage a question mark hung over the accuracy of the content of the forgotten May 2015 email received by Fitzgerald, which was the primary focus of controversy. This did not, however, lower the political temperature.

Fitzgerald remained subject to criticism and an Opposition target. The political hyperbole and dramatics, to which truth rapidly became irrelevant, was reminiscent of my experiences in the first half of 2014 and rapidly evolved into Opposition calls for Fitzgerald's resignation. The Dáil was yet again back in kangaroo court mode with Sinn Féin tabling a motion of no confidence in Fitzgerald and one threatened by Fianna Fáil, on whom the minority Government was dependent for its Dáil majority and to remain in office. Fianna Fáil's Justice spokesperson, Jim O'Callaghan, who ten months earlier had spoken of the importance of fair procedures and due process, joined the calls for Fitzgerald's resignation. Varadkar resisted and the prospect of a general election loomed.

Under Opposition pressure to resign, with Varadkar stating she had done no wrong and expressing his full confidence in her, Fitzgerald engaged in a bit of fantastical historical revisionism, incongruously claiming that both she and 'my party' had 'always supported due process in every situation' proclaiming the importance of 'the principle of natural justice'. In the background I awaited the Supreme Court hearing Guerin's appeal denying that I had any right to challenge the manner in which he had conducted his inquiry and his condemnation of me.

Following events from the outside I regarded the whole controversy as half-baked, riddled with confusion, politically opportunistic and unfair to Fitzgerald. Without fully knowing what occurred during the confidential O'Higgins Commission hearings on an issue subject to inquiry by the Disclosures Tribunal, both Opposition TDs and most media commentators had adopted McCabe's February 2017 narrative that he had been badly treated during the Commission's hearings and concluded that both Nóirín O'Sullivan and Frances Fitzgerald were complicit in his alleged ill treatment. No one cared to consider if that were true why Judge O'Higgins had not intervened to protect McCabe or had criticised his treatment by the Garda Commissioner or her counsel in his report.

The critical political and media juggernaut gathered speed uninhibited by the fact that McCabe had asserted the email to be inaccurate and ignoring the fact that it would have been entirely wrong for Fitzgerald to intervene in any way whatsoever with the legal strategy pursued by the Garda Commissioner and the garda organisation before the O'Higgins Commission. It was also wrongly based on an assumption that the only function of the O'Higgins Commission was to validate not investigate and test the credibility of McCabe's claims.

Over a weekend Varadkar and Martin engaged in discussions to try and avoid a general election. Then on the day before the Dáil reconvened with the prospect of the Government falling and a general election imminent, new emails of relevance to the controversy and the work of the Disclosures Tribunal not previously discovered and provided to it emerged out of the Department of Justice. They included one received by Fitzgerald on 4 July 2015 that she had also forgotten. It contained a query from John Burke of RTÉ Radio 1's Sunday lunchtime news programme *This Week* asking whether it was the Garda Commissioner who instructed counsel to adopt an 'aggressive stance' towards Sergeant McCabe before the O'Higgins Commission. Fitzgerald was to appear on the programme the next day and the advice to her contained in the email properly suggested that due to the confidentiality of the O'Higgins hearings she should not directly answer the question but that she should simply state that both she and the Commissioner 'have made it clear that Sgt McCabe is a valued member of the force'. As it turned out the question never arose on the interview.

The email was published on Monday evening, 27 November 2017. It resulted in a tsunami of criticism that Fitzgerald clearly knew well before May 2016 of Commissioner O'Sullivan's alleged 'aggressive' strategy to attack McCabe and challenge his motivation before the O'Higgins Commission which was alleged to be totally inconsistent with public expressions of support for McCabe by both Fitzgerald and O'Sullivan. All of the commentary assumed McCabe had been wronged, Fitzgerald should have intervened by requiring the Commissioner to instruct her counsel to behave differently, that she was complicit in a disreputable garda strategy and that she was untruthful when stating she knew nothing of it until publication of the leaked selective O'Higgins transcripts in May 2016. The email's content was perceived as validating the narrative derived from the leaked O'Higgins transcript of May 2016 and the McCabes' February 2017 statement that Maurice McCabe had been wrongly treated and unfairly and aggressively cross-examined at the O'Higgins Commission. It did not matter that this very issue was a subject for inquiry before the Disclosures Tribunal and that Fitzgerald was being damned by fragments of information and without any knowledge of the full transcripts of the O'Higgins Commission hearings.

Throughout the course of the controversy Varadkar was supportive of Fitzgerald, for whom he once briefly worked as a political intern, and correctly asserted her right to due process and a fair hearing, as did other Fine Gael members of Cabinet. On 28 November 2017, during a Cabinet meeting she announced her resignation 'in the national interest' to avoid a general election. When informing the Dáil that afternoon of her departure from Cabinet, Varadkar complained that 'a good woman was leaving office without getting a full and fair hearing'. He referred to 'a feeding frenzy' which made it impossible for her 'to get a fair hearing based on the full facts' but carefully avoided any criticism of the Opposition's or the media's dramatics. Describing the Department of Justice as dysfunctional, he held it responsible for Fitzgerald's departure from Cabinet in its failure to provide full answers to Dáil questions originally tabled by Labour's Alan Kelly and its tardiness in identifying and producing internal emails relevant to the controversy and to the work of the Disclosures Tribunal. Subsequent to Varadkar's Dáil comments, Noel Waters, a good and decent man, who in difficult circumstances succeeded Brian Purcell as Secretary General of the Department, announced his immediate retirement, bringing it forward from February 2018.

The issues central to the entire controversy fell within the terms of reference of the Disclosures Tribunal and Varadkar stated his hope that the Tribunal would determine that Fitzgerald had at all times behaved appropriately and would have her good name vindicated. Like Micheál Martin, having spoken on the phone to Maurice McCabe at the height of the 'crisis', Varadkar assumed that McCabe had been badly treated during the O'Higgins Commission proceedings and asserted that 'these events have reminded us of some of the ways in which Maurice McCabe was undermined when he shone a light into some very dark places'. This appeared to confirm that the Taoiseach accepted the veracity of McCabe's February 2017 statement and the then prevailing narrative that McCabe had been wrongly and aggressively questioned before the O'Higgins Commission and that his character and integrity had been unfairly challenged. While Varadkar was happy to assert his hope that Fitzgerald would be found to have behaved appropriately, he expressed no such hope about any findings that the Disclosures Tribunal might make about the conduct before the O'Higgins Commission of former Garda

Commissioner Nóirín O'Sullivan and the barristers who represented her. The extent to which both in public comment and off the record briefings he and those around him nourished the 'feeding frenzy' which undermined my credibility, profoundly damaged my reputation and contributed to my political demise in 2014 I am sure never crossed his mind.

Prior to Fitzgerald's resignation, Judge Charleton in a statement issued by the Disclosures Tribunal noted that both the Dáil and Seanad had determined that the Tribunal's public inquiry was 'the most appropriate way' in which to address the matters 'of public disquiet at issue in its terms of reference'. He announced that it would commence public hearings on 8 January 2018 on the module requiring it 'to investigate whether the false allegations of sexual abuse or any other unjustified grounds were inappropriately relied upon by Commissioner O'Sullivan to discredit Sergeant Maurice McCabe' at hearings of the O'Higgins Commission. This included addressing what instructions were given by Nóirín O'Sullivan to her counsel appearing before the O'Higgins Commission, whether they behaved appropriately, Fitzgerald's knowledge of what occurred and the propriety of her inaction. Unlike me, she would not have to live for a long time under the shadow of false allegations. Within six weeks of her resignation Fitzgerald was destined to have all of the issues surrounding the political and media frenzy that led to her resignation revisited in public hearings before the Disclosures Tribunal and would have an opportunity to publicly give evidence on the controversy in which she had become entangled. As we entered January 2018 and I concluded this chapter, I anticipated that the credibility of the allegations which resulted in her resignation would not withstand 'vigorous' cross-examination and legal scrutiny and that within a few months of giving evidence she would be vindicated.

For me the circumstances of Fitzgerald's resignation from Government were a depressing action replay of what I had experienced in 2014. Yet again there had been a rush to judgement in a McCabe-related controversy. A minor offence, forgetting the contents of emails on which she could take no relevant or appropriate action, had been elevated into a scandal, become an unnecessary Government crisis and resulted in Fitzgerald being another Cabinet casualty. The only mystery was how she could have forgotten the content of the 2015 internal Justice emails in the context of continuing controversy relating to Maurice McCabe and her receiving them just a year after my forced departure from Cabinet.

Fitzgerald had completely ignored my criticising Guerin's condemnation of me without affording me due process and a fair hearing and which had resulted in my resignation. She had now unexpectedly suffered a fate similar to mine but I took no pleasure in it. For me, it simply revived stressful past events and resulted in reoccurring headaches and sleepless nights.

CHAPTER 44

The Disclosures Tribunal Reports

When Bunreacht Na hÉireann guarantees fairness of procedures in removing or diminishing fundamental rights, including the right to a good name, it applies that guarantee in the name of the people not just to the courts but to all the organs of government and administration –Judge Peter Charleton's *Disclosures Tribunal Report*, October 2018

The Disclosures Tribunal read the O'Higgins Commission's transcripts in full and listened to audio recordings of its proceedings. When commencing its hearings on 8 January 2018 into allegations relating to the Commission, one of the Tribunal's counsel, Kathleen Leader, BL, in her opening statement categorically stated that at no stage during the Commission's proceedings had Maurice McCabe been accused of 'false allegations of sexual abuse'. Just over ten months later, the Tribunal's report, published in October 2018 definitively asserted that such allegations had 'never happened' and was critical of the fact that the transcripts had not been 'fully considered' nor any audio recording listened to prior to the 'expenditure of public money on a Tribunal'.

The Tribunal detailed that 'leaked snippets of a transcript' and a Justice Department email 'had somehow transmogrified over time into an allegation that Maurice McCabe had been maliciously accused before the O'Higgins Commission of multiple and false sexual assault offences with a view to damaging his creditworthiness; that the Garda Commissioner had authorised this; that the Minister had been informed and that the Minister had stood back and allowed it to happen'. Referencing its obligation to inquire into whether McCabe had been subject to 'false allegations of sexual abuse', the Tribunal found that 'no one, never mind the Garda Commissioner, before the O'Higgins Commission ever accused Maurice McCabe of any crime or hinted at it or attempted any innuendo about it'.

While acknowledging that at the initial stages of the O'Higgins Commission hearings there had been some confusion that was subsequently resolved about the general approach being taken by the Garda Commissioner's counsel, the Tribunal concluded that any 'error' that occurred 'did not commence with the Commissioner'. It found that 'Maurice McCabe was not traduced' before the Commission, no attempt was made to undermine his integrity or his character and that he had not been subjected to 'a series of attacks'. 'Any challenge to him never went beyond putting issues to him, asking if he could support the serious allegations of corruption which he had repeatedly made with facts. This involved tabling a proposition that he had become mistrustful of authority in consequence of his colleagues having the deeply unpleasant duty of investigating an allegation of what was claimed amounted to a sexual assault.'

The Tribunal recalled that claims made by McCabe addressed by the O'Higgins Commission were not just of 'inattention to duty by Gardai on the ground, but corruption under the direction of Garda management'. The 'allegations of corruption were as serious as could be made against any police officer'. The allegations of corruption the Tribunal stated 'lacked a substratum of fact on which to base them' and Commissioner Callinan was found by the O'Higgins Commission 'to be not guilty of corruption' and these 'potentially devastating charges against the other officers were found to be without any factual foundation'. The Tribunal noted that O'Higgins found McCabe 'to be honest' in 'making these charges' as 'he believed them'.

Referencing the approach taken before the O'Higgins Commission by Garda Commissioner O'Sullivan's counsel, the Tribunal asserted that 'where an allegation of a serious kind is made without evidence, it is … completely proper to ask the person making it why it had been made without evidence in the first place'. Subsequent to the Tribunal listening to audio extracts of the O'Higgins Commission hearings, McCabe withdrew an allegation that he had been shouted at by O'Sullivan's counsel a year after making it. The allegation had caused the Tribunal extreme concern as it 'impacted not only on the barrister in question but also on the judge'. The former being 'accused in explicit terms of unprofessional conduct' and the latter 'as having lost control of the proceedings'. The Tribunal, rejecting McCabe's solicitors' contention that the allegation was due to an office error, concluded that McCabe was not shouted at and that 'There was nothing in the nature of bullying conduct either attempted or permitted' during the O'Higgins Commission hearings.

The Tribunal's conclusions unequivocally established that the political and media frenzy which had targeted the manner in which Judge O'Higgins had conducted his Commission, the conduct of Garda Commissioner O'Sullivan and her barristers before it and the conduct of Frances Fitzgerald was built on falsity, hyperbole and political opportunism. There was no malicious legal strategy to denigrate McCabe. Although Charleton did not address the issue, it was also clear that he was not treated when before the O'Higgins Commission as depicted in his February 2017 statement. He was also not attacked nor were attempts made to ambush him before the O'Higgins Commission as alleged in Michael Clifford's biography of him. Moreover, it was established that the flawed report received by TUSLA was not used before the Commission to undermine McCabe's character or integrity. Reading the O'Higgins Commission's transcripts and listening to audio extracts could have established this without the necessity for a Tribunal inquiry.

How the allegations made came to be 'somehow transmogrified over time' was something the Tribunal did not address. Its remit did not include a full inquiry into and expressing any opinion about the interaction during 2016 and 2017 between McCabe and those members of the Oireachtas and the members of the media who promoted falsity. The Tribunal in its report did not expressly reference the McCabes' public statement of 13 February 2017 which resulted in Micheál Martin rushing to their home and then criticising the O'Higgins Commission, supporting the McCabes' rejection of the creation of another Commission of Investigation and their demand for a public inquiry. The Tribunal was also not tasked with inquiring into who engaged in what it described as the 'deception' and 'manipulation of the media with selected extracts' leaked of the O'Higgins Commission transcripts. It stated it had 'no view as to responsibility for this conduct', while acknowledging 'the selective leaking caused serious public disquiet', a 'truly unfortunate impression' and 'a rush to judgment in the public mind'.

Having referenced the O'Higgins Commission's synopsis of its findings relating to McCabe's complaints and its view of him as a man of 'integrity', 'never less than truthful' but 'prone to exaggeration', the Tribunal acknowledged that: 'this caution as to exaggeration is not misplaced. It has meant that the Tribunal has had an especially difficult task'.

Describing McCabe as 'a public spirited, decent and kind individual but one suffering from the effects of strain' the Tribunal stated he is 'someone who tries his very best to tell the truth as he sees it'. Observing that it should always be remembered that he 'is an ordinary human being who can make mistakes' the Tribunal acknowledged that 'at times [he] is prone to grasp the wrong end of an issue. Because he is so intent on his task and feels matters so deeply he is not a completely reliable historian'.

As with any other witness, his evidence 'cannot just be accepted at face value but requires to be tested'.

Implicitly excusing any exaggeration, mistaken or false allegation or complaint made by McCabe, the Tribunal expressed its understanding 'that through a process of strain, the ability of a person to see matters objectively may be affected'. It also described him as a police 'officer of exemplary character', 'a person of exemplary fortitude', who was a 'genuine person who has at all times had the interests of the people of Ireland uppermost in his mind' and had 'done the State considerable service'. No criticism was expressed of complaints or allegations made by McCabe for which there was no evidence or which were simply false. The Tribunal did not address the impact on others of McCabe's 'very best' attempts 'to tell the truth as he sees it'. No attempt is made in the Tribunal's narrative to explain at what point a false or exaggerated accusation which results from strain evolves into deceit or calumny nor how to distinguish a false or exaggerated charge maliciously made from one that is delusional, mistaken or based on a 'belief' for which there is no evidence. The Tribunal also did not explain how to differentiate between a belief that is the result of strain from one that is not, nor did it address in its Report the emotional, physical and possible life changing impact of wrong allegations made against anyone other than McCabe.

The Tribunal, as I expected, concluded that Frances Fitzgerald had at all times behaved properly in not interfering with the approach taken before the O'Higgins Commission by Nóirín O'Sullivan as both the Garda Commissioner and the Department of Justice were under investigation by the Commission. 'As a matter of ethics' any 'hint of working things out between them ... had to be avoided', it stated. This conclusion of the Tribunal unknowingly articulated exactly why when Minister for Justice I had refrained from corresponding or communicating directly with Sean Guerin prior to his completing his report in the absence of his directly asking me to answer questions posed or asking me to address any specific concerns. For ethical reasons any 'hint of working things out' between us 'had to be avoided'.

Fitzgerald had made an honest appraisal of the situation and her approach was 'not a lazy dodging of issues but rather a considered response to the information' contained in the May 2015 email that she had initially forgotten receiving. Accusations made both inside and outside the Dáil that she had behaved wrongly towards McCabe or that she had in some way conspired with the Garda Commissioner or was complicit in a malicious plot to wrong McCabe were blown apart by the Tribunal's conclusion. In its report the Tribunal noted she had 'selflessly' resigned from Government 'in the national interest'.

The catalyst to renewed public controversy relating to Maurice McCabe which ultimately resulted in the creation of the Disclosures Tribunal were the Protected Disclosures made by McCabe and Superintendent David Taylor in September 2016. Inquiring into these occupied a substantial portion of the Tribunal's time and resulted in unexpected revelations.

Taylor alleged that when Garda Press Officer he had been directed to organise a smear campaign to discredit McCabe by Garda Commissioner Martin Callinan and that Nóirín O'Sullivan, when Deputy Commissioner, was aware of this 'strategy'. He also alleged that he had 'face to face' meetings with her and gave her 'updates' where he discussed the strategy and his media briefings against McCabe. He claimed the campaign involved briefing journalists that McCabe was motivated by 'maliciousness and revenge' when making allegations of garda wrongdoing, that his complaints had no substance and that he 'was driven by agendas'. Taylor also claimed that he was 'directed to draw journalists' attention to the complaint of sexual assault made against Sgt McCabe and that this was the root cause of his agenda-revenge against the Gardai'.

In three different formal interviews conducted over three days by Tribunal investigators he failed to supply definite details of the journalists and of the nature and date of such briefings. In a subsequent letter to the Tribunal of 17 April 2017, he listed nine journalists as recipients of his negative briefings, including Paul Williams (*INM*), John Mooney (*Sunday Times*) and Paul Reynolds (RTÉ). Over five months later he added another two, Eavan Murray (*Irish Sun*) and Debbie McCann (*Irish Mail on Sunday*) following their being identified to the Tribunal as having visited Ms D's parent's home seeking to interview her. Bizarrely, it emerged that the reporter with whom Taylor had most contact by way of texts and phone calls was Eavan Murray, who was responsible for the *Irish Sun*'s fake news 'Runway Exclusive' published in August 2014. Following a former *Irish Daily Mirror* journalist, Cathal McMahon, giving unexpected evidence of a conversation he had with Taylor, he was added by Taylor to the list on day 94 of the Tribunal hearings, the second last day of Taylor's evidence.

In the days preceding his appearance before the Tribunal evidence was given that, at the time of his Protected Disclosure, Taylor was suspended, under criminal investigation and facing a disciplinary hearing. He was accused of furnishing confidential information to journalists and of acting as a rogue press officer after his transfer to the Garda Road Traffic Unit by Nóirín O'Sullivan, following Martin Callinan's retirement. When giving evidence he was unable to identify the exact content or location of the briefings he had allegedly conducted with any journalist he named and he could not recall any reaction to his briefings, which he contended were unplanned and 'opportunistic'.

Following his meeting with Taylor in September 2016, McCabe made his Protected Disclosure substantially based on what he had allegedly been told by Taylor of the orchestrated 'smear' campaign. McCabe's Disclosure derived from two meetings between him and Taylor at which Taylor, he claimed, told him that hundreds, if not thousands, of text messages had been sent by him to O'Sullivan, journalists and other senior garda officers containing 'vile' messages about McCabe which were prepared by Martin Callinan. The journalist, Michael Clifford, who had first reported the content of the Protected Disclosures, claimed Taylor had told him the same story as did TDs Mick Wallace and Clare Daly, who had spoken about the alleged smear campaign in the Dáil in October 2016 and called for Nóirín O'Sullivan to resign. Taylor denied saying any such thing and insisted all his negative briefings about McCabe were oral and to journalists only.

Substantial resources were expended and time spent by the Tribunal in trying and failing to identify the texts smearing McCabe that Taylor had allegedly received from Callinan and then sent to journalists but none were discovered. Having previously alleged he had been investigated and suspended because he knew too much, towards the end of his evidence, Taylor acknowledged that he had wrongly operated his own unofficial rogue press office for over a year from the Garda Traffic Unit and that he resented Nóirín O'Sullivan transferring him to Traffic. In response to a question from Judge Charleton, he also acknowledged that there were no texts implicating Martin Callinan or Nóirín O'Sullivan in any kind of plot to traduce McCabe. It was also established that an affidavit he had sworn in a High Court action he initiated to stop disciplinary proceedings taken against him was riddled with untruths.

By the time Taylor's evidence concluded his veracity and the credibility of his Protected Disclosure was substantially undermined. The Tribunal concluded that in order to scupper the disciplinary proceedings and the danger of a criminal prosecution, Taylor had 'dressed up lies in a legal syrup that cloyingly garnered public sympathy'. It also found that by telling lies he had attempted to minimise 'his whole role in the scandal'. While concluding that Taylor had sent no texts smearing McCabe to the journalists he named, the Tribunal concluded that it believed McCabe's evidence of Taylor telling him that he had done so. It also concluded that Taylor's allegations of Garda Commissioner Callinan drafting such texts and of O'Sullivan, when Deputy Commissioner, being complicit in a strategy to undermine McCabe's credibility were false.

Despite rejecting most of Taylor's evidence as lies and deceit and depicting him 'as a witness whose credibility was undermined by his own bitterness', in reliance on the evidence of others the Tribunal ultimately concluded that Callinan and Taylor had participated in a campaign of calumny against McCabe in which O'Sullivan had no involvement. Its particular focus was 'late 2013 through 2014' and, in particular, the period leading into the January 2014 hearings of the Public Accounts Committee into the ticket charge issue and the time of the hearings. Evidence of general rumours circulating about McCabe was given to the Tribunal by John McGuinness, Micheál Martin, Pat Rabbitte and Eoghan Murphy. According to McGuinness, Martin and Rabbitte, the rumours connected McCabe to child sexual abuse, and according to Murphy there was a rumour that both McCabe and John Wilson were odd. Murphy heard no rumours about child abuse.

In a statement made by me to the Tribunal and in evidence before it on 17 May 2018, I dealt with what I knew about issues that fell within its terms of reference and detailed background information. One concerned a phone conversation in 2013 between me and Callinan shortly after publication of the *O'Mahoney Report*.

As I told the Disclosures Tribunal, the background to the conversation was the difficulties I was experiencing in dealing with McCabe's complaints and allegations and what I perceived to be the erratic nature of his engagement. The difficulties included his failure to reply to letters sent to his solicitors seeking McCabe's consent to release documents to Callinan for his response to facilitate my determining whether there was a need for a public inquiry or Commission of Investigation to address McCabe's complaints and allegations; McCabe's adamant insistence that every ticket charge allegation made by him stood up, even though some patently did not; his puzzling complaint that he had not been interviewed by John O'Mahoney on the ticket charge issue, when he had insisted on anonymity as the complainant; his strange communication to Taoiseach Enda Kenny of being alarmed during a phone call he made when invited by O'Mahoney to meet a member of his team prior to his report's publication and his capacity to perceive events through a distorted perspective. In the period leading into the phone conversation there was continuing public controversy, I was subject to continuing criticism and Callinan was being demonised. Giving evidence I said that 'there was this feeling when dealing with issues he [McCabe] raised of sinking in quicksand'.

I told the Tribunal that I asked Callinan if there was something in the background I should know. In response he advised me that an allegation of a sexual nature was made in relation to McCabe, that it had been fully investigated and that the DPP had directed that there was no basis for a prosecution. When I asked him whether any similar further allegations had been made, he said 'No' and then speculated that perhaps McCabe was upset at the manner in which the issue was dealt with. I informed the Tribunal that I interpreted that to mean that what had occurred impacted in some personal way on McCabe and this was affecting his perception of how he should or could engage with the gardaí. The conversation was very brief and Callinan had not made a big deal out of it. He had not detailed to me the nature of the 'sexual allegation', and my perception was that the allegation was not a major issue. I took it that the DPP had decided that it was baseless and it was something that we never again discussed.

Although McCabe's Senior Counsel, Michael McDowell, was present, it was his Junior Counsel, Breffni Gordon who questioned me on his behalf. His main focus was on my Dáil reference to McCabe's lack of co-operation with the O'Mahoney investigation. He challenged my reference to McCabe's wish for anonymity, as if it was something I fabricated, but when pressed by Judge Charleton acknowledged that McCabe had in fact sought anonymity. His questions travelled up some highways and down some byways and revisited evidence I had already given but to no particular benefit.

The Tribunal fully accepted my evidence as truthful and my testimony that I had never heard any rumours in Leinster House or elsewhere about the issue of sexual abuse. However, it stated that my evidence as 'to the attitude of Commissioner Callinan' contrasted markedly with other evidence it heard. The reason for this, it determined, was because my conversation with Callinan had occurred in late spring 2013 and other conversations had occurred in the lead up to Christmas

2013 and in January 2014. At that time contentious correspondence was being exchanged between Callinan and John McGuinness concerning documentation the PAC had received from McCabe on the ticket charge issue and, thereafter, Callinan made his 'disgusting' comment when answering questions before the PAC and a dispute arose concerning McCabe appearing before it. The Tribunal believed that there was 'particular pressure on Commissioner Callinan' and that an allegation of 'serious abuse of police power' put into the public arena by McCabe 'added to the ordinary strains of those in garda headquarters'. It was this 'matrix' which the Tribunal concluded resulted in a series of damning 'utterances' by Callinan in conversations with McGuinness and three others, Philip Boucher Hayes (RTÉ), the C&AG Seamus McCarthy and John Deasy. Callinan's utterances and evidence given by Taylor led the Tribunal to conclude that they had been jointly involved in a 'campaign of calumny' against McCabe.

McGuinness told the Tribunal that in conversation with Callinan after his appearance before the PAC in January 2014, Callinan alleged that McCabe 'fiddles with kids' and described McCabe and John Wilson as 'fucking headbangers'. Taylor gave evidence that he overheard Callinan say McCabe was 'a kiddie fiddler'. The next day, when McGuinness and Callinan met in the car park of Bewley's Hotel, McGuinness testified that Callinan had said that McCabe 'was not to be trusted' and that 'he had sexually abused his family and an individual' and that he was led to believe 'there was an investigation ongoing in relation to the allegations' and it was 'at an advanced stage'. Micheál Martin gave evidence that shortly after the PAC meeting McGuinness briefly informed him of the car park meeting and conversation with Callinan.

Seamus McCarthy told the Tribunal that prior to the PAC meeting attended by Callinan, in a brief conversation, the Commissioner told him McCabe was not to be trusted, that he had questions to answer and that there were sexual offence allegations against him.

John Deasy told the Tribunal that in a conversation before the PAC meeting that lasted less than a minute, Callinan told him that McCabe 'was not to be believed or trusted with anything'. Nothing was said about sexual abuse.

Philip Boucher-Hayes told of an encounter with both Callinan and Taylor in December 2013 in RTÉ studios preceding an interview with Callinan for the *Crime Call* programme. A disagreement occurred relating to discussion topics. Boucher-Hayes wanted to include the ticket charge issue. Callinan did not want it included. Boucher-Hayes stated that during the course of their conversing, Callinan spoke of McCabe as having 'some well known grievances' and of 'psychological, psychiatric, issues with this man' and of there being 'more' and 'an awful lot worse' he could tell him. He could tell him 'the worst kind of things' but 'we'll leave it there'. Continuing Boucher-Hayes said 'As far as I remember, it was actually the most horrific kind of things, which I didn't believe … my imagination went to where I assumed it was being directed to an allegation of child sexual abuse or rape perhaps.' He recalled that Callinan, in a parting shot, told him if there was anything else he wanted to know, he could talk to David Taylor who had accompanied him to RTÉ. Taylor, he told the Tribunal, then said to him 'now do you understand what the position is with Maurice McCabe?'

Callinan denied the utterances attributed to him by all four and Taylor denied overhearing the conversation with Boucher-Hayes and making any comment. The Tribunal concluded that neither of them had told the truth and viewed Boucher-Hayes's testimony as 'confirmation in a material respect of the existence of a plan of campaign' between Callinan and Taylor who were 'acting together' in attempting 'to denigrate the character of Maurice McCabe'. The Tribunal also rejected a claim made by Taylor for the first time when giving evidence that he was acting under 'orders' when he negatively briefed journalists against McCabe.

Most of the journalists who gave evidence to the Tribunal said they had heard rumours about McCabe. All of those named by Taylor did so, with the exception of RTÉ's John Burke, but none stated Taylor to be the source of the rumours. Three *Irish Examiner* journalists, relying on journalistic privilege, refused to answer any questions about any engagement with Taylor, despite his waiving any claim to the protection afforded by the privilege. Debbie McCann of the *Irish Mail on Sunday* adopted the same approach. The Tribunal stated that it was 'not convinced that any of the original nine journalists' listed by Taylor 'were ever egged on in publishing negative stories about Maurice McCabe or even in thinking less of him'. No stories traducing McCabe had ever been published. However, it concluded that journalists Eavan Murray and Debbie McCann, who had both separately called to Ms D's parents' home, had been 'encouraged' by Taylor to 'seek out Ms D and to publish a negative story' about McCabe 'in relation to her allegation'. Cathal

McMahon, it found, having 'innocently' made an inquiry after hearing a rumour, was told by Taylor 'he might find out more by going to Cavan' where Ms D's parents lived. McMahon had not acted on the advice. McCann and Murray were described by the Tribunal as 'committed journalists who were looking for news' and 'very unfortunate to have come within the orbit of Superintendent David Taylor'.

Remarking on the stance taken by those journalists who relied on journalistic privilege to refuse to answer questions as to whether or not Taylor had briefed them negatively about McCabe, the Tribunal, referring to Taylor's waiver of journalistic privilege remarked that it 'considers the privilege waived' and that the 'bizarre aspect' of it being claimed was that 'the journalist, having refused to give evidence to the Tribunal, is quite free to write whatever he likes about any alleged encounter he may believe he had with a Garda source ... how that might serve the public interest is hard to fathom'.

The Tribunal determined that Taylor intended 'to cause as much trouble for McCabe as possible'. He had pursued a scheme to traduce McCabe that 'somehow evolved out of his cheek by jowl working relationship' with Callinan by the use of 'much nodding and winking and references to a historic claim of sexual abuse'. As the PAC public hearings came to a climax, 'in terms of the emotional disquiet that they were causing Commissioner Callinan' the Commissioner had 'personally felt the need to supplement the efforts of his press officer' by speaking to both John McGuinness and John Deasy and the C&AG 'in the most derogatory way about Maurice McCabe'. The engagement of Callinan and Taylor with Philip Boucher-Hayes as detailed in his evidence was pivotal in the Tribunal concluding that Callinan and Taylor were 'working together' to denigrate McCabe 'for no more than being a good citizen and a good police officer'. Nóirín O'Sullivan, the Tribunal concluded had played no 'hand, act or part' in their campaign.

I was surprised to first learn during the Tribunal hearings of the alleged conversations in which Callinan had engaged during my time as Justice Minister and of Taylor's gross misconduct. When Minister for Justice no concerns resulting from their encounters with Callinan had been communicated to me by Deasy, the C&AG or Boucher-Hayes and neither Callinan nor Brian Purcell had informed me of Callinan's meeting with McGuinness, nor had McGuinness. It emerged in evidence that Callinan had first discussed arranging such a meeting with Purcell and that he had subsequently informed Purcell of his version of how it went. It is extraordinary that this meeting was both arranged and took place without any prior discussion with me at the height of the controversy surrounding the PAC's consideration of the ticket charge issue.

In the context of what is now known, it is surprising that McGuinness, as Chairperson of the PAC, did not after the car park meeting inform me of what occurred. There was no barrier to McGuinness doing so, and our meeting could have been easily arranged. He simply briefly informed Micheál Martin of his conversation with Callinan who chose not to pursue it. Anything I knew of the meeting, prior to the hearings of the Disclosures Tribunal, derived from media reports and Dáil exchanges two years after my resignation and subsequent to publication of the *O'Higgins Report*. Based on my personal experiences I believed little reliance could be placed on such sources of information.

As I expected, the Tribunal concluded that the report dealt with by TUSLA containing a false allegation that McCabe had committed a rape offence had resulted from a genuine mistake made in August 2013 by a counsellor using a template which in error resulted in her report containing allegations which had no connection of any nature to either Ms D or McCabe. The letter received by McCabe from TUSLA in January 2016 was the result of 'complete and absolute incompetence' by the body which had been informed of the error by the counsellor in mid-May 2014 and 'the astounding inefficiency of that organisation and the inertia of its management in Cavan/Monaghan'. There was no garda conspiracy found to be involved in the dreadful and distressing allegation contained in TUSLA's letter to McCabe. The political and media frenzy of February 2017 alleging Garda collusion with TUSLA in a plan to destroy McCabe was entirely undermined by the Tribunal's report. The failure of TUSLA to contact McCabe to inform him of the error that had occurred at an early stage, the distress caused by TUSLA's letter to him and his family and its taking almost six months for TUSLA to explain to his solicitors how the false allegation of rape occurred, was rightly trenchantly criticised by the Tribunal.

There is a possibility that TUSLA's incompetence would have been discovered much earlier and some of the upset avoided had Frances Fitzgerald, as I proposed, included the issue of the garda investigation into Ms D's complaint against McCabe within the O'Higgins Commission's terms of reference. A series of stories written by Paul Williams had appeared in the *Irish Independent* recounting that a young woman was complaining that a sexual assault perpetrated on her in Bailieboro had not been properly investigated. She was reported in May 2014 to have met Micheál Martin and asked that the manner in which the investigation was conducted be addressed by what ultimately became the O'Higgins Commission. Martin was reported to have subsequently forwarded her request to Taoiseach Enda Kenny. About a month after my resignation, in June 2014, Williams phoned me saying she wished to meet me and I agreed. My meeting with the woman, who became known (through the Disclosures Tribunal) as Ms D, took place in the Merrion Hotel a few days later and both Williams and Jane Lehane were present.

At our meeting, Ms D was greatly distressed, explained that she had great personal difficulty coping with the media praise of McCabe, was unable to focus on her third level studies and had postponed taking her exams. She wanted my help in ascertaining how the Garda investigation into her complaint against McCabe had been conducted. I knew nothing about the investigation and made no judgement on its efficiency. Believing that if I made any such request to Frances Fitzgerald or Enda Kenny it would be dismissed as some vengeful false claim made against McCabe, I advised her to again contact Micheál Martin. As he had made false accusations against me in February 2014 after meeting McCabe and following his receipt of documents from him, Martin's motivation in raising her concerns would not be questioned.

I was deeply affected by Ms D's level of stress and her circumstances. After our meeting I reread Williams's articles and decided that I should not ignore her plight. A Dáil debate on the Cooke Report was imminent and I intended to use it to discuss both it and the *Guerin Report*. I decided by first making a short, considered reference to one of Paul Williams's reports and Ms D's meeting with Micheál Martin in the debate I could follow up our discussion without provoking another media backlash and a frenzy of new false allegations. Towards the end of the debate that took place on 19 June 2014, referring to what ultimately became the O'Higgins Commission, I said its inquiry should include 'all cases dealt with in Bailieboro Garda Station which have given rise to complaint' and continued 'I understand from the newspaper report that Deputy Martin was to provide information on this matter to the Taoiseach and I presume he has done so. This case should clearly form part of any statutory inquiry.'

Frances Fitzgerald neither responded to me in her Ministerial reply to the debate nor in any later communication nor, when established, did the O'Higgins Commission's terms of reference allow it to examine Ms D's concerns. During hearings of the Disclosures Tribunal in 2017 I first learnt that Fitzgerald subsequently had referred the file to be independently reviewed by the Independent Review Mechanism established in May 2014 to examine alleged inadequacies in Garda misconduct. Barristers conducting such reviews on 10 November 2014 had concluded that Ms D's complaint had been properly investigated. Judge Charleton, who read the file, expressly agreed with that conclusion as, it emerged, did GSOC in response to a complaint made by Ms D prior to our meeting. Of course, had Ms D's concerns come before the O'Higgins Commission in 2015, the difficulties caused to Maurice McCabe by TUSLA's total incompetence may have been avoided, no false allegation would have been made of some sort of conspiracy between TUSLA and the garda authorities, the controversy in which the Government became entangled after Katherine Zappone met the McCabes would not have occurred, Enda Kenny would not have broadcast a fictitious story on RTÉ in February 2017 that led to his resignation and one of the modules that occupied the time of the Disclosures Tribunal would have been unnecessary.

The extent to which events can become distorted was for me starkly illustrated by that part of the Disclosures Tribunal's terms of reference which required it to 'investigate' whether Nóirín O'Sullivan, when Garda Commissioner 'using briefing material prepared in garda headquarters, influenced or attempted to influence broadcasts on RTÉ on 9 May 2016 purporting to be a leaked account of the unpublished *O'Higgins Commission Report* in which Sergeant McCabe was branded a liar and irresponsible'.

RTÉ's experienced and respected crime reporter, Paul Reynolds, had acquired copies of the Commission's report and two days prior to its publication in a series of broadcasts had accurately detailed its conclusions on a variety of issues it addressed. These broadcasts included referring to O'Higgins's praise of McCabe, his conclusions validating McCabe's complaints of garda failures in relation to a variety of incidents and his findings that allegations of corruption McCabe had made against Martin Callinan and other senior garda officers were unfounded. O'Higgins's findings in my favour contradicting Guerin had also been broadcast as had the findings that some of McCabe's claims were unfounded, exaggerated or withdrawn. McCabe's solicitors had complained on the day of the broadcasts that some references to McCabe were defamatory. It emerged that particular objection was taken to a broadcast by Reynolds which recounted that McCabe was found to have lied when stating in a report to a senior officer that a complaint had been made to GSOC about an alleged garda failure. The Commission had determined what he said to be 'untrue' and objection was taken to the use of the word 'lie'.

In his 2016 Protected Disclosure McCabe alleged 'the disgraceful series of broadcasts on RTÉ' on the 9 May 2016 'in which he had been branded as a liar and irresponsible' had contributed to him going on stress-related sick leave. He claimed 'that he was satisfied on impeccable authority that those RTÉ broadcasts were planned and orchestrated' by Nóirín O'Sullivan personally 'using briefing material prepared at garda headquarters'. When giving evidence to the Tribunal, McCabe identified the 'impeccable authority' for his accusation as John Barrett, the civilian head of Human Resources in An Garda Síochána. He claimed the accusation derived from a comment Barrett had made to him at a meeting between them both which took place in McCabe's home three weeks after publication of the *O'Higgins Report*.

Reynolds gave evidence over three days of the research he had undertaken in the day's preceding his broadcasts, of the care taken to ensure they were accurate, balanced and fair to all parties and of the fact that the content of his broadcasts derived entirely from the *O'Higgins Report*. His evidence was corroborated by others in RTÉ involved at editorial level and the Tribunal viewed and listened to all the relevant broadcasts. It was clear that in no broadcast had Reynolds referenced McCabe as 'irresponsible'. O'Sullivan had previously denied any involvement in the broadcasts and, following Reynolds giving evidence, Barrett denied ever making to McCabe the comment attributed to him on which McCabe based his allegation that O'Sullivan had orchestrated Reynolds's broadcasts.

Charleton did not believe Barrett's denial and other evidence given by him. Despite it becoming clear during the Tribunal's hearings that there was no basis for McCabe's depiction of the broadcasts as 'disgraceful' nor for his allegation they were 'planned and orchestrated' by O'Sullivan, McCabe declined to withdraw his allegation against O'Sullivan. The Tribunal concluded that O'Sullivan had neither influenced nor attempted to influence the broadcasts and that Reynolds had not 'branded' McCabe 'irresponsible'. In circumstances in which the O'Higgins Commission had determined McCabe to be untruthful in relation to a particular incident, no valid objection could be made to Reynolds's reporting that O'Higgins found McCabe to have told a lie.

When the Tribunal was established, I regarded it as extraordinary that both the Dáil and the Seanad, without a single objection voiced, required the Tribunal to conduct an inquiry into a series of RTÉ broadcasts which had faithfully and accurately reported the *O'Higgins Report* and, in doing so, saw fit to adopt McCabe's allegation that he had been 'branded a liar and irresponsible' by Reynolds. Just listening back to the broadcasts would have established the falsity of that allegation and reading the *O'Higgins Report* should have confirmed that the broadcasts were simply an example of good, well-researched journalism. The reality is that no member of either House of the Oireachtas was prepared critically to address any allegation made by McCabe for fear of adverse political consequences or to logically and rationally address the likelihood of a Garda Commissioner and RTÉ's premier crime reporter conspiring together to bring about inaccurate and distorted broadcasts of a Commission of Investigation report a short time before its official publication.

While required to inquire into Paul Reynolds's leaked account of the unpublished *O'Higgins Report*, the Tribunal was not empowered to inquire into the leaking of selective extracts from the O'Higgins Commission transcripts to the *Irish Examiner*'s Michael Clifford four days after Reynolds's broadcasts and subsequent to the Commission's report being published. The latter leak was of much greater consequence as it laid the foundation for false allegations that McCabe had been wrongly treated during proceedings before the Commission, that his character and integrity had been attacked, that Nóirín O'Sullivan and Frances Fitzgerald had in some way conspired to do him down and that Judge O'Higgins had failed to properly control the Commission's hearings. To require a Tribunal inquiry into who was responsible for that leak was clearly perceived to be politically too hot to handle.

The *O'Higgins Commission Report* was delivered to Justice Minister, Frances Fitzgerald on 25 April 2016. She was legally obliged to publish the report 'as soon as possible'. This requirement usually results in publication within a week. Ten days later there was no sign of its publication. It was over three months since the February 2016 general election, a new Government had not yet been formed and I believed its publication was being deliberately delayed to ensure that neither the Taoiseach nor any of my former Government colleagues became embroiled in any controversy. Still subject to occasional media vilification almost two years after publication of the *Guerin Report*, still stressed by the High Court's dismissal of my court proceedings and just over a month away from the Court of Appeal hearing, I was understandably anxious that the O'Higgins Commission's conclusions should be published. After all, Guerin's report had been published three days after its receipt by Enda Kenny. For me, Paul Reynolds's broadcasts of 9 May 2016, coincidentally on the second anniversary of the publication of Guerin's report, partially lifted a cloud I had been under for two years and alleviated some of my stress. In delaying publication of the report, neither Kenny nor Fitzgerald or any of my former Fine Gael colleagues in Government gave any thought to the predicament and stress of all of those subject to false and mistaken allegations which had damaged careers, reputations and upended lives nor to the impact of the delay on Maurice McCabe. Had the report been more speedily published none of the controversy surrounding Paul Reynolds's broadcasts would have arisen, Noirin O'Sullivan would not have been subject to a clearly false allegation and the broadcasts would not have occupied any of the Disclosures Tribunal's time nor that of any of the witnesses who made statements to it and gave evidence on the issue. It is also possible that selective extracts from the O'Higgins Commission hearings would not have been leaked.

Amongst its many conclusions the Tribunal stated that 'the improvement most needed in our police force is adherence to honesty'. The same improvement is long overdue in the cut-throat, self-absorbed cultish bubble of Irish politics.

CHAPTER 45

Closure and a Pyrrhic Victory

Guilty before the trial, punished by loss of career, then found to be innocent after all ... With the possible exception of what happened to Alan Shatter, I can't think of any instance in political life, either here or elsewhere, where that sequence of events applies
–Fergus Finlay, 'O'Sullivan and Fitzgerald have both been victims of rough justice', *Irish Examiner*, 16 October 2018

It was reminiscent of what happened to ... Alan Shatter who was similarly hounded from office on the basis of a range of accusations that also turned out to be false. He was one of the most energetic and reforming ministers in the history of the State but that was no defence once the remorseless tide of scapegoating had begun
–Stephen Collins, 'How the truth became irrelevant to Fitzgerald's fate', *Irish Times*, 18 October 2018

On the day the Disclosures Tribunals Report was published, Maurice McCabe welcomed its conclusions and Frances Fitzgerald understandably welcomed her exoneration. Some journalists acknowledged she had been badly treated but no Opposition leader or TD apologised for false allegations made that she had wronged McCabe or had colluded in his alleged ill treatment before the O'Higgins Commission. No media outlet or newspaper apologised for her being hounded out of office. TUSLA yet again apologised to McCabe for its shocking incompetence. Taoiseach Leo Varadkar reiterated his description of McCabe as a 'distinguished' public servant, thanked him for his bravery and tweeted that Opposition deputies who forced the resignation of Frances Fitzgerald and the early retirement of Nóirín O'Sullivan should 'reflect on their judgement'. In the Dáil the following week he urged Opposition deputies to do 'the decent and right thing by correcting the record of the Dáil' in respect of 'the false charges against Nóirín O'Sullivan and the unfair allegations and accusations made against Deputy Fitzgerald'. The *Irish Examiner* reported him in an interview as demanding that they apologise. On the day the Tribunal's report was published independent TD, Denis Naughton, resigned from the Cabinet on an unconnected issue. Two days later Varadkar elevated Joe McHugh, a Fine Gael Minister of State, to Cabinet to fill the vacancy but did not reinstate Fitzgerald.

Justice Minister Charlie Flanagan formally apologised to McCabe on behalf of the State for the manner in which he was treated and expressed his hope that Fitzgerald would 'return to high office'. Demands that Opposition deputies either correct the Dáil record or apologise for false allegations made fell on deaf ears while McCabe was praised by all, both within and outside the Dáil. Minister for Health Simon Harris in a Tweet on the day the *Disclosures Tribunal Report* was published criticised the charges made against Fitzgerald as 'a rush to judgement for political gain and a refusal to afford due process by some'. He was obliviously partially but somewhat inaccurately repeating my critique of the *Guerin Report* which all my Fine Gael colleagues chose to ignore. I had not mentioned 'political gain'.

Simon Coveney who had told the *Irish Examiner* in November 2016 that Enda Kenny need offer me no apology after I had won my Court of Appeal case against Sean Guerin and earlier been exonerated by O'Higgins, joined in the calls for an Opposition apology to Fitzgerald and told the Fine Gael parliamentary party that she had been 'completely vindicated'. Clearly his perspective on the role of an apology had evolved over two years. He was reported to have criticised 'the silence of the cheerleaders who called for her head'.

Flanagan was critical of Nóirín O'Sullivan 'having been subject to a concerted campaign to undermine her position' and of the manner in which she had been questioned in various Oireachtas committee hearings but no apologies were volunteered by any Oireachtas committee member for her treatment. McCabe, interviewed on RTÉ's *Prime Time*, accepted all the conclusions of the Disclosures Tribunal, expressed his relief that it was over and gave no apology for any false or mistaken allegation he had at any time made based on 'belief' or as a result of stress or strain. He stated he had expected the Tribunal's conclusions in relation to Callinan and Taylor and accepted those in relation to O'Sullivan. New Garda Commissioner, Drew Harris, visited McCabe in his home and apologised for the manner in which he had been treated by An Garda Síochána. No one suggested McCabe need apologise to anyone for the collateral damage inflicted by wrong allegations which damaged reputations, contributed to the end of careers and caused stress to those against whom they were made. Three weeks later Maurice McCabe retired from

An Garda Síochána. On the same day, it was announced by the Secretary General of the UN, Antonio Guterres, that Nóirín O'Sullivan had been appointed the UN's Assistant Secretary General for Safety and Security. The position had been advertised some months earlier and women candidates had been 'strongly urged to apply'. Her appointment did not result from a Government nomination. The next day an *Irish Times* article by journalist, Jack Power, reported that when asked by him whether 'Ms O'Sullivan or Ms Fitzgerald had been forced to resign from their posts unfairly given the Tribunals findings', Sergeant Maurice McCabe said, 'I cannot comment on anything like that.'

Callinan and Taylor were universally condemned. Taylor was suspended from duty and a week later retired having served in the gardaí for over thirty years. No consideration was given to the impact on Callinan of being wrongly accused of corruption by McCabe in January 2012, being wrongly demonised and publicly pilloried both prior to and after the *O'Mahoney Report* was published, constantly attacked in the Dáil during 2013 and to the fact that the Disclosures Tribunal stated the O'Mahoney investigation to have been carried out 'in good faith'. Also ignored was the Disclosures Tribunal wrongly assuming Callinan's unfortunate 'disgusting' comment before the PAC was intended to apply generally to McCabe blowing the whistle on garda failures. The Tribunal, like many critical commentators, ignored his acknowledging immediately in his next sentence that deficiencies had been exposed in the administration of the Fixed Charge Notice Processing System. Of course none of that could justify what the Tribunal described as a campaign to denigrate McCabe.

Ten days after publication of the *Disclosure Tribunal's Report* an article in Fitzgerald's name appeared in the *Sunday Independent* entitled 'I was exonerated – but we must stop the avalanche of lies and vilification.' It bemoaned that those who have their 'lives' and 'their reputations wrongly destroyed' are 'expected to simply shrink away and sit in the wreckage of their career'. Referencing the 'political/media interplay – which often now functions in a destructive way for individuals and for our democracy', the article continued: 'Those who have experienced it first hand have, by definition, had their credibility so shredded that no one will listen. Those who have not experienced it cannot begin to know what it is like when the hydra turns its sole focus on you.'

Fitzgerald's article criticised the media publishing unsubstantiated attacks and 'the most egregious of unsupported defamation' being 'walked into our national press wrapped in the cloak of Dáil privilege'. Politicians are using the shelter of parliamentary privilege to defame, the article asserted and 'defamation laundering is not what this privilege is designed for'. She rightly criticised her being 'daubed with believed complicity in events which never happened'. Four days later, Fitzgerald speaking in the Dáil on the *Disclosures Tribunal Report* asserted that 'Those who think that due process and fair procedures can be cast aside for reasons of political expediency do a disservice to the values of democracy'.

Fitzgerald, when Justice Minister, had inexcusably turned her back and chosen not to listen to what I said about the importance of due process and fair procedures in the Dáil in June 2014 after publication of the *Guerin Report*. We had worked together, been friends and known each other long enough for her to trust the truth of anything I said. Within six weeks of Fitzgerald's resignation from Government, public hearings of the Disclosure Tribunal had commenced. Her reputation had been fully restored ten months later and she was still a TD. Two years had elapsed from my resignation before the *O'Higgins Report* was published. Frances Fitzgerald had unnecessarily delayed the Commission's establishment and also publication of its report and I was no longer a TD. When reading the *Sunday Independent* article, I was awaiting the outcome of Guerin's Supreme Court Appeal in which he was seeking the court's approval for the process he applied to shredding my reputation four and a half years earlier. While I agreed with many of Fitzgerald's insights, still awaiting the Supreme Court's decision on Guerin's appeal, it was difficult to take seriously her belated outrage and demand for 'change in how our legislature, media and public interact'.

✳✳✳✳

If this book was a novel or television series, the conjunction of personalities, issues, events, controversies and bizarre coincidences would present as too far fetched even for fiction. The *Disclosures Tribunal Report* eloquently illustrates how fact can be stranger than fiction in recounting how the flawed report containing a false accusation of rape against Maurice McCabe was created and how it catastrophically found its way into TUSLA files and was dealt with by TUSLA. Much of what occurred relating to it coincided with the ticket charge controversies, the Guerin Inquiry and the O'Higgins Commission's investigation. Yet it had no connection to them. This was, as the Tribunal concluded, 'an incredible coincidence' and 'despite its bizarre nature … a genuine mistake'. For me, it was a bizarre coincidence that it emerged that Peter Charleton was one of the five judges sitting to hear Sean Guerin's Supreme Court appeal and that he took time out from the Tribunal's hearings. I had already referenced his insightful book, *Lies in a Mirror* in earlier parts of this book. He was now destined to play an unexpected role in my life.

The one-day Supreme Court appeal hearing took place on 3 May 2018. My role was to simply sit in court and listen as legal arguments were conducted by the contesting teams of barristers and as each were subjected to questioning by the five judges appointed to hear Guerin's appeal. The judges, in addition to Charleton were William McKechnie, Donal O'Donnell, Elizabeth Dunne and Iseult O'Malley.

The central argument of Guerin's lawyers in the Supreme Court moved from contending that, as a former Minister for Justice, I had no entitlement to take proceedings against Guerin to contending that, as Guerin's Inquiry was only the start of a process, as he had recommended the creation of a Commission of Investigation and as I had been vindicated by the O'Higgins Commission, my proceeding were premature and should not have been taken. This was a strange argument. It sought to rely on the *O'Higgins Report*'s conclusions praising my ministerial conduct to set aside the Appeal Court's declaration that my right to a fair hearing had been violated, and to preserve-in-being Guerin's critical and damaging conclusions contradicted by O'Higgins. It was based on a perspective that the devastating impact on my life over a period of four years of the *Guerin Report* should be ignored and was of no importance. In the middle of it all the issue of whether Guerin had violated my right to a fair hearing and the impact of his conclusions on my reputation was debated back and forth as I struggled, sitting at the back of the court, to contain myself from furnishing repetitive notes detailing the blindingly obvious to my Senior Counsel, Paul Sreenan and my solicitor, Brian Gallagher. My past experience of the Supreme Court was as an advocate representing litigants and I found being a spectator in my own proceedings enormously difficult. Upon the hearing concluding, Judge Donal O'Donnell announced that the Court's decision would be delivered on some unspecified future date.

As occurred with the previous court hearings, Seán Guerin was not present in court. As I awaited the court judgement I read with some bemusement a newspaper report in early June 2018 of a case in which he and Remy Farrell appeared as Senior Counsel. Guerin was reported as representing, before the Court of Justice of the European Union, a Polish citizen charged with drug trafficking offences in Poland who was resisting being returned from Ireland to Poland for trial pursuant to a European Arrest Warrant, on the grounds he would not receive a fair hearing before the Polish courts. Farrell was reported as representing Ireland and asking the court to determine whether the rule of law had been so eroded in Poland by recent laws impacting on its judiciary as to create a strong risk the accused would not receive a fair trial. In circumstances in which Guerin had condemned me without a fair hearing and Farrell had publicly excoriated and ridiculed me for criticising Guerin for doing so, there was something truly surreal about it all.

Almost ten months passed from the hearing of Guerin's Supreme Court appeal before the Court scheduled its decision to be given and judgements delivered on Tuesday 26 February 2019. The wait was excruciating. I had expected to know the outcome of the appeal by mid-October 2018 at the latest and became increasingly anxious as time passed. When, as Justice Minister, I had promoted the creation of the Court of Appeal, a major objective had been to reduce the pressure on the Supreme Court and to speed up the hearing and completion of appeals that came before it. It is frequently said that justice delayed is justice denied and I wanted to reach the end of what had become a five-year saga. By an extraordinary coincidence, the court sitting was scheduled for the day after the fifth anniversary of the announcement of Guerin's inquiry. It was Tuesday 25 February 2014 when Enda Kenny first informed me of Guerin's intended appointment and informed the Dáil of the inquiry he was to undertake.

Having attended all of the court hearings and at both the High Court and the Court of Appeal when judgements were delivered, Carol and I decided to stay home to await word of the outcome of Guerin's appeal. Despite my favourable Court of Appeal decision, the spectre of Judge Seamus Noonan's dismissive High Court judgement started to again erode my confidence in my own understanding of the law. The Supreme Court's unusual delay resulted in it looming large and my becoming increasingly pessimistic. Neither of us wanted to be on public display should Guerin's appeal be successful.

The Court sat at 10am and at about 10.17am my phone rang. It was Brian Gallagher. He sounded very emotional. Momentarily we feared the worst and then 'You have won. Guerin's appeal has been dismissed. All five judges have found in your favour.'

It was finally over. There were no further appeals Guerin could take. I expected a moment of elation but there was none. Yes, it was a relief that the court case had ended but, for me, it was a Pyrrhic victory. The clock could not be turned back. There was little likelihood of resurrecting my political career. Multiple reports of Guerin's damning conclusions would forever be accessible online and I knew my reputation remained damaged. I also knew that few outside the legal profession would learn of the Supreme Court's judgements or be interested in the complex legal analysis contained in them. I correctly anticipated they would receive minimal media reportage compared to the sensational condemnatory reports and commentaries that followed publication of the *Guerin Report* and that there would be no public reaction to them by the Taoiseach, Leo Varadkar, any of my former Fine Gael colleagues or any Opposition politician or political commentator who had gorged at the trough of Guerin's condemnation.

In total three written judgements were delivered. The one I was most anxious to read was that of Judge Peter Charleton as I assumed he would be the member of the Court with the greatest insight into the issues involved, having presided over the Disclosures Tribunal. His judgement proved me correct.

Dismissing the submission of Guerin's counsel that the conduct of his inquiry was not justiciable, that is amenable to review by the courts, and was not 'an exercise in public law' he stated,

'Publicly reducing the reputation of a political figure through a formal process of inquiry and report by a government appointed expert may be seen as … an exercise of significant power.'

He observed that judicial review is available 'as a remedy against the overarching power of the State where that power has been unfairly exercised'. When recommending in his report that there be a statutory inquiry, Guerin had made 'a public declaration' as 'to the inadequacy of [my] stewardship of the Department of Justice and Equality referable to the treatment of a particular police officer' (Sergeant Maurice McCabe). This was an issue, he asserted, 'directly relevant to the public question of the ordering of society and the regulation of discipline within society'. Charleton continued,

> Here any negative comment against Alan Shatter could predictably have the effect of calling into sharp focus his competence and application to duty as a member of government. This was not a private, or internal administrative, or even, confidential exercise. At all times that report was either going to be published, or would otherwise come to public attention. With the attention directed at the underlying issues that the report otherwise properly addressed, its official nature, which was publicly proclaimed as such, and the fact that the government openly turned to an outside source for an expert viewpoint and with public focus on this matter of extreme public interest, this is ... a matter of public law.

Charleton next addressed whether there had been 'substantial procedural injustice' or whether Guerin had exceeded the 'boundaries of jurisdiction', that is, gone further than permitted, by his terms of reference. Central to the first issue was whether 'any conclusion' arrived at by Guerin 'adverse' to my right to my 'good name ... respected, at least to a minimum degree' my 'entitlement to make a representation as to any issue concerned'. Charleton, together with Judge Donal O'Donnell, concluded that Guerin had 'exceeded the boundaries of the task assigned to him' and that Guerin's publicly appointed function was to solely determine 'whether some form of statutory inquiry was necessary'. His terms of reference 'never mandated' his deciding on 'the rights and wrongs of the oversight by Alan Shatter of the Department of Justice and Equality' nor his commenting 'in the public sphere on any individual'. The process in which he engaged, Charleton explained, 'was not set up as that but came, nonetheless, to a negative conclusion'. Had it been so set up, he asked, 'would anyone then doubt that fairness in coming to a decision was required?'

Such fairness, he determined, as a minimum, required that Guerin ascertain what I had to say about any issue of concern and that he include my response in his report without endorsing any point of view or voicing any criticism. He had not done so and as a result, Charleton held, there had been a 'material impairment' of my constitutional rights.

Charleton described Guerin's task as being 'of an exploratory kind in defining important issues' and identifying what should be addressed by a statutory judicial inquiry. It had boundaries and 'it was never expected that facts would be found and condemnations issued'. It was Charleton's judgement that *Guerin's Report* in its 'likely to be headline statement' that as Minister for Justice I did not seem to be able to heed the voice of Maurice McCabe 'exceeded its mandate and did so without any aspect of fairness being afforded' to me. As a minimum my views should have been sought and recorded and no determination made other than to say 'that there was an issue which only some form' of statutory inquiry could address 'to sort out where the truth is to be found'.

Charleton also acknowledged that the 'definitive and damaging conclusion' contained in *Guerin's Report* had an 'immediate public effect' undermining my position. Guerin's counsel had argued that no court order should be made, as what he had said publicly 'had no legal effect' and I was ultimately vindicated by the O'Higgins Commission. Rejecting that argument, Charleton asserted that Guerin's remit was solely to conduct a scoping exercise 'not a public scrutiny of what went right or wrong'.

'A public declaration was made as to the competence and application of a Minister in the Government. That opinion was always likely to be publicised and it was of its nature damaging to the good name of Alan Shatter. Even still, he was neither asked what his side of the story was and no such contradictory view was included in this public report. That is not what the law has consistently required in the public space.' Charleton concluded that

> There is no reason why it was ever necessary to say of the Minister for Justice and Equality that 'despite his having an independent supervisory and investigative function with specific statutory powers' he did not seem 'to have been able' to heed 'the voice of a member [of the gardaí] whose immediate supervisors held him in high regard which Sergeant McCabe was held'. That was not the brief given to Sean Guerin.

It was, of course, that damning conclusion wrongly reached by Guerin that received the most prominence in the immediate aftermath of his report being published and that had continued to contaminate media commentary and damage my reputation, even after his criticism had been discredited by the *O'Higgins Report*. Earlier in his judgement, Charleton remarked that 'Like every other country, from time to time in Ireland matters of public moment are invested with an emotional overlay as to the issues and the real facts become difficult to see.' Referencing the importance of there being a 'concise' statement of any issue identified to be addressed by a public inquiry, he warned of 'temptation' caused by 'the potentially febrile nature of public discourse'. Almost five years had passed since Judge Cooke had partially explained GSOC's failures with regard to the fake bugging controversy as attributable to 'the somewhat febrile world of covert intelligence'!

Judge Donal O'Donnell, critically referencing the same damning conclusion, observed: 'No one who is required to write a report, adjudication, or, indeed, a judgement is likely to be unaware of, or entirely immune from, the temptation to pontificate, and few, as perhaps this sentence illustrates, entirely succeed in resisting it.'

O'Donnell also described Guerin's function as being confined to identifying 'those issues which are truly in dispute, if any, so as to provide focus for any inquiry' and to advise 'whether a further inquiry should be established'. It is 'desirable,' he asserted, 'that any person appointed to produce a preliminary report on whether or not a further inquiry is necessary should avoid expressions which suggest he or she has come to any conclusion on the matters which remain in dispute'. He agreed that Guerin was engaged in 'a significant exercise of power' having been appointed by government. As such, his report was properly subject to judicial review.

O'Donnell determined that 'in the normal course' a person conducting a preliminary inquiry, to report on whether a more formal inquiry into an issue is necessary, is not required to comply with fair procedures but that 'the final public reporting of adverse conclusions requires that fair procedures are accorded to the person the subject matter of the report'.

In the context of a preliminary inquiry, O'Donnell stated 'the court should only intervene when it can be said the report has clearly exceeded the boundaries set in a manner which was unfair to the individual who was the subject of the commentary'. He concluded that various adverse conclusions expressed, and 'the impression thereby created' were damaging to my reputation and 'exceeded the scope of the inquiry' Guerin 'was authorised to conduct'.

Both Judges Iseult O'Malley and Elizabeth Dunne agreed with Judge O'Donnell's judgement and, together with Judge Charleton, agreed that Guerin's appeal be dismissed and that the court make a declaration that specified critical conclusions reached by Guerin were 'outside the scope' of his terms of reference. They included Guerin's conclusion that I had been unable 'to heed' McCabe's voice.

Judge William McKechnie travelled a somewhat different route prior to deciding also that Guerin's appeal be dismissed. Agreeing with his judicial colleagues that Guerin's task was 'overwhelmingly public in nature' he witheringly rejected Guerin's contention that he was engaged in a private law matter not subject to judicial review, describing it as a 'hindsight suggestion' that his 'engagement and process was akin to that which occurs by virtue of counsel's retention to advise a client on a legal issue'. As far as McKechnie was concerned, there could 'be no comparison between the nature of a barrister's advisory work and the task required of and carried out by Mr Guerin'. *Guerin's Report* was prepared with the foreknowledge it would be published and would be laid before both Houses of the Oireachtas. It thus became part of the official record. These steps, he held, 'in themselves' rendered the report determinative and subject to judicial review. He described Guerin's critical conclusions as 'damning' of me 'personally, professionally as a lawyer and in his capacity as Minister for Justice'. Unlike the other members of the Supreme Court, he held Guerin to have stayed within the overall parameters of his obligation and not to have exceeded his mandate. However, he determined Guerin's mandate did not oblige him to reach any critical conclusions on disputed issues. Doing so in relation to me required that I be afforded an opportunity to engage with Guerin's concerns. As I was not, there was a breach of fair procedures. 'Respect for rights with legal or constitutional protection' McKechnie asserted, 'must be adhered to.'

A curious aspect of O'Donnell's judgement was his reference to 'some ambiguity' in Guerin's terms of reference, the approach of the government and the absence of any clear legal definition of the 'function and role he was to perform and its limits'. He rightly stated the desirability of 'the precise legal function of a preliminary inquiry be[ing] clarified at the outset on the appointment of a person to inquire'. Of course, if Guerin believed there was some 'ambiguity' over the task he was to perform he could have sought clarification from Enda Kenny at any time after his appointment. I am not aware of his ever having done so.

And so ended almost five years of litigation. The *O'Higgins Report* taken together with the Supreme Court verdict established Guerin had no mandate to evaluate my ministerial conduct, he should not have done so without according me, as a minimum, 'an opportunity to express my views' and his damning criticism of me was wrong. In essence, my resignation from government and the reputational damage which resulted from his report should never have occurred. My life should not have been turned upside down. What remains a mystery is why Guerin behaved as he did and why, after publication of the *O'Higgins Report* in May 2016, which clearly established that his criticism was unjustified, he did not simply acknowledge his serious mistakes and lacked the decency to apologise for them. After all, Enda Kenny when informing the Dáil of his preliminary inquiry, described his objective as 'to have the truth established'. By May 2016 'the truth' had been established but Guerin's appeal to the Supreme Court delayed a final resolution until almost three years later.

In the immediate aftermath of the dismissal of Guerin's Supreme Court appeal, no public comment was made on behalf of the Fine Gael party nor by any member of government, nor did I receive any private congratulatory message from any former Fine Gael colleague. Taoiseach and Fine Gael Leader Leo Varadkar's speedy call on Opposition TDs to apologise to Frances Fitzgerald for false charges made against her and to correct the Dáil record after publication of the *Disclosures Tribunal Report* was not followed by any public apology given by him for the manner in which I had been treated. Tánaiste, Minister for Foreign Affairs and Trade and Fine Gael's Deputy Leader, Simon Coveney, did not feel compelled to inform the Fine Gael parliamentary party that I had been completely vindicated and to call on Opposition TDs to apologise for their past conduct. Neither Varadkar nor any member of government took any steps to correct the Dáil record by acknowledging in the Dáil chamber that Guerin's damning conclusions were mistaken, that I was wrongly deprived of any opportunity to address his concerns and that my right to my good name and reputation had been violated. No apology of any nature was given by Frances Fitzgerald for entirely ignoring the concerns I had voiced in the Dáil on 19 June 2014 about my being condemned without any hearing nor apology and explanation given by Enda Kenny for ignoring those and earlier concerns expressed by me. It was senior Fine Gael figures evident lack of moral compass, core values and basic decency together with an obsessive focus on self-promotion and manipulative media spin which had resulted in my quietly letting my party membership of thirty-nine years lapse in the spring of 2018. I know that I made the right decision.

No Opposition TD nor media commentator pondered on how Guerin could have reached conclusions totally contradicted by the *O'Higgins Report* nor why he condemned me unheard. No demand was made that the transcript of Guerin's nineteen hours of conversation with Maurice McCabe when conducting his inquiry be published nor that Guerin publicly apologise to me for the manner in which he conducted his inquiry and the devastating impact on my life of his discredited conclusions. No article appeared in the *Irish Independent* written by Guerin's Law Library colleague, Remy Farrell SC, apologising for his scurrilous diatribe which the paper published in June 2014 in which he depicted me as engaging in 'public ravings' when deriding my criticism of Guerin's failure to fairly engage with me. Neither the Irish Human Rights and Equality Commission nor any other human rights organisation broke almost five years of total silence to issue any statement welcoming the Supreme Court's decision that no one should be criticised or condemned in a report resulting from a preliminary inquiry in breach of its mandate or in breach of fair procedures. No journalist, broadcastor, political commentator or media outlet critically publicly reflected on and apologised for their part in the vicious abusive feeding frenzy of false allegations and the promotion of fake news in which they had engaged and which generated 'the febrile nature of public discourse' that was a prelude to the *Guerin Report*. There was nothing to indicate that either within the world of Irish politics, journalism nor broadcast media any lessons had been learned or that the importance of ethics, values and principle would be fully recognised. The toxic mix of political and media exaggeration, falsity and hysteria and the febrile atmosphere created, which resulted in my political assassination, was not something anyone involved wanted to address. All had a vested interest in impunity and not saying anything or drawing attention to any past conduct which might attract criticism. At the time of writing, in the words of William Shakespeare's Hamlet, 'the rest is silence'.

Truth Matters

We live in a political culture that is deeply ambivalent about truth
–Jeremy Elkins and Andrew Norris, *Truth and Democracy*

Trust is the critical aspect of the relationship between a newspaper and its readers –Fionnan Sheahan, *Irish Independent*, 1 September 2018

A disregard for facts, the displacement of reason by emotion and the corrosion of language are diminishing the very value of truth –Michiko Kakutani, *The Death of Truth*

Truth matters. The neglect of factual, empirical evidence-based or objective truth can have dramatic and significant consequences for individuals, for society and for democratic politics. It can also result in a slow and imperceptible erosion of the rule of law, undermine democratic values and constitutional norms. The need to fact-check, in so far as is possible, and to ascertain the truth of claims and allegations made should never be abandoned on the altar of partisan political opportunism nor sacrificed in the search for popularity and attention.

There is a need for less instant media-generated excitement over the sensational nature of claims and allegations made and for more serious attention to be given by mainstream media and the responsible press to checking their plausibility to avoid giving credibility to falsity, fabrication and propagating myths. The media too frequently gives equal weight to competing politically partisan and opportunistic sound bites without conducting any independent factual assessment of the veracity of what is said and confuses balance with truth telling or adopts to itself the most appealing version of events it believes will catch readers' or viewers' attention. As Tom Crosbie wrote in July 2018, the day after ownership of the *Irish Examiner* transferred to *The Irish Times*, 'ultimately a free press is about ensuring the public are fully and honestly informed, so that they can make their own decisions, whatever they may be'. As a news junkie and an admirer of good journalism, of which there are myriad examples in Ireland and elsewhere, my complaint is that, too frequently, the obligation to 'fully and honestly inform' is forgotten by some in the rush to publish or broadcast or due to the excitement generated by a perceived scandal.

In the early days of his presidency of the United States Donald Trump outrageously and dangerously depicted the media as 'an enemy of the people'. To this day he continues to proclaim this Stalinist construct beloved by tyrants and dictators. A free press and media are critical to a functioning constitutional democracy and is intrinsic to both respecting and protecting the constitutional right to freedom of expression. However, this does not require that we ignore the fact that one that publishes, propagates and promotes untruths, and gives a distorted perception of reality to all of those who rely on it to form their views and opinions, undermines democracy. This is rapidly becoming an era of fabricated truth – such 'truth' being a lie so regularly repeated that it assumes a life of its own, is popularly believed to be true and anyone who denies its truth is branded and denigrated as a liar. It is already an era in which beliefs are too frequently preferred to facts and opinions too often more valued than knowledge.

In the realm of Irish politics, when controversy arises, some in the media simply play a prosecutorial rather than an inquisitorial or investigative role. All too often the objective is to sensationalise, vilify and convict, not to ascertain objective or factual truth or to expose deceit and hypocrisy. The difficulty is compounded by the tendency of journalists to refrain from criticising and to protect confidential sources even when it ultimately emerges that a source has spread a story that is simply mistaken or false and/or malign and clearly self serving. Some also have a theological or ideological tendency to simply accept as true every allegation made by a person proclaimed by themselves or others to be a whistle-blower and assume malign intent behind any questioning, criticism, denial or disproof of the claims they make.

Researching the evidence and evaluating the credibility of information received or allegations made, in so far as is possible, should be an essential prerequisite before such information or allegations are proclaimed as 'revelations', and relied upon by journalists or politicians – some of whom are too easily beguiled and seduced by a 'confidential' source or become so personally invested in a story as to lose all critical faculties and sense of proportion. Establishing the incontrovertible facts of a contentious claim or an issue should always be prioritised as it is the 'facts' as reported which largely shape public opinion and perception. 'Facts' can too easily be distorted or manipulated for personal or political advantage or be asserted by an individual who is deluded, mistaken or has been misled.

Addressing this is not helped by the extent of the disconnect between how well some journalists perceive or claim they or their news outlets research or validate stories prior to publication and the actual approach taken. I know this to my cost.

As for claims of journalistic privilege, such privilege has a crucial role in ensuring the confidentiality of sources who provide journalists with accurate information that exposes or sheds light on issues of public interest and in speaking truth to power. However, there can be no justification for relying on the doctrine and concealing the identity of a source who makes patently false allegations for which there is no credible evidence; or who provides false information because deluded, mistaken, misled or for their own personal benefit; or in order to maliciously and wrongly damage others, or for continuing to rely on or promote clearly false or mistaken allegations or complaints. It is an issue that gave rise to discussion and differing views during the course of the Disclosures Tribunal in the context of the Tribunal addressing the false claims originating from Superintendent David Taylor. However, it gave rise to no discussion following the Cooke and Connaughton reports on the GSOC controversy, nor in relation to publication of selective leaked extracts from the transcripts of the O'Higgins Commission which gave a partial and distorted insight into the O'Higgins hearings. The Disclosures Tribunal was not empowered to inquire into the provenance of the leaked extracts and did not do so. It did, however, note that while the Protected Disclosures Act protects the discloser by provisions relating to anonymity, it provides no effective protection for individuals referred to in a protected disclosure. Nor does it preserve the confidentiality of allegations disclosed to public representatives and journalists. Parliamentary privilege, when abused, also provides no such protection. Both privileges too readily facilitate false allegations being made public before a person accused of wrongdoing has any opportunity to consider the content of any disclosure and how it can be properly addressed before being publicly pilloried and suffering permanent reputational damage without due process.

If the principal objective of both privileges is to establish truth, there is no public interest in either of them being available as a shield to spread lies. There can be no public benefit or interest in politicians or journalists being enabled or manipulated into weaponising falsity or deceit – and protecting its source by using privilege to preserve his or her anonymity. Used in this way, a privilege simply confers impunity on those who lie or mislead or simply make unfounded or baseless allegations that damage others and incentivises their conduct. This is an issue that should not be ignored in an age in which there is a daily difficulty in separating fact from fiction and in which 'fake news' published by mainstream or social media can trump truth, with instant and dramatic impact.

It has been my personal experience that too many prominent members of the Irish media, with some honourable exceptions, are more comfortable ignoring instead of acknowledging the clear consequences of truth found where that truth totally undermines an all pervasive and false previously favoured and popularised narrative. It is noteworthy that the finding of such truth rarely generates any recrimination, soul searching or investigation into how or why a false narrative came to be actively promoted, published or broadcast and widely believed. It also rarely adversely impacts on the creator of falsehood or deceit. Even when a favoured narrative is acknowledged to be false, it can be so ingrained that, over time, amnesia or cognitive dissonance sets in and there is a reversion to the clearly discredited original popularised story.

It has also been my experience that Irish politicians inhabit an amoral world in which politically uncomfortable and inconvenient truths that contradict allegations previously made or which are personally or politically embarrassing are ignored and, if possible, deemed disposable. It is rare for any TD who made false allegations and unjustly called for resignations in the Dáil under the protection of Dáil privilege to publicly admit, following an inquiry or commission of investigation, that what they did was wrong and to apologise for the consequences of their action. For too many involved in politics it is all a game and truth only has a value if it is perceived as politically advantageous and does not risk criticism or opprobrium. Where all members of the Oireachtas have subscribed or surrendered to a false narrative there will never be contemporary political pressure within the Houses of the Oireachtas to acknowledge and apologise for the falsity. The imperative and mutual interest on all sides is to look the other way and avoid embarrassment.

The health of a democracy can be judged by the capacity of politicians, journalists and society in general to acknowledge and accept uncomfortable and inconvenient truths that challenge and upend their publicly stated beliefs and opinions. My personal experience of the last five years is that our democracy is badly in need of care and of a realignment of the moral compass and values of many of those who are politically active or reporting and commenting on politics if fakery, truthiness, popularism, attention seeking, simplistic media friendly sound bites, emotion and mob rule are not to win out over truth, decency, knowledge, integrity, logic and reason. There is a vital and urgent need for the State, its institutions, agencies, Government, Oireachtas members, civil society groups, political activists and journalists to renew their commitment to and recognise the importance of the rule of law, constitutional norms, fair procedures and due process.

There is also a need to recognise and reaffirm the importance of incontrovertible facts and indisputable and objective truth and to recognise the danger of giving excessive credibility to beliefs, perceptions, opinions and unverified allegations made by unidentifiable sources or whistle-blowers before passing judgement on others. The fact that a source or whistle-blower justifiably and accurately discloses some wrongdoing, negligence or maladministration should also not automatically lend credibility to and require automatic acceptance of all claims made, no matter how serious, without independent verification or corroboration. It should also not result in the instant vilification and ridicule of those who factually dispute allegations made.

Before something is sensationally proclaimed in front-page headlines or at the top of talk news or current affairs broadcasts and podcasts or revealed in the Dáil chamber, the importance of independent confirmation of its truth, where possible, should not play second fiddle to the excitement of its anticipated impact and the public attention it is likely to attract. All too frequently it does.

Timeline of Key Events

9 March 2011 Alan Shatter appointed Minister for Justice, Equality and Defence.

14 June 2011 Oliver Connolly appointed Confidential Recipient.

23 January 2012 The Department of Justice receives Sergeant Maurice McCabe's anonymised Protected Disclosure from Oliver Connolly detailing various alleged garda failings which occurred in the 2007–2008 period, alleging Garda Commissioner Martin Callinan behaved corruptly and making other serious allegations against senior gardaí.

24 January 2012 The Department of Justice transmits McCabe's Protected Disclosure to Garda Commissioner Martin Callinan for his response.

30 January 2012 The Department of Justice receives the Garda Commissioner's response.

3 February 2012 Minister for Justice Alan Shatter sends his response to the Protected Disclosure to Oliver Connolly.

9 February 2012 McCabe and Connolly meet to discuss Shatter's response. Unknown to Connolly, McCabe records their conversation.

September 2012 The Department of Justice receives (i) from McCabe's solicitors a letter with documentation containing further complaints and allegations and (ii) from the Taoiseach's Department and the Department of Transport, Tourism and Sport, letters from McCabe with documentation containing allegations in relation to fixed charge notices (ticket charges) and penalty points.

October 2012 The Department of Justice commences correspondence with McCabe's solicitors in relation to their letter. Assistant Commissioner John O'Mahony and his team commence investigating McCabe's ticket charges allegations.

28 November 2012 Interim Report of Assistant Commissioner John O'Mahoney on McCabe allegations received by Minister for Justice Alan Shatter.

15 May 2013 The *O'Mahoney Report* is published.

20 May 2013 Mick Wallace TD complains to data protection commissioner that Minister for Justice Alan Shatter violated Wallace's Data Protection Act rights

30 September 2013 Seamus McCarthy, the Comptroller and Auditor General (C&AG) publishes critical report on the Fixed Charge Notice Processing System which is transmitted to the Public Accounts Committee (PAC).

23 January 2014 The Garda Commissioner appears in public before PAC to answer questions on the Fixed Charge Notice Processing System and his criticism of whistle-blowers generates controversary.

9 February 2014 *Sunday Times* front-page story asserts GSOC under high-tech surveillance.

18 February 2014 Former European Court and High Court Judge John Cooke is appointed to conduct preliminary non-statutory (informal) inquiry into alleged surveillance of GSOC.

25 February 2014 Sean Guerin SC appointed to conduct a preliminary non-statutory (informal) inquiry into McCabe's allegations of garda failures and corruption.

1 March 2014 Fine Gael Ard Fheis.

3 March 2014 Minister for Justice Alan Shatter receives Garda Inspectorate Report into Fixed Charge Notice Processing System.

12 March 2014 Garda Inspectorate Report on Fixed Charge Notice Processing System discussed by Cabinet and published.

20 March 2014 Leo Varadkar, Minister for Transport, Tourism and Sport delivers a speech praising McCabe when opening one day conference of Road Safety Authority.

25 March 2014 Commissioner Callinan prematurely retires. The same day government issues statement on recordings of phone conversations in various garda stations for over 30 years.

30 April 2014 A Commission of Investigation presided over by former Supreme Court Judge Niall Fennelly is formally established to investigate garda recordings issue and circumstances surrounding Commissioner Callinan's retirement.

6 May 2014 The Guerin Report is transmitted to the Taoiseach. The Report of Data Protection Commissioner published.

7 May 2014 The Taoiseach, Enda Kenny, informs Shatter that he will no longer be able to express confidence in him. Shatter resigns from government.

9 May 2014 The *Guerin Report* is published.

10 June 2014 The *Cooke Report* is published.

July 2014 Shatter issues High Court judicial review proceedings against Guerin in relation to his report, having earlier appealed Data Protection Act Commissioner's decision to Circuit Court.

21 January 2015 Circuit Court Judge Jacqueline Linnane dismisses Shatter's appeal against findings and decision of Data Protection Commissioner as to Mick Wallace's Data Protection claims.

3 February 2015 The Commission of Investigation recommended by Guerin commences its work presided over by retired European Court and High Court Judge Kevin O'Higgins.

14 May 2015 The O'Higgins Commission commences its hearings.

20 May 2015 High Court Judge Seamus Noonan dismisses Shatter's judicial review proceedings taken against Sean Guerin in relation to his report.

1 September 2015 The Interim Fennelly Report on circumstances surrounding Martin Callinan's premature retirement is published.

15 February 2016 The O'Higgins Commission circulates drafts of extracts from its report to interested parties for their observations.

26 February 2016 Dáil general election. Shatter fails to get re-elected.

11 May 2016 The *O'Higgins Report* is published.

10 November 2016 The Court of Appeal reverses the High Court decision dismissing Shatter's judicial review proceedings against Guerin. Finds Guerin failed to afford him a fair hearing.

17 February 2017 The Disclosures Tribunal is established to be presided over by Supreme Court Judge Peter Charleton.

6 April 2017 The Final Report of Fennelly Commission published on the recording of phone calls in garda stations.

17 May 2017 Enda Kenny announces his resignation as leader of Fine Gael.

14 June 2017 Enda Kenny resigns as Taoiseach and is replaced by Leo Varadkar who has been elected leader of Fine Gael.

10 September 2017 Nóirín O'Sullivan resigns as Garda Commissioner under a cloud of false allegations that she had treated McCabe badly.

9 November 2017 Judge Charles Meenan reverses Circuit Court decision dismissing Shatter's Data Protection Act appeal, finds Shatter was denied a fair hearing and did not violate any Data Protection Act rules.

28 November 2017 Frances Fitzgerald resigns from Cabinet amidst controversy resulting from a false allegation that McCabe was badly treated during the O'Higgins Commission hearings.

3 May 2018 The Supreme Court hears Sean Guerin's appeal against his Court of Appeal reversal.

11 October 2018 The Disclosures Tribunal publishes its third interim report concluding its inquiry into all Sergeant McCabe-related issues.

26 February 2019 The Supreme Court unanimously dismisses Sean Guerin's appeal. It finds that he exceeded his mandate, damaged Shatter's constitutional right to his good name and reputation and failed to accord him fair procedures and a chance to be heard.

Acknowledgements

I believe when something bad happens in your life it is important to move on. Obsessing on the past instead of living your today and endeavouring to make tomorrow better can achieve little of value. However, when the past intrudes into today and erects barriers to enjoying tomorrow your options are constrained. It can be difficult to be optimistic for tomorrow if you fear nothing will likely change.

This book focuses on past events and, in particular, on the first half of 2014 and its aftermath. If not for the Commissions of Investigation established to investigate the various garda-related controversies, the court cases I believed I had no choice but to initiate and my being continuously publicly denigrated and vilified, this book would not have been written. Had I been simply able to move on, I would have done so.

As a participant in as well as a witness to many of the events I describe, the writing was not easy. It required my forensically reliving stressful occasions better forgotten, interrupted my sleep and unsettled my equilibrium. It also led me to understand that the difficulties I had experienced and I was living through were minor compared to the catastrophes that unexpectedly impact on the lives of many others.

Despite all outward appearances, I would not have held it together without the unstinting love, understanding, insights and support of my wife Carol for which I thank her from the bottom of my heart. The kindness, encouragement, guidance, and editorial skills of my long-time friend Jane Lehane, shortly to become Jane Freedman were, as always, invaluable. So was the friendship and good counsel of my former legal partner, Brian Gallagher, who was burdened by being my solicitor in the Guerin proceedings and by my discussing with him a variety of issues relevant to the book. I will be forever in their debt.

Jerry O'Brien maintained extraordinary good humour and a permanently optimistic demeanour as my solicitor in the proceedings taken against the Data Protection Commissioner and in dealing with other related matters. He also deserves much thanks as do Paul Sreenan SC and Cathal Murphy BL who represented me throughout in the Guerin case and Eileen Barrington SC and Emily Gibson BL who represented me in the Data Protection Commissioner case. I also thank Tom Cooney with whom, during our many walks in Marlay Park, I discussed and explored the complexity of the relationship between the Irish media and politicians and the way politics is daily portrayed. I am also grateful to him for his helpful suggestions on the final manuscript. I also want to recognise and extend thanks to the many distinguished authors from whose attributed works I have quoted and whose extraordinary intellectual prowess, insights and literary skill I greatly admire.

The records I maintained of my time as both a Government Minister and a TD were invaluable in ensuring the accuracy of my story. So also was the assistance I received in tracing material of relevance from the librarians in the Leinster House library and Departmental officials. To all I give my thanks and, in particular, Seamus Haughey.

I have been careful in my narrative to preserve the confidentiality of evidence given in private before Commissions of Investigation which is not in the public domain and information contained in Commission and Tribunal documentation not originally part of my own personal papers and not revealed in published reports. As I quote extensively from their reports, I thank retired Judges Niall Fennelly, Kevin O'Higgins and John Cooke and also Supreme Court Judge Peter Charleton for their public service. I also thank retired Judge Iarlagh O'Neill for the impeccable approach he took to the preliminary inquiry he undertook which was a prelude to the Disclosures Tribunal. Both it and that of Judge Cooke are valuable precedents for future such inquiries. My thanks also go to those members of the judiciary who determined the various court appeals in which I was involved for the care taken in addressing the complex and difficult issues on which they adjudicated and for restoring my faith in our legal system.

My publisher, Merrion Press, and its Managing Director, Conor Graham, deserve a special mention. As is my habit, I did not seek a publisher until the book was substantially finished although somewhat raw. Conor's interest and enthusiasm at a time when I was feeling low was enormously encouraging and propelled me into some crucial editing to make the book more succinct and an easier read. He also understood that, for the sake of accuracy and to preserve the integrity of the narrative, it was in some areas necessary to get into some technical detail that the Irish media previously bypassed to avoid issues of complexity and tell simple stories that did not accurately portray important events. I also thank Fiona Dunne, Managing Editor, for all the vitally important work undertaken on my manuscript to enable you, the reader, best follow my story.

It was my forced resignation from Government on 7 May 2014, following my receipt of the *Guerin Report,* that began one of the most difficult periods of my life. From early February 2014, I felt that I had become entrapped in a world prone to collective madness which no longer valued truth. That 7 May date five years ago symbolised its apotheosis. However, as I have written elsewhere, life is a funny business. For Carol and me, 7 May has now become a day of celebration and hope as it marks the birth in 2016 of Riley Shatter, our first grandson. To his parents, my son Dylan and his wife Gaby, thank you for bringing the joy of Riley into our lives and to Dylan and my daughter Kelly thank you for all your concern and support during a difficult time.

Alan Shatter
April 2019